A Land Afflicted

Scotland and the Covenanter Wars 1638–1690

God have mercy on this Afflicted Land

– *James Graham, Marquis of Montrose*

*This book is dedicated to the memory of
my grandmother, Agnes McLetchie Campbell,
a lifelong Covenanter.*

A Land Afflicted

Scotland and the Covenanter Wars 1638–1690

RAYMOND CAMPBELL PATERSON

JOHN DONALD PUBLISHERS LTD
EDINBURGH

ISBN 0 85976 486 9

British Library Cataloguing in Publication Data.

A catalogue record for this book is available
from the British Library.

Typesetting & origination by Brinnoven, Livingston.
Printed & bound in Great Britain by MPG Books Ltd, Bodmin, Cornwall.

Contents

Preface   vii

1. From Rebellion to Revolution   1

2. No Bishop – No King?   21

3. Newburn   36

4. The Armies of God   53

5. Marston Moor   71

6. Montrose – The Scourge of Heaven   89

7. From Auldearn to Philiphaugh   109

8. The Engagement   130

9. Preston and the Whiggamore Raid   151

10. Dunbar   173

11. Worcester and the End of the First Covenanter War   197

12. Rullion Green – The Agony of the Covenant   221

13. Drumclog and Bothwell Bridge   245

14. The Cameronians and the Killing Time   264

15. Dunkeld and the End of the Covenanter Wars   279

Select Bibliography   294

Index   303

List of Maps

1. The Covenanter Wars, 1639–1689   xi

2. The Battle of Marston Moor   xii

3. The Battle of Aberdeen   xiii

4. The Battle of Auldearn   xiv

5. The Preston Campaign   xv

6. Edinburgh: The War of Manoeuvre   xvi

7. The Battle of Dunbar   xvii

8. The Battle of Inverkeithing   xviii

9. The Battle of Worcester   xix

10. The Battle of Rullion Green   xx

Preface

Close to the entrance of Saint Giles Cathedral in Edinburgh there is a metal plaque inserted in the floor with the following inscription:

> Constant Oral Tradition Affirms that near this Spot a Brave Scotch Woman Janet Geddes on the 23 July 1637 Struck the First blow in The great struggle for freedom of conscience which after a conflict of half a century ended in the establishment of civil and religious liberty.

While the existence of Janet – or Jenny – Geddes is now generally disputed, the events of that Sunday morning in the summer of 1637 are real enough. The riots that greeted the first public reading of the new Anglican style Prayer Book, introduced on the insistence of Charles I, were the start of a great upheaval that was to embrace England and Ireland as well as Scotland. The stool thrown at the unfortunate Dean Hanna may have missed its immediate target; but, in the end, it took off the head of a King.

In the February following the riot the political community, with a few important exceptions, pledged itself to the defence of the Reformed faith in the National Covenant, arguably the most complete expression of the spirit of Scottish self determination since the Declaration of Arbroath in 1320. The implications of this document were immediately obvious to Charles, who complained that as long as it existed he had no more power than the Doge of Venice.

In late 1638 the General Assembly of the Church of Scotland not only upheld the Covenant, but it also went on to sweep aside the rule of the bishops and all the other innovations in religious practice that had been introduced by Charles and his father, James VI. Out of the ashes emerged a new Presbyterian Phoenix.

Presbyterianism comes from the Greek word *Presbuteros*, meaning elder. It entails a system where there is no ecclesiastical hierarchy: where all minister are equal, subject only to the discipline of a series of church courts, ending in the General Assembly, the highest court of all. Presbyterians held that

Episcopacy – government by bishops – could not be justified by reference to scripture; and as bishops were agents of royal power, the rejection of Episcopacy was also the rejection of all state interference in the church.

This was not a challenge the King could ignore. In 1639 he prepared to use the power of England and Ireland to suppress Scotland, the country of his birth. Thus began what contemporaries were to label the *Bellum Episcopale* – the Bishops' Wars, the first stage in a more widespread British struggle. They were a disaster for Charles; but in a deeper sense they were also a disaster for Scotland. The easy successes the country enjoyed in this early conflict, combined with a dangerous sense of religious mission, were to pull it ever more deeply into economically and politically ruinous wars in the rest of the United Kingdom.

The tensions caused soon exposed the Covenanter movement itself as an uneasy alliance between competing factions. Through fifty years of conflict it moved in ever decreasing circles, until the pure ideal of 1638 was represented in the end by a fanatical rump known as the Cameronians, after Richard Cameron, one of their spiritual guides. Although the Revolution of 1688–1690 finally established a Presbyterian national church, it was a shadow of the system envisaged in the 1640's.

Charles I's religious policies and the crisis they induced, exposed the fragile nature of the United Kingdom in the early seventeenth century. Although the crowns of England and Scotland had been joined in 1603, when James VI succeeded Elizabeth I, both countries retained their separate Parliaments and political institutions, and custom controls remained in place. While Scots were proud that it was their monarch who occupied the throne of England, the limitations of the new arrangement were quickly apparent. When the real centre of power shifted to London, few of the traditional ruling groups in Scotland shared in the benefits. As long as James, a skilled manager of men, was in control things went reasonably well. Charles, in contrast, was in all respects an alien King who knew little of Scotland or its customs. From the very outset of his reign in 1625 he managed to antagonise whole sections of the community, ending with the ill-conceived attempt to introduce the new Prayer Book with only the minimum of consultation. For the Covenanters, the defence of Scotland's national integrity was as important as the attempt to defend her religion.

Before the start of the Covenanter Wars, Scotland and England had been at peace for almost a hundred years. However, many people in both lands had kept abreast of the latest military thinking by taking part as mercenaries in the major conflicts on the Continent. The long Dutch Wars of Independence against the Spanish, and the great contest in central Europe that in time was to be known as the Thirty Years War, had introduced important innovations, associated with Prince Maurice of Nassau and, above all, with the champion of Protestant Europe, Gustavus Adolphus, King of Sweden.

The growth of firepower had rendered old medieval battle formations, like the Scottish schiltron, obsolete. In their place had come smaller, more mobile regiments and companies which demanded a higher degree of training and uniform drill. In place of the bow and spear, the musket had become the main infantry weapon. Its rate of fire was far less than the traditional English longbow, but it was much quicker to master. Musketeers, however, were vulnerable to cavalry attack. To guard against this, each infantry regiment had a contingent of pikemen, who formed up to a third of its strength, until the introduction of the plug bayonet later in the century, when the pike finally disappeared.

Cavalry tactics had also changed. Troopers were armed with sword and pistol for the most part, although the lance continued to be important in the lighter Scottish cavalry formations. Realising the advantage of concentrated cavalry attack, Gustavus taught his horsemen to carry their attacks right into the enemy ranks, rather than firing their weapons and wheeling back before they made contact, a practice common in the previous century. He also introduced the mounted infantryman known as the dragoon, a kind of distant cousin of the medieval Scottish hobelar. Field artillery, moreover, became lighter and more manoeuvrable.

Scots from all ranks of society fought with Gustavus Adolphus in Germany against the Imperial armies of Wallenstein and Tilly, and performed particularly distinguished service at the Battle of Breitenfeld in September 1631. One soldier, Alexander Leslie, served in the Swedish army for thirty years, rising to the rank of field marshal. He came back to Scotland in 1638, ready to take the leading role in the army of the Covenant.

This book completes the story of Scotland's early wars that that I set out to tell in *For the Lion* and its sequel *My Wound is Deep*.

None of this would have been possible without the help of my wife, Fiona, and the continual stimulation provided by my children, Stephanie and Edward, whose battles are fought on different fields. My thanks are also due to Russell Walker and all at John Donald Publishers.

R.C.P.
Edinburgh, 1998

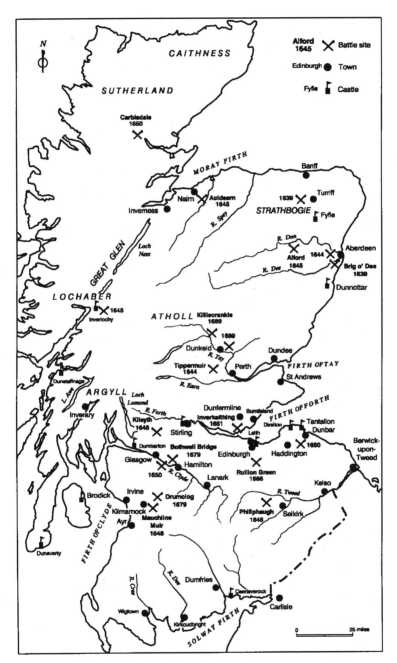

Map 1. *The Covenanter Wars 1639–1689.*

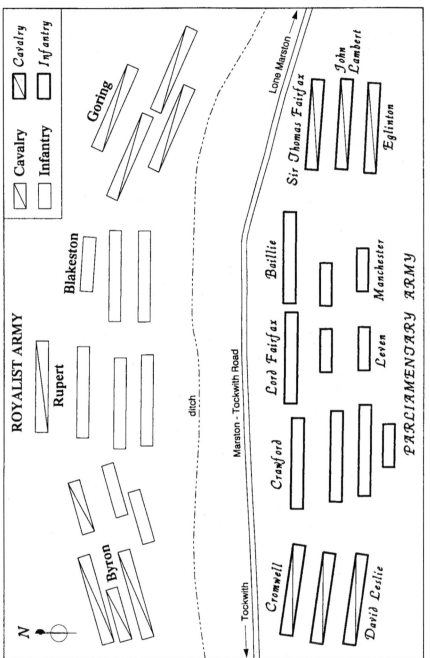

Map 2. The Battle of Marston Moor.

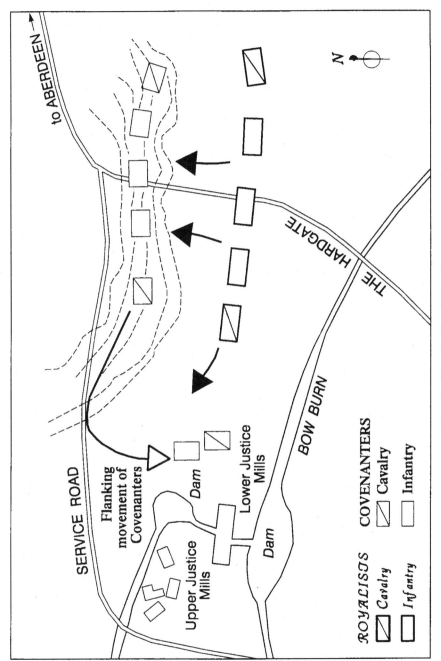

Map 3. *The Battle of Aberdeen.*

xiii

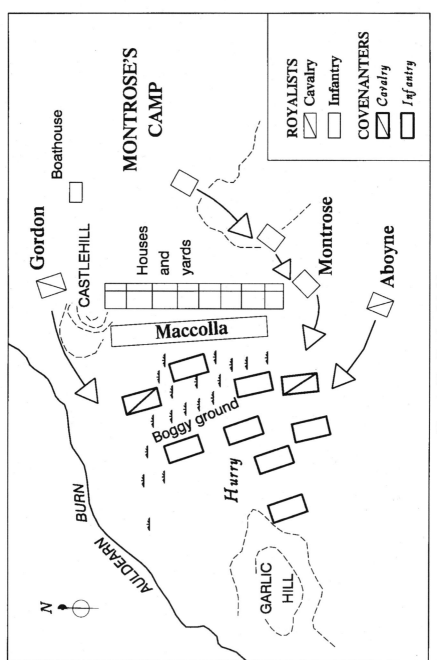

Map 4. *The Battle of Auldearn.*

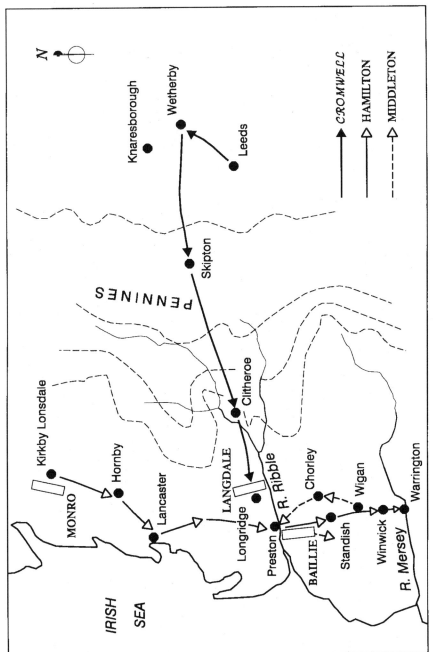

Map 5. *The Preston Campaign.*

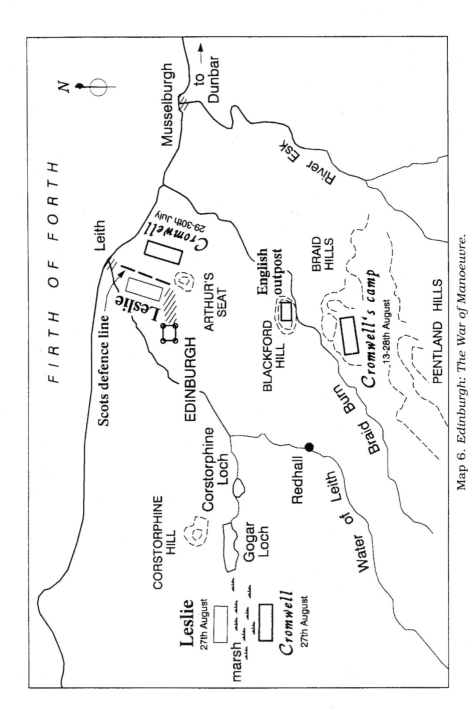

Map 6. *Edinburgh: The War of Manoeuvre.*

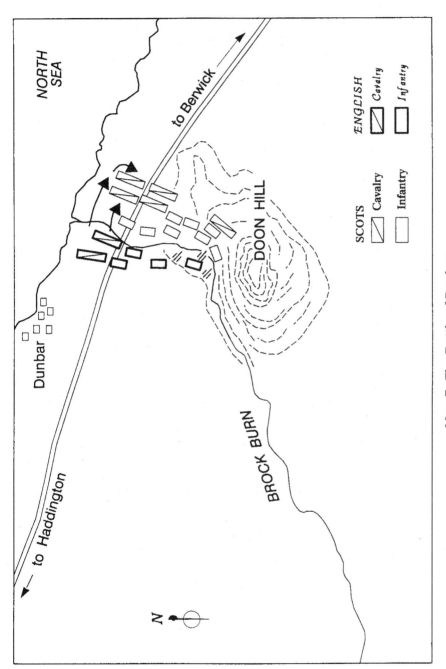

Map 7. The Battle of Dunbar.

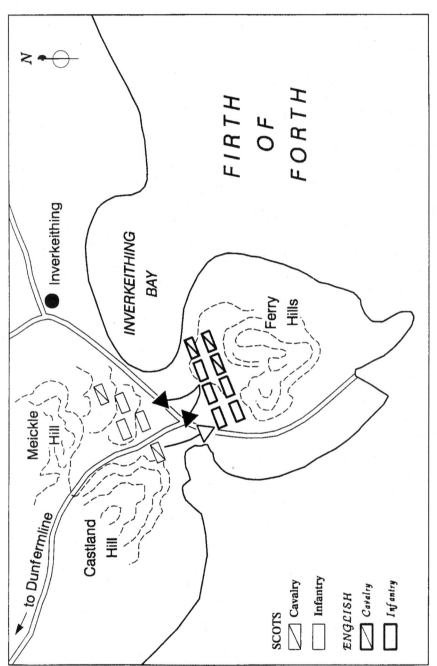

Map 8. *The Battle of Inverkeithing.*

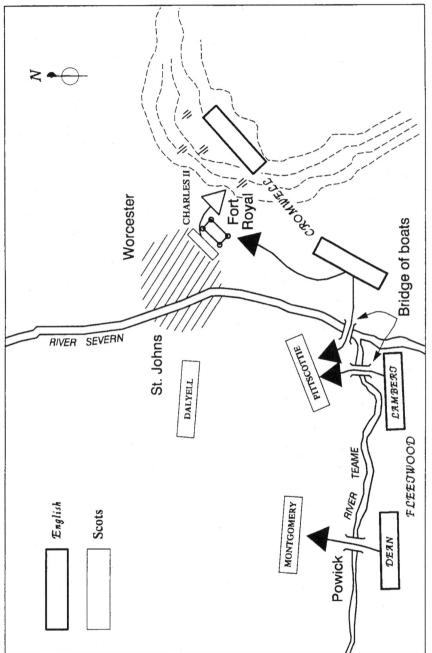

Map 9. *The Battle of Worcester.*

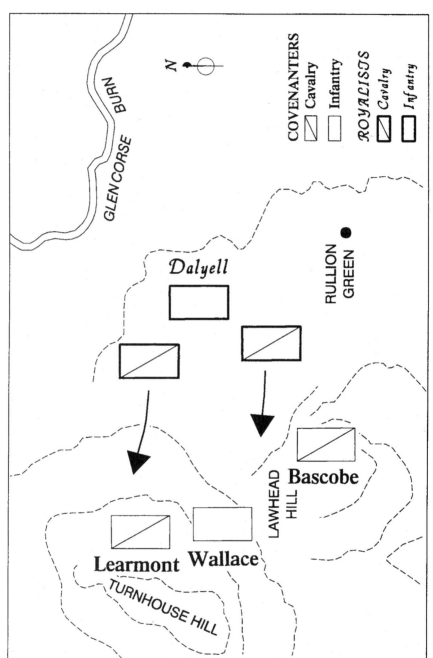

Map 10. The Battle of Rullion Green.

CHAPTER 1
From Rebellion to Revolution

In the spring of 1625 few Scots can have had any real knowledge of their new sovereign, King Charles I. Although James VI, who died on 27 March, had spent the last twenty two years of his reign in England, apart from one brief visit back to his native land in 1617, he had been King of Scots since 1567 and was known and understood by all the leading men of the land. Charles had been born in Dunfermline and had spent the first four years of his life in Scotland, but it was soon apparent that he knew little and cared less, for the ancient kingdom of the Stewarts. In manners, attitude and religion Charles was Scotland's first English King.

It's difficult to imagine a greater contrast than that between the father and the son. James had been easy going, slovenly and vulgar; Charles was cold, distant and formal. James had been a king for almost all of his life, and had a comfortable familiarity with the role. Charles, who was painfully shy and suffered from a speech impediment, had only become his father's heir in 1612, on the premature death of his much admired older brother, Henry. All too aware of his personal shortcomings, he hid himself behind a rigid armour of protocol and ceremony. He had, however, been influenced by his father in one particularly dangerous direction. James invented the concept of the Divine Right of Kings, but Charles was the first to take it seriously.

In 1599 James had published *Basilicon Doron*, a manual on the art of kingship written for Prince Henry. It opens with the following sonnet:

God gives not Kings the stile of Gods in vaine,
For on his throne his septre doe they sway;
And as their subjects ought them to obey
So kings should feare and serve their Gods againe.
If then ye would enjoy a happie raigne
Observe the statutes of your heavenlie king,
And from his house make all your lawes to spring,
Since his Lieutenant heere ye should reacive
Reward the iust, be stedfast, true and plaine,
Repress the proude, maintayning aye the right
Walk alwaies, as euer in his sight.

1

James went on to outline a doctrine of royal absolutism, with the monarch as the supreme arbiter in both civil and ecclesiastical matters, answerable to God alone. This doctrine was shaped in the King's long contest with Andrew Melville, champion of Presbyterianism and author of *The Second Book of Discipline*. Melville was to James what John Knox had been to his mother, Queen Mary. In conversation with the King at Falkland Palace in 1596, Melville made a remarkable assertion:

> Thair is twa Kings and twa Kingdomes in Scotland. Thair is Christ Jesus the King, and his kingdom, the Kirk, whase subject King James the Saxt is, and of whase kingdome nocht a king, nor a lord, nor a heid, but a member!

For James, the pretensions of Melville and the extreme Presbyterians placed intolerable restrictions on royal power. Melville had successfully persuaded the Kirk that the office of bishop, which the King considered to be an essential prop of royal government, was contrary to scripture. After a prolonged struggle, the Church of Scotland appeared finally to be established on a firm Presbyterian basis by Act of Parliament in 1592. James spent much of the remainder of his reign, both as King of Scots and latterly as King of Great Britain, steadily undermining Melville's triumph. The notion of the Divine Right of Kings was the first step along this road, acting as a kind of royal declaration of independence.

But Divine Right for James was really only an ideal; he had spent long enough on the throne of Scotland to recognise that there were restrictions on the exercise of the royal will. He acquired very real skills in the management of men and institutions. The Scots nobility was won over to his side by generous grants of land, which had belonged to the old Catholic Church. General Assemblies of the Kirk were held only at a time and place of the King's choosing, and were packed with his own nominees. Little by little, Episcopalian government was re-established, beginning with Parliament downwards. The pretensions of the Melvillian clergy were simply ignored. In late 1596 a pro Presbyterian riot in Edinburgh collapsed in the absence of noble support; and in 1611 Andrew Melville was exiled to France. He never returned.

James had a simple view of the church: in essence, it would become an adjutant of royal absolutism, presided over by the bishops, policing the conscience and determining the duty of the King's subjects. Two courts of High Commission were established in 1610 – united into one five years later – to try all offences against the clerical establishment. But up to this point James had only established the rule of bishops on a church that, in terms of its basic practice, remained puritan in doctrine and direction. After the high watermark of 1610, when the General Assembly approved his innovations in the Kirk, he began to move into more dangerous territory.

After the austerity of Scotland, James was impressed by the wealth and spectacle of England. He was particularly attracted to the English church and the beauty of its rituals. Unlike Scotland, the Reformation in England had been a partial, state directed process, retaining some of the elements of the old Catholic Church. Most gratifying of all, it acted as a mirror to the majesty of the King. James had failed to create a closer political union between England and Scotland; but at the very least he could ensure that the Church of Scotland moved closer to the Anglican ideal.

So far James' ecclesiastical policy in Scotland had been a notable success. He had managed to exploit the differences between the conservative and radical elements to the detriment of the latter. Most ministers had accepted the steady increase in the power of the bishops. Melville's two states moved further into the background, as the Kirk was firmly subordinated to government authority – a process known as Erastianism, after Thomas Erastus, who first defined the concept.

By 1617 James was confident enough to move beyond shaping the government of the church into the area of doctrine, proposing to introduce five new ceremonies: kneeling at Communion, private Communion for the sick, private baptism, observance of the principal Holy Days of the Church, and confirmation of children by bishops. All of these were contrary to strict Presbyterian practice, and, for many, gave all the appearance of popery. To make matters worse, James returned to Scotland the same year with a number of English clerics in tow, including William Laud, then Dean of Gloucester and future Archbishop of Canterbury. By way of example, services were performed at the Chapel Royal of Holyrood with all the splendour of the English system, the ministers bedecked in white surplices. All of this was done against the advice of John Spottiswood, Archbishop of St

Andrews, who tried to argue that the time was not right for controversial innovations. James refused to listen.

A year later James' five reforms were approved, with some reluctance, by the General Assembly meeting in Perth. But it was soon apparent that the 'Five Articles of Perth' were meeting with widespread resistance. The following Christmas, the first of the Holy Days after the Assembly, many stayed away from church, and tradesmen opened for business as usual. In many parts of the country men and women refused to kneel at Communion. Some ministers were prosecuted for defying the royal will; but James was quick to realise that he had taken a step too far. The Five Articles remained in place, and were confirmed by Parliament in 1621. Beyond that, though, no uniform attempt was made to enforce them. Divine Right was in practice limited by the exercise of the popular will. There were no further attempts at reform for the remainder of James' reign, and the General Assembly of the Kirk was not to meet for another twenty years.

So, in the end, the Divine Right of Kings, as James interpreted it, was simply a principle constantly modified by practice. But for Charles the principle was all. He was essentially a mediocrity with few political skills; a man of great charm, but little imagination and a large degree of obstinacy. Any form of criticism or resistance to his will was deeply resented, and all too often viewed as little better than treason. Before long he was on a collision course with his Scottish subjects. It began, fatally for him, not on the question of religion, but over the property rights and political privileges of the nobility.

In October 1625 Charles introduced an Act of Revocation. Measures of this kind were a common feature of Scottish history, intended to return to the crown all grants of land made during royal minorities. As Charles' own minority, by seventeenth-century standards, was due to run out on 19 November – his twenty fifth birthday – he introduced the measure without any attempt at consultation. But the most alarming feature of the new Revocation was that it was to be backdated to 1542, wiping out at a stroke all of the lucrative gains in church lands made by the nobility since the Reformation, and before. Charles' motives were noble enough. He intended, amongst other things, to improve woefully inadequate clerical incomes by establishing them on a sounder financial basis; but for Scotland's nobles, whose own incomes were declining because of long term inflation, the psychological impact of this measure was profound. It was particularly worrying for a new class of noblemen – the Lords of Erection – whose wealth was almost exclusively based on James' grants of former church lands.

In the end the shock of the Revocation was more important than its practical implications. Though no one was forcibly deprived of their lands, almost the whole of the Scottish nobility had been deeply shaken by the proposal and never fully trusted the King thereafter. Charles' proposed revolution in property relationships had been blown in on the cold wind of Continental despotism; if he had had his way, title to property would not have been governed by law but subject to royal whim. It resembled a similar edict introduced in Germany by the Habsburg Emperor Ferdinand II a few years later, which helped to usher in the bloodiest phase of the Thirty Years War. The alliance between crown and nobility that had provided a secure background for James' unpopular ecclesiastical innovations, was weakened beyond repair.

Apart from a few prominent Scots in London, most of the leading men in the land had never seen their new King. It was expected that he would come north for his coronation at the earliest opportunity; but it was eight years into his reign before he came to Edinburgh. He left London on 8 May 1633, and, demonstrating no sense of urgency, he made a painfully slow progress to the north, not entering Scotland until 12 June; he stayed for no longer than it had taken him to complete his journey.

Charles' coronation was carried out with all the grandeur Scotland could muster; but his visit to his ancient kingdom was not a happy affair. The suspicions and fears aroused by the Act of Revocation had been deepened by the time he left. He was accompanied, as his father had been in 1617, by William Laud, soon to be appointed to the See of Canterbury. Services were carried out at both Holyrood and St Giles according to the English fashion. Most Scots failed to appreciate the subtleties of Anglicanism, with its devotions to ceremony; and when it came to a Pope in Rome or a Pope in Canterbury, there appeared to be little practical difference. But Charles now envisaged a much more elevated role for his Scottish bishops, soon to be joined by a new colleague from Edinburgh, now elevated to an Episcopal See by royal edict.

When the first Parliament of the reign gathered, the bishops were appointed to a prominent position on the Lords of the Articles – a vetting body that screened all legislation to be put before the full assembly. Once legislation was introduced it was not followed by debate in the manner of the Parliament of England; those in attendance were simply required either to vote for or against. On this occasion a negative vote could easily prove dangerous; for the King himself was present, openly noting down the names of all those in opposition to his measures. In the course of a single day no fewer than 168 measures were rushed through, including the Revocation, new taxes and fresh confirmation of the Five Articles of Perth. The King was also given authority, in terms of an Act of 1609, to prescribe clerical dress.

It was quickly made plain that the King would countenance no appeal against any of his measures. Soon after Charles returned to England, William Haig, a prominent solicitor, drew up a protest against the innovations in ecclesiastical legislation, to be presented to the King. Not only did Charles refuse to hear the petition, but he also ordered the arrest of John Elphinstone, Lord Balmerino, simply for possessing a copy. Haig fled abroad, while Balmerino was charged with treason, and, after a carefully managed trial, sentenced to death. The whole proceedings caused such anger that, as a precaution against any attempt to free him, the nobleman was accompanied by a heavy escort each day on his way to the court from his prison in Edinburgh Castle. Public opinion was so violent that John Stewart, Earl of Traquair, a senior figure on the King's Scottish Privy Council, advised strongly against any attempt to have the sentence carried out. Charles reprieved Balmerino, which he no doubt intended to do, even without Traquair's intervention; but his clumsy attempt to intimidate noble opposition had been a serious error of judgement. Writing years later Gilbert Burnet, Bishop of Salisbury during the reign of William of Orange, said, with some justice, that the ruin of the King's affairs in Scotland was in great measure owing to the prosecution of Balmerino.

During the period of Balmerino's arrest and trial a new threat to the nobles steadily took shape. In 1634 the powers of the Court of High Commission were greatly extended. The following year the bishops began a steady political ascent under the patronage of King Charles, who clearly saw them as the most efficient instruments of royal policy. John Spottiswood, Archbishop of St

Andrews, was appointed as Chancellor, the highest office of state, and the first time a cleric had held the post since the pre Reformation days of Cardinal David Beaton. In the wake of this, more and more bishops were appointed to the Privy Council, the chief executive body in the land, thus depriving many nobles of their traditional influence on the affairs of state. Scotland's aristocracy, faced with economic ruin and threatened with death as the price of political opposition, could not ignore this fresh challenge. In his *History of the Rebellion,* Edward Hyde, Earl of Clarendon, highlighted the dangers of Charles' favourable treatment of the bishops;

> ...this unseasonable accumulation of so many honours upon them to which their functions did not entitle them...exposed them to the universal envy of the whole nobility...

The most serious consequence of Charles' political promotion of the bishops was the tension it introduced into the heart of the Privy Council itself. Traquair, the Lord Treasurer, was far from pleased by the growing power of the bishops, fearing for the security of his own position. Others, like Archibald, Lord Lorne, the acting head of the great Clan Campbell, neither trusted nor liked their clerical colleagues. This weakness at the heart of government affected the ability of the Council to deal with the dangerous crisis of 1637.

The failure of the Presbyterian riots of 1596 had shown the weakness of the Kirk party when deprived of aristocratic support; and the Balmerino trial had demonstrated that the nobles could not mount a challenge to the King without the backing of the rest of the nation. Against a background of growing discontent with Charles' arbitrary rule, all that was needed was a unifying force to bring Scotland to the threshold of rebellion. The banner that was eventually raised was for the defence of the Reformation itself.

After 1603 Scotland had been ruled by an absentee King, which inevitably involved some loss of national esteem. But Scotland's religion, too plain and vulgar for the taste of King Charles, provided her with a unique sense of identity which could not be easily tampered with, as the opposition to the Perth Articles had shown. By the 1630's the country had largely settled for the role of a junior partner in the regal Union in all matters but religion. Most Scots were proud of their Reformed faith, which had been introduced from below against the wishes of a Catholic sovereign. At the end of 1638 this spirit was summed up in the following words;

> ...this ancient kingdome, though not the most flourishing in the glory and wealth of the world, hath been so largely recompensed with the riches of the Gospel in the reformation and purity of religion from the abundant mercy and free grace of our God towards us, that all reformed kirks above us, did admit our happinesse. And King James himself of happy memory, gloried that he had the honor to be born, and to be king, in the best reformed kirk in the world.

No doubt King James would have expressed the matter differently, but he at least had the political sense to ensure that his religious innovations had the support of the General Assembly and Parliament. In 1635 Charles, caring nothing for Scots' sensibilities or established constitutional practice, and not even troubling to consult his own Privy Council, issued a royal warrant authorising a new set of clerical rules – the *Book of Canons* – published early the following year. The new rules began by asserting royal supremacy over the Church of Scotland. In the most remarkable statement of that supremacy, they went on to require the church to receive a new Liturgy or Service Book – sight unseen – to replace Knox's *Book of Common Order*, in use since the Reformation. In a heavy handed pun, Bishop Juxon of London remarked the canons would 'make more noise than all the cannons of Edinburgh Castle.' His prophecy was to prove sadly correct.

The Service Book which emerged was known by contemporaries – and for generations afterwards – as 'Laud's Liturgy'; but it was, in reality, the work of the Scottish bishops, anxious not to offend the sensibilities of the nation that the straightforward use of the English Prayer Book – Laud's own favoured solution – would inevitably have caused. Spottiswood and some of his colleagues were far more sensitive to Scottish opinion than is often assumed. On more than one occasion the venerable Archbishop had tried to get Charles to moderate his more extreme proposals. But the work carried out in secret by a small body of men, subject to the final approval of Laud and the King, inevitably incited suspicion and, more damaging, some wild speculation. It was widely reported that the Service Book, which every parish was enjoined to obtain before Easter 1637, was even more popish than the English Prayer Book. John Row was to call it a 'Popish–English–Scottish-Mass-Service Book.'

Rumours of discontent reached the ears of the King, but Charles was not his father: there would be no back tracking, no search for a face-saving compromise. This was the apogee of Divine Right. Always a dangerous doctrine, it was soon to be exposed in all its political folly.

Throughout late 1636 and the early months of 1637 Scotland was beset by a mood of tense anxiety. To make matters worse, new rumours about the Revocation had begun to spread, claiming that the King intended to restore so much property to the church that it would soon posses a third of the kingdom's wealth. Easter came and passed; still the long expected Service Book had not appeared. Finally, it was announced by the Archbishop of St Andrews on 16 July that the inaugural readings of the new book would be held in the Edinburgh churches the following Sunday.

According to Henry Guthrie, Bishop of Dunkeld after the Restoration of Charles II, opposition to the Liturgy was co-ordinated by Alexander Henderson and David Dickson, two leading Presbyterian divines, who came to Edinburgh as early as April to enlist the support of the mob. During this time, according to Guthrie, they consulted with Sir Thomas Hope, the Lord Advocate, and Lord Balmerino to obtain approval for their plans. But, as with all conspiracy theories, the intention is often to blacken the names of enemies, rather than to establish the facts. There is no other source to support Guthrie and the truth will never be known for certain. All that can really be said is that there was a great build up of popular resentment in the days prior to Sunday 23 July, and what followed is more likely to have been caused by a spontaneous outburst of anger, rather than a carefully preconceived plan.

Samuel Rutherford, the minister of Anwoth in Galloway who had been exiled to Aberdeen in 1636 by Bishop Sydserf, for his opposition to the Perth Articles, wrote to his old parishioners on 13 July, no doubt expressing the feelings of many like-minded people;

> I counsel you to beware of the new and strange leaven of men's inventions, beside and against the word of God, contrary to the oath of this Kirk, now coming among you. I instruct you of the superstition and idolatry of kneeling in the instant of receiving the Lord's Supper,

and of crossing in baptism, and of the obeying of men's days without any warrant for Christ our perfect Lawgiver. Countenance not the surplice, the attire of the mass priest, the garment of Baal's priests. The abominable bowing to alters of tree (wood) is coming upon you. Hate, and keep yourselves from idols. Forbear in any case to hear the reading of the new fatherless Service-Book, full of gross heresie, popish and superstitious errors, without any warrant from Christ, tending to the overthrow of preaching. You owe no obedience to the bastard canons; they are unlawful, blasphemous, and superstitious. All the ceremonies that lie in Antichrist's foul womb, waves of that great mother of fornication, the kirk of Rome, are to be refused.

On the Sunday in question St Giles was packed. Amongst the congregation were many serving women, seated on three legged stools, keeping places for their mistresses. To show support for the Prayer Book, the members of the King's Privy Council were also present, with some ominous exceptions: Traquair, the Treasurer, said that he had a prior engagement, and Lord Lorne pleaded sickness. When Dean John Hanna appeared carrying a brown leather book the murmuring began. As soon as he started to read many people, lead by the serving women, raised their voices in protest. Loud hand clapping and yells drowned out Hanna's words. Bibles flew towards the Dean, accompanied by Jenny Geddes' famous stool. David Lindsay, Bishop of Edinburgh, entered the pulpit to try to quieten the unseemly tumult. This only made matters worse. The cries became ever louder, ever more offensive – 'false Christian'; 'wolf'; 'beastly belly-god'; 'crafty fox.' Lindsay was told he was the offspring of the Devil and a witch, and that it was better that he had been hanged as a thief than live to be a pest to God's church. The scenes in St Giles that morning have been compared to the witches swarming out of the church at Alloway in pursuit of Tam o' Shanter.

With some difficulty the mob was forced outside by the town guard; but the riot continued in the streets, with stones being thrown at the cathedral windows. When the Bishop tried to leave after the service, his carriage was pursued by missiles and curses, causing the poor man to shit himself in fear. He was only rescued from further indignities by the intervention of the Earl of Weymss.

From Edinburgh, resistance to the Prayer Book spread outward across Scotland like a great tidal wave. When the synod of Glasgow met in August to introduce the Liturgy, a mob of women descended on the cathedral. One minister, William Anna of Ayr, who had been brave enough to preach in favour of the Prayer Book, was grabbed by the women in the streets and almost killed. For his own safety he had to be escorted out of town by the guard. On the way, he stumbled and fell headlong into the mud and filth in the streets, to the delight of the howling mob. In Brechin, the Bishop entered the pulpit with the Prayer Book in one hand and a pistol in the other, accompanied by his wife and servants, also armed. James Graham, Earl of Montrose, made the feelings of many of his fellow aristocrats plain when he described the Book as emerging from the bowels of the whore of Babylon. The mood of the nation was summed up in more moderate terms by Robert Baillie, the minister of Kilwinning in Ayrshire who wrote;

> ...there was in our Land never such ane appearance of a sturr; the whole people thinks Poperie at the doores...no man may speak any thing in publick for the King's part, except he would have himself marked for a sacrifice to be killed one day. I think our people possessed with a bloody devill, farr above any thing that I ever could have imagined...

There were some areas, however, that resisted the general feeling. The Highlands and Islands, outwith the Campbell territories, remained apart from the main currents of national life, preserving, in places, some loyalty to the ancient Catholic faith. Similarly in the south west, the lands of Robert Maxwell, first Earl of Nithsdale, provided a haven for Scotland's persecuted Catholic minority. But the most important centre of resistance was undoubtedly Aberdeen, where a group of conservative clerics held out against the condemnation of the Prayer Book, supported by one of Scotland's senior noblemen, George Gordon, second Marquis of Huntly.

In Edinburgh the Privy Council was in an almost impossible position. Charles' first reaction was to blame it for not putting down the disorders with greater efficiency; but the Council, already weakened by fatal divisions between the clerical and lay representatives, had no armed force at its disposal to ensure that the King's decrees were obeyed. Rather lamely, it tried to pass the responsibility for dealing with Edinburgh's disorderly mob to the town council, who were also ordered to ensure that protection should given to all readers of the Prayer Book in the city's churches. Not surprisingly, no one could be found who was brave enough to undertake the reading. Offers of money by the Privy Council to any hardy individuals prepared to volunteer for the task failed to get any takers.

Petitions, expressing hostility to the King's church policy, began to arrive in Edinburgh from many parts of Scotland. One group of ministers went so far as to describe the Prayer Book as part of a plot to destroy the Kirk. Many of the petitions shared a common theme: the innovations in religion had not been approved by either Parliament or the General Assembly. Faced with this depth of opposition the Council, on its own initiative, suspended the reading of the Liturgy, and made efforts to open the King's mind to the extent of the crisis. True to character, Charles simply refused to listen. Bit by bit, he increased the political temperature. Not prepared to retreat on any of the issues at stake, Charles chose to stand on his own authority and Majesty. He had no means of enforcing his unrealistic demands and the whole crisis rapidly escalated out of control. Before long it was the role of the bishops and the government of the King that were in dispute, not simply the Prayer Book. Charles turned a rebellion into a revolution.

In all, sixty-nine petitions were received against the Service Book. The protesters – nobles, ministers and burgesses – all crowded into Edinburgh to back up their demands. In September, three of the petitions, together with a list of the rest, were sent to the King. All waited with great anticipation for the answer. It came in mid October. Charles refused to consider the petitions until the atmosphere was more peaceable; all petitioners were ordered to leave the capital within twenty-four hours, or risk being accused of treason; the Privy Council and law courts were to move out of Edinburgh, in emulation of a measure taken by James VI to deal with the riots of 1596. The city was a powder keg; Charles threw in the match.

With the refusal of the petitions, and the insulting treatment of Edinburgh, fresh riots swept the town on 18 October. Thomas Sydserf, Bishop of Galloway, a particularly unpopular figure, was attacked in the streets, along with Sir William Elphinstone, the Lord Chief Justice. Traquair, too, was badly manhandled. He was knocked to the ground and in risk of being trampled to death, finally escaping from the embrace of the mob with the help of some of the opposition nobility.

The protesters, headed by John Leslie, sixth Earl of Rothes, John Campbell, Lord Loudoun, and Lord Balmerino, old opponents of royal policy in Scotland, decided that the King's answer to the petitions merited an even grander response, which emerged towards the end of the year as the General Supplication, in which all of the individual currents flowed into a single torrent. An attack was made not just on the Service Book, but on the Canons of 1636 and, more seriously, on the bishops in general, who were accused of misleading 'so good a King.' In this we can detect traces of the age old protest directed against 'evil counsellors', intended to allow the monarch to save face by escaping from the errors of his own policy. It was soon apparent that Charles was not prepared to accept this bait.

The General Supplication was bad enough; but by far the most serious consequence of the October riots for the battered authority of the King was the formation of an executive body from amongst the various classes of the petitioners that, by December, was to be known as 'The Tables'. In face of the Privy Council's continuing impotence, the Tables were, by the end of the year, acting as an alternative government.

After his bruising experience in the Edinburgh riot, Traquair, in a mood of frustration and despair, wrote to James, Marquis of Hamilton, Charles' principal Scottish courtier;

> My Lord believe that the delay in taking some certain and resolved courses in this business has brought business to such a height and bred such a looseness in this kingdom that I daresay was never since His Majesty's father going into England. The king is not pleased to allow any of us to come to inform him...No man stays here to attend or assist the service; and those on whom he lays or seems to entrust his commandments in this business, most turn back upon it whenever any difficulties appear. I am in all things left alone, and God is my witness, never so perplexed what to do. Shall I give way to the people's fury, which without force and the strong hand cannot be opposed?

Traquair finally obtained permission to come to the King early in the new year. He told Charles frankly that he must either abandon the Liturgy or come to Scotland with an army of 40,000 men. Instead of an army, the King gave the Treasurer yet another proclamation. Still believing, after all the turmoil of the previous year, that a simple assertion of royal authority was enough to dispel the opposition, Charles took the most fateful step of all. He decided to set matters straight: it was he, and not the bishops, who was responsible for the Service Book. There could be no more pretence. Charles was offering a direct challenge to his opponents, fully expecting them to stand down. Sadly for him, they did not.

The new proclamation was read in Edinburgh on 22 February. It was greeted, not with reverence, but with hoots and jeers. A rival protestation was read out in the presence of the King's heralds, who could not escape the throng. Urging on the crowds, the Earl of Montrose, a man who always managed to balance depth of thought with vain and histrionic gestures, stood on a barrel which had been placed on the town scaffold, causing his mentor, the Earl of Rothes, to remark that he would not be content until he had been raised there three fathoms above the rest; a humorous remark that turned out to have the force of prediction.

In responding to the King's intransigence, the Tables took one of the most important steps in Scottish history. It was decided that answer should be made in the form of a Covenant, an age old device of biblical origin, used most recently in 1581 by James VI, during one of the periodic outbursts of anti Catholic hysteria. The Tables decided to resurrect this so-called Negative Confession, to be updated and used as the basis of a new National Covenant. The task was given to two men: Alexander Henderson, the minister of Leuchars in Fife, and a young lawyer by the name of Archibald Johnstone of Warriston.

Johnstone of Warriston is one of the most fascinating figures of the Covenanting period. He left behind a diary which details his inner struggles and the intensity of his relationship with God. It also shows a personality verging on the threshold of disintegration. He compensated for his sense of emptiness and self doubt by filling himself with the power of God. In the process, he acquired a single minded sense of mission, which often blinded him to political reality. He was to be the Robespierre of the Scottish Revolution.

The National Covenant was prepared with some care. As the opposition to Charles was by no means united, the document could not be too revolutionary in its general direction. Many ministers, for example, were not convinced that Episcopacy was contrary to divine law, so no mention was made of the bishops. At the heart of the document lay a simple assertion: that all signatories pledged themselves to defend the Reformed religion and to resist all innovations, unless tried by free Assemblies and Parliaments.

On Wednesday 28 February 1638 the newly completed document was read to the barons and nobles assembled in Greyfriars Church. The signing began at 4 in the afternoon and continued until 8 o' clock, on what Johnstone called the glorious marriage day of the kingdom with God. Next day, 300 ministers signed at Tailor's Hall; and on 2 March at Trinity College Church at the foot of Leith Wynd, it was read to a gathering of the ordinary people of Edinburgh, who subscribed to it that day and the following. From Edinburgh copies were carried across Scotland to be signed in local parish churches. Some, it is said, signed in their own blood. What is certainly true is that the surviving copies convey the heightened emotion that greeted the Covenant – 'John Cunynghame till daith'; E. Johnestoun with my heart.' Scotland witnessed scenes of acute religious fervour, described by the minister, James Gordon of Rothiemay;

> And such was the zeale of many subscribents, that for a whyle, many subscrybed with teares on their cheekes...Such ministers as spocke most for it wer heard so passionately and with such frequencye, that churches could not containe ther hearers in cittyes; some of the devouter sexe (as if they had keeped vigills) keeping ther seates from Friday to Sunday, to gett the communione givne them sitting; some sitting allway let befor such sermones in the churches, for feare of lossing a rowe or place of hearing; or, at the least, some of their handmaides sitting constantly ther all night till ther mistresses came to tack upp ther places and to releeve them; so that severall (as I heard from a very sober and credible man) under that relligiouse confynment, wer foeced to give waye to ther naturall necessityes, which they could no longer containe, bedewng the pavements of churches with other moysture than teares.

In Ireland, the English Lord Deputy, Thomas Wentworth, took steps to stop the fervour spreading in Ulster, where a strong Scots community had been settled since the beginning of the century. All were required to subscribe to an oath renouncing the Covenant, a cause of much resentment against the dictatorial Wentworth.

15

The wave of the Covenant did, however, break against some obdurate shores, principally Aberdeenshire, where the Marquis of Huntly enjoyed great power, partly as a Highland chief and partly as a Lowland magnate; but elsewhere, refusal to sign was accompanied by threats, and sometimes by outright violence. David Mitchell, a dissident Edinburgh minister, was accompanied through the streets by a party of people who muttered murderous threats against him; the minister at Torphichen was attacked in his own church. The unfortunate Bishop Sydserf was subject to further indignities, when he was stoned on his way to Edinburgh by a gang of women from Falkirk.

Archbishop Spottiswood, a man who had warned time and again against Charles' rashness, was quick to realise the implications of the Covenant. 'Now,' he is said to have remarked, 'all that we have been doing these thirty years is thrown down at once.' Later that year, in fear of his life, he left Scotland, never to return. Deposed by the Glasgow Assembly in December 1638, he died in exile the following November.

All to late, Charles began to waken to the danger in which he had placed himself. The Covenant was clearly a treasonable document because it had been subscribed without royal warrant; but no amount of empty threats would make the Tables back down. As early as October 1637 the Catholic Earl of Nithsdale had urged him to use force against his opponents in Scotland. The King, already suspicious of the involvement of Balmerino in the opposition, was all too ready to listen to people like George Conn, a papal agent, that the Covenanters were part of an international Calvinist conspiracy against monarchy itself. But Charles was in no position to take any more active steps at this stage. He had ruled in England without the aid of Parliament for almost ten years and did not have enough money for a large scale military operation.

Summoning an English Parliament was a risky enterprise. The last assembly, dismissed in 1629, had been highly critical of royal policy both at home and abroad, refusing to grant the King the taxes he desired. More recently, the opposition to the unconstitutional tax known as Ship Money – demonstrated in the famous case against the former MP John Hampden – had shown widespread discontent in much of England. Deciding it was more prudent to delay militant action for the time being, he sent his kinsman and favourite, the Marquis of Hamilton to Scotland, as

Royal Commissioner, with instructions to negotiate with the Covenanters.

It's difficult to know what to make of James Hamilton. A man of limited political talents, he was often too subtle for his own good. He had an incoherent mind, indulging in elaborate conspiratorial games when only plain words were needed. With a strong stake in Scotland, he had too much to lose to be a completely selfless agent of the King. Essentially, he was a compromiser, with no strong views on religion, sent to deal with a complex problem already past compromise. He had the capacity to change his mind with bewildering rapidity, turning mountains into mole hills and back into mountains again. Robert Baillie, generally well disposed towards Hamilton, said that his ways were so ambiguous that no man understood him. It is only fair to say that he genuinely tried to do his best; but he had a reverse Midas touch, in the end turning all to lead.

Hamilton was certainly anxious to avoid war. Soon after he arrived in Scotland in June he wrote to Charles, attempting to flatter and warn him at the same time;

> ...you Majesty uood dou ueill of cumming heir in persone with a royall armie, and of victorie make no doubt; bot when itt is obtained itt is bot ouer you oune poure people, and hou fare your Majesty in you great uisdome uill think it fit to uink at their madnesis, I doe not nor presume to aduise, onlie this much, give me leave to say I dare assure you till some part of their madnes hes left them, that they will sooner loose ther lives than lieve the Covenantt...

Over the next few months Hamilton laboured to improve the King's position in Scotland, travelling back to London to consult with him when necessary. But none of his schemes and plots had any effect. He even managed to persuade Charles to reissue the Negative Confession of 1581, and sought signatories for this document, which he hoped would replace the National Covenant, with very limited success. Schemes like the revival of the Negative Confession did little more than increase the general distrust of the King; but another of Hamilton's plots had far more dangerous long term consequences.

Earlier in the century the Campbells, acting as agents of the King, had seized the last of the lands of the southern branch of Clan Donald – the Kintyre Peninsula and the island of Islay. For some time prior to this the southern MacDonalds – often known as Clan Ian Mor, after their founder – had been linked by ties of blood and kinship to the McDonnells of Antrim. The McDonnells had never been reconciled to the dispossession of their Scottish kin, and their present head, Randal McDonnell, Earl of Antrim, claimed to be the rightful heir to the lands of Clan Ian Mor. Hamilton was aware of this claim and suggested that Charles might use Antrim's ambitions against Lord Lorne, the heir of Clan Campbell. This was an amazing suggestion, for Lorne, although never a wholehearted supporter of the King, was still a member of the Privy Council, and had not signed the Covenant. Hamilton may very well have thought that the Antrim threat would be enough to stop Lorne taking this final step; but, if this is the case, it was hardly necessary. Lorne's father, the seventh Earl of Argyll, was still alive and, as a Catholic convert, was living in London, estranged from his son and exiled from his clan. Nevertheless, it was open to Charles to use the seventh Earl to challenge the authority of Lorne; and as long as his father was alive the Campbell chief would not break with the King. Playing with Antrim's ambitions was hardly the way to win over a man of whom Hamilton said 'itt feares me that he will prufe the dangerousest man in this state.' This ill judged proposal was revealed to Lorne and virtually ensured that the most powerful Scot of his generation was one day guaranteed to be an opponent of the King.

On Hamilton's advice, Charles finally accepted that he had no other recourse but to summon an Assembly. He did so on the understanding that the bishops would be allowed to attend, and that no minister would be debarred from attending for refusing to sign the Covenant. Pleased that he had obtained this concession, Hamilton, after he had returned from his consultation with the King, found that events had, once again, marched ahead of him. Rothes and the other leading Covenanters made it all too clear that the bishops would only be allowed to appear as criminals before the bench and that leading laymen intended to be present as elders of the church. It was also clear that the elections would be so managed that no opponent of the Covenant had any chance of appearing in the Assembly.

Even the choice of Glasgow as the venue was another of Hamilton's miscalculations. He hoped that the close proximity of his tenants and kinsmen on his Lanarkshire estates would be enough to intimidate the Assembly; but these were under the control of his mother, the formidable old dowager, Lady Anna Cunningham, a committed Covenanter.

When the Assembly met on 22 November all Hamilton's worst fears were realised. No bishops attended, all having followed Spottiswood into exile. All the leading lay Covenanters were present as elders, many of them armed. Archibald Campbell, whose father had recently died, attended as the eighth Earl of Argyll, along with the other Privy Councillors. A protest had been prepared in advance on behalf of the truant bishops, which Hamilton, as the King's Commissioner, tried to have read; but his interventions were simply ignored as the Assembly proceeded to elect Alexander Henderson as Moderator and Archibald Johnstone of Warriston as Clerk. Hamilton fought a futile rearguard action against the legitimacy of the Assembly. As a final gesture he declared the gathering illegal, commanding all present to depart on pain of treason. The Commissioner and the other royal officers withdrew, a moment of high drama reduced to low comedy when the door was found to be locked and the keys temporarily missing. Hamilton finally exited with as much dignity as he could muster; Argyll, ominously, declined to follow.

After the Commissioner's departure, the Assembly, now technically illegal, continued to meet until 20 December. Its proceedings showed how much more radical feelings had become since the Covenant was signed in February. It swept away all that James and Charles had worked for in the church over the preceding forty years: the Liturgy, Canons, Five Articles of Perth and Court of High Commission were all rejected. Episcopacy itself was abolished and the bishops condemned and excommunicated one by one. Presbyterianism was restored as the true government of the Kirk of Scotland. This was a political as well as an ecclesiastical revolution: the bishops stood condemned not just as church officers, but also as officers of the absolutist state; instruments, in other words, of the King's will.

The Glasgow Assembly was only outwardly a clerical forum: in practice it was a gathering of all the dissatisfied elements in the state, lay as well as clerical. It was one of the most important gatherings in British history; a body which defied a King and began a revolution, with consequences so far reaching that none of those present could have imagined the outcome. The German historian, Leopold von Ranke, compared its defiance to that moment, a century and a half later, when the French National Assembly for the first time resisted the commands of Louis XVI.

In London the King condemned the Assembly as a gathering of traitors. Both sides openly prepared for conflict. 'I am affrighted,' Robert Baillie wrote, 'with a bloody civil war.'

CHAPTER 2
No Bishop – No King?

For Charles, war with his Scottish subjects was a major gamble. He had no army and insufficient resources to mount a serious campaign of conquest. Both Scotland and England had been at peace with one another for almost a century, and the Border defences at Carlisle and Berwick were in a poor state of repair. Yet there could be no backing down. If he agreed that the Scottish General Assembly was supreme in all ecclesiastical matters, the dream of Andrew Melville, it would not be long before an English Parliament would make similar demands; and this would inevitably lead to a challenge to royal supremacy in other areas of state policy. Soon after the conclusion of the Ship Money case against John Hampden, William Laud wrote;

> It is not the Scottish business alone that I look upon but the whole frame of things at home and abroad, with vast expenses out of little treasure, and my misgiving soul is deeply apprehensive of no small evils coming on...I can see no cure without a miracle.

Charles himself remained childishly perplexed by the events of the previous year, refusing to accept that his whole policy had collapsed as a result of his obstinate blindness to political reality. He was all too ready to believe that he was the victim of conspiracies engineered by the puritans and Cardinal Richelieu, the chief minister of Louis XIII. He simply could not believe that the Scots would not give in to a determined show of royal authority, and from beginning to end his plan of campaign for the coming war was little more than a gigantic bluff. Early in the conflict he stated his position in unambiguous terms;

> The question is not whether a Service Book is to be received or not, nor whether episcopal government shall be continued or presbyterial admitted, but whether we are their King or not.

He also made ready to conjure up ancient rivalries. The English shires were informed that the Scots had risen in arms in order to invade England. On 27 February 1639 a proclamation was read in every parish church in England, summoning the northern barons and their vassals to meet the King at York by 1 April, an antiquated device of feudal origin, intended to overcome some of the King's financial problems in raising a professional army. All of the English preparations gave an appearance of obsolescence. The county militia – known as the trained bands – resembled a kind of seventeenth century Dad's Army. In the north they were even armed with longbows and brown bills, last used with any effect by English infantry at the Battle of Flodden in 1513.

The obvious solution was to summon Parliament to vote the necessary war funds; but Charles did not trust his subjects. During the early part of his reign his experience of Parliament had not been a happy one. His early wars with Spain and France had been lamentable failures, in sharp contrast to the great military successes of Elizabeth I, leading to major criticism of royal government by the puritan gentry, who were heavily represented in the Commons. The Bishops' War was to be the first major conflict started since 1399 without first calling Parliament.

As both sides made ready for the first Anglo-Scots conflict since the 1550's, Sir John Suckling wrote to a friend in Norfolk, telling him that 'this northern storm (like a new disease)...hath not yet been given a name.' But by the summer it was reported to Sir John Lambe, the agent of Archbishop Laud, that some were styling it the *Bellum Episcopalae* – the Bishops' War.

In Scotland preparations for war had been underway since the previous summer. Alexander Leslie, the senior Scottish soldier serving in the German wars, had signed the Covenant and returned home with many of his comrades. These men were to form the basis of a professional officer corps, and soon managed to shape their raw recruits into a well organised, disciplined army. Leslie himself had a European reputation as a soldier, arising from his skilled defence of the town of Stralsund against Wallenstein in the Thirty Years War; but his talents were, at best, limited – he was a good sergeant major rather than a great captain.

While most Scots were committed to the cause of the Covenant, few can really have welcomed the prospect of a full scale war. The country had no navy and a very long coastline. In early February Robert Baillie recorded his own feelings in a mood of some apprehension;

We look for no other bot in the Spring the King to come in person, upon Louthian and Edinburgh, with a great land army; that one part of his navie shall go to Aberdeen and joyn with Huntley, another to the coast of Fyfe and Louthian, a third to land from Ireland on us in the West some little armie.

In January Rothes, Montrose, Balmerino and the other leading Covenanters met in Edinburgh to finalise their preparations. Although Argyll had not yet signed the Covenant – he was not to do so until April – he mobilised Clan Campbell to meet the expected threat of an invasion from Ireland.

The accession of Argyll to the cause was a considerable boost to the Covenanters. With an estimated 20,000 men at his disposal he was by far the strongest nobleman in Scotland, a figure of considerable influence in both the Highlands and the Lowlands, known to his kin in Gaelic as *MacCailen Mór* – son of Great Colin – after the founder of Clan Campbell. Although, as time was to show, he had absolutely no military talents whatsoever, he was a skilled politician, the first man to understand the rising power of the Scottish middle classes organised in the Kirk. Patrick Gordon of Ruthven, no friend of the Campbells, composed a fair pen portrait of the great Argyll;

For his extrenall and outward disposition, he was of homely carriage, gentle, myled and affable, gratious and courteous to speake too. Naturallie, he had a large and understanding heart, a jealous and far reaching apprehension and yet his presence did showe him of such plaine and homely aspect, as seemd rather inclyned to simplicitie then any wayes tented with a loftie and unsatiable ambition.

It was inevitable that his power and influence would eventually carry him into the leading role in the Covenanter movement. Argyll, however, did not intend to make himself into a dictator, an accusation to be made against him by nobles of the second rank, like the much more ruthlessly ambitious Montrose, jealous of his political advance.

In making their preparations against an English invasion, the Covenanters had to be mindful of the opposition they faced within Scotland itself. Although there were some Catholic noblemen in the south, they had no real power beyond the enclave of Nithsdale. Huntly, secretly appointed as the King's lieutenant in the north east in early 1639, was potentially far more dangerous, with the power of the Gordons and the prosperous port of Aberdeen behind him. But George Gordon, for all his unshakeable loyalty to the King, was not the man for the moment. If Argyll was a bad soldier, Huntly was a disastrous one. He had no leadership skills whatsoever. Quite incapable of firm and resolute action, he embarked in a series of half hearted, aimless enterprises which allowed the energy of Clan Gordon to drift and dissipate.

Charles' plan of campaign involved an ambitious three pronged attack on Scotland. A naval task force under Hamilton, who had returned to England after leaving the Glasgow Assembly, was to carry 5,000 men from the eastern counties of England to the support of Huntly. The King would march with the main army to the eastern Border, while the Marquis of Antrim, with the support of Deputy Wentworth, would launch an attack on Argyllshire from Ireland.

The Antrim plan involved considerable political risks for the King. Distrustful of puritans of all descriptions, Charles, firm in his high Anglican convictions, enjoyed the company of George Conn and the other Catholics in the retinue of his French Queen, Henrietta Maria. Although his Catholic subjects suffered from various social and legal restrictions, they were at least loyal to the King, in sharp contrast to the Presbyterian Scots. The Earl of Nithsdale had first proposed that Irish troops might be sent to Scotland, with a possible landing at Ayr to be supported by himself, Hamilton of Abercorn, the Marquis of Douglas, Herries, Seton of Winton and Semple, the chief Catholic nobles of the south. But a landing in the south west of Scotland was not a realistic prospect: the Covenanters here were far stronger than the Catholic loyalists. In invading the western Highlands, Antrim, also a Catholic, could at least count on the support of his kinsmen and other clans who hated the domination of the mighty Campbells. But the effect of a Catholic Irish invasion of Argyllshire on wavering Protestant opinion was likely to have a serious impact on the future prosperity of the King's cause in Scotland.

In January Charles wrote to Wentworth to express his warm support for Antrim's scheme;

> I should be glad if you could find some way to furnish the Earl of Antrim with arms, though he be a Roman Catholic; for he may be of much use to me at this time, to shake loose upon the Earl of Argyll.

24

But Wentworth, by far the most skilled of Charles' ministers, was not enthusiastic. He distrusted Antrim, and, as a staunch Protestant, was deeply opposed to arming the Catholic Irish 'as many O's and Macs as would startle the whole Council board.' His lack of co-operation ensured that Antrim's plan never got off the ground; but it did not go away, and eventually found its greatest supporter, ironically, in a Covenanter General who was at present making ready to lead an army against the Gordons.

The Covenanters were quick to mop up all pockets of resistance in southern Scotland before the King could appear on the Border. Edinburgh Castle, the most powerful in Scotland, was taken with some ease from a Royal garrison which lacked the will to fight. Dumbarton fell soon afterwards. At Dalkeith Castle, where the Scottish regalia was stored, the Earl of Traquair hoped to make a stand; but although his garrison was well provided with powder and ammunition, the castle itself was not defensible and was taken with ease by a Covenanter force led by the Earl of Rothes and others. By the end of March, Caerlaverock Castle, a property of the Earl of Nithsdale, was the only defensive position untaken south of the Tay. It was now time to deal with the more dangerous situation in the north.

Early in the year Aberdeen made ready to resist the Covenanters by arming and training its citizens. Huntly also made his own preparations, and by February had some 2000 men under arms. He learned of a meeting of the local Covenanters at Turriff on 14 February. Considering this as a threat to his prestige, Huntly set off with his men, intending to frighten his enemies off. Instead they accepted the challenge. When Huntly arrived, he found that the Earl of Montrose was there before him. To balance the preparations of Aberdeen and the Gordons, Montrose had raised forces in his native Forfarshire, confronting the rebels at Turriff with 800 well armed men. Huntly faced his first great challenge, and failed. Although he heavily outnumbered his opponents he was not willing to risk an armed encounter, and promptly drew off after being allowed to ride through the town as a face saver.

The following month Huntly finally received his commission from Charles in a proclamation which made clear that the King stood by Episcopacy and the Prayer Book. This helped to breath fresh life into the northern resistance, deflated by the fiasco at Turriff, and the city of Aberdeen made ready to resist. By 25

March Huntly had gathered an army of 5,000 men at Inverurie. On his instructions the soldiers wore red ribbons as a mark of their loyalty to the King. This theatrical gesture was as much as Huntly was able to accomplish. Learning that Montrose, accompanied by Alexander Leslie, was advancing from the south, he decided not to resist and disbanded his forces before retiring to his castle of Bog of Gicht in Strathbogie. Demoralised by Huntly's obvious lack of backbone, Aberdeen decided to offer no resistance, allowing the Covenanter army to enter unopposed on 30 March. Never slow to learn from others when it came to the grand gesture, Montrose ordered his men to march in wearing blue sashes across their chests and blue ribbons in their bonnets, in response to Huntly's red ribbons. The blue bonnet was to survive as the badge of the Covenanters, long after Montrose had found another cause.

Leaving an occupying force under the Earl of Kinghorn in Aberdeen, Montrose continued his advance towards Inverurie. On the way his men raided the property of known opponents of the Covenant, and the verb 'to plunder' was introduced into the English language, brought by Leslie and his followers from the German wars. It was a kind of warfare with which the area was to become all too familiar before it saw the last of Montrose.

With no sign of the promised support from the King, Huntly, with an inadequate force at his disposal, had no choice but to open negotiations. An agreement was reached on 5 April, allowing Huntly to remain at liberty, provided he offered no further resistance. It's possible that Huntly, who had little taste, and less aptitude, for war, may have kept to this agreement; but he was not trusted by the Covenanters of the area, and Montrose was obliged to break the agreement. A few days later on a visit to Aberdeen, Huntly and his eldest son, Lord George Gordon, were effectively arrested and taken south with the rest of the army to Edinburgh. This action was quickly to prove to be a major error of judgement; the Gordons may have been quiet, but they were not pacified. Huntly was such a poor leader that he was more of an asset than a danger to the Covenanters. Angered by the kidnapping of their chief, the Gordons were soon to find leadership from more determined men. Huntly's arrest also had more serious long term consequences for the royal cause in Scotland. As Gordon of Rothiemay records;

...it bredde such a distaste in Huntly against Montrose, that afterwards when Montrose fell off to the Kinge and forsooke the Covenanters, and was glad to get the assistance of Huntly and his followers, the Marquesse of Huntly could never be gaind to join cordially with him, nor to swallow that indigniyye.

On 30 March, the day the blue bonnets entered Aberdeen, Charles arrived at York. Already his grand strategy had almost completely unravelled. Wentworth's hostility towards Antrim and arming the Catholic Irish, had ensured that their would be no diversionary attack on Scotland from the west. The occupation of Aberdeen and the arrest of Huntly meant that their was no party north of the Border on which to base a royalist resistance. Wentworth had promised to raise his own force for an advance up the Firth of Clyde; but the fall of Dumbarton Castle, and the capture by Argyll of Brodick Castle on the Island of Arran, a property belonging to Hamilton, nullified the prospect of this supplementary invasion.

Argyll also took the opportunity to strengthen his own western flank, seizing the island of Colonsay, the last toehold in Scotland of Clan Ian Mor. In the process Campbell troops imprisoned Antrim's principal supporter, Coll MacGillespick MacDonald – usually known as Coll Coitach – and two of his sons. The remaining two, Alasdair and Ranald MacColla, managed to escape to Ireland. Alasdair, in particular, nurtured a furious hatred of the Campbells, which was soon to bare a bloody fruit.

Faced with these strategic failures, and an acute shortage of money with which to pay their English troops, a mood of paranoia gripped the King and his chief advisers. Charles continued to see the hand of Richelieu in the northern rebellion. When Edinburgh Castle was taken, the Earl of Dorset accused Hamilton of treason in open Council. Huntly was also believed to be a traitor for the tame surrender of Aberdeen; and no sooner had Traquair set foot in York than he was arrested for the fall of Dalkeith.

Sir Edmund Verney recorded his own feelings of despair shortly after the fall of Aberdeen;

...soe now all Scotland is gone. I would it were under the sea, for it will aske a greate time, and cost much bludd, to reduce them againe...

By the middle of April Hamilton's naval expedition was ready to sail from Great Yarmouth. He had in all some twenty-eight ships and 5,000 men. However, the quality both of his men and their equipment was far from good. No more than 200 of them had ever held a gun before. What is worse, the muskets provided were of poor quality, and were not all of the same calibre. Hamilton reckoned that it would take at least a month to prepare his men for combat. But with Aberdeen gone there was now nowhere for him to land and make his force fighting fit. He was given orders to sail to the Firth of Forth – with what purpose it is not clear.

Mindful of the English seaborne descent on Leith and Edinburgh in 1544, the Scots had taken steps to defend the Forth estuary. The defences of the vital port of Leith had been strengthened, with women coming from Edinburgh to help carry earth and stones to improve the fortifications. In the Lothians and Fife thousands of people turned out to defend their homes. All was ready by the time the English force appeared in the Forth on 1 May. Even Hamilton's mother, Lady Cunningham, had turned up armed with a brace of pistols, saying that she was ready to shoot her son if he attempted to land.

Faced with this determination, and having an inadequately prepared force, all Hamilton was able to do was to take possession of the small islands of Inchkeith and Inchcolm, in a rather desperate attempt to improve the military skills of his men, while opening fresh negotiations with the Covenanters, which met with no success at all. He failed in attempts to have another proclamation by the King published; and when he asked for fresh water Leslie, with grim humour, said he should come and fetch it. Making absolutely no attempt to conceal his feelings, or to improve the King's morale, Hamilton wrote to his master on 7 May;

> Your Majestie's affaires ar in ane desperatt condition. The inraged people heir runes to the height of Rebellion and walkes with a blind obedience, as by ther tratrous leaders they ar commanded, and resolved they ar rather to obay then to embrace or exsept of your profered grace in your last most gratious proclamation...You will find itt a woorke of greate difficultie and of vast expens to curb them by force, ther power being greatter, ther combinatione stronger than can be imagined.

Charles needed no reminder of this from Hamilton. He had managed to raise a reasonably sized force of 18,000 infantry and

3,000 cavalry; but, like Hamilton's marines, much of this army was of dubious quality. It wasn't just Hamilton who was advising against invasion; from Ireland Thomas Wentworth urged him to delay his campaign for the time being. But too much of the King's personal prestige was invested in the enterprise for him to step down without some kind of concession from the Scots. In a slightly more conciliatory tone he issued a proclamation from Newcastle on 14 May, saying that he intended to give his Scottish subjects full satisfaction in Parliament as soon as the disturbances were quietened, and that he had no intention of invading, provided the Scots kept their army at least ten miles from the Border. Charles, moreover, still refused to believe that the Scots would not back down when faced with an assertion of kingly power. Before long he was to receive some morale boosting news from the distant north.

Learning of the arrival of Hamilton's fleet in the Forth, the Gordon's decided that the time had come to avenge Huntly. Gathering in strength the local gentry, headed by Sir George Ogilvie of Banff, pledged themselves to defend the King for the 'honour and service we owe to the house of Huntly.' The Marquis' second son, James, Viscount Aboyne, was sent to Newcastle to appeal to the King for aid, while a force of 800 men under Colonel Johnstone was detached to attack the Covenanters at Turriff, the scene of Huntly's earlier humiliation.

Turriff was a dangerous position to attack. It was guarded from the south and west by steep slopes above the Deveron and Idoch Water, giving the defenders a good view of the surrounding countryside. Johnstone decided that the best plan was to launch a surprise strike. Advancing along the Banff road on the night of 13/14 May, the Gordons arrived before the town at dawn. The assault commenced at once. Taken by complete surprise the Covenanters, who did not have the time to organise their superior forces, were driven from the town by a discharge of musket fire, followed by a charge of pikemen. Under the leadership of the Earl of Errol a few attempted to make a stand, but were forced to surrender after Johnstone brought up some cannons. This affair, the first serious clash of the Covenanter Wars, was to be known as the Trot of Turriff.

Hugely elated by this small victory, the royalists proceeded to occupy Aberdeen. There was some talk of carrying the campaign further south into the Mearns. However, fears for the safety of the captured Huntly prevented any serious escalation of the conflict, and after a few days the Gordons left Aberdeen, which was reoccupied by a force led by the Earl Marischal on 23 May. Two days later Montrose arrived with a larger army of Covenanters. This second occupation of Aberdeen was a little less gentle than the first. Discontent with the royalist city expressed itself in some limited plundering. The city dogs, which had been decorated with blue ribbons to mock the Covenanters, were all rounded up and killed. After fining the city 10,000 merks for its disloyalty, Montrose went north to track down the Gordon lairds; but he was soon called back by a new crisis.

At Newcastle the King was gratified by the arrival of Aboyne with news of the exciting events in Aberdeenshire. Here was an ideal opportunity to revive the scheme for landing a diversionary force in the north of Scotland. Aboyne was at once sent on to join Hamilton in the Firth of Forth, with the recommendation that he be supplied with men and munitions for a return to Aberdeen.

Hamilton did not receive the young nobleman in the best of humours. Many of his men were falling sick of smallpox; and whatever enthusiasm he ever had for the enterprise was long since gone. He was also aware of the limitations of the force at his disposal, the bulk of which had been detached to join the King at Berwick some days before; but it is also fairly clear that he had no desire to engage in any serious military operation. Hamilton undoubtedly shared the King's belief that the Covenanters would back down in the face of royal authority, and reach a negotiated settlement. Serious bloodshed in the north would obviously have made this much more difficult. He continued to send the King gloomy dispatches from the Forth, saying that the Scots would accept no peace unless the acts of the Glasgow Assembly were ratified; otherwise they were resolved to give battle. His letter of 21 May is fairly typical;

> Resolued they are to force your Majestie to a battle, being confident that they ar much stronger in infantry...All that is to be fearedis that they may pass by your army, and so gett betwixt Newcastle and you, by which means they cutt of your victuals...

The arrival of Aboyne was, therefore, less than welcome. Hamilton, however, yielded to the King's command by doing the very minimum: Aboyne was given a ship with some guns and men, but hardly enough to make any real difference. He was also given the services of a military expert, Colonel William Gunn from Sutherland, a man who was to prove so incompetent that he was later accused of deliberate treachery. In the company of Gunn, and the Earls of Glencairn and Tullibardine, Aboyne sailed for home. On the way he was met by Sir George Ogilvie and other Gordon partisans, who had sailed from Aberdeen after it was occupied by the Covenanters.

News of the arrival of Aboyne's little force in early June spread quickly through Buchan, and before long the Gordons were back in arms. Aboyne was joined by his thirteen year old brother, Lord Lewis Gordon, with the men of Strathbogie and their allies, the Farquharsons. The Earl Marischal, with insufficient force to resist, abandoned Aberdeen, retiring to his stronghold of Dunnotar Castle, just south of Stonehaven, and sent for aid to Montrose, who at this time was in Angus seeking fresh recruits.

Despite their early success in reoccupying Aberdeen, the royalists had no clear plan of action. Gunn quickly proved himself to be of no value at all. An advance was made on Megray Hill, close to Stonehaven, with what purpose is not clear. The army was left in this exposed position, without artillery support, while Gunn took Aboyne off to breakfast. Marischal, now with the support of Montrose, advanced to the foot of the hill and opened up with his artillery. Few were killed, but the noise of the fire unsettled the royalists, especially the Highlanders, who began to draw off in large numbers.

Undismayed, Aboyne took the remainder of his army back to Aberdeen on 18 June, and made ready to defend the entrance to the town across the Brig o' Dee against the advancing Covenanters. Colonel Johnstone was appointed to lead the detachment defending the bridge. A barricade of earth and stones was erected behind the gatehouse at the southern end. Montrose's artillery opened fire. The bombardment continued all day, but little damage was done, as most of the shot went overhead. An attempt to rush the bridge by some companies from Dundee was beaten back with ease.

Under cover of darkness Montrose moved the artillery closer to the Dee; and when battle recommenced the following morning, the fire from the Covenanter guns, under the direction of Colonel Henderson, was much more accurate, falling with devastating effect on the bridge. Seton of Pitmedden had the top part of his body blown off as he sat on his horse. Colonel Johnstone was wounded by a piece of flying masonry, whereupon the defence of the bridge was entrusted to Captain Nathaniel Gordon and his company from Strathbogie. Advancing under the cover of the guns, an assault party led by Major John Middleton managed to drive Gordon and his men back, giving the Covenanters possession of the bridge. Just to the north, the Gordon Cavalry, under the command of William Gunn, were urged to counter attack; but Gunn refused to listen. The royalists drew off, allowing the Covenanters to occupy Aberdeen for the third time. Middleton and Henderson's contribution to the victory was celebrated in ballad;

> His name was Major Middleton,
>   That manned the Brig o' Dee;
> His name was Colonel Henderson
>   That let the cannons flee.

Thus concluded the Battle of the Brig o' Dee, the only serious military clash of the First Bishops' War. On the very day it took place the King and the Covenanters made peace at Berwick.

Charles finally arrived at Berwick on 28 May. Two days later he joined the rest of his army camped at a place called Birks, three miles west of Berwick on the English side of the Tweed. Although the men's morale was boosted by the appearance of the King, all was far from well. Most of the troops were badly prepared, food was scarce, and disease had broken out. The Scots also had an important psychological advantage, in that the English believed themselves to be numerically weaker than their opponents, although this was almost certainly untrue. Earlier in the month Sir Edmund Verney had written;

> Our army is but weake, our purce is weaker, and if wee fight with thes foarces wee shal have our throats cutt; and delaye fighting longe wee cannott, for want of monny to keepe our army togeather...I dare saye ther was never soe raw, soe unskilful, and soe unwilling an army brought to fight.

The command structure of the army was also a cause of some concern. It had been expected that the cavalry would be put in the charge of the Earl of Essex, a senior nobleman who had some military experience. Instead it was given, at the special request of the Queen, to the lightweight Earl of Holland, a court favourite who had no military experience whatsoever. This was a cause of considerable resentment amongst the other noblemen, which did little to improve the army's fighting efficiency.

Following the arrival of Hamilton in the Forth the main Scots army had been reluctant to move far from Edinburgh. However, when it became clear that he represented no real danger, Leslie took up a position at Dunglas between Berwick and Dunbar, to see how the situation developed.

Once on the Border Charles sent a small party across the Tweed to the town of Duns, to publish his Newcastle proclamation. Reacting to this provocation, Leslie detached part of his own force and sent it to Kelso, within the King's proscribed ten mile limit. On June 3 Holland was sent with a force of 3,000 foot and 300 horse to drive them out. Riding too far ahead of his infantry, struggling to keep up with the cavalry on a hot day, Holland found himself confronted by a much larger Scots detachment. With no infantry support he was immediately obliged to make a hasty withdrawal. Indeed, the Scots were so well prepared for Holland's incursion, that rumours began to spread that the enemy was being kept informed of every move the English army made. Following Holland's retreat, the morale of the army, the King's included, slumped to a new low.

Soon, even more alarming news arrived. Leslie had broken his camp at Dunglas and marched on Duns Law, a commanding position close to the Border, that enabled him to intercept any move on Edinburgh, either from Berwick or Kelso. Charles sent an urgent message to Hamilton to abandon his operations in the Firth of Forth – such as they were – and join the King at Birks. Once Hamilton arrived, he was told that the King had abandoned any offensive intention. All that was left was to settle down and await events.

The English soldiers at Birks were in an increasingly miserable position. Most were tormented by lice, which in the grim humour of the camp were known as 'Covenanters.' When the weather turned bad few had any shelter, and for miles there were no trees with which to build huts. Smallpox was an ever present hazard. Desertions were frequent. Thomas Windebank, a son of the King's Secretary of State, carried his own frustrations to an explosive extent. The only thing that kept out the cold and the wet, he wrote, was the hope of;

> Rubbing, fubbing, and scrubbing those scurvy, filthy, dirty, nasty, lousy, itchy, scabby, shitten, stinking, slovenly, snotty-nosed, logger-

headed, foolish, insolent, proud, beggarly, impertinent, absurd, grout-headed, villainous, barbarous, bestial, false, lying, roguish, devilish, long-eared, short-haired, damnable, atheistical, puritanical crew of the Scottish Covenant.

Morale was certainly much better in the Scottish camp at Duns Law, as Robert Baillie reports;

> Our sojours grew in experience of armes, in courage, in favour dailie; everie one encouraged another; the sight of the nobles and their beloved pastors dailie raised their hearts; the good sermons and prayers, morning and evening, under the roof of heaven, to which the drumms do call them for bells; the remonstrance verie frequent of the goodness of their cause; of their conduct hitherto by a hand clearlie divine; also Leslie his skill and fortoun made them all so resolute for battell as could be wished...such was the wisdome and authoritie of that little, crooked souldier, that all, with ane incrediible submission, from the beginning to the end, gave themselves to be guided by him as if he had been the Great Solyman.

Baillie, filled with the righteousness of the cause, no doubt exaggerated. Soldiers, after all, are only soldiers; and the lice were surely no kinder to the Scots than they were to the English, only a few miles to the south. What is certain is that this stand off could not continue indefinitely. As Archibald Johnstone of Warriston relates, Leslie was short of money, horses and provisions. Moreover, the Scots were unwilling to cross the Border and arouse English national passions, or to incur the odium of possibly defeating the King in battle. Neither able to advance or retreat, the only alternative was to open negotiations.

At Birks Charles had reached a dead end. His last hope disappeared when he received a letter from Wentworth, saying he could expect no help from Ireland, and urging him to delay his campaign for a year. The Earl of Bristol, and several other noblemen, told him frankly that he would have to summon Parliament if he wished to proceed with his war against the Scots. Realising that that his whole strategy was failing, he decided to accept the Scots' request to open negotiations.

Talks began in the Earl of Arundel's tent on 11 June, with six Scots commissioners – headed by Rothes, Henderson and Warriston – facing a similar number of Englishmen. Soon after they began, the King himself appeared, at first frosty, then becoming slightly more relaxed. All responded to his charm, with the exception of Warriston, as stiff and as fanatical as ever. After Charles promised a new Assembly and Parliament to settle the church question, Warriston responded, to the embarrassment of his colleagues, by accusing the King of playing for time; to which Charles replied in anger 'The Devil himself could not make a more uncharitable construction', no doubt unsettled more by Warriston's candour than by the accuracy of his assessment. But nobody was fooled. Both sides agreed to disband their armies; and Charles, while refusing to accept the decisions of the 'pretended' Glasgow Assembly, agreed to summon a new Assembly to meet in Edinburgh on 20 August, followed shortly afterwards by a Parliament. On this basis the Pacification of Berwick was signed on 18 June. It was only to be a breathing space.

CHAPTER 3
Newburn

The First Bishops' War had settled nothing. Charles still refused to concede any of the fundamental issues at stake, and saw the Berwick settlement as little more than a temporary halt in hostilities. It brought with it, however, an artificial sense of relief, which only postponed the final struggle, much like the Munich settlement prior to the Second World War. Robert Baillie recorded his own feelings;

> Many whereof I was one, was glad at their heart of this divine conclusion...Many secret motives there was on all hands that spurred on to this quick peace. What to have done when we came to Tweedside we were very uncertaine: the King might have been so wilful, as rather to have hazarded his person than to have raised his camp. Had he incured any skaith, or become disgraced with a shameful flight, our heads had been broken for it; and likelie all England behooved to have risen in revenge.

But things started to go wrong almost from the start. Hamilton arrived in Edinburgh on 24 June to receive the keys of Edinburgh Castle, one of the conditions of the peace. He was jostled by an angry mob, who called him a traitor, an enemy to both God and his nation. Charles, with an astonishing lack of tact, had a proclamation read in the capital on 1 July, inviting the exiled bishops to attend the forthcoming Assembly. Strictly speaking he was entitled to do so, as the acts of the Glasgow Assembly were not officially recognised; but in the circumstances it was a piece of political folly. It was almost as if everything the Covenant stood for meant nothing; as if Leslie had been defeated in battle. Scotland was still in a dangerous mood, and a riot inevitably followed the King's announcement. Aboyne, showing greater courage than sense by appearing in Edinburgh, was chased through the streets; Traquair's coach was pierced with swords and his unfortunate coachman beaten up; Sir William Elphinstone, a senior judge, was punched and kicked.

In deep distrust of the King, the Scots began to break the terms of the Pacification of Berwick one by one: the Tables were not dissolved; the fortifications of Leith were not dismantled; two regiments still remained under arms; and Leslie retained his commission. Although Patrick Ruthven, one of the King's officers, was allowed to take possession of Edinburgh Castle, the Covenanters began to interfere with the delivery of military supplies to the garrison.

Charles, who had remained at Berwick with the intention of coming to Edinburgh to attend the Assembly, was angered at these developments. The leading Covenanters were summoned to his presence to explain the situation. Some refused, notably Argyll, fast taking over from Rothes as the head of the movement. Only six eventually agreed to come, including Rothes, Montrose and Warriston. The meeting was far from happy. Charles and Rothes had a particularly angry exchange, in which the nobleman bluntly told the King that if he insisted on retaining bishops in Scotland, the Scots would be forced to get rid of them in England and Ireland, a forecast of what was to come. It was perfectly clear to Rothes – and presumably to the others – that Charles intended to use any means at his disposal to restore Episcopacy, regardless of the outcome of the Edinburgh Assembly. Another meeting was held, but Charles decided that he would not, after all, come to Edinburgh.

Charles seems to have enjoyed one small success in his first meeting with the Covenanter leadership: Montrose, in the words of John Buchan, fell under the spell of the King's personality. It is most certainly true that, within a short space of his meeting with Charles, he was no longer trusted by his colleagues. Within a few weeks someone pinned a Latin motto to the door of his Edinburgh chamber: *Invictus armis, verbis vincitur* – 'he conquered by arms and is conquered by words.'

To the end of his life Montrose maintained that he was opposed to the bishops. He can have had no doubts – after the proclamation of 1 July and Charles' exchange with Rothes – what the King's long term intentions were, no matter what he said to the contrary. Moreover, there was no pretence at this stage that he was alarmed by the ambitions of Argyll. Yet if anyone could be turned by flattery, it was Montrose. His vanity had been badly wounded when the King snubbed him during their first meeting in 1636; now Charles made good the damage. Charles would have been aware of the reports that during the troubles of 1638 there 'was none more vainly foolish than Montrose.' Such a man would be easy to win over with the right choice of words and a little fuel to feed the fires of his ambition. Greatly exaggerating his importance and influence in Scotland he soon promised Charles, according to Gilbert Burnet, that he could turn the whole kingdom; but it was only with the aid of a Catholic Irish army, the darkest of all the fears of the Covenanters, that Montrose came anywhere near turning the kingdom.

It was perfectly obvious to all that the new Assembly was simply going to be a re-run of that held in Glasgow the previous year. Hamilton declined the dubious honour of continuing in the post of Royal Commissioner, and the long suffering Traquair was appointed in his place. Sensing the strength of Covenanter opinion, Traquair advised the King not to insist on the presence of the bishops in the coming Assembly and Parliament. In their absence neither gathering could be said to be properly constituted in the legal sense, so any measures they passed could simply be disregarded, when the time was appropriate. But to the embarrassment of both Traquair and the King, one bishop did turn up, George Graham of Orkney, who immediately resigned his office, and denounced Episcopacy as an erroneous doctrine.

When the new Assembly opened on 12 August no mention was made of its predecessor in Glasgow; but all the measures adopted by that rebel gathering were quickly confirmed. The members went on to take an even more serious step, by returning to the doctrine outlined by Andrew Melville in the 1580's: Episcopacy was declared to be contrary to scripture, and therefore had always been wrong. Charles had accepted Traquair's argument that Episcopacy could be set aside in the Scottish church as a temporary political expedient. However, to declare it to be against the law of God meant that its rejection could not be limited by space or time. If Episcopacy were held to be universally unlawful, how could it be maintained in England and Ireland? Charles quickly wrote to Traquair telling him to resist this measure. It was already too late. Bending to pressure, the Commissioner confirmed all the acts of the Assembly in the name of the King. No sooner had the Assembly dissolved than Parliament began to gather, ready to give its measures legal substance. All Traquair could hope for was a successful rearguard action in Parliament.

The Assembly adopted one further measure, also raised in Glasgow. To ensure that no attempt was made to retreat from the ideals of the Covenant, it was agreed that annual church gatherings should be held, an ideal expressed in the Golden Act of 1592, but never carried into practice. From this point forward Assemblies met every year until 1653, by which time a new force had intruded into Scottish politics.

The abolition of Episcopacy presented Parliament with an immediate problem. In the absence of the bishops, how were the Lords of the Articles to be chosen? Scotland's Parliaments, unlike those in England, were little more than gatherings of the ancient feudal estates, called on to support the monarch. In tackling the question of the Articles, the Parliament of August 1639 broke out of its medieval chrysalis and began the process of transforming itself into a modern legislature.

For some hours, the nobility, reserving the matter to itself, debated the issue. Traquair argued that the bishops should be replaced by as many ministers chosen by the King. But this was simply the old Trojan Horse that had enabled James VI to reintroduce parliamentary and then diocesan Episcopacy in the early years of the century. As an alternative, he suggested that the King should be allowed to appoint nobles instead, a position supported by Montrose. But Argyll, supported by Loudoun, argued that in future each estate should nominate its own representatives to the Articles, an astonishingly democratic suggestion for the times. This meant that King would no longer be able to manipulate parliamentary procedures. It would also mean a decisive shift in power away from the nobility towards the lesser gentry and the burgesses, both groups far stronger in their Presbyterian convictions than the self interested aristocracy. Argyll's motion was passed by a narrow majority.

Although members of the committee of the Articles were at that time all chosen by the nobles, it was far from being the packed house that Traquair had wished. With the exception of Montrose, the Covenanter party was still fairly united in its aims. One by one Traquair lost important votes. Attempting to stop the Covenanter revolution in its tracks, he prorogued Parliament from 30 October until 14 November, and then, on a command from the King, until June 1640. Loudoun and others attempted to persuade Charles against this, but he refused to see them.

Even before he left Berwick, Charles turned his mind to a fresh campaign against the rebel Scots. From Ireland, he sent for Thomas Wentworth, soon to be the dominant figure on the royal council, with dangerous consequences for both him and the King. Wentworth, created Earl of Strafford in the new year, had a simple view of the Scottish problem; and religion had little to do with it. For him, the Covenanters were rebels who aimed at the power of the monarchy itself. Scotland was best conquered and governed, in the manner of Ireland, by the English Privy Council.

Wentworth was a strong personality with a clear appreciation of the priorities facing the King. He laboured to lift Charles out of his self imposed difficulties; but for all his intelligence and strength of will, Wentworth was a disastrous choice for the King. If Charles understood little of the mood of the Scottish people, Wentworth understood absolutely nothing. Fatally for him, and Charles, he misunderstood the mood of England itself. Outraged by the arrogance of the Scots, he firmly believed that all loyal Englishmen would share his view. The First Bishops' War had emptied Charles' treasury; therefore, Wentworth reasoned, the English Parliament would have to be summoned to provide fresh funds. He seems to have forgotten the early Parliaments of Charles' reign, and his own role in them, when the Commons had been highly critical of the incompetent war efforts against Spain and France. Over the intervening eleven years since the last Parliament had been dismissed in 1629, many grievances had built up against arbitrary royal rule, which were waiting to be released, like a great political volcano. In late December 1639 Charles held a Council of War to discuss ways of raising money for a new war against Scotland. Various options were explored; but on the insistence of Wentworth, supported by Laud and Hamilton, the King agreed to summon Parliament.

Early in the new year fresh tensions began to build. In February Ships arrived at Leith with a party of English soldiers to reinforce the garrison of Edinburgh Castle. It was feared that any attempt to refuse them entry might provoke the governor, Patrick Ruthven, to open fire on the city. It was also known that Charles had recently appointed the Earl of Northumberland to command a fresh army to be raised against Scotland. Repairs were carried out to the fortifications at Carlisle and Berwick, and armaments began to stockpile in the royal arsenals. Charles justified his military preparations by referring to the breach in the terms of the Pacification of Berwick, saying that he had

> ...to take care that the gangrene be cut off before it spread too farre, to the endangering of this our Kingdome of England.

The Scots made their own preparations. Officers were appointed to military districts, and a chain of outposts were placed near the Border. In April, in the letter renewing Alexander Leslie's commission, it was declared that the kingdom was;

> ...not only threatened with warres concludit against it in the counsall of England and parliament of Irland most unjustly, without any offence given to either of these nationnes, but also the warres already begunne by the governor of the Castell of Edinburgh and garisoun of Englishmen thairin, who hes schot att the burgh of Edinburgh and slapped housses, and killed some people without any injury done him or them...

Charles looked forward to the new Parliament, due to meet in April. He had in his possession the copy of a letter addressed to Louis XIII and signed by Rothes and the other leading Covenanters, asking for the French King's mediation in the crisis. Charles chose to put a treasonable interpretation on this document, a view he was convinced most Englishmen would share.

The assembly, destined to pass into history as the Short Parliament, finally met on 13 April. Proceedings were opened by the Lord Keeper, Lord Finch of Fordwick, who launched an immediate attack on the disloyalty of the Scots. To defend the kingdom it was necessary, Fordwick continued, to raise an army. In asking the assembled members for the necessary funds he produced Charles' trump card, the letter to Louis XIII, and cited this as evidence of Scots treachery. To the amazement of the Royal Council, the letter made no impression at all. In the Commons the first member to speak, Harbottle Grimston, said that bad as a Scottish invasion might be, the invasion made upon the liberty of the subject at home was far more dangerous. This set the whole tone for the Short Parliament. The following day John Pym, a long standing opponent of royal absolutism, rose to his feet and took up the attack launched by Grimston. In a two hour speech he captured the spirit of the Commons, defending civil and religious liberty, the very principles for which the Scots were fighting. Making no progress in his pleas for money, Charles was forced to dissolve the Short Parliament on 5 May. Politically and financially he was worse off than ever.

The proceedings of the Short Parliament had been an enormous boost to the morale of the Scots, showing that Charles did not have the support of the English nation. While the English

Parliament was in session, a Convention of Estates – a parliament held without royal warrant – was held in Edinburgh to prepare against any surprise attack. Lord Eglinton was appointed to watch the west coast from the Clyde to the English Border in case of an attempted landing from Ireland, where it was known that Wentworth had raised a fresh army, including many Catholics as well as Protestants. Argyll was entrusted with the defence of the western Highlands. The country was now effectively in a state of war. Ruthven had opened up a desultory fire on Edinburgh, killing some thirty of its citizens in the streets. At sea English warships were patrolling the coast, seizing Scottish merchantmen as prizes.

Besides Edinburgh, only three Lowland castles were held for the King – Dumbarton in the west and the Earl of Nithsdale's strongholds of Caerlaverock and Threave in Galloway. Aberdeenshire was a little more secure than it had been in 1639, because Huntly and the other leading royalists of the area had left for England; but to make sure that it remained peaceful, the Earl Marischal occupied the city of Aberdeen on 5 May.

The following month Parliament reassembled in Edinburgh. Traquair, acting on the King's instructions, tried to have it prorogued once more, with no success, despite the support he received from Montrose. All the radical measures planned in 1639 were carried into law. Measures were also taken for the further defence of the realm. The Tables were replaced by a new Committee of Estates, to fulfil the executive functions of government between Parliaments, which, it was decided, should meet every three years. A sub committee was appointed to assist Leslie in making military preparations 'for a just and lawful defence of their religion, laws, lives, liberty and country.'

As in the First Bishops' War, steps were taken to strengthen the internal security of Scotland. From Aberdeen the Earl Marischal, aided by Major General Robert Munro, raided the country of the Gordons, capturing strongholds and sending all who resisted as captives to Edinburgh. Further south, Argyll, authorised by a commission of fire and sword against the Earls of Atholl and Airlie, set out from Inverary with 4,000 of his clansmen on 18 June, and marched across central Scotland, subduing the Drummonds, Stewarts and Ogilvies. Atholl was seized and sent as a prisoner to Edinburgh, as Huntly had been the year before. About this time rumours began to circulate that

Argyll was in favour of deposing the King, based on a conversation he is alleged to have had with the gentry of Atholl. John Willcock, Argyll's biographer, says of this;

> ...it is quite absurd to imagine that a grave and subtle politician like Argyll would sit and prate to his enemies about the deposition of the King as a matter practically decided upon by himself and his political associates, while they took the greatest care in all their public utterances and proclamations to express loyalty to the sovereign...

All that really needs to be added is that this story has about as much substance as the persistent allegations that Hamilton, a descendent of James II, planned to set himself up as King of Scots.

Argyll continued his punitive raid through Perthshire on into Angus, to Airlie Castle, the stronghold of the Ogilvies. The Earl of Airlie was in England, leaving his son, Lord Ogilvie, and Lady Helen Ogilvie in possession of the castle. Aware of Argyll's approach Montrose, a neighbour and friend of the family, persuaded Lord Ogilvie to allow him to send in his own garrison to try to deflect the Campbells from their destructive course. Ogilvie was then allowed to make his way to England. Argyll simply ignored Montrose's arrangement. In early July the Campbells approached Airlie Castle, situated on a high promontory above the River Isla, closely observed by Lady Helen, as the famous ballad relates;

Argyll has raised an hunder men,
   An hunder harness'd rarely,
And he's awa' by the back of Dunkell,
   To plunder the castle of Airlie.

Lady Ogilvie looks o'er her bower-window,
   And O but she looks Warely!
And there she spied the great Argyll,
   Come to plunder the bonnie house of Airlie...

'Gif my gude lord war here this night
   as he is with King Charlie,
Neither you, nor ony ither Scottish lord,
   Durst avow to the plundering of Airlie...

The Castle was destroyed and the Ogilvie lands were systematically plundered. Munro and Argyll's punitive expedition ended any prospect of a northern diversion on behalf of Charles before the Border war began anew.

Already jealous of Argyll's steady ascent in the ranks of the Covenanters and angered by the incident at Airlie Castle, Montrose was further alarmed by a rumour of a proposal to carve up Scotland into two spheres of influence, with Argyll controlling the north of the country beyond the Forth and Hamilton all the lands to the south. The only source of this information was Lord Lindsay. It is difficult to know what to make of this. Hamilton, after all, was a senior royal councillor and a member of the English war cabinet. Nobody could seriously have considered giving him control of all of southern Scotland with its vital Border defences. Argyll was surely not so lacking in political skill that he could delude himself into believing that such a proposal would be acceptable to the other leading Covenanters.

It's interesting the way in which one accusation quickly followed upon the other: Argyll, having told Atholl that he intended to depose the King, now apparently aimed at a Roman style dictatorship. At no point in his career, not even when he was at the height of his power, did he come anywhere near establishing complete political control of Scotland. So why would he attempt to do so now, when he could easily be confronted by a combination of his fellow nobles? Why, moreover, was Montrose – very much in the second division of the Scottish nobility – told of this plan when no other senior nobleman seems to have been aware of it?

Argyll was not confronted; instead Montrose and a group of his political allies met at Cumbernauld House, a property belonging to the Earl of Wigtown, and signed a secret bond 'against the particular and indirect practicking of a few.' The Cumbernauld Bond was the first serious rent in the fabric of the Covenant; and although in terms of practical politics it was too vague to have any meaningful effect, Montrose is likely to have felt that he had at least kept some of the exaggerated promises he had made to Charles at Berwick in the summer of 1639.

Suffering from a serious shortage of cash, the King's preparations for war were not going well. Apart from the garrisons at Berwick and Carlisle, the only English troops close to the Border were some advance cavalry and infantry units at Newcastle, who arrived there from late April onwards under the command of Edward Lord Conway. Elsewhere recruitment was not going smoothly. Instead of calling out the trained bands, men were pressed into service, with disastrous consequences. The trained bands, inefficient as they were, at least had some discipline; the forced recruits had none at all. Over a wide area of southern England there were reports of riot and murder. In the east, ill disciplined recruits broke into churches and burned Communion rails, a symbol of Archbishop Laud's high Anglican innovations. Officers suspected of Catholicism were murdered, and the disorders became so bad that many commanders were too frightened to march with their men. At Newcastle, Conway reported on the quality of his own troops in a spirit of black humour;

> I am teaching cart-horses to manage and making men that are fit for Bedlam and Bridewell to keep the ten commandments; so that General Lesley and I keep two schools, he has scholars that profess to serve God, and he is instructing them how they may safely do injury an all impiety; mine to the utmost of their power never kept any law either of God or the King, and they are to be made fit to make others keep them.

Despite these alarming signs Charles was encouraged in his resolve by the determination of Wentworth, newly created Earl of Strafford. But Strafford had already badly damaged the King's cause by misjudging the mood of the nation. Continuing a military build up without the necessary funds made a bad situation infinitely worse. If England was ill prepared for war in 1639 she was even less so in 1640. But whatever difficulties Charles had at home, Strafford assured him after the dissolution of the Short Parliament, he still had an army in Ireland 'you may employ here to reduce this kingdom.' He clearly meant Scotland; but the notes of the meeting, taken by Sir Henry Vane, were so vague that they were destined to bring Strafford to the scaffold within a year.

Strafford's had been a highly efficient ruler of Ireland. However, his dictatorial methods were far from popular, particularly amongst the northern Protestants, forced to sign 'the Black Oath' against the Covenant. A company of them under Captain Fulk Ellis came across the North Channel to join the Scots army, now massing on the Border.

In Scotland the preparations for war were going even better than they had been the previous year. In contrast to Charles' problems in England, recruitment was good, with each parish providing their allotted quota of men and arms. While the recruits were trained by the professional officer corps, shiploads of arms were arriving from the Netherlands. The women of Edinburgh were busy turning thousands of sheets into tents for the army. Leslie was, once again, proving himself to be the great organiser. The English were becoming more aware of the strengths of the old commander, of whom it was written in some bitterness;

> ...Leslie...would be found to be one who, because he could not live well at home, took up the trade of killing men abroad, and now is returned to kill, for Christ's sake, men at home.

From early July the army began to build up in some strength at Choicelee Wood – now Campmoor – about four miles from the old camp at Duns Law. This time there was no diversion in the Firth of Forth, and the north was generally quiet. In the south, Edinburgh Castle, ably defended by Ruthven, continued to be a problem, as did Dumbarton; and in the south west, the Earl of Nithsdale placed a garrison of two hundred men in Caerlaverock Castle which managed to hold out, despite heavy bombardment, until commanded by the King to surrender in late September. But these were no more than irritants, which did not deflect from the main military preparations.

While morale amongst the Scots troops was good, Leslie's supply situation was not much better than it had been in 1639. He could not afford to wait on the Border to see what the English were going to do. Apart from Conway's force at Newcastle, the main English army was as far south as Selby in Yorkshire, and the King, showing no sense of urgency, had not even left London. Exposure and hunger would eventually drive most of the Covenanter army home if nothing was done. John Livingston, a minister with the army, detailed his own miserable experience of the unusually cold summer nights;

> ...having lain several nights with my cloaths on, I being wearied with want of sleep did ly one night with my cloaths off; that night was very cold, and while I slept all the cloaths went off me; so that in the morning I was not able to stir any part of my body, and I had much ado, with the help of my man and a baggage man to get on my cloaths. I caused them to put me on my horse and went to Dunse, and lay down in a bed, and caused them to give me into the bed, a big tin

stoup full of water, wherby a sweat was procured; so that before night I was able to rise and put on my cloaths.

Rather than risk disintegration of the army it was decided to launch a pre-emptive strike into northern England, with the aim of taking Newcastle, where the coal of Northumberland and Durham was shipped to London, providing the main source of the capital's fuel supply. There was much in favour of this. Charles' difficulties with the Short Parliament had shown how divided England was. The main English army was too far to the south to intercept any drive through the north east, and the Earl of Northumberland was showing himself to be an indifferent commander. Conway's forces were not sufficient to both garrison Newcastle and take to the field; and the port's defences were only partially complete because of shortage of cash. Most important of all, there was now no risk of having to face the King in battle.

At Newcastle Conway was confident, despite his own problems, that the Scots had no intention of crossing the Border in strength. On 27 July he wrote to Sir Francis Windebanke, saying;

> I am still of the same opinion that the Scots will not come to England, it will be the greatest madness that may be for them to think to subsist by robbing and to make a conquest of England, they have not the forces to come into England to do it...

Less than a fortnight later he changed his mind; and by 10 August he was reporting in alarm that an invasion was immanent, and that he feared Newcastle would be lost. At Selby Sir Jacob Astley, an experienced soldier, now had about 12,800 men, about half the number with which the Scots were preparing to cross the Tweed. Of this number 3,000 were still without arms, and many were on the point of mutiny because of lack of pay. Few, moreover, had the will or desire to fight with the Scots. He wrote to Conway on 11 August;

> I am persuaded if Hannibal were at our gates some had rather open them up than keep him out...I think the Scots had better advance a good way into Northumberland without resistance than we send this army to encounter them without pay; for then, without all question, they will prove more ravenous upon the country than the Scots, who, for their own ends and to gain a party here, I believe will give the country the fair quarter that may be, which our men neither can nor will do.

In desperation Conway pressed the townspeople of Newcastle into building up the inadequate defences; but it was now too late. The Earl of Northumberland, unable to cope with the pressures placed upon him, retreated into illness. Strafford, now ill himself, was appointed in his place. Confident as ever he simply refused to believe Conway's gloomy reports. Even when he learned that the Scots were over the Border he was not dismayed. Surely, he reasoned, no loyal subject would tolerate the presence of an ancient enemy on English soil? In this, as in many other matters that year, he was mistaken.

On 17 August the advanced guard of the Scots army waded through the Tweed, followed three days later by Leslie and the bulk of the troops crossing at Cornhill, Wark and Carham. In all 20,000 infantry and 4,000 cavalry marched into England, the largest Scots' army to cross the Border since that led by James IV in 1513. Leslie, it is said by a hostile English source, addressed them as follows;

> We are now with Caesar past the Rubicon and this night you are to lie on English soil. This is the land of promise which as yet ye see but far off. Do but follow me and I will be your Joshua.

That same day the troops marched past Flodden Field, perhaps watched by the ghosts of their ancestors. On the following morning the River Glen was crossed, and the army moved on towards Wooler, where an English skirmishing party was sent hurrying back to the safety of Berwick. The advance continued, without any further opposition, towards the River Tyne. Meanwhile, the King, who left London the day Leslie forded the Tweed, arrived at York.

Both before and after the invasion of England the Scots had been waging a relentless propaganda offensive, designed to win over English opinion. One of their most effective pamphlets was issued just after the Border was crossed. Entitled *Six Considerations of the Lawfulness of our Expedition into England Manifested*, its declarations of loyalty to the King were tinged with some touches of humour, perhaps unconscious. The Scots were merely coming to see the King and warn him against the Canterburian faction of papists and prelates who were deliberately misleading him. England was their highway; and the English were probably unaware that it was an ancient custom of the Scots to be fully armed when visiting their sovereign.

Newcastle was better defended to the north than the south of the Tyne, so Wentworth wrote to Conway ordering him to hold the passage of the river at all costs. The nearest ford upstream from the city was at the village of Newburn, four miles to the west. It was here that King David II had crossed in 1346 on his way to the Battle of Neville's Cross. If the Scots forded the Tyne Newcastle would not be defensible; but rather than concentrating all his forces at Newburn, Conway attempted two objectives at the same time, leaving a good part of his army in the in the city, while taking the remaining 3,000 foot and 1500 horse west to the ford.

Newburn was not a good position to have to defend. Flat meadows lay on the southern bank of the Tyne, which were overlooked by wooded slopes to the north. To improve his position Conway ordered the construction of two earthworks close to the ford, and placed 400 men and some guns in each, with the cavalry drawn up a slight distance to the east. Leslie arrived late on the evening of 27 August, occupying Heddon Law, the height above the village of Newburn. To his experienced eye the advantage was immediately obvious. Under cover of darkness he moved his artillery into a commanding position on the forested area of the northern height. Newburn itself was occupied, and some of the lighter cannon were placed in the steeple of the church to cover the earthworks opposite.

At dawn on 28 August the river was running too high for the Scots to attempt a crossing. For some time nothing happened, both sides simply keeping a close eye on one another. Then, in the early afternoon, a Scots officer came out of one of the houses of Newburn to water his horse in the Tyne. This provocation was too much for a watching English sniper, who promptly opened fire, wounding the officer. Scots' musketeers positioned in and around the village responded, followed soon after by the artillery. Conway's own gunners were quick to reply. The Battle of Newburn had begun.

The exchange of cannon fire continued for some time before the Tyne was fordable. Considering that Leslie had forty to eighty guns of various sizes to Conway's eight, it was far from being an equal contest. Besides, firing from low ground, the English could do little damage against the Scottish gun emplacements, which were mostly hidden from their sight. Once the water level fell, Leslie ordered across an advance party of 300 horse; but they were beaten back by a wall of ferocious fire from the English soldiers in the two earthworks. Leslie then ordered a concentrated bombardment of the English emplacements. The cannon in the church steeple were particularly effective. Soon the earthwork closest to the Tyne took a direct hit, which killed several officers and men. Colonel Thomas Lansford managed to keep his frightened soldiers in place with the greatest of difficulty, but was forced by the concentrated fire to retreat from the forward position. Fearing that they were about to be overwhelmed by the Scottish horse, many of the panicking soldiers fled off to the east towards Stella Haugh, where Conway had placed his cavalry.

Scots' artillery fire was now directed against the sole remaining earthwork. When another shot descended into their midst, Lansford was unable to do any more. Musketeers and artillerymen both fled, abandoning their weapons in their fear. The Scots' cavalry regiments now began to cross in strength. Seeing this, the English cavalry, which had hitherto remained out of the range of the enemy guns, prepared to counter attack. Anticipating such a move, Leslie had moved a number of his lighter guns closer to the river bank. The gunners then fired into the royal horse as they deployed on the meadows to the south. In spite of this, part of the cavalry under Commissary-General Wilmot and Sir George Vane pressed the attack, forcing the Scots to fall back for a second time; but without the support of their comrades they were compelled by superior numbers to withdraw.

Leslie then ordered a general advance, with the infantry crossing in support of the forward cavalry units. Moving up the higher ground, the Scots intercepted Wilmot's disorganised regiment which broke in confusion, the panic spreading to Conway's own regiment. By now the whole English army, horse and foot, was in full scale retreat. With his army now across, and not wishing to damage English prestige any more than was necessary, Leslie sensibly called a halt; there would be no murderous pursuit of the routed enemy. Two days later the Scots entered Newcastle, now abandoned by its defenders, and took possession of the most important port in England after London and Bristol. On the same day Durham was occupied by a force under the Earl of Dunfermline. The Second Bishops' War was effectively over.

In military terms the Battle of Newburn was a minor affair, little more than a large scale skirmish. Only twelve Scots and sixty Englishmen had been killed. Politically, however, it had an impact far beyond its tactical importance. By carrying the war into England, putting an English army to flight and establishing a hold of London's coal supply, the Scots had virtually ensured the calling of a new Parliament, with profound consequences for the history of both kingdoms.

Newburn considerably increased Scottish military prestige and confidence; perhaps fatally so. Conway was outnumbered and outgunned. With such advantages in their favour it would have been a catastrophe if the Scots had lost the battle; a miracle if the English had won. Yet it is important to realise what a huge gamble the advance on Newcastle was. The Scots army was seriously short of both money and supplies. Moreover, it had no siege equipment. The King's main army, which had moved to York, was now in much better shape and very well provisioned; as indeed had been the soldiers at Newcastle, whose abandoned stores helped save the Scots from starvation. If Newcastle had been properly fortified – as it was when the Scots next came this way – Leslie's hungry army could have been caught between the city walls and the approach of the King at the head of a relief force. But these considerations were set aside in the flush of victory, quickly followed by a rapid collapse in the royal war effort. In his *Memoirs*, Sir James Turner, a Scottish soldier of fortune, wrote of Newburn some years later;

> ...Generall Leslie haveing marchd into England, with a numerous armie at the Lambs (Lammas) before, and put my Lord Conway with some of the king's forces to a shameful retreat at Newburne, had made himself master of Neucastle, and all the Bishoprick of Durham. I found this successe had elevated the minds of my countreymen in generall to such a height of vanitie, that most of them thought, and many said, they sould quicklie make a full conquest of England; but time hath shoune them since that they made their reckoning without their host for the very contrarie fell out.

If some Scots thought that they could conquer the rest of the country after the victory at Newburn, so did some of the English. With the Scots occupying the line of the River Tees, many feared an advance on London. Charles' army, powerful as it was, lost the will to fight. Calls began to be heard for a new Parliament. In Scotland the last traces of royalist opposition were eliminated one by one. Dumbarton Castle surrendered on 29 August. On 15

September, the garrison of Edinburgh Castle, weakened by scurvy, finally gave up the fight, and were allowed to depart in peace, despite the many deaths they had caused amongst the inhabitants of the city. Before the end of the month, Caerlaverock Castle, the last royalist stronghold, capitulated.

Peace negotiations opened up with the Scots at Ripon on 2 October. Charles hoped for a new personal treaty like the Pacification of Berwick; but the Scots were having none of it. Having no trust in the word of the King they insisted that a final peace would have to involve the English Parliament. A provisional treaty was agreed towards the end of the month. The Scots were to be paid £850 a day in expenses and were to occupy the northern counties of England until the final treaty was concluded in London. Only Parliament could approve the sums agreed. On November 3 one of the most momentous assemblies in English history met for the first time – the Long Parliament of the Civil War. The puritan gentry were well represented in the Commons – amongst others John Pym, John Hampden and an as yet little known MP for Cambridge by the name of Oliver Cromwell.

CHAPTER 4
The Armies of God

Charles returned to London with the lingering hope that all true Englishmen would be angered by the Scots' occupation of the north. There was some minor encouragement for this belief. In September a group of Scots' raiders had been defeated at Stapleton in County Durham. After a summer of disappointments, this small success was celebrated in a patriotic ballad *Good News from the North*;

I'll daily pray and hourly
As it doth in my power lie
To him by whom kings reign; that with success
King Charles go on and prosper may
And (having made the Scots away)
Rule o'er his lands in peace and happiness.

In his opening speech to the assembled members, the King immediately took the offensive. Parliament was called upon to provide assistance in chasing out traitors and rebels for the safety and well being of the kingdom. To Charles' dismay, the bait was not taken. In the Commons the first to speak was John Pym, who immediately defined a higher form of treason than the Scots' invasion – a design to alter the religion and government of the kingdom. With this the battle lines were drawn, leading two years later to the outbreak of the Great Civil War.

For the puritan party, headed by Pym, the presence of the Scots' army, and the financial demands this made on the crown, ensured that there would be no early dissolution of Parliament. When the Scots' Commissioners arrived in London on 19 November to continue the discussions adjourned at Ripon, they were well received. For divine worship, they were given Saint Antholin's Church, a well established centre of puritanism. Here their preachers, especially Alexander Henderson, soon attracted large crowds of sympathetic English hearers. Out of this alliance between Presbyterians and Puritans the English Revolution began to take shape.

Almost at once things started to go wrong for the King. His

principal minister, Strafford, was impeached by Parliament and sent to the Tower. This was followed a few weeks later by the arrest of Laud. Charles had hoped to take part in the peace discussions, as he had at Birks in 1639; but neither the English nor the Scots' Commissioners would agree to this. Negotiations which were nominally carried on between the crown and the Scots were, in reality, between the Scots and Parliament.

The London peace talks, which continued for some months, did not always go well, despite the initial enthusiasm for the Covenanters. Amongst other things the Scots placed increasing emphasis on unity of religion between the two realms. This was due not to any great crusading zeal – important as that was for some – but to a desire to increase the security of the political settlement at home. In other words, the Covenanters did not feel safe as long as the bishops continued to rule the English church, which might, at some future stage, lead to the reintroduction of Episcopacy into Scotland. After all, it had been differences over the question of church government that had been the cause of the recent wars.

While there was a growing party in the English Parliament in favour of a wholesale reform of the church, few were prepared to be dictated to on this matter by the Scots. Most Englishmen were happy to retain Episcopacy, free from some of the high Anglican innovations introduced by Laud. There was also a minority of puritan radicals, headed by a group known as the Independents, who believed in the autonomy of each congregation, free from the central control of either bishops or Presbyterian church courts. Of those who did accept the Scottish confession, none believed in Melville's notion of the two states, with a church theoretically free of Parliamentary control.

Encouraged by the reception given to Henderson at St Antholin's, the Scots overestimated the strength of Presbyterian feeling in London. When Henderson published a pamphlet in February 1641 calling for the abolition of Episcopacy it roused deep resentment against a perceived attempt to interfere in English affairs. In the ensuing political storm, national opinion united for a time against the perceived arrogance of the Covenanters. Even their friends in Parliament criticised the rashness of the Scots. It was made apparent to Henderson and his fellow Commissioners that;

...though they loved not the bishops, yet for the honour of their nation they would keep them up rather than we as strangers should pull them down.

Henderson was forced to issue an apology. This whole affair should have warned the Scots that the English would not have reformation out of the barrel of a Scottish gun; unfortunately it did not.

The peace discussions were punctuated by some dramatic events. Strafford was put on trial, essentially as a scapegoat for all the wrongs of the King's period of personal rule, although he had only really played an important part in national government in the previous few months. The impeachment failed because of lack of evidence; but his enemies brought him back before the high court of Parliament on a Bill of Attainder, a terrible measure which required only a presumption of guilt. Strafford's advice to the King, after the dissolution of the Short Parliament, that he had an Irish army with which to reduce this kingdom, was interpreted to mean that this army was to be used against England. Strafford's enemy, Sir Harry Vane, the man who had taken the notes at the meeting, confirmed that this was the case; although this was denied by Hamilton and the others who had been present. No-one, not even the King, could save the beleaguered Earl. He was duly condemned and executed on 12 May. Archbishop Laud, in lonely confinement in the Tower, confided to his diary that the King, for whom he and Strafford had given so much, had not been worth serving.

The death of Strafford, one of the most powerful subjects in the land, had a sobering effect on the Marquis of Hamilton. Ever mindful of his own personal safety, he was deeply concerned that he too might be defined as an 'incendiary' or a 'malignant', terms used with increasing frequency against many of the King's chief advisors. If Charles had not the power to save even his chief minister, what hope had the others? As an act of personal insurance, he began to move closer to Argyll and the leading Covenanters, although always, at least in his own mind, with the intention of serving the King.

The execution of Strafford was the first act in a summer of intense political drama. Six days after the Earl's death the King announced that he intended to go to Scotland to open the new Parliament, scheduled to meet in August. Under increasing pressure at home he hoped, at the very least, to build up a new party in the north as a counter-weight to the puritan opposition in England. Now close to achieving all their political and religious demands in Scotland, serious splits were beginning to show in the Covenanter movement. Hamilton's approach to Argyll might, Charles hoped, produce a more favourable climate in Edinburgh; but even if it did not, there was a scheme underway to humble *MacCailein Mór.*

Since the signing of the secret Cumbernauld Bond Montrose had continued his cloak-and-dagger intrigues against Argyll; but he did so with such a lack of subtlety and political skill that, bit by bit, his party slowly disintegrated. He had already been in trouble for corresponding with Charles during the Ripon negotiations; and when the details of the Bond were finally revealed in November, his personal standing in the Covenanter movement was reduced still further. But there was nothing Montrose was not prepared to do in his increasingly bitter vendetta against Argyll.

In February 1641 he met with the Earl of Atholl and John Stewart of Ladywell, commissary for Dunkeld, a figure of no political importance. This unfortunate man, conveniently produced by Atholl, his feudal chief, seems to have been nothing more than a catspaw in a slowly evolving conspiracy. He was prepared to repeat the stories, spread the previous year, that Argyll planned to depose the King, and to say that, during the raid through Atholl, his soldiers had said that they were 'King Campbell's men, no more King Stewart's.' On no better evidence than this Montrose prepared to challenge Argyll.

With his usual lack of discretion he began to spread the story. By May the allegations that Argyll intended to depose the King and set himself up as a dictator were reported to the Committee of Estates. When challenged on these matters, Montrose immediately revealed Stewart and Lord Lindsay as his sources. Stewart duly appeared before the Committee and reminded Argyll what he had said 'in the presence of a great many people,' none of whom were named or cited as witnesses. Argyll responded with anger, denying everything. Stewart was tortured and immediately retracted his statement, saying that the Earl had referred, more blandly, to kings in general. Having admitted to perjury the friendless Stewart, of no more use to anyone, was tried and executed. Lord Lindsay was also examined and it was concluded that Montrose had no grounds for his misconception.

It's almost impossible to reach any definite conclusion about this sordid intrigue. Beyond John Stewart's word, there was no definite evidence against Argyll. His torture obviously makes the retraction of his original evidence suspect; but there was no one prepared to corroborate his statement either then or later. We either accept that Argyll had a unique capacity, unlike Montrose, to remove all trace of his double dealing, or that the whole thing was little more than an elaborate fabrication. Before Stewart's death a document was found, along with a letter from the King to Montrose, apparently promising him a pension. For this, and the belief that he could count on the support of Atholl and Montrose, he gambled, and lost.

While Argyll's intrigues could not be proved, Montrose's certainly could. Without a single dissenting voice amongst the Committee of Estates, his fellow noblemen or the Commissioners of Parliament, he was arrested on 11 June by the Earl of Lothian and imprisoned in Edinburgh Castle. Lothian dismissed him with some contempt;

> In Winter, when his band was burnt, I did what I could to quiet matters and bring him off, and he thought I did him good offices. But now I took not so much pains; for his often relapses are not to be endured, and his practices will be found much to the prejudice of the public, and very malicious against particular men, who, to my knowledge, deserve it not at his hands...

News of the arrest of Montrose caused a stir in London. Details of a plot by reactionary elements in the army had recently come to light. It was rumoured that the King's planned visit to the north was to allow him to link up with discontented elements in the English army and the conspirators in Scotland. Charles did his best to dispel this. He wrote to Argyll, saying that his visit had nothing to do with Montrose, and he had not planned to offer him any office. But Charles had at least been successful in winning over far more useful allies than the deeply compromised Montrose.

John Leslie, Earl of Rothes, one of the Scots' Commissioners in London, was also resentful of the rise of Argyll. An ambitious man, he had seen his position at the head of the Scottish Revolution gradually eroded away by the great Earl. Rothes was essentially a political pragmatist rather than an ardent Presbyterian. For him the object of the Covenant had been the elimination of the bishops as political rivals, rather than the establishment of a purer form of church government. As far as his own interests were concerned he was always ready to reach a working compromise. Possessing a far higher degree of skill than the impulsive Montrose, he soon convinced the King that he would be able to build up a royalist party in Scotland, not tainted by half baked intrigues.

The Anglo-Scottish peace negotiations finally reached a conclusion, and the Treaty of London was ratified by the King in August 1641. Charles undertook to withdraw all his declarations against the Covenanters and to ratify the decisions taken by the Edinburgh Parliament in June 1640. He further agreed to withdraw the garrisons from Berwick and Carlisle, and to place Edinburgh Castle under the control of the Estates. Reparations of £300,000 were agreed, the Scots' army to begin the withdrawal from northern England on receipt of the first instalment.

With this matter settled the King made ready to visit Scotland for the first time in eight years. If he hoped for some relief from his troubles in London, he was to be sadly disappointed. Rothes, who had been ill for some time, was unable to accompany Charles on his journey north. He died at Richmond upon Thames on 23 August, ending any immediate prospect of the King building up an alliance amongst the middle ranking nobility. Charles was left to depend upon the relationship Hamilton had constructed with Argyll.

No greater contrast can be imagined between the Scotland of 1633, when Charles had last come, and that of 1641. All the King's hopes for a uniform British Church were gone. Parliament, which had been sitting for a month, had transformed itself from a subservient feudal gathering into a true national assembly. All of the radical legislation of 1640, which had effectively destroyed the royal prerogative, was immediately approved by Charles. Keeping his true thoughts to himself, he dutifully attended the Presbyterian services.

The King was, however, very well received, and soon deluded himself into believing that all his troubles in Scotland were over. But it was quickly apparent that the new axis between Hamilton and Argyll was not working in his favour. Argyll had taken on the mantle of John Pym, demanding that no political or judicial office should be filled without Parliamentary consent. He was supported in this by a clear majority of members. When Charles attempted to fill the office of Chancellor, long vacated by Archbishop Spottiswood, with his own nominee – the Earl of Morton – he met with a blunt refusal. Apparently abandoned by Hamilton, and lacking the political support that Rothes would have provided, Charles soon allowed himself to be seduced by wilder counsels.

On 29 September Lord Ker, the son of the Earl of Roxburgh, appeared in Edinburgh at the head of a large party of armed retainers, at the very peak of the political wrangle over the Chancellorship. He then proceeded to accuse Hamilton of treason and challenged him to a duel. Parliament immediately summoned him to explain his conduct. Although he came, and promptly apologised to Hamilton, the sight of his men was a cause of considerable concern, perhaps recalling an occasion in 1522 when Hamiltons and Douglases had fought each other in a pitched battle in the centre of the city. Passions were roused, and rumours of royalist plots began to circulate. Charles tried to quieten the situation by immediately giving in to Parliament, appointing Argyll's kinsman Loudoun as Chancellor. But fear of royalist treachery was now acute.

Before long a murky plot began to take shape amongst the group of professional soldiers who had accompanied the King to Edinburgh. From his prison cell, Montrose was busy writing to Charles, suggesting that Hamilton was guilty of treason. His letters were carried to the King by William Murray, a gentleman of the royal bedchamber, who had visited Montrose in the Castle. Even the King realised that Montrose was a source too tainted to command any credibility; but after he received a second letter from Montrose, Charles had a private interview at night with Colonel John Cochrane, the commander of one of the three Scottish regiments that had remained under arms after the withdrawal from England, and a man with strong royalist sympathies. Soon after Cochrane and the Earl of Crawford, the leading officer in the King's entourage, were busy planning with a number of other men to arrest both Hamilton and Argyll, carry them to a ship at Leith and confront them with Montrose's charges. The details became known to Sir John Hurry, another professional soldier with a higher degree of intelligence than many of his comrades, who promptly told General Leslie. On October 14, Hamilton and his brother William, Earl of Lanark, together with Argyll all fled the city. Next day Argyll let it be known that there was a conspiracy against their lives, and hinted that the King himself might not be ignorant of the details.

It's difficult to know what to make of this clumsy plot, known in Scottish history as the Incident. The degree of Montrose's involvement is uncertain; it seems that his accusations simply acted as a spur to men even less scrupulous than himself. Charles, too, managed to keep clear of any direct involvement; but his behaviour looked suspicious, especially his cloak-and-dagger interview with Cochrane. When he appeared before Parliament, accompanied by a strong armed retinue, he affected an appearance of injured innocence. He convinced nobody. His popularity was now gone, as was any chance he had of building up a party. The only real beneficiary was Argyll, who soon returned to Edinburgh, carried to new heights of power and popularity by the malice of his enemies.

In attempting to make good the political damage caused by the Incident, Charles was forced to make major concessions. A new Council was appointed consisting of the principle Covenanters, including Argyll and the King's old opponent Lord Balmerino. Soon after Argyll was created a Marquis and Loudoun an Earl. Alexander Leslie was elevated to the peerage as the Earl of Leven. Even the firebrand Archibald Johnstone of Warriston was knighted, although this did nothing to moderate his more extreme views. The Covenanters had achieved the kind of political victory that Pym and the English Puritans could only dream of. It was now no longer in anyone's interest to rake over the details of the Incident, so in November the chief plotters, including Montrose, were all released.

Before he returned to England, Charles received news of serious developments in the last of his three kingdoms. On 23 October the Catholic Irish in the north had risen in rebellion under the leadership of Sir Phelim O' Neil. The rebellion, which quickly spread to other parts of Ireland, was accompanied by terrible stories of the wholesale massacre of the Protestant settlers. A report made by Sir John Clotworthy, a Protestant landowner in Ireland with close associations with John Pym, is fairly typical of the kind;

> ...cutting off privie members, hands and feete; dashing out the braines of young children, driving divers naked before them, ripping upp womens bellies; driving multitudes over bridges and causing

them to fall in the water and be drowned; and beating out the brains of such as escaped with Poles, deflouring virgins, and then having forced them to renounce their religion, did marry them to their basest followers.

Many of these rumours were grossly exaggerated, or simply untrue. However, they served a purpose. Suspicion centred on some of the Catholics in the royal household, and some went so far as to blame Henrietta Maria, describing the Irish rising as the Queen's Rebellion.

To make matters worse, in early November O'Neil claimed that he was acting on commission from the King. This turned out not to be true; but it had the immediate effect of increasing suspicion of Charles in both Scotland and England.

The cause of the Irish Catholic rising had roots deep in the island's history. Of all the three Stewart kingdoms, Ireland had by far the most cause to be resentful. Since the middle ages the English had been consolidating their hold on the island, which became little better than a colony of the crown. For centuries the Irish had been viewed with suspicion and hostility by their English masters, a situation made worse by the Reformation. Most Irish people remained loyal to the old faith, suffering from various civil and political disabilities as a consequence. Wentworth, Charles' dictatorial Lord Deputy, did nothing to disguise his view that Ireland was a conquered nation. Irish resentment in Ulster was particularly acute. Here, since the beginning of the century, the Catholic inhabitants had been steadily replaced in many places by Protestant settlers from England and Scotland. The Covenanter Revolution both encouraged and alarmed the Irish. On the one hand they saw that it was possible to gain religious concessions from the King; but on the other they were frightened by the intense anti-Catholic rhetoric of the Scottish Covenanters and the English puritans. Rebellion seemed to be the only way to ensure that they were able to defend their interests in the great political reorganisation of the British Isles.

Charles returned from his disastrous trip to Scotland, uncertain what to do about the Irish crisis. The following year the rebels, having extended their control over most of the island, formed a new state, the Irish Catholic Confederacy, with a capital at Kilkenny. Loyal forces under James Butler, Earl of Ormonde, managed to hold on around Dublin and parts of the south, as did the Protestant settlers in the north. Armed reinforcements would have to be sent, however, to prevent further deterioration in the military situation. Despite obvious Scots' interest in the fate of their co-religionists in Ulster, Ireland was an English problem, and so any initiative in the matter would have to come from London. But as neither the King nor Parliament was willing to trust the other in raising an army, both sides appealed to the Scots. Only too willing to extend their influence to another part of the British Isles, the Covenanters agreed to send an army to Ireland, to be paid for by the English Parliament.

On 15 April 1642 Colonel Robert Munro, like Leslie a veteran of the Swedish service, landed at Carrickfergus Castle with 2,500 troops, the first part of a force which rose to 10,000 men in August. Against the inexperienced Irish rebels they soon enjoyed some quick successes. Large parts of Down and Antrim were quickly reoccupied, and communications were re-established with Dublin. On 29 April O' Neil's forces were defeated at Kilwarlin Wood near Lisburn, and the town of Newry was recaptured the following month. After these setbacks the Irish guerrillas, realising their weakness in the face of professional forces, refused to be drawn into battle, disappearing into the interior of the country where ground conditions and supply problems did not allow the Scots to follow. The war now settled down to a prolonged stalemate, although the Irish received a considerable boost to their morale and organising ability with the arrival in July of Owen Roe O'Neil, a professional soldier who had served for many years in the Spanish army.

Argyll had a close interest in the progress of the army in Ulster. He sent over one of his own regiments to occupy Rathlin Island, from where it proceeded across to the mainland, joining Munro at Ballycastle to help clear the rebels from the Glens of Antrim. Argyll's old enemy, Ranald McDonnell, Earl of Antrim, had remained loyal to the King. Even so, the opportunity to get him out of the way was too good to pass. He was arrested at Dunluce Castle and sent as a prisoner to Carrickfergus, where he remained until October, when he finally managed to escape to join the King in England. By this time Civil War had broken out between Charles and Parliament.

After the King returned to London his political struggle with Parliament intensified. In January 1642 he went so far as to enter the Commons in an attempt to arrest five of his most prominent critics, including Pym and Hampden. Forewarned, the Five Members all managed to escape. Having lost all credibility Charles was forced to abandon London. Slowly, over the remainder of the year, the two sides drifted towards war, with the King finally raising his standard at Nottingham on 22 August. England divided into two armed camps. From the Continent the King was joined by his nephew Prince Rupert a talented, if impetuous, soldier. Scotland remained neutral; but many individuals came south to offer their services to one side or the other: men like Sir John Hurry, who had revealed the details of the plot against Hamilton and Argyll. Over the next few years Hurry, a man seemingly of no great political conviction, had a remarkable career, changing sides with bewildering frequency, before ending up on the scaffold with Montrose in 1650. He saw his first action on 23 October at the Battle of Edgehill, the first major conflict of the Great Civil War, and a victory, on points, for the King.

The month after Edgehill Parliament made its first request to the Scots for military aid. In its letter it accused Charles of favouring Papists and of intending to use foreign troops against his own subjects. Hamilton and his brother Lanark, now representing moderate opinion amongst the Covenanters, were successful in having this letter suppressed for some weeks. When a letter arrived from the King refuting the 'horrible scandals' laid against him, it was immediately published on the insistence of the Hamiltons, a political miscalculation of breathtaking proportions. Not surprisingly, everyone immediately wanted to know what the alleged scandals were, and the Council had no alternative but to publish Parliament's letter also. In the uproar that followed the Parliamentary agent in Edinburgh wrote 'The coals now want only blowing from England, and this Kingdom will soon be on fire.' The only royalist response was a petition urging restraint sponsored by the Earl of Home. Soon called the Cross Petition because it crossed with the policy of the Covenanters, it was condemned by the Kirk and denounced from the pulpits of Edinburgh.

Argyll initially hoped for a negotiated settlement between the two parties to the conflict, rather than armed intervention on either side. On his initiative the Privy Council wrote to Charles offering mediation. Following this up, Loudoun and Henderson came to see Charles at Oxford, his temporary capital. But they were received coldly by the King and deliberately insulted by the Cavaliers in the streets of the town. Faced with the King's intransigence, the Scottish Privy Council decided to summon a Convention of Estates. Charles' objections to this were simply ignored.

From early in the new year Montrose was convinced that it was only a matter of time before the Covenanters intervened in the Civil War on behalf of Parliament. In his view it was necessary to forestall this by a pre-emptive military strike. He came to England in February 1643 and met with Queen Henrietta Maria, newly returned from a mission to acquire military supplies on the Continent. The Queen had already suggested to Charles the necessity of raising a loyal army in Scotland, and was receptive to Montrose. Full of his usual confidence, he told the Queen that there were thousands of loyal subjects in Scotland waiting for an opportunity to rise against the Covenanters. However, his mission was frustrated by the prompt arrival of Hamilton at York, ready to warn of the acute danger that Montrose's ill-considered proposals entailed. Gilbert Burnet reports as follows;

> The earl of Montrose and a party of high royalists were for entering into an open breach with the country in the beginning of the year 1643, but offered no probable methods in managing it; nor could they reckon themselves assurance of any considerable party. They were full of big words and bold undertakings: but when they were pressed to shew what concurrence might be depended on, nothing was offered but from the Highlanders; and on this wise men could not rely; so duke Hamilton would not expose the king's affairs by such a desperate want of proceeding.

Hamilton was now trying to negotiate his way through a political minefield. His relationship with Argyll was much cooler than it had been at the time of the Incident, and he undoubtedly believed that it was only a matter of time before the Scots allied themselves with Parliament. The situation in Scotland required all his diplomatic skills. Charles was not trusted by most Scots, who believed that a royal victory against Parliament would be followed by an attempt to reverse the results of the Covenanter Revolution. Hamilton, as the leading moderate amongst the Covenanters, could only delay Scots' intervention in the war; but they could not be kept out indefinitely. Much depended on a full royal victory in the course of 1643; beyond that, no promises could be made. If Montrose was given his head at this stage, then disaster must inevitably follow. Hamilton did not believe that he would be able to muster the promised support; and, as it turned out, Montrose's first military adventure in the spring of 1644 was a fiasco. Charles showed his continuing support for Hamilton by awarding him a dukedom; and then proceeded to cast all his schemes down into the dust.

Charles had already started to fish in Irish waters, with disastrous consequences. Looking for ways to break the deadlock in England he began to consider the possibility of a cease-fire with the Irish Confederates, which would release Ormonde's troops for service in England, and, more dangerously, might even lead to an alliance with the Kilkenny government against Parliament. In late April 1643 the King authorised Ormonde to conclude a cease-fire with the Catholics. Negotiations were kept secret for fear of pushing the Scots further into the Parliamentary camp; for if this happened, as Will Murray put it,

> ...the two kingdoms will shatt upon him in despight of what his best servants can do.

Queen Henrietta Maria was closely involved in these Irish schemes. She was also involved in another plot which had the effect of nullifying Hamilton's success in heading off Montrose.

The Convention of Estates was scheduled to assemble in Edinburgh on 22 June to consider the general situation. Hamilton realised that it was fear of the King's future intentions that might conceivably push the Estates into an alliance with Parliament. On his advice the King issued a manifesto on 1 June, saying that the rumours that he intended to overturn the Presbyterian settlement in Scotland were groundless slanders perpetuated by his enemies. At Charles' request wide publicity was given to this declaration. Any effect it may have had was destroyed a few days later when details of a new plot by the Earl of Antrim were made public.

Attempting to return in secret to Ireland, Antrim was captured by Monro's soldiers in late May on the coast of County Down. He was found to be carrying letters from Viscount Aboyne and the Earl of Nithsdale. After Antrim and his servants had been examined, details of an elaborate conspiracy emerged. Arms were to be sent to the north of Scotland for the use of Aboyne and the

Gordons. Antrim was to raise a force of his own clansmen in Ireland to join their comrades in Scotland, and all others who hated the Campbells. Alisdair MacColla was to return with the McDonells from his Irish exile; and Montrose, it was hoped, would also be drawn in to the scheme. Another shipment of arms was to be sent to Nithsdale and his associates in southern Scotland. The aim was to bring as much force as possible to bear on Scotland; to destroy the Scots' army in Ireland; and to bring Irish troops to mainland Britain to fight against the Covenanters and Parliament.

The details of this intrigue were worked out when Antrim met the Queen in York, shortly after the departure of Montrose and Hamilton. Antrim, who had a similar personality to Montrose, and whose hatred of Argyll was even more profound, promised Henrietta Maria that he would be able to raise 20,000 men for his proposed campaign. The degree to which the King was involved is uncertain; but it is difficult to accept that he did not have some knowledge of the scheme.

As soon as the details emerged, Hamilton's diplomatic manoeuvres in Scotland counted for nothing. The Privy Council, while not implicating the King directly, made some significant remarks;

> Nor is it to be passed without observation that whill his Majesty is making a publick declaration of his intentions to defend and maintaine the religoun, rights, and liberteis of this kingdome according to the lawes, civill and ecclesiastick, the papists ar conspiring, plotting and practising against the lyves of his Majesties good subjects, wherby they doe reallie mainfest to the world what the Kings Majestie against all his declarations and his subjects against their confidence grounded thereupon, may looke for frome their malice and power if they sall continue in armes, and, which God forbid, if they sall prevaile in the end.

Antrim's plot was more of a schematic project than a detailed plan; but it was enough to outrage opinion in Scotland. When the Convention of Estates assembled, it was presented with a paper drawn up by the Commission of the General Assembly, saying that the country was in greater danger from Papists now than it had been at the time of the Spanish Armada. Robert Baillie expressed his own feelings of horror;

...a commission was given to Antrim to treat with the Irish rebells, that the English and they might agree...the first service of the reconciled Ireland and England should be the disposal of the dissafected Scots; that they should goe by sea to Carlile, wher Nithsdale and other Southland lords should joyne; that Colekittoch's sones should waken our Isles; that McClaine and Gorrum, and the other clanes dissafected to the Campbells, should goe to armes; that Huntly and his son Aboyne, with Bamfe and Airlie, Montrose and Marshall, should raise our North...that so in a trace we should become a field of blood...

Politically Hamilton was now in an impossible position. He knew that in the Convention of Estates he would be able to count on the support of most of the senior nobility. But Argyll, whose position in the western Highlands had been so threatened by the Antrim conspiracy, would be strongly backed by the lairds and the burgesses, now in favour of an alliance with Parliament. The beleaguered Hamilton made every attempt to maximise his influence by persuading Montrose and his royalist friends to attend the Convention. Montrose agreed only on condition that if they failed to stop Scottish intervention in the English Civil War, then Hamilton would take up arms with him against the Convention. Hamilton refused to accept this, and Montrose did not come.

When the Estates assembled Hamilton fought a desperate rearguard action, attempting to have discussion limited to domestic affairs, to no avail. On 26 June the members declared themselves to be a free Convention. Two days later they decided to send the details of the Antrim plot to Westminster. Sir Symond D'Ewes commented in his diary;

The discovery of the plot did more work upon most men than anything that happened during the miserable calamities and civil wars of England, because it seemed now that there was a fixed resolution in the Popish party utterly to extirpate the true Protestant religion in England, Scotland and Ireland.

Realising the game was up, Hamilton and Lanark withdrew from the Convention. The way was now free towards a military alliance against the King. News from England convinced the Convention of the urgent necessity of a Parliamentary alliance; for Charles seemed to be winning the war.

On 30 June the Parliamentary army in Yorkshire, under the command of Fernando, Lord Fairfax and his son, Sir Thomas Fairfax, was crushingly defeated by the Marquis of Newcastle at the Battle of Adwalton Moor. This left the Cavaliers in control of almost all of northern England outside the port of Hull. A few days after this alarming development, the Scots sent a proposal for an alliance to Westminster.

From the beginning of the war, John Pym had realised that an alliance with Scotland was essential if Parliament was to prevail against the King. His view was not shared, however, by the majority of his fellow Parliamentarians, in either the Lords or the Commons. With fresh memories of 1640, few welcomed the prospect of the return of a Scottish army to English soil. Events now moved opinion towards Pym. Adwalton Moor was quickly followed by the defeat of the western army under Sir William Waller, first at Lansdown, and then again at the Battle of Roundway Down. John Hampden had been killed in a clash with Rupert at Chalgrove Field; the northern royalists were pressing into Lincolnshire; and, towards the end of July, Bristol, the second port of the realm, fell to the Cavaliers. As Robert Baillie aptly put it 'for the present the Parliament side is running down the brae.'

With no further hesitation Parliament agreed to send a deputation to Edinburgh asking for a Scots army. It was felt that a price would have to be paid for this, not just in money, but one of the things that the Scots had pressed for unsuccessfully in the peace negotiations of 1641 – the reform of the Church of England. In furtherance of this the Scots were to be invited to send representatives to an Assembly of Divines to meet at Westminster. This was destined to become the basis of a great misunderstanding. In the aftermath of the Antrim Plot and Adwalton Moor, the Scots were no less eager for a military pact than the English. There was no suggestion in the Convention that religious reform was a precondition for armed assistance. By bringing the two elements together, the Parliamentary negotiators raised a spectre in the mind of the Covenanters that led to disaster.

The Parliamentary delegation, headed by Sir Harry Vane the younger, the son of the King's former Secretary, arrived in Edinburgh on 7 August. Approaches were made not only to Argyll and the Convention, but also to the General Assembly, meeting in St Giles. Vane informed the gathering that Parliament had abolished Episcopacy, and invited them to send delegates to the Westminster Assembly, which had been called to help in the reconstruction of the Church of England.

In their mutual urgency to do business, both sides quickly concluded an alliance which was called the Solemn League and Covenant. Vane, having raised the possibility of religious uniformity between England and Scotland, made sure that the document, drawn up by Henderson, made no definite commitment to a Presbyterian system. The final form of church government in England was left deliberately vague by the insertion, on Vane's insistence, that it would be 'according to the word of God and the example of the best reformed churches.' England wanted a military alliance; the Scots had been led into the mistaken belief that they could have a religious Covenant. Here were the seeds of a future tragedy. The Scots believed that they were to enter England to impose a religious settlement in their own image; essentially what Charles had tried to do so disastrously in 1639 and 1640. But there was no party in England willing to support a Presbyterian settlement, at least in the sense that the Scots understood it. Without doubt, the Solemn League and Covenant was one of the greatest political errors in Scottish history. Its basic aim could not be fulfilled; but throughout the remainder of the Civil War, up to the invasion of England in 1651, the Scots tried to win one side and then the other over to its aims, becoming ever more divided in the process.

Ever mindful of the horrors that were to be unleashed upon them by the Antrim plot, the Scots looked for guarantees for their own safety from the Solemn League. In return for their assistance it was promised that if Scotland was threatened from Ireland then;

> Parliament would maintain a guard of ships at their own charge on the coast of Scotland for the security of that kingdom from an invasion of Irish rebels or other enemies during such time as the Scottish army shall be employed in the defence of England.

This clause was broken, with disastrous consequences for Scotland. Of course, no one was able to look into the future; but the promise to pay the Scots army £30,000 a month for its maintenance while in England should, perhaps, have raised some questions. Parliament was already experiencing considerable difficulties in ensuring that its own armies were regularly paid; and the Scots army in Ulster, which was to be maintained at English expense, had received almost nothing, with serious effects on its operational ability. In the three years he had served in Ireland, James Turner claimed to have received no more than three months pay. But this was clearly not the time to focus on any of the details of the alliance; for in September Charles finally concluded a truce with the Irish Confederates. The Solemn League and Covenant had come just in time.

Charles' truce with the Confederates – known as the Cessation – theoretically released some 20,000 troops under Ormonde's command for service in England. It should be emphasised that most of these soldiers were Englishmen serving in Ireland; but it suited Parliamentary propaganda to depict them as Catholic Irish. On 25 September, ten days after the Cessation, the Solemn League and Covenant was ratified at Westminster. It was the last great political act of John Pym, who died of cancer in December, believing his revolution to be safe. In fulfilment of its terms, the Earl of Leven crossed the Border in January 1644. The war in England was now about to enter one of its bloodiest phases.

CHAPTER 5
Marston Moor

By the end of 1643 both sides in the English Civil War had fought each other almost to the point of exhaustion. The summer successes of the Cavaliers had led to no definite conclusion; and their attempt to defeat the main Parliamentary army under the Earl of Essex had been frustrated at the first Battle of Newbury. Parliament had authorised the formation of county defence leagues, the most famous of which was the Eastern Association, commanded by the Earl of Manchester, with Oliver Cromwell as his cavalry general. Together they managed to head off the royalist invasion of Lincolnshire, with Cromwell, in particular, showing himself to be a courageous and intelligent soldier. But for both sides the picture was not encouraging. Recruitment was proving difficult, and losses could not easily be made good. Many regiments refused to fight outside their own locations; so outside intervention was necessary to end the deadlock. It remained to see who would make the greatest impact: the Scots or the King's army from Ireland.

On paper the royal forces in Ireland were almost as strong as the army the Scots were able to raise. But the Cessation had not been well received by many of Ormonde's Protestant troops. Their discontent increased when they arrived in England to find themselves shunned as 'papists'; even some of the King's own forces refused to serve with them. Many of Ormonde's officers raised major difficulties. Lawrence Crawford, a Scottish professional soldier, committed in equal measure to war and Presbyterianism, simply refused to transfer the troops under his command to England. He was arrested. So, too, was George Monk, an officer from Devonshire, with whom Scotland was destined to acquire a particularly close acquaintance. Crawford was eventually able to make his way to England, where he joined Manchester and the Eastern Association, providing Cromwell with a rival and an unwelcome taste of Scottish Presbyterianism. Monk, in contrast, overcame his scruples, agreeing to serve with the royalist army in England.

In Ulster the Scots refused to recognise the Cessation. They were joined in their opposition by government troops and Protestant settlers in the area, who described the truce as the work of the Devil. It suited Charles that the Scots should now bear the full weight of the war against the Irish Catholics; for an extra 10,000 Covenanter troops in England would seriously upset his calculations. By January several of the King's Irish regiments were safely in England, particularly in Cheshire, but with nowhere near the concentrated strength of the army descending from the north.

After the truce with Ormonde the Confederates turned to consider ways of ejecting the Scots, their most implacable opponents, from Ulster. They were aided in this by the Earl of Antrim, who had managed to escape, yet again, from Carrickfergus. In November 1643 a meeting was held at Waterford at which it was agreed that an expeditionary force, drawn from Antrim's tenants, should be sent to the west of Scotland, in the hope that Monro would be drawn out of Ulster. In December Antrim crossed to England to put the details of this plot to Charles at Oxford. His latest intrigue was basically a re-run of that of 1643. There would be no slip-ups this time, though, and the co-operation of Montrose was assured.

Leven's army entered England on 19 January 1644, carrying the hopes of a nation. Much was expected of them; too much. Since 1640 Scots' arms had enjoyed an excellent reputation, far in excess of what had been achieved that fateful year. People in both Edinburgh and London did not just expect military success; they expected a miracle. The royalists had a firm hold on Newcastle, depriving the freezing Londoners of their much needed coal supplies. News sheets in the capital were jubilant,

> We may here fall to rigging up old and new ships to fetch the coals which by the time they (the Scots) get thither, no doubt there will be coals ready to take in; therefore let those that howe wood sell good pennyworths, lest they repent it.

But much had changed since 1640. The defences of Newcastle had been considerably improved, especially on the vulnerable southern side. Her citizens, moreover, having experienced one lengthy bout of Scots occupation, were anxious to avoid another. The ford at Newburn was also well fortified, so there would be no easy passage of the Tyne. Leven certainly came with an impressive army: 18,000 foot under the command of William

Baillie; 3,000 horse commanded by Leven's namesake David Leslie; 500 dragoons and 150 field guns, far greater than the forces his chief opponent, William Cavendish, Marquis of Newcastle, could pitch against him. But the season itself favoured defence, rather than attack. Leven's army advanced slowly over roads and through passes choked with snow. He had only just over £10,000 in his war chest, which was exhausted by late February. Supplies were always to be a problem, sometimes serious, at other times acute. The Scots' invasion did make a difference, but not in the way expected. There was no quick campaign followed by a decisive battle. The difference they made was slow and incremental, rather than dramatic; and it would be others who would reap the benefits.

Soon after Leven crossed the Tweed, the royalist commanders in the north met at Alnwick, under the chairmanship of Sir Thomas Glenham. Accepting that they were far too weak to offer any effective resistance, they decided to retreat back to Newcastle, after destroying the bridge across the River Aln. Some of the Yorkshire gentry suggested laying waste to the area before retiring; but, naturally enough, this did not meet with the approval of their Northumbrian counterparts.

Because of the adverse weather conditions, Leven's advance was painfully slow. Baillie and the infantry did not reach Wooler, only a few miles over the Border, until 23 January. It was five days after that before the advanced units of the army reached Morpeth, where a halt was made to allow the rearguard to catch up. The Marquis of Newcastle reacted much more promptly, getting some of his own forces under his Scottish general, Lord Eythin, into Newcastle a few hours before Leven's vanguard arrived. It had taken the Scots over two weeks to march from the Tweed to the Tyne, not an encouraging start to the campaign. Leven, having expected no opposition, was amazed that his opponents had won the race to occupy the city. Newcastle could not be taken, and the Scots had met their first real problem. There would be no coal for London that winter.

Despite this minor success, Cavendish was not blind to his strategic difficulties. In facing Leven he had to turn his back on the Fairfaxes and Manchester's Eastern Association. He wrote to Prince Rupert on 28 January requesting reinforcements. This was followed up on 16 February with a letter to the King;

...the seat of the war will be in the north, a great army about Newark behind us, and the great Scottish army before us, and Sir Thomas Fairfax very strong in the West Riding of Yorkshire, as they say, and his father master of the East Riding: so we are beset, not able to encounter the Scots, and shall not be able to make our retreat for the army behind us...If your Majesty beat the Scots your game is absolutely won; which can be no other way but by sending more forces, especially foot...

With Newcastle drawn off to the north, Sir Thomas Fairfax was able to make useful account of the greater manoeuvrability this allowed. Advancing across country into Cheshire, he defeated a royalist force, including some of the newly arrived Irish regiments, commanded by Lord John Byron, at the Battle of Nantwich on 24 January. George Monk found himself amongst the prisoners. Struggling through the frozen wastes of Northumberland the Scots contribution to Nantwich cannot be measured; but it was real enough, notwithstanding.

Angered by the presence of the Covenanters on English soil, Charles called an 'alternative' Parliament to Oxford. In his opening address to this assembly, Charles accused the Westminster Parliament of inviting a 'foreign power' into England. Responding to the cues from the King, the members of the Oxford Parliament declared the Scots to be invaders. Their denunciation was echoed by Montrose and the other Scots lords in attendance, who condemned their 'traitorous countrymen.'

Montrose was not the only Scot who had come to see the King that winter. Hamilton had arrived at Oxford in December, expecting to be thanked for all the political effort he had made in Scotland. Instead, he was thrown in prison, on the basis of charges drawn up by Montrose, largely on the basis of innuendo, malice and spite. Hamilton was never called to answer these accusations. He remained in prison, without trial, until liberated by victorious Parliamentary troops in 1646. For advice on Scottish matters the King now turned to the Young Turks – Montrose, Aboyne and Lord Ogilvie.

During those gloomy winter days, Oxford was particularly rich in peacocks. Antrim appeared, proudly declaring to all that he had been appointed as General in Chief of the Irish. This turned out not to be true; but at least he could count on the support of his own McDonnell clansmen, unlike Montrose, who could count on virtually nobody. With Charles' blessing the two men put their heads together to work out a plan to further the King's cause in Scotland. On 28 January a bond was drawn up between them, with Montrose as Lieutenant-General of Scotland, and Antrim as General of the Highlands and Islands. Montrose promised to raise the north, the east and the Borders of Scotland by 1 April, while Antrim was to raise his own supporters in Ireland – 10,000 men, so he said – and the Isles and attack Argyll by the same date. Montrose, with no power base of his own in Scotland, was clearly relying on his ability to raise some of the more conservative noblemen in the south and the Gordons in the north, a perilously uncertain basis for an adventure of this kind, especially in view of his less than perfect relations with Huntly.

To further the aims of the Solemn League, the Church of Scotland sent an impressive delegation of ministers and elders to attend the Westminster Assembly. This included some of the heavyweight figures of the Covenater movement: Henderson, Baillie and Rutherford amongst the ministers; John Lord Maitland and Warriston amongst the elders. A number of separate lay commissioners were also sent who took part, along with some of the elders, in the Committee of Both Kingdoms, an executive body set up to co-ordinate the war effort. Ready to decide the fate of England, all now waited for news from Leven's army.

The Scots' invasion had stalled before Newcastle. Old General Leven was now showing his limitations as a commander. Not expecting any resistance, he had left his artillery behind. Even when it arrived, he was slow to start operations, in contrast to Cavendish, who had burnt all of the suburbs of Newcastle, to deny the Scots cover. With Scots' attention firmly fixed on the city, their base at Corbridge was successfully raided by a royalist cavalry column headed by Sir Marmaduke Langdale.

As his casualties began to mount, Leven, after some hesitation, decided to break off his operations before the town, rather than tie up the army in a lengthy siege. Leaving six regiments behind, he moved off in late February to find a way to cross over to the south bank of the Tyne. Although Cavendish had taken the precaution of fortifying Newburn, he did not have sufficient force to guard all of the other fords across the river between Newcastle and Hexham. Leven finally managed to cross on 28 February by the fords at Ovinghame, Bydwell and Altringhame. By 4 March he had crossed the Wear and entered Sunderland. Strengthened by twelve troops of horse under Sir Charles Lucas, Newcastle set off in pursuit.

At Sunderland the way was open to Leven to continue his advance south to link up with Fairfax and Manchester; but his communications were now dangerously over-extended, and fresh supplies were not easy to obtain in a country ravaged by winter. Although Newcastle was weak in infantry, he now had a strong cavalry force, all mounted on good English horses, far superior to their lighter Scottish counterparts. Learning of the approach of the English on 7 March, the Scots took up a strong position on the Bowden Hills, just outside Sunderland. Here the armies faced each other for two days, engaging in no more than light skirmishing. Unable to provoke the Scots into an attack, or to launch an attempt on their own position, Newcastle finally withdrew.

Leven resumed his snail-like progress to the south a few days later, reaching Durham by 13 March. But supplies were now a major problem, especially fresh fodder for the horses, so the army marched back to Sunderland. Here Leven contented himself with cutting off the city of Newcastle from the south, attacking and capturing the small fort at South Shields. He also won a minor engagement with the royalist forces at Chester-le-Street. At Sunderland, Leven's supply problems were slightly improved by the capture of incoming English ships, and he was able to maintain contact with both Scotland and London.

So far Leven had achieved nothing of distinction. He could not remain at Sunderland indefinitely. Supply difficulties would be eased by an advance into Yorkshire, and a link up with the Parliamentary forces to the south would put him beyond the reach of Newcastle's cavalry. Cavendish's task was to prevent any such move; so he decided to attempt another engagement. On 24 March, recently joined by Montrose, he moved his army to Hilton, close to Sunderland on the north side of the Wear. Leven immediately responded by moving to Cleadon Hill, between Hilton and the sea. Between both positions the ground was intersected by hedges and ditches.

The so-called Battle of Hilton began as an artillery duel at 5 o' clock on the evening of 24 March. Fire continued for six hours, well into the dark, and recommenced the following morning. But because of the difficult terrain between the two positions, the armies could not draw any closer. Some musketeers were sent forward to man the hedges by both commanders, the closest the two sides came to direct contact. Newcastle's casualties from the artillery contest were slightly higher than Leven's; so rather than continue the futile encounter, he withdrew to Durham the next day. With the weather now greatly improved, Leven set off in pursuit. By 8 April he approached Durham, and made ready to cut off Newcastle's retreat. Soon Newcastle received even more serious news from the south.

While Leven and Newcastle were duelling with each other, the planned royalist rising in Scotland went off half-cocked. In the north east some of the Gordons, straining at the leash of the Covenant, and frustrated by the inactivity of the diffident Huntly, rose under the leadership of Sir Gordon Haddo on 19 March and launched a raid on Aberdeen. But the clan was not united. Huntly's eldest son, Lord Gordon, a nephew of Argyll, had declared for the Covenant, and attempted to raise forces against his rebel kinsmen. However, Haddo's Raid had the effect of pushing Huntly out of his lethargy. At the head of two hundred horsemen, he reoccupied Aberdeen, driving out all of the leading Covenanters. Recruits were raised in the city for the King and organised by Nathaniel Gordon, one of Huntly's best soldiers. Huntly himself spent his time indulging his taste for melodrama, giving his men black cockades as a sign that they were prepared to fight to the death.

Montrose, newly created a Marquis, had left Oxford at the beginning of March, riding north in the company of the Earls of Nithsdale and Crawford, together with the Lords Aboyne, Ogilvie and Reay. His little party made its way towards Newcastle's army, hoping to obtain support for an invasion of southern Scotland. But Newcastle, now hard pressed by the Scots, did not have the men to spare. Anxious to meet his April deadline with Antrim, Montrose was, however, given the authority to raise the militia of Westmorland and Cumberland for an advance into Galloway.

Almost from the start this ill thought out scheme began to collapse. No sooner had they advanced into Annandale than most of the English levies mutinied, and promptly turned back home. Despite this Montrose, with Nithsdale's encouragement, advanced towards Dumfries, with absolutely no idea of what kind of support he was likely to attract. He entered the town on 15 April, and was warmly received by the provost, an act of generosity that was to cost him his life; but the only reinforcement he attracted was from the Catholic Lord Herries. Montrose now settled down in Dumfries and waited, with increasing anxiety, for news of Antrim.

On receiving news of Huntly's rising, Argyll left the army in England. Settled at Perth, he made ready to deal with the crisis facing the Covenanters from opposite ends of the country. It was imperative to stop Montrose linking up with Huntly, which without doubt would encourage the rest of the wavering royalist nobility to rise against the government. Argyll remained at Perth to keep an eye on the Gordons, while the regiment of Campbell of Lawers was sent south to deal with Montrose. Heavily outnumbered, Montrose had no choice but to retreat back towards Carlisle. Antrim had failed to keep his side of the bargain.

To prevent any further incursion from the south, the Earl of Callendar, who, as Lord Almond, had been one of the signatories of the Cumbernauld Bond, stationed army units along the Border. But Leven's force was now seriously overextended, operating between Newcastle and York, and vulnerable to attacks in the rear.

In the north, things were not going well for Huntly. Following the example of Lord Gordon, his clan had not risen as he had hoped. All he had been able to achieve was a pointless raid on the port of Montrose. By April 26 Argyll had arrived at Dunnotar Castle, at the head of 5,000 men – levies from Perthshire, Fife, Angus and the Mearns, as well as his own Campbells. As Huntly's country was systematically ravaged, the spineless Marquis, black cockades and all, fled to Strathnaver, where he remained in hiding for the next eighteen months. Haddo was arrested and taken back to Edinburgh, where he was executed along with the unfortunate provost of Dumfries. For the time being, the royalist rising in Scotland was over. Its future revival lay in the hands of the dilatory Antrim.

Far to the south, the Scots' Commissioners were increasingly unhappy. They had been well received by the people of London, who expected great things from their army; and to please them Parliament had immediately banned the observation of Christmas Day, as a festival unwarranted by scripture. But as time passed, and Leven's army failed to live up to its expected promise, criticism began to grow. The general sense of gloom grew worse when news came that Prince Rupert had won an important engagement at Newark, cutting London off from the north. Baillie recorded the mood of disappointment;

> ...our armie, after two moneths abode in England, hath done so little; that they had left the siege of Newcastle; that when the enemie came to their quarters, they let them go without fighting; that their provision of victuals is so extremlie small, that their money and munition is so inlacking...so much misorder among the sojors, as some English hath written to their friends...all here thought all was done, if once the Scotts had past Tweed.

Moreover, the Westminster Assembly was not turning out as envisaged. The perceived failures of the Scottish army to deliver the promised knock out blow greatly weakened the political weight of Baillie and his colleagues. The English Presbyterians, such as they were, could only be described as pale Erastian shadows of their northern brethren, failing to accept the notion of a church equal, or superior, to Parliament. To make matters worse a small group of Independents, headed by Philip Nye and Hugh Peters, were determined to resist any attempt to replace Episcopacy with Scottish Presbyterianism. Debates were spun out endlessly, and even the smallest points were argued into the ground. For the Scots, the Independents – and the puritan sects in general – were soon perceived to be an even greater threat than the King. Although they were only a minority in the Assembly, in Parliament and in the country at large, they had the support of Oliver Cromwell and many of the cavalry officers of the Eastern Association. In the end, this was to be decisive.

To help end the log jam in the north, Sir Thomas Fairfax was ordered to assist the Scots. On 9 April he joined up with his father, Lord Fairfax, and beat Sir John Bellasis at Selby, commanding that part of his army that Newcastle had left behind to guard Yorkshire. Soon after this important victory Fairfax wrote;

> This good success put them into great Distraction and Feare att York, who speedily sent to the Earle of Newcastle to hast back thither...leaving the Scotts who...were reduced to great Extremity, but who advanced without delay after this.

Threatened from the rear, and with York itself in danger from the Fairfaxes, and the Eastern Association not far behind,

Newcastle had no choice but to abandon his operations against Leven. He retreated at once towards York, closely pursued by the Scots army, who joined with the Fairfaxes on 20 April at Wetherby. From here they moved to lay siege to York, the most important royalist stronghold in northern England. Newcastle sent an urgent appeal to the King for help;

> ...the Scots and Fairfax have joined near Wetherby, are now too strong for us in matters of the field...they have already put themselves in such a posture as will soon ruin us, being at York, unless there is some speedy course taken to give us relief, and that with a considerable force, for their army is very strong...We shall be distressed here very shortly.

Before the ring closed round him, Newcastle sent out Sir Charles Lucas and most of the cavalry to join the King in the Midlands. He also provided Montrose with 2,000 foot and 500 horse, hoping to draw Leven off by creating a diversion in the north. Montrose used this force to attack the Scots at Morpeth Castle, which fell after a two week siege. He went on to take the fort at South Shields, threatening Leven's base at Sunderland. But, in the end, all of this counted for nothing. On 3 July he met Prince Rupert, who brought news of a disastrous royalist defeat near York.

At York the combined forces of the Fairfaxes and Leven, whose army was now considerably reduced since crossing the Border in January, were not large enough to complete the circle around the city. They wrote to the Earl of Manchester for help, and, in response, the Eastern Association marched out of Lincolnshire in late May, joining their comrades before the city on 3 June. Lawrence Crawford was now Manchester's second-in-command, much to the discontent of Oliver Cromwell. Lines of investment were opened on the east bank of the River Ouse – but, in spite of the combined strength of the three armies, York was still open to the north.

In this emergency, Charles turned to Rupert. Leaving his base at Shrewsbury on 16 May, and gathering all the available forces, the Prince began a march north into Lancashire. The Parliamentary stronghold of Bolton was taken on the 28th of the month, and Rupert was joined by Lord George Goring with Newcastle's cavalry. After completing his operations in Lancashire, Rupert finally crossed the Pennines on 28 June. Two days later, he was at Knaresborough, only twelve miles from York. Learning of his presence, the allies abandoned the siege and formed their combined army to the west of the city at a place called Marston Moor, fully expecting that Rupert would approach by the direct route from Knaresborough. But the Prince was not ready to oblige.

Making a feint towards York from the west, Rupert immediately drew off towards the north, crossing the Ouse at Boroughbridge early on the morning of 1 July and marched southwards to the unguarded gate on the northern side of York. With the Ouse now between him and the allies, he sent a party to seize the bridge of boats that they had constructed across the river to aid communications. Rupert had won an important tactical victory: with a smaller army he had outmanoeuvred his enemies and relieved York with almost breathtaking ease. Leven, Manchester and Fairfax could only look on in impotent frustration as the royalist army advanced towards the city.

Rupert's march on York was a brilliant manoeuvre; but, in itself, it wasn't enough. Something more was demanded of him. At Oxford the King, with only modest forces, was in serious danger from the Parliamentary army of Sir William Waller. Rupert could not simply return to the south to assist him and leave York to be reinvested, as it surely would have been; the north had to be secured first. The only way to do this was by a quick victory over the three opposing armies. Although he was still weaker than the allies, his junction with Newcastle's infantry at York had done much to close the gap. Allied morale, moreover, was likely to be deflated by the relief of York; so the time was right for a battle. The weak link in this thinking was the condition of Newcastle's army: they had undergone the rigours of a siege for almost three months and were in no mood for an immediate fight with the enemy. Newcastle himself, moreover, while pleased by the arrival of Rupert, soon found himself annoyed at the younger man's peremptory manner.

With the royal army at York commanding both banks of the Ouse, the undefended counties of the Eastern Association were in clear danger if Rupert continued his advance to the south east. In the early hours of 2 July the allied generals decided to prevent any move of this kind by marching south to Tadcaster. Slowly the infantry and artillery drew off, leaving a cavalry screen behind with Cromwell and Thomas Fairfax to keep an eye on the enemy. As the day progressed the two men realised something was happening on the other side: Rupert's troops were crossing the Ouse and gathering in strength to the north on Marston Moor. Word was sent to Leven and Manchester, whose leading columns were now just short of Tadcaster. Immediately the order was given to march back towards the north.

From early on in the day Rupert had been ready to attack. With the Parliamentary army dangerously strung out on the road to Tadcaster, he might have achieved an overwhelming victory. Any such surprise attack was overruled by the late arrival of Newcastle and Eythin with the infantry from York. It wasn't until 4 o' clock in the afternoon that the royal army was fully assembled; and by this time their opponents were ready.

As each of the Parliamentary regiments returned they were put into line of battle, which led to a complex intermixture of Scots' and English units. To mirror the dispositions of the royalists, the allied army was drawn up over a one and a half mile front between the villages of Tockwith and Long Marston. They occupied a slightly superior position – a rye field, which sloped gently down towards the Cavaliers, positioned on the moor, a slight distance to the north. A shallow ditch lay between both armies, just beyond the road between Tockwith and Long Marston, on Marston Moor itself. Apart from this, there were no natural obstacles in the open country, save on the eastern side of the armies, where some furze bushes and ditches made the ground more difficult for cavalry.

In accordance with the military thinking of the time, the infantry of each of the armies was placed in the centre, with the cavalry on the wings. The cavalry on the right of the Parliamentary army, close to Long Marston in the east, was commanded by Sir Thomas Fairfax, supported by Colonel John Lambert and three Scottish regiments to the rear under the Earl of Eglinton. Next, to the left of Fairfax, came the main body of the Scottish infantry under Lieutenant General Baillie, six regiments in all – four in the first line and two in the second. To their rear, a third line was formed by two infantry regiments from the Eastern Association. In the centre stood Lord Fairfax, with two English foot regiments in the front, supported by four Scottish foot regiments, two in the centre and two in the rear. To their left were the remaining four infantry regiments of the Eastern Association, commanded by Crawford, with four Scottish regiments in the second line, and four of Fairfax's regiments in the third. Two Scots regiments were held in reserve. Finally, on the left, came the cavalry of the Eastern Association, commanded by Oliver Cromwell, in two lines, with David Leslie in charge of a third line of three Scottish regiments. There was a company of Scottish dragoons on this wing under Colonel Fraser. Overall command was given to Leven, who had some 27,000 men at his disposal.

Opposite Fairfax, on the Cavalier left, was a cavalry force under the command of George Goring – a brave, if rather quixotic soldier – supported by Sir George Lucas and Sir Richard Dacre. To their right came the infantry regiments of Rupert and Lord Byron, with Newcastle's own regiments to the rear, including a crack force known as the Whitecoats. The royalist foot were supported by a cavalry brigade led by Sir William Blakeston. Finally, on the right, Rupert positioned his remaining cavalry regiments, under Lord Byron. Commanding one of the leading regiments was Sir John Hurry, whom we last met fighting for Parliament at Edgehill. He had since quarrelled with his allies and switched sides. On both wings the cavalry were interspersed with dragoons, a Swedish innovation intended to throw an attacking enemy force off balance. Rupert also held some of the cavalry units back to fight under him as a mobile reserve. In all, Rupert had something over 17,000 men, considerably weaker than the enemy. Even so, Leven's superiority was in infantry; in cavalry the gap was not so wide. Both sides were evenly matched in field guns – Rupert had twenty-eight pieces to Leven's twenty-five. Artillery, however, played a part of no great significance in the coming battle.

On both sides the standard infantry weapon, apart from the pike, was the matchlock musket. At the beginning of the century, this weapon had been so heavy that the musketeer required a long forked rest, which was planted in the ground and used to support the weight of the barrel. In introducing a much lighter weapon, Gustavus Adolphus had dispensed with the need for the rest; but the firing technique had remained the same. The match was a long length of slow burning cord, impregnated in saltpetre, lit at both ends as a precaution against one being extinguished. It was held in a device known as a 'serpantine', which resembled the hammer of a gun, and lowered to a touch hole by a lever, acting in the same way as a modern trigger. Each musketeer carried two powder horns, the nozzle of which contained an exact charge. One horn contained priming powder, which was placed in the pan below the serpantine; the other held the ordinary gunpowder for pouring directly down the barrel.

Loading was a detailed operation. First, the lighted match was removed from the serpantine and held in the left hand, well away from the powder horns. The butt was then placed in the ground. With the right hand the powder flask was tipped up, the mouth blocked by the forefinger. A spring thumb-catch was then pressed to allow the nozzle to fill. Then the thumb-catch was released and the measured charge poured down the barrel. Wadding and a musket ball were rammed down afterwards. The weapon was then lifted off the ground and some priming powder poured into the touch pan; after which the pan was closed by its cover and the loose powder blown away. Then the match was screwed back into the serpantine, and the gun was ready to fire. All of this sounds impossibly complex; but with some practice the trained musketeer could fire off approximately two shots a minute. Not surprisingly, there was also a tendency to cut corners. Rather than replacing the match, the harassed musketeer would often place it directly into the pan with his fingers; and the gun was frequently fired off from the waist, rather than carefully aimed from the shoulder. Accuracy, needless to say, was not high, and there were many accidents.

Firing was by a procedure known as the 'countermarch', allowing for a continuous rate of fire. Each rank of a musketeer regiment was organised in files of six men. As the front rank fired they fell back to the rear to reload, the new front rank firing and falling back, and so on. As an alternative, to allow a more concentrated fire, the muskets could be shot off in ranks of three – the front rank kneeling, the second rank stooping and the third rank standing. As a secondary weapon, each man carried a sword, although this was rarely used. When it came to close quarter fighting with enemy infantry regiments, it was more usual to use the musket butt as a club. For the musketeer the greatest danger was a sudden cavalry attack. To guard against this the pikemen would break their own solid formations and form squares, within which the musketeer could take cover. For the pikeman, close quarter fighting with his enemy counterpart was by a gruesome operation known as 'push of pike.'

By late afternoon all was ready. The day was overcast, punctuated, from time to time, by heavy falls of summer rain.

84

Neither side seemed willing to move, simply keeping a wary eye on each other at a distance of no more than half a mile. There had been an exchange of artillery fire, which gradually petered out. Apart from the sound of psalm singing from the Parliamentary side, no other noise disturbed the quiet of the evening. Finally, at about 7 o' clock, the tension was relieved by a tremendous thunder storm. The heavy rain that followed no doubt extinguished matches and soaked gunpowder, causing many muskets to misfire. Rupert gradually began to relax, accepting that there would be no battle that day. He called for his supper, as Newcastle retired to his nearby carriage for a smoke. All along the line, the reserve regiments began to stand down. This was clearly the sign Leven had been waiting for; the signal was given and the allied army moved slowly forward. The Battle of Marston Moor was about to begin.

Picture the scene. The clouds were dark and heavy, and visibility already poor. On both sides the musketeers began firing. Before long great clouds of smoke arose, reducing the visibility still further. To aid identification, the Parliamentary cavalry all wore white cockades in their hats. Leven's unexpected advance had taken the Cavaliers by surprise, allowing the Parliamentary army to clear their opponents quickly from the ditch, the only serious obstacle in front of them, and advance to a close quarter engagement before the enemy was able to fire off more than a couple of volleys. Under pressure from musketeers and pikemen, the front ranks of Rupert's infantry began to crumble. On both wings the cavalry also moved forward, riding at a fast trot rather than at the gallop, each trooper keeping abreast of his neighbour. The initial advance had gone well; but, on the right, Sir Thomas Fairfax was soon in serious trouble.

Like their comrades elsewhere along the line of battle, Fairfax's cavalry successfully fought their way across the main ditch in the face of enemy musket fire. No sooner had they crossed than their real difficulties began. North of the ditch, the ground was dotted with bushes and intersected by smaller ditches, which broke the line and made a further advance difficult. Fairfax managed to fight his way clear at the head of his own troop, but the rest of his cavalry was swept away in a sudden counterattack by Lord Goring, sweeping through the front ranks, cutting into Lambert's second line and on into Eglinton's reserve. Eglinton attempted to make a stand; but his force was too weak to stem the flood of Goring's heavy cavalry. Two troops from Ayrshire did, however, manage to fight their way through to join their comrades on the left. Cut off from the rest of his men, Sir Thomas ordered the troopers with him to remove their badges of identification, thereby remaining undetected in the general confusion. He, too, made his way to the left, riding across the rear of the royalist army.

Meanwhile, Goring's charge carried him right through the Parliamentary lines, on to the baggage train at the rear. To the left of Fairfax, the Parliamentary infantry were also in difficulty. Sir Charles Lucas broke away from Goring's wild career to attack Baillie and the Scots, now exposed on the flank. Lord Fairfax's own foot, after their initial success, were fought to a standstill by the advance of Newcastle's Whitecoats. Seeing an opportunity, Sir William Blakeston charged with his own cavalry regiments, scything through Fairfax's beleaguered infantry, and on into the four Scots regiments behind them. Panic began to spread. In ever increasing numbers the infantrymen dropped their weapons and fled. Arthur Trevor, riding from Skipton with dispatches for Rupert, came across;

> ...a shoal of Scots crying Wey is us, we are all undone...and anon I met with a ragged troop reduced to four and a coronet; by and by with a little foot officer without hat, band, sword or indeed anything but feet and so much tongue as would serve to inquire the way to the next garrison...

Fairfax, too, ran away. Leven, after trying in vain to steady the line, joined him, ending up in Leeds. Manchester was also seriously unsettled, joining this flight of the generals; but he managed to compose himself sufficiently to return to the field. Soon the news of a great royalist victory spread across the country with the fleeing soldiers; and at Newark the church bells rang out in joy. But the battle was not yet over.

For the Parliamentary side the position looked desperate. On the right their army had virtually disintegrated. Only one thing saved them: the stand being made by William Baillie and the rest of the Scots' infantry; men from Fife, Ayrshire, Strathearn and Mid-Lothian. Attacked in the front and on both flanks, the musketeers fought off the enemy footmen, while the pikemen repelled the cavalry. No fewer than three enemy charges were repulsed, during which Sir Charles Lucas himself was unhorsed and taken prisoner. The regiments of Lord Maitland, commanded by Lieutenant-Colonel Pittscottie, and Lord Lindsay performed particularly distinguished service. But, faced with unrelenting pressure from the enemy, they could not hold out forever. Lord Goring was returning with his cavalry from the rear, threatening to surround the struggling Scots, when out of the gathering darkness, from the position Goring had started the battle, rode Oliver Cromwell and the cavalry of the Eastern Association.

Marston Moor was a complex and confused battle, perhaps best pictured as a giant swing door, with Baillie's foot regiments forming a pivot in the centre. While the Parliamentary offensive on the right had stalled and then collapsed, the picture was quite different on the other side of the field. Fraser's Scots dragoons had quickly cleared the ditch of the royalist musketeers, allowing Cromwell's cavalry to cross in good order. Rupert had intended Byron to remain on the defensive, to allow the musketeers scattered amongst them to inflict maximum casualties on the approaching enemy. But the sight of Cromwell was simply too much for Byron, who ordered an immediate counter charge, masking the fire of the snipers. With sword and pistol Cromwell's men fought their way through, routing Byron's first line and part of his second. Seeing the danger, Rupert rode forward with his reserves, steadying the fleeing royalist cavalry in the process.

In the fierce fighting that followed, Cromwell received a slight neck wound, and had to retire to have it dressed. His cavalry began to give way; but, at this crucial point in the battle, Rupert was charged in the flank by David Leslie and his three regiments of Scottish lancers, who swept in from the left of Cromwell's men. With no more reserves, Rupert began to give way. Cromwell returned to lead a second assault. The royalist cavalry broke and Rupert fled, hiding from his pursuers in a bean field.

Unlike their royalist counterparts on the right, the allied cavalry preserved perfect discipline. There was no disorderly pursuit of the broken enemy. Instead, Leslie followed the fugitives for a while, to prevent them rallying, while Cromwell wheeled to the right, across the centre part of the battlefield, now covered in darkness, relieved only by the light cast by the fire of the guns. The allied infantry to his right, the mixed force commanded by Lawrence Crawford, had also fought their way forward, turning the flank of their opponents. Crawford immediately informed Cromwell of the crisis on the far right. News of the situation was also brought by Sir Thomas Fairfax. Leslie had now returned, and it was decided to follow Fairfax back across the rear of the royalists to attack Goring and ease the pressure on Baillie. When assaulted from a totally unexpected direction, Goring's disorganised troopers simply collapsed in bewilderment. The rout spread to the royalist infantry in the centre. All were gone, save Newcastle's Whitecoats, who, assailed on all sides, fought on with fierce courage until hammered to death. By midnight all was over.

Marston Moor was the biggest battle of the Civil War; more than that, it was one of the largest fights in British history, exceeded only by Flodden, and perhaps Towton in the Wars of the Roses. Parliamentary losses were fairly light; but the King had lost 4,000 men killed, many of whom could not be replaced, especially amongst the infantry. News of the triumph was brought to the fugitive General Leven, who made a shamefaced return to his army, saying 'I would to God I had died upon that place.' His actions were to be a cause of some embarrassment for the Covenanters. He had shown considerable skill in organising and directing the allied army; but he left too early, and retired too far, to earn much but ridicule. The most novel explanation for his behaviour was provided by his pastor, Robert Douglas, who recorded in his *Diary;*

> God would not give the victorie to so great a multitude, we were then 24 thousand, the enemy 20, therefore he dismayed more than the halfe; they that fled ran fast away; they that stood, God stood to it indeed. God would not have a generall in the army, he himself was Generall.

The Battle of Marston Moor was the great watershed of the war in England. Before it Parliament had been fighting for survival; after it the road to total victory was opened. Concern over the implications of the complete defeat of the King was soon to cause major political divisions on the allied side. This led to the formation of a force that was to be the victor over the King, the Scots and even over Parliament itself – the New Model Army.

CHAPTER 6
Montrose – The Scourge of Heaven

The effects of Marston Moor were immediate: Charles had lost the north. Soon after the battle York surrendered, and the Marquis of Newcastle left for the Continent, fearing the scorn of the court, and taking no further part in the war. The three allied armies separated. Leven returned to complete the siege of Newcastle, where he was joined by a second Scottish army under the Earl of Callander. Rupert gathered together all the royal cavalry that had managed to escape from the debacle. Meeting Montrose at Richmond, he not only refused his request for reinforcements 'to cut into the heart of Scotland', but immediately deprived him of the troops he had been given by Newcastle earlier in the year.

In London Marston Moor was about to be fought anew. Baillie and the other Scots' Commissioners were delighted to receive news of the triumph, which fully justified the presence of their army in England. Yet, in spite of the crucial part played by the Scots, and the outstanding courage shown by Baillie and Leslie, the Independents were soon claiming all the honours for Cromwell, their favourite soldier. Cromwell certainly did nothing to correct this impression. In a letter written shortly after the battle he said that 'Our horse, save for a few Scots in our rear, beat all the Prince's horse.' Admittedly, this was said not in a battle report, but in a letter of condolence written to his brother-in-law telling of the death of his son in the fight. Even so, Cromwell certainly emphasised the importance of his own cavalry, and his description of Leslie's role is neither fair nor accurate. The first report of the battle was carried to London by one of Cromwell's own men, Captain Thomas Harrison, who said that God and the Independents had carried the day. Baillie wrote in frustration that, according to the Independents;

> ...all the glory of that night was theirs; that they and their Generall-major Cromwell had done it all there alone...but a Scottish captain Stuart arrived in London with the true story, showing...the vanitie and falsehood of their disgracefull relation.

This came at a particularly frustrating time for the Scots. In the Westminster Assembly, progress on the new Directory of Worship had been held up for weeks by Philip Nye and his colleagues – or the 'sectaries', as the Scots called them. Increasingly, demands were made for the toleration of all Protestant dissenters, anathema to the Presbyterian Scots. The steady rise of Cromwell appeared to make the situation even more dangerous. Here was a man who was absolutely convinced that God was on his side and this added to his outstanding natural ability as a military commander, made a deadly combination. As time passed, the Scots became worried by the forces raised in England, and, unable to win the war, began to turn their thoughts more towards securing a peace. They were supported in this by some of their more conservative English allies, including Cromwell's superior, the Earl of Manchester.

Leven in the north east set about reversing the damage done by Montrose before Marston Moor. Morpeth was recaptured, as was the fort at South Shields. This was followed on 24 July by the capture of Hartlepool and Stockton. Serious effort was now given to the reduction of Newcastle. The city finally fell to an assault on 19 October, which helped to restore some of the battered credibility of the Scots army. But, by this time, Leven and his men were becoming increasingly alarmed by a new crisis at home.

Antrim had not forgotten his pact with Montrose. He had not been able to raise the lavish numbers mentioned at Oxford, but he had assembled some 1600 tough and reliable men, mostly drawn from amongst his own tenants. Under the overall command of Alisdair MacColla this force was to be sent to the Highlands to act as a core – it was hoped – of a larger Celtic army. Antrim's force was organised in three regiments: the first headed by his brother Alexander, the second by Magnus O' Cahan and the third by James McDonnell. Subsequent events were to show these men to be superb soldiers, courageous, disciplined and controlled under fire. They were also to be capable of epic feats of endurance, indicating that some, if not all, had served in Continental armies, rather than being lifted straight from the farm. Perhaps because of this they were also men of a bloodthirsty temperament. Even before they left Ireland there were reports of atrocities committed against the people of Roscommon and Galway, all boding ill for Scotland. Patrick

Gordon of Ruthven was eventually to record his own impressions of these men;

> ...the Irishes in particulare ware too cruell; for it was everiewhere observed they did ordinarely kill all they could be maister of, without any motion of pitie, or any consideration of humanitie; ney, it seemed to them there was no distinction betwixt a man and a beast; for they killed men ordinarily with no more feeling of compassion, and with the same carelesse neglect that they kill ane henn or capone for ther supper.

In late June Antrim's regiments, with their wives and children in tow, set sail for Scotland in three ships the *Christopher*, the *Angell Gabriell* and the *Jacob*. All were equipped and supplied at the expense of the Kilkenny government, for whom the success of the enterprise would be determined by how fast it took to remove Monro from Ulster.

In early July, about the time of Marston Moor, MacColla and his men landed in Ardnamurchan, on the mainland opposite Mull, without interception by the English navy, a breach of one of the terms of the Solemn League and Covenant. They enjoyed some quick successes, capturing the Campbell castles of Lochaline and Mingarry. But early optimism soon gave way to concern; for the royalist clans did not come to join them, as had been expected. MacColla sent messages to the Earl of Seaforth, the chief of the MacKenzies, now, after the defeat of Huntly, the most important royalist in the north. But Seaforth was no greater as a leader of men; and while Huntly had at least been prepared to take risks, he, in contrast, valued his safety too much to embark on any rash enterprise. Unable to remain for long in hostile Campbell territory, MacColla and his men set off in search of recruits. Far away in London Baillie wrote of their coming;

> We trust they shall not doe much hurt, but that God, who has defended hitherto our land, shall deliver these idolatrous butchers to our swords.

At first the Covenanters did not take this invasion seriously. Argyll, who prevailed so effortlessly against Huntly, was given the task of destroying MacColla's small army. News of his landing had reached Montrose in England. Rupert, however, had taken away all the men he had, so he was unable to hold to his own side of the bargain with Antrim. But as every other royalist rising

91

in Scotland had been a miserable failure, it was important to seize this last opportunity. Montrose returned in secret to Scotland, ready to place himself at the head of a Catholic Irish army, as far away from the original principles of the National Covenant as it is possible to imagine.

Once back in Scotland, Montrose kept his presence secret by hiding in Methven Wood in Perthshire. Here he waited for news of the Irish. In late August he learned they had advanced into Atholl. Hurrying north to meet them, he arrived just in time to prevent a clash between them and the local clansmen, the Stewarts and Robertsons. Armed with the King's commission, and little else, both sides immediately agreed to serve under him. Soon after he was joined by Lord Kilpont at the head of a force of archers, supposedly raised to fight for the Covenanters.

Although Argyll had assembled a force at least equal in strength to that of MacColla by mid July at Dunstaffnage Castle, he did not set off in pursuit, concentrating, rather, on a time consuming attempt to retake Mingarry and Lochaline castles. This had allowed the Irish to penetrate the centre of the country, dangerously close to the Lowlands. The link up with Montrose had now turned a serious situation into a critical one. Without doubt *MacCailein Mór* was the most talented politician of his generation; he was shortly to prove himself to be one of the worst soldiers.

On 28 August the government decided to organise a new scratch force to oppose the rebels. In the Perthshire lowlands, the area of the immediate emergency, all men between 16 and 60 were called up. A cavalry force was provided by the local gentry. Command of this army – some 6,000 men in all – was entrusted to David, Lord Elcho, the eldest son of the Earl of Wemys. With him was the Earl of Tullibardine, a confirmed Covenanter, and James, Lord Drummond, a former signatory of the Cumbernauld Bond. Drummond was in command of the Covenanter's 800 horsemen. As Montrose had no horse or pikemen to fight off a cavalry attack, the coming battle should, in conventional military terms, have been an easy victory for his opponents.

Elcho drew up his army on the plain of Tippermuir on Sunday 1 September, intending to deny Montrose entry into Perth. Considering that most of the men had only been raised a few days before, and the untrained infantry were presumably still fumbling with the complex musket drill, the Covenanters were surprisingly confident. All shared the Lowlander's general contempt of the Highlanders and the Irish, an attitude strengthened by the ministers in the army. In *A Short Abridgement of Britane's Distemper*, by far the most accurate contemporary account of Montrose's campaigns, Ruthven notes;

> ...they ware so confident, that when the marquise sent to them desyring the battell might be deferred till the nixt day, because that was the Sabboth, there answere was, they had made chose of the Lordes day for doeing the Lords worke; and they war the more incouraged to this, because a holy Covenanting minister, with whose seemeing sanctitie they were much takein, esteeming all his sentences as divine oracles, had promised them in his sermones chosen for that day ane famous and undoubted victorie...

Montrose's mixed Highland and Irish force numbered about 3,000 men, half the size of their opponents. MacColla and the Irish infantry – all musketeers – were placed in the centre; Kilpont's bowmen were on the left; and on the high ground on the right Montrose took command of the men of Atholl and Badenoch, swordsmen in the main, some with muskets, but the only missile weapon for most were the stones they found scattered around. The whole line was lengthened by making the ranks only three deep, instead of the usual six, to avoid being outflanked by Elcho's stronger force. Kilpont's force and the Highlanders were, for the most part, no better trained than their Lowland counterparts, so the key to the battle lay with the Irish.

To the east the Covenanters stood waiting under a banner bearing the motto 'Jesus and no quarter', a device which sadly set the tone for the wars of Montrose. Elcho, a man of no military skill, took charge of the right wing; the Earl of Tullibardine was given the centre; and the left to Sir James Scott, opposite Montrose. In conventional fashion, Drummond's cavalry force was divided between each end of the army.

As the enemy approached, Elcho tried to knock them off balance by a cavalry probe, but this was beaten back by the fire of the musketeers. The inexperienced Covenanter infantrymen began to panic, firing off their weapons at too great a range to do any damage. Unpreturbed by their amateur opponents, desperately struggling to reload, the Irish infantry advanced ever more closely, and then began a disciplined and continuous fire into the enemy ranks. Clearly outgunned, the Lowland levies started to give way. The infantry and cavalry under Sir James Scott on the left was assailed by a single musket volley and a shower of stones, before the enemy charged into their ranks with drawn swords.

Neither Ruthven nor George Wishart, Montrose's future biographer, make any mention of Kilpont's role in the battle; but his bowmen, with a much higher rate of fire than the half trained musketeer, must have caused as much damage and panic in their sector as MacColla and Montrose elsewhere along the line. In any event, the whole of Elcho's army crumbled, rushing back to the illusory safety of Perth. The fight had been short and battlefield casualties few; but now the real killing began in the murderous pursuit of the defeated Covenanters. So many were butchered on the road between Tippermuir and Perth, that it was said to be possible to cover the route by stepping on corpses all along the way, without once setting foot on the ground. Montrose entered the defenceless town of Perth in triumph. Here he waited for several days, in confident expectation that his longheld belief that Scotland was about to shake off the yoke of the Covenant. But there was no sign of any support from the south.

News of the shocking outcome of the Battle of Tippermuir spread quickly across Scotland. A stronger army had been defeated by a weaker opponent. That was bad enough; but what is worse, Montrose had no cavalry. William Baillie was in no doubt that Lord Drummond, who showed neither skill nor determination, was chiefly responsible for the disaster. It is certainly surprising that there was no massed cavalry attack. Drummond's horsemen, however, were only the local gentry, not professional soldiers; so their courage under fire was likely to have been little better than that of the raw infantry. The real lesson of Tippermuir is that the rebellion was best handled by experienced troops, concentrated in strength, rather than by local levies. It was to be some time, though, before this was learned.

There was one late casualty of the Battle of Tippermuir. Soon after the fight Montrose entered the house of Alexander Balneaves, the local minister, and asked for a drink of water, which was promptly supplied. When later called to account by the local presbytery for his conduct that warm September afternoon, Balneaves responded in spirited terms that there was not one of those present, if they had been there that day, who would not have kissed Montrose's arse, if so commanded.

On September 12, as the rebels were approaching Aberdeen, a price was put on Montrose, to be taken dead or alive because he had

> ...joined with a band of Irish rebels and mass-priests, who had, this two years bygone, bathed themselves in the blood of God's people in Ireland, and in a traitorous and perfidious manner has invaded this kingdom, taken possession of some royal burghs, thereof, apprehended, killed and cruelly murdered divers of his Majesty's subjects.

Despite the unexpected success against Elcho's horse, Montrose realised that his army was not equipped for a prolonged campaign in the Lowlands without cavalry and trained pikemen. Besides, as Hamilton had predicted at York in 1643, he was soon abandoned by most of his Highland irregulars, who had returned home laden down with booty; and with Argyll approaching from the west, he could not remain in Perth. To make good his loss, he decided on a swing to the north to recruit in the country of the Gordons. He hoped to gain the support of Lord Gordon and his much needed horsemen, without which, as Ruthven says, 'he should not be able to keepe the low country, but must of force retyre to the mountains.'

From Perth Montrose marched eastwards, camping close to Dundee. Here he received a serious blow when Lord Kilpont was murdered by James Stewart of Ardvoirlich, one of his own retainers. Stewart escaped from the camp, later joining with the Covenanters. The exact circumstances of this murder have never been made clear; but it would seem that Kilpont's decision to join the royalists was not universally popular amongst his men, especially as they all now insisted on leaving Montrose to take their chief home for burial.

Montrose now had little more than his three Irish regiments. He hoped to find additional recruits in Angus, an area widely known for its royalist sympathies. Most were unwilling to take the risk, apart from the Earl of Airlie and his second son Sir Thomas Ogilvie, at the head of a much needed party of forty horsemen. Airlie, of course, was a long standing royalist, who nurtured a special hatred of Argyll for the damage inflicted on his property in 1640. Nathaniel Gordon also arrived with another party of horse, bringing the total strength up to about ninety. However, there would be no widespread support from the Gordons: Huntly was still in hiding, and, in any case, bitterly resentful of Montrose; Aboyne, his most reliable ally amongst the clan, was in Carlisle, under siege by the Covenanters; and Lord Gordon and his brother Lewis were, at this time, with the Covenanters.

Argyll arrived at Stirling on 4 September, in the mistaken belief that Montrose would head south after Tippermuir. On discovering the enemy's true direction, he advanced to Perth, arriving in time to receive news of a new disaster from the north.

The defence of Aberdeen, which had been under continuous military occupation since the failure of Huntly's rising, had been entrusted to Robert Arnot, Lord Burleigh, who had some 2,500 men, stronger by at least 1,000 than the fast approaching enemy. But if Elcho knew little of war, Burleigh knew nothing. Failing to take account of the lessons of Tippermuir, he drew up his army outside the town, rather than occupying defensive positions within; and as his troops were little more experienced than those who had fought with Elcho, this was to be a fatal mistake.

Finding the Brig o' Dee held against him, Montrose marched to the west, fording the river at the Mills of Drum, and then along the northern bank, arriving before the city on Friday 13 September. Burleigh had placed his army on a slope to the west of the city, near the Justice Mills astride the Hardgate, the main road into Aberdeen from Deeside. His dispositions that day are not entirely clear. It would seem that Lords Fraser and Crichton held the left, Sir William Forbes of Craigevar the centre, with Lord Lewis Gordon on the right. Montrose entrusted his own left to Nathaniel Gordon and Colonel James Hay with thirty horsemen and one hundred musketeers; MacColla and the Irish held the centre; and the right, with the remainder of the cavalry, was placed under the Earl of Airlie and Sir William Rollo. There is no mention in the records of Montrose's position. It may be that he took a more central location than he had at Tippermuir, a victory that owed more to MacColla than Montrose. Before the battle commenced a parlay was held after which a royalist drummer boy was shot dead by the Covenanters, an act that was used to justify the horror to follow,

The Battle of Aberdeen began as contest over some houses and gardens, lying between the two armies. There was also an exchange of cannon fire. With the wind blowing from the south west, the smoke from the guns was carried into the eyes of Burleigh's army, severely restricting their view of the enemy. Burleigh then appears to have ordered some cavalry probes on Montrose's left close to the houses, with a possible view of turning the enemy flank. The first attack was easily beaten back by the musketeers. A party of 100 horse and 400 foot was then sent out, moving round the side of the hill to try to escape detection.

MacColla's Irish regiments had now pushed well forward, so this new probe by the Covenanters was well positioned to roll up Montrose's entire flank from the left. Amazingly, no attempt was made to exploit this advantage. Soon the opportunity passed. Nathaniel Gordon detected the move and alerted Montrose, who detached another 100 musketeers to reinforce his left. Once strengthened, both musketeers and cavalry advanced uphill towards their opponents, and, in Ruthven's words, 'cutes all these fooles in pieces.' Covenanter attacks on the right fared no better. Fraser and Crichton charged twice; but, without the support of the other cavalry units on this wing, their attempts failed. The overwhelming superiority the Covenanters enjoyed in cavalry was being slowly frittered away in a series of appallingly co-ordinated attacks. Finally, in an attempt to redress a deteriorating situation, Cragievar charged with his own cavalry troop straight towards the Irish infantry in the centre, who responded with an astonishing degree of self control. Ruthven describes the scene;

> ...the Irishes, throw whom he charged, being well trained men as the world could afford no better, oppins there rankes receiving him, and closes againe immediately by command of their worthie McDonald and then on all quarters gives fire upon.

Burleigh's remaining cavalry were badly shaken by the destruction of Craigevar's charge. The initiative had now passed firmly to the royalists, who pressed their attack with greater savagery. In increasing numbers the Covenanter horsemen began to ride off, leaving the frightened infantry to their inevitable fate. A regiment from Fife tried to draw away in good order towards the Dee. This move was spotted by MacColla, who ordered his men to intercept. In the rush back towards Aberdeen the disorganised Covenanter infantry were cut down in hundreds;

but the killing did not stop there. No sooner had the Irish troops entered the city than they began a three day orgy of plunder, rape and murder, detailed by John Spalding in *The History of the Troubles*. In his account, Montrose returned to camp soon after the battle;

> ...leaving the Irishes killing, robbing and plundering of this toune at thair plesour. And nothing hard bot pitifull houling, crying, weiping, murning, throw all the strettis...sum wemen thay pressit to defloir, and other sum thay took peforce to serve thame in the camp...The men that thay killit thay wold not suffer to be bureit, bot tirrit thame of thair clothis, syne left thair naikit bodeis lying above the ground. The wyf durst not cry nor weip at her husbandis slauchter befoir hir eyes, nor the mother for the sone, nor dochter for the father; whiche if they war hard, then war thay presentlie slayne also.

There can be no accusation of exaggeration or bias here; for Spalding was a royalist as well as an Aberdonian. The sack of Aberdeen shocked contemporaries not because of its scale – there were to be far greater outrages committed in England and Ireland – but because it seemed to confirm all of the horror stories that had accompanied the rising of 1641. Here, on Scottish soil, a Papist army was cutting the throats of innocent Protestant civilians. All the more shocking, that this should be done in Aberdeen, the most loyal of all the royal cities, as Montrose well knew. Aberdeen had been Covenanter by force, never by its own free choice. But the city had no reason to welcome the heroic Marquis, either in his Covenater or in his royalist guise. The damage down those September days was more serious than Montrose can have conceived at the time: it ensured that the vast majority of Scots would never rally to the cause of King Charles while he was his champion. Aberdeen's suffering was ended by the approach of Argyll, at the head of another Covenanter army. When word arrived of his approach 'mony who lovit the king wes glad of thir news,' so wrote Spalding, 'utheris of the covenant was no less sorie.'

As Montrose set off into the Gordon country on a recruiting drive, Argyll re-established Covenanter control in the shattered city of Aberdeen. Although he failed to show the necessary sense of urgency as a commander, Argyll did at least ensure that Montrose was not given the leisure to settle down in the territory of the Gordons. He advanced through Huntly to the Bog of Gicht, plundering on the way to deprive the royalists of a secure base, pushing the patience of Lord Gordon to extreme limits in the process. Montrose, himself, continued to elude the Covenanter forces, and the government in Edinburgh became ever more dissatisfied with Argyll's conduct of the campaign. But towards the end of October he came close to trapping his enemy at Fyfie Castle, in the process exposing a fatal weakness in Montrose's conduct as a soldier that, in time, was to destroy him – his failure to appreciate the importance of reconnaissance and military intelligence.

In late September MacColla left Montrose, taking away some of the Irish units, to check on his bases in the west, and to recruit more men from among the anti Campbell clans. Believing his enemies to be far to the south, Montrose settled down at Fyfie on 27 October. No scouts were sent out to scour the surrounding countryside. But Argyll was not far away: he was just over the next hill. When the Covenanters approached, most of Montrose's available cavalry was out foraging. He was alerted to the enemy presence only just in time. With only O'Cahan's Irish regiment and a small cavalry force, he was in no position to face Argyll in battle. Not wishing to be caught in Fyfie Castle itself – a home rather than a good defensive strongpoint – he took up a strong position to the east, protected by the River Ythan and the woods of Fyfie Glen. With a stream to his front and some walled enclosures to the left, Montrose drew back from Argyll like a snail drawing into its shell. Three attempts were made to tease him out, before the Covenanters finally drew off in frustration.

Montrose, who had only narrowly escaped from a trap of his own making, marched off to the north to plunder Turriff and Rothiemay. Dutifully, Argyll, once again, set off in pursuit; but his heart was clearly no longer in the seemingly endless chase of the elusive Highland fox. As Montrose withdrew along the Deveron towards Balvenie Castle in Glen Fiddich, his opponent fell back, mentally and physically exhausted, to Aberdeen, where he sent most of his Campbell army home for the winter. He then returned to Edinburgh and resigned his commission. In accepting this the Committee of Estates could not resist a touch of irony, thanking him for his services 'all the more deserved because there had been so little bloodshed.' But *MacCailein Mór* was to get no peace that winter; for MacColla had rejoined Montrose with a new scheme in mind.

In England the initial enthusiasm which had greeted the Solemn League and Covenant was all but gone. The fall of Newcastle, so eagerly expected earlier in the year, was the cause of still further dissension. Angered by the failure of Parliament to provide the promised financial support for Leven's army, the Scots refused to send the much needed coal to a fuel starved London, unless they were allowed to claim the revenues of the trade to meet their expenses. Pressure was also put on Parliament to settle the long standing question of church government. With so much at stake politically, the Covenanters were in no mood to send the main part of their army back north to deal with the irksome Montrose. They were also soon to be drawn into a serious clash between Cromwell and Manchester.

Marston Moor had opened a door which many were anxious to see closed again. The victory had a sobering effect on the Earl of Manchester, one of its architects. Soon after he began to have serious doubts about the course of the war. He was particularly alarmed by the rise of political and religious radicalism amongst his own soldiers in the Eastern Association. The personal and political capital Cromwell and the Independents had made out of Marston Moor had unsettled him, as it had the Scots. For a time he seemed to have withdrawn from the conflict altogether; and when he was finally pushed into taking the offensive, his conduct at the indecisive second Battle of Newbury, fought as Argyll was marching to meet Montrose at Fyfie, was less than satisfactory.

For Cromwell, the poor performance of the Parliamentary armies at Newbury was to be the turning point of the war. It was clear to him that neither the Scots, nor the county associations, nor any of the other assorted and badly paid formations were in a position to win the war. Manchester and Essex, the leading Parliamentary generals, and their Scots allies may have wanted to give the King a bloody nose; but only to persuade him of the value of negotiation and compromise. Cromwell and the Independents wanted to hammer the King into the ground, and then dictate the terms of the peace. From September, when he first raised the question of toleration for the sects in the Committee of Both Kingdoms, Cromwell was firmly at the head of the war party. In opposition a new peace party began to take shape, consisting of the Scots, the House of Lords, and the Presbyterians in the Commons; a powerful coalition which pressed for immediate negotiations with the King. At the same time Cromwell and his allies introduced two crucial measures into Parliament – the Self Denying Ordinance and a proposal for the formation of a New Model Army.

In late 1644 Archbishop William Laud, a ghostly figure long since banished from the stage, was put on trial for his life. The outcome was inevitable: he was finally done to death in January 1645. This vindictive act, intended to unify Presbyterians and Independents against a common enemy, did virtually nothing to disguise the huge divisions within the allied camp. In the increasingly bitter quarrel between Manchester and Cromwell after the second Battle of Newbury, the Presbyterian Earl had accused his cavalry commander of threatening to take up arms against the Scots. For a time, the Committee of Estates in Edinburgh even considered instructing their commissioners in London to have Cromwell impeached before Parliament. Instead, they united with the Presbyterian party in the Commons, headed by Denzil Holles, in making secret overtures to the King. With the aid of the Earl of Loudoun, Holles approached the French, asking them to act as intermediaries with Charles. Once a treaty was concluded, it was hoped, then all parties would unite to destroy the Independents. The chief demand made of the King was that he abandon Episcopacy. Negotiations between the peace party and the royalists finally opened at Uxbridge in late January 1645: they were doomed, almost from the start.

For the moderates these negotiations, known as the Treaty of Uxbridge, were the last chance to secure a peace, short of the complete victory of one side or the other. In many ways it was a Scottish initiative. Angered by the continuing neglect of their armies in England and Ireland, an agreement with the King would settle the question of church government in the British Isles, with the added benefit of side-stepping Cromwell and the Independents. But, in the end, neither side was willing to compromise on any of the fundamental points under consideration. Charles, moreover, refused to settle anything concerning Scotland without first consulting Montrose, a figure now loathed by all but the most extreme royalists in the north. The leading Scots' Commissioners, John Maitland, who had recently succeeded his father as Earl of Lauderdale, and the Earl of Loudoun, both attempted to persuade the King to agree to a Presbyterian settlement, with absolutely no success. Making no progress on this or any of the other matters under discussion, the talks were finally abandoned on 22 February. The Scots and their Parliamentary allies left for London in a mood of gloom. Charles, in contrast, was reasonably optimistic; for he had just received news that led him to believe that if might be possible to win the war outright.

While these negotiations were underway, Cromwell and the war party, now gaining the upper hand in Parliament, were fashioning an instrument that was destined to prevail over all. On 9 December in the House of Commons, Zouch Tate, the member for Northampton, following a speech by Cromwell, moved that while the war lasted no member of either of the Houses of Parliament should be allowed to hold a commission in the armed forces. This proposal came to be known as the Self Denying Ordinance. It was always open to Parliament to make exceptions to this rule – and Cromwell himself was eventually to be the chief exception – but at a single stroke control of the army was removed from its traditional aristocratic leadership, men like Manchester and Essex. Recognising a challenge to their authority, the House of Lords – or, rather, the small minority that had not deserted to join the King – attempted to resist this new measure for some time, eventually giving way in April 1645.

After approving the Self Denying Ordinance, the Commons passed a measure for the formation of a 'new modelled' Army. This was intended, unlike most of the existing Parliamentary forces, to be a truly national army, to fight anywhere as directed. It incorporated some of the existing formations, including the elite cavalry of the Eastern Association, known since Marston Moor as the Ironsides. Philip Skippon, the commander of the London militia, was chosen as Major General, and Sir Thomas Fairfax as Commander-in-Chief. Command of the cavalry was not decided whilst the Lords continued to resist the Self Denying Ordinance; but the post was eventually filled by Cromwell. By Easter Day 1645 the New Model Army had been born. Uniforms were issued for the first time: all the infantry were given red coats, which was to become the standard dress of the British army until the Boer War. As far as religion was concerned, the army took its cue from Cromwell's Ironsides, where the Independents and the other Protestant Sects were dominant. Parliament, in creating its saviour, had also created its master.

Ever since the Cessation, Charles had been considering ways

of concluding a full peace with the Confederates, which would allow him to obtain the services of Catholic Irish troops in England. Antrim's force in Scotland was the first step along this road. But the Irish refused to commit further forces to Britain until they had derived some benefit from the venture in Scotland. As a first step the Scots had to be forced out of Ulster. At the same time as MacColla was sent to Scotland, the government in Kilkenny had reinforced Owen Roe O'Neil's army with an additional 4,000 infantry and 300 cavalry. But instead of giving overall command to the experienced O'Neil, it was handed instead to James Tuchet, the Earl of Castlehaven, a man with few qualities as a soldier.

Although Castlehaven invaded Antrim in July 1644 with a sizeable force of 10,000 men, nothing definite was achieved. At the approach of Monro and the Scots, the Confederate army drew back to the fortified camp at Charlemont, where they remained for seven weeks, until forced by shortage of provisions and poor weather to retreat back to winter quarters in Leinster. After this humiliating retreat, there were no further military operations in Ulster until the summer of 1646. While the Kilkenny government must have been gratified by news of the battles of Tippermuir and Aberdeen, it refused to send MacColla much needed reinforcements, despite Antrim's pleading, as long as the Scots retained their hold on the north. But the Scots under increasing pressure from Montrose, were starting to withdraw forces from both Ireland and England, in a way that was to alter the balance of power in all three kingdoms.

In late November 1644 MacColla rejoined Montrose in Atholl. He came with some welcome reinforcements – the MacDonalds of Clanranald, Glengary, Keppoch, Sleat and Glen Coe, all the main branches of the great Clan Donald, as well as the Stewarts of Appin, some of the Camerons and other west Highland clans. Montrose was delighted to receive them all. Despite his successes at Tippermuir and Aberdeen, he had so far failed in his main aim of drawing the Covenanters back from England. With these new forces he was ready to risk a push into the lowlands. But for MacColla and the clansmen the war for King Charles was far less important than the war against King Campbell. Montrose's plan was immediately challenged by MacColla, who argued instead for an advance through the mountain passes to Inveraray, the very heart of Campbell country. If Montrose refused, all would go home. Needless to say he yielded to the force of MacColla's argument, later claiming all the credit for the operations of his army in Argyllshire for himself. The MacDonalds were now ready to revenge themselves on Clan Campbell, their age old persecutors. MacColla had a more personal motive: he was ready to pay his enemies out for the imprisonment of his father and the destruction of Clan Ian Mor. Father James MacBreck, a Jesuit priest attached to the Irish regiments, was jubilant at the prospect;

> The Catholic regiments...and their leader Alexander Macdonald, longed earnestly to fight it out with the Campbells, who had been their fiercest persecutors, and, whenever they could, the murderers of the Catholics, in the north of Ireland and the whole of Scotland. The entire conduct of the war, and the whole hazard of their cause, turned upon this single point, and they considered that they would effect nothing worthy of their efforts unless they crushed the Campbells, devastated Argyll with fire and sword, and administered a terrible and telling chastisement to that hideous receptacle of bandits, plunderers, incendiaries and cut-throats.

The march began in early December, along by Loch Tay into Bredalbane. On the way, the army paused to plunder the lands of Argyll's kinsman, Campbell of Glenorchy. At the head of Loch Tay they were joined by the Macnabs of Glen Dochart and the MacGregors, the children of the mist. Argyll himself had returned from Edinburgh, believing that his enemies would be trapped in the snow bound passes leading in to the Campbell kingdom. At Inveraray he waited patiently, only to be brought the amazing news on December 13 that the rebels were advancing down Glen Shirra, only a short distance from his capital. With insufficient force gathered to resist this unexpected invasion, and not willing to be trapped at Inveraray Castle, Argyll retired to his galley on Loch Fyne. Left defenceless, the town of Inveraray and all the surrounding countryside was devastated. The plundering was also accompanied by a massacre, more diffuse but even more devastating than the destruction of Aberdeen. All men capable of bearing arms were killed outright: some 900 in all are said to have died. The priests who accompanied the army celebrated mass in Argyll, for the first time in fifty years. Montrose, delighted by the dramatic success of MacColla's scheme, wrote to the King, making no mention of his ally;

I was willing to let the world see that Argyll was not the man his Highlandmen believed him to be, and that it was possible to beat him in his own Highlands.

Early in 1645 the army began the withdrawal from Argyll, around the head of Loch Awe and westwards through the narrow Pass of Brander, where Robert Bruce had defeated the MacDougalls in 1308 during the Wars of Independence. The only resistance they met was from Campbell of Inverawe, who was quickly beaten back to the safety of Dunstaffnage Castle. At Connel at the mouth of Loch Etive boats were obtained to ferry the army across to the northern shore, the friendly country of the Appin Stewarts. More boats were obtained to carry the army across Loch Leven on 8 January. A halt was made at Inverlochy Castle, close to the site of the modern town of Fort William, and the site of a MacDonald victory over Lowland forces in 1431.

The march continued onwards in a north easterly direction, through the Great Glen towards Inverness, with the intention, perhaps, of beginning a fresh campaign in Gordon country. Another halt was made at Kilcumin – now Fort Augustus – at the foot of Loch Ness. Here Montrose received some disturbing news. Seaforth was advancing towards him from Inverness at the head of a Covenanter army. To his rear, the Campbells had recovered from the December raid, and marched into Lochaber with Argyll, taking possession of Inverlochy.

While the Uxbridge negotiations were under way, part of the Scottish army in England was sent home with General William Baillie, who had distinguished himself at Marston Moor. He was given overall command of the home army in place of Argyll. He accepted with some reluctance, and only on condition that he did not have to take orders from the Marquis. Argyll agreed to this, with no good grace; Baillie, after all, was well down the social hierarchy of Covenanter Scotland, whatever his skills as a soldier. But Baillie did not expect to command in Argyll's own country. Instead he detached 1100 men from his Lowland army, mostly newly raised levies, to serve under the Campbell chief, while he returned to the rest of his forces at Perth. This did much to make good the Campbell losses in December; but as far as their fighting qualities were concerned, these men were best left at home. Argyll was also strengthened by Sir Duncan Campbell of Auchinbreck, newly arrived with some of the professional

Campbell soldiers from Monro's army in Ireland. The chief of the clan had recently injured his face and arm in a riding accident, so command was entrusted to Auchinbreck. As the army – now some 3,000 strong settled down to spend the night of 1 February at Inverlochy, Argyll retired to his galley *An Dubh Luidneach*, which lay at anchor on Loch Linnhe.

Montrose now faced some serious choices. If he attempted to retire eastwards, Argyll and Seaforth would be able to join forces behind his back, while Baillie advanced from the south. A march on Inverness risked him being caught by Argyll in the rear. With the Highland troops always anxious to get to grips with the Campbells, he decided to turn back to Inverlochy. But the direct route past Loch Lochy was bound to be spotted by the Campbell scouts. Instead he decided to make an epic flanking march, across a route that was difficult enough in summer, and thought to be impossible in winter.

The army entered Glen Tarff, turning south west and marching parallel to the Great Glen, their movements concealed by the ridge of Meall a'Cholumain. At the head of Glen Buck they crossed the pass of Allt na Larach, two thousand feet into the mountains, struggling through deep drifts of snow. From there it was downwards into Glen Roy, on to Keppoch, where the Roy joins with the Spean. The Spean was forded at Dalnabea. Then they continued on to Inverlochy Castle, arriving by nightfall on 1 February, after a journey of some thirty six hours. Hungry, tired and cold the army stood to arms all through that long night. There was some skirmishing with the enemy, who assumed that they were faced with no more than small raiding parties. But on the following morning the Campbells awoke to discover the whole of Montrose and MacColla's army poised on their flank.

Montrose divided his army – about 1500 men – in four. MacColla with one of the Irish regiments commanded the right, while Magnus O'Cahan held the left with his own regiment. Montrose placed himself in the centre with a mixed force of Highland clansmen. The remaining Irish regiment was held in reserve under Colonel James McDonnell. There were also a few horsemen led by Sir Thomas Ogilvie, who had managed to survive the long march, their hooves worn to pieces. Auchinbreck placed the main body of his clansmen in the centre. Some companies were also placed on both wings to stiffen the Lowland levies, who were divided between them. A small party also held Inverlochy

Castle. Before the battle began, the Catholic soldiers prayed for the assistance of the Virgin Mary and Saint Brigid, whose festival was then being kept. Whom Montrose appealed to is not recorded.

Both Irish regiments advanced on the Lowlanders, holding their fire until they were within close range. No sooner had they shot off their muskets, creating considerable confusion among the raw levies, than the Irish emerged suddenly out of the clouds of gunsmoke. Armed with swords and the light Highland shield known as a targe, they fell amongst their opponents, who quickly dispersed across the field. Now exposed on both flanks, the Campbell militia were soon assailed on the front by Montrose and the Highlanders. For a time they fought back with extreme bravery. Finally, under great pressure, the forward ranks fell back on the rear; but instead of opening to receive them, and thus present the enemy with a fresh front, they broke. Many headed towards the safety of the castle, only to be intercepted by Ogilvie and the horsemen. The remainder ran up the side of Loch Linnhe to escape the pursuit, where they were either killed or drowned under the eyes of their despairing chief. Hundreds were cut down in the chase, which continued for eight miles. Auchinbreck himself was amongst the dead. Iain Lom, the bard of Clan Donald, celebrated the victory over the blood enemy in his poem, *The Battle of Inverlochy;*

> The most pleasing news every time it was announced
> about the wry-mouthed Campbells, was that every company
> of them as they came along had their heads battered with
> sword blows.

> Were you familiar with the Goirtean Odhar? Well was
> it manured, not with the dung of sheep or goats, but by the
> blood of Campbells after it had congealed

> Perdition take you if I feel pity for your plight, as I
> listen to the distress of your children, lamenting the company
> which was in the battlefield, the wailing of the women
> of Argyll.

Inverlochy gave rise to an altogether less bloody victory. Seaforth's army took fright and scattered, the gallant Earl leading the way. The day after the battle Montrose wrote to Charles in a mood bordering on megalomania, urging him to break off the Uxbridge talks;

...I am in the fairest hopes of reducing this kingdom to your Majesty's obedience. And, if the measures I have concerted with your loyal subjects fail me not not, which they hardly can, I doubt not before the end of summer I shall be able to come to your Majesty's assistance with a brave army, which, backed by the justice of your Majesty's cause, will make the Rebels in England, as well as Scotland, feel the just rewards of Rebellion. Only give me leave, after I have reduced this country to your Majesty's obedience and conquered from Dan to Beersheba to say to your Majesty then, as David's General did to his master 'Come thou thyself, lest this country be called in my name.'

Montrose's success did irreparable damage to the Covenanters in England, without weakening their determination in Scotland. But there was a deeper irony at work. The Covenanters had ceased to be the most radical political force in the British Isles, and were now allied with the more conservative elements in the Parliamentary camp. With their power steadily weakening, they were less and less able to determine the shape of the peace, or to offer any practical help to their Presbyterian allies. Montrose's triumph was, in a way that he cannot have imagined, also the triumph of the Independents. Scotland's army steadily weakened as the prestige of the New Model began to grow. In the months that followed the Battle of Inverlochy, with the Scots increasingly preoccupied by the crisis at home, it won the war in England, virtually single-handed. It would hardly be possible after this to keep them out of the peace, as King Charles was fated to discover. Ultimately, this was the political cost of Montrose's empty victories.

CHAPTER 7
From Auldearn to Philiphaugh

In Edinburgh the government at last began to wake up to the danger it faced. Neither Tippermuir nor Aberdeen had caused any permanent withdrawal of Scottish troops from the other theatres of war. The humiliation of Argyll, the strongest oak of the Covenant, was different. Fearing that the rebels were about to descend on the Lowlands, the Committee of Estates transferred 1,500 troops from England and 1,400 from Ireland. Accompanying the contingent from England was none other than Sir John Hurry, whom Baillie had last faced across the battle lines at Marston Moor. After escaping with Rupert and the royalist cavalry on that fateful occasion, Hurry had concluded that the King was going to lose the war; so he offered his services to the Covenanters. Because of his experience as a soldier, he was appointed to be Baillie's second in command; hardly a comfortable arrangement, as neither man could stand the other.

In many ways Hurry was a typical example of the amoral professional soldier, with whom the modern world is only too well acquainted. Another such was Sir James Turner, who wrote of himself;

> I had swallowed without chewing in Germany, a very dangerous maxim, which military men there too much follow: which was, that so we serve our master honestly, it is no matter what master we serve...

After the Battle of Inverlochy, Montrose resumed his march up the Great Glen. His army skirted round the southern end of Loch Ness. Inverness, too strong to be attacked, was by-passed, and the royalists continued on into Moray, plundering the property of known Covenanters and all others who refused to join the rising. Montrose was joined by small bodies of recruits, including some three hundred men from Clan Grant; but by far the most welcome was Lord George Gordon, who now abandoned his former commitment to Argyll and the Covenanters. Gordon came into Montrose's camp at Elgin on 19 February, together with his youngest brother Lewis, and 200 much needed horsemen.

Huntly, who continued to loathe Montrose, perhaps even more than he loathed the Covenanters, held aloof. Lord Gordon's accession, however, opened the prospect of further recruiting amongst the clan. Seaforth also joined the army at Elgin, most likely fearing the destruction of his lands, only to desert soon afterwards. From Elgin the army moved on to Turriff. Rumours of its approach had reached Aberdeen, prompting the badly frightened citizens to send a delegation pleading for mercy. Responding to this, Montrose forbade his Irish troops to approach within eight miles of the city.

Nathaniel Gordon was sent to Aberdeen on a foraging expedition with Donald Farquharson and a party of eighty horsemen. But unknown to the royalists, Sir John Hurry was close by. As soon as he learned of the rebels' presence in the city he rode in, taking them by surprise. Farquharson was shot dead, as were a number of others. Gordon managed to escape to carry the news to Montrose. Hurry's force was not strong enough to face the full weight of the rebel army, so he withdrew back to the south with his prisoners, leaving the unfortunate Aberdonians to face the anger of the royalists. They at once sent another deputation, pleading that it was not their fault. There was to be no retribution; but this time MacColla and the Irish were allowed to advance close to the outskirts of the town, camping at Brig o' Dee. Farquharson's body was recovered and buried with military honours.

News of Inverlochy reached Charles just before the Uxbridge discussions broke up. Quick to seize on this new possibility, the King wrote to the victorious Marquis, telling him that he intended to come north to join him in the Lowlands. The fear of a link up between the royalists soon began to dominate the strategic thinking of the Scots' army in northern England. Leven was continually urged to march south to complete the war against the King; but this would have meant leaving Scotland uncovered, a risk he was not prepared to take. In the Committee of Both Kingdoms, Sir Harry Vane the younger, openly taunted his Scottish counterparts with the poor performance of their army, conveniently forgetting that they had received only a fraction of the promised financial aid.

In spite of the capture of Newcastle, Leven's hold on the north was far from secure. Carlisle still held out against him, seriously weakening the safety of the western Border. With Montrose threatening to break out of the Highlands, it would simply not be prudent to take the main army any further south. Appeals were sent from the Committee of Both Kingdoms, urging a march into Yorkshire, where cavalry units under Sir Marmaduke Langdale were causing problems. Money, Leven was assured, would be forthcoming for the campaign. But with the King promising to relieve Carlisle and join hands with Montrose behind Leven's back, there was no possibility of the Scots playing a decisive part in the coming campaigning season in southern England.

The problem was that Scotland was a small nation with great ideas, now acting well beyond its military and economic capacity. In almost every aspect, the English had broken the terms – and the spirit – of the Solemn League and Covenant. In particular, the Irish had been allowed to enter Scotland without interception; and the Scots armies in both Ireland and England were starved of essential aid, and then criticised for living off the land. It would have been perfectly understandable if the Committee of Estates had simply ordered Leven and Monro to return home. But the country was now holding the wolf by both ears, afraid of what might happen once it let go.

With the exception of Montrose, most Scots clearly realised that a victory for the King would also signal the end of Presbyterianism in Scotland. But it was looking more likely that, in the absence of a Scottish contribution, the victory of Parliament would also be the victory of the Independents and the other sectaries. In the minds of the Covenanters, this prospect was as much a threat to the safety of the Presbyterian Revolution as the return of the bishops. Yet, in trying to achieve everything, they ended by achieving nothing. Montrose was a good soldier, no more than that. He was allowed to acquire the status of a military genius quite simply because the forces sent against him were not adequate for the task. Rather than raising army after army of badly trained levies, it would have been better if Leven had come back to deliver a knock-out blow, and only then return to the southern war. As it was, all he did was to remain in the north of England, moving ineffectually from one side of the country to the other, while battles were won and lost on either side of his impotent army.

Montrose was greatly encouraged by the King's letter. In an attempt to bridge the gap between him and his royal master, he advanced further south, arriving at Dunkeld, in the hope of crossing the River Tay. Anticipating his moves, Baillie was quick to block the way. Montrose was suffering, yet again, from a problem that was to bedevil all of his campaigns: his irregulars, tiring of the endless marches, once again made for home. Frustrated that the grand promises he made to the King just after Inverlochy were further off than ever, he had no choice but to reverse his march back to the north. But before he did so he decided to take Dundee, to demonstrate to the Lowlanders that there had been some purpose in the march to the Tay. It was an ill-judged venture, bringing him even closer to disaster than he had been when he met Argyll at Fyfie.

Believing that Baillie was still south of the Tay, Montrose sent the bulk of his army north to Brechin in early April, while he advanced on Dundee with the Irish infantry and some Gordon cavalry. Even with Baillie and Hurry to the south, this operation involved a high degree of risk, because the army would not be able to make a quick retreat to the cover of the hills. Dundee was taken by assault on 5 April. There was none of the slaughter that had accompanied the fall of Aberdeen, but the town was widely plundered. Before long a high proportion of the Irish infantry were drunk, sinking into incapacity as danger marched in from the west.

Baillie was not to the south, as Montrose mistakenly believed: he was at Perth. As soon as he learned of the rebels' whereabouts, he marched off after them. By late afternoon, Montrose was shocked to see Baillie making a rapid approach, only a mile from the town. With some difficulty the army was reassembled, only just in time, and a fighting retreat was made to the east, the royalists suffering a number of losses in the process. Closely pursued by Hurry and the Covenanter cavalry, Montrose finally managed to slip back into the hills under cover of night. His pointless raid on Dundee had brought the army to the threshold of destruction.

Montrose had received a bloody nose, no more. For the Covenanters, however, depressed by his continuing success, the retreat from Dundee was a God send, which they quickly amplified out of all proportion. In London the Scots' Commissioners had the church bells wrung to mark a 'victory', of which Baillie wrote;

It wes a matter of exceeding joy unto us to hear of the great and first real disaster that Montrose gott at Dundee, and the posture of our countrie at last, according to our mind, after the flight of the enemie, the killing of four or five hundred of the best of the Irishes, the dissipating of most of the Scots highlandmen, the loss of their ammunition, and most of their arms, the returning of the remnant to the hills and the woods.

His joy was not to last. For Montrose, though, the recent triumph at Inverlochy seemed a long way off, and there was to be no more talk of biblical victories.

Back in the hills near Dunkeld, Montrose's demoralised army badly needed fresh recruits. Lord Gordon was sent to his own country, while MacColla marched off back to the west Highlands. Montrose's own spirits were raised when he was joined at Cardross, near the Lake of Mentieth, by Viscount Aboyne, whom he had last seen at Carlisle the previous summer. Excited by the news of the Marquis' successes, Aboyne had broken through the Scottish siege lines at Carlisle and made his way north. Soon after the royalists were also joined by the seventeen year old Archibald, Master of Napier, who had managed to escape from Edinburgh, where he and his father had been held prisoner.

Montrose was now more aware than ever that there could be no proud advance into southern Scotland without the cavalry reinforcement promised to him by the King. He wrote to one of Charles' advisors on 20 April urging that these men be sent as quickly as possible, because, with their support for one month, he would soon be able to come to the King with 20,000 men. But it was to the north, not the south, that he was called.

After the encounter at Dundee, Baillie decided to divide his forces in two, sending one part north under Sir John Hurry to ravage the country of the Gordons, while he remained with the other part at Perth. Depending on the support of the Gordons, especially for cavalry, Montrose could not ignore this new threat. From his base in the Trossachs, he slipped past Baillie on a rapid march to the north east. He was joined on the way by Lord Gordon and MacColla, both of whom had brought reinforcements; and by 1 May the whole force had reached Skene, seven miles west of Aberdeen. From there Aboyne led a raid into the city, carrying off much needed supplies of gunpowder. Hurry, in the meantime, was busy ravaging Strathbogie. Montrose set off in this direction on 2 May. To his rear, Baillie, who had been raiding Atholl, began a march through the Grampian Mountains.

Hurry had based himself at Buckie. On receiving news of the enemy's approach, he remained only long enough to tempt them, then quickly retired across the Spey, into territory hostile to the royalists. Hurry behaved with great strategic skill, drawing Montrose ever deeper into the country around Nairn, an area strong in Covenanter sympathies, where the rebels could not expect the support or intelligence of local people. 'Hurrey,' Ruthven says of his actions, 'that wes left to draw them in, did his pairt so weell, as he did show himselfe ane expert, subtill, and craftie warriour.' Having almost trapped Montrose at Dundee, he was clearly aware of his enemy's tendency to neglect the importance of military intelligence, which he proceeded to exploit.

In falling back towards Inverness, Hurry knew he would also be able to call on a concentration of anti-royalist clans and other local levies, raised by the ever hesitant Seaforth, as well as the more reliable Earls of Sutherland and Findlater. He was also joined by another three professional regiments: Campbell of Lawers' – recently returned from Ireland – Buchanan's; and Loudoun's; bringing his total strength up to about 300 horse and 4,000 foot. With these reinforcements he returned to the east, searching for the royalists. Not until he reached the River Nairn on the night of 8/9 May did he discover that they had camped by the village of Auldearn, two miles east of Nairn.

It was a miserable night. Rain fell incessantly. With no tents, the soldiers sought cover wherever they could find it, some in the cottages of Auldearn itself and others in the outlying areas. Taking solace from the night and the rain, Montrose did not take the elementary precaution of sending out scouts. Ruthven comments on this negligence;

> ...it cannot be refuised but the generall was to blame, who, drawing neir to his enemies, should not have bolded his confidence upon a generall report, but above all things should have bein cairful of intelligence, either by disguysed espyeles...or a partie send forth to catche ane centrie, or bring in a prisoner; for want of which intelligence, if God had not prevented it beyond all expectation, all ther throates had been cutt.

Montrose's main camp was situated in a hollow above Boath House, to the north and east of Auldearn, hidden from the west by a low ridge, where the houses lay. To the south the ground was boggy and covered in scrubby woodland. Auldearn itself was occupied by some of the Irish and Gordon infantry.

Hurry approached the town from the south west, advancing over the high ground between Kinnudie and Newmill. His men were tired and wet; but in his anxiety not to lose the advantage of surprise, he pushed his regiments forward as rapidly as possible. It's quite probable that his musketeers were having trouble keeping their match alight. What is certainly true is that they decided to test fire their guns before closing with the enemy. To muffle the noise they pointed in the direction of the sea before firing; it was a fatal mistake. The report was picked up by some scouts sent out by MacColla, who hurried back to camp. MacColla immediately gathered all his available men and prepared a defensive screen, while the alarm was carried to the rest of the disorganised camp. It was not a moment too soon; for the leading enemy regiments were now emerging from the dark.

In his eagerness to gain maximum advantage from his surprise attack, Hurry appears not to have formed a line of battle. Each regiment, rather, was sent in piecemeal as it arrived on the field – the professional units to the fore, the militia following on behind. The first to engage was that of Campbell of Lawers, with some detachments from Loudoun's and Lothian's. Lawer's spearhead had the additional help of two troops of horse. Montrose's force was soon pressed so hard that there was no possibility of the kind of fighting retreat they had made at Dundee.

MacColla took up a defensive position just in front of the town close to the marsh and some bushes, which gave good cover against a cavalry attack. Gathering his men under his yellow banner, he immediately counter attacked Campbell of Lawers' regiment, drawn up on the open ground to the west of the village. For a time the shock of MacColla's onslaught stopped the advance of the Covenanters; but, despite fierce and prolonged resistance, he was pushed back to the village by sheer force of numbers. A stand was then made in the gardens and enclosures at the back of the houses, which allowed the musketeers to keep up a steady fire from under cover. This appears to have had the effect of disorganising Lawers sufficiently for MacColla to mount a second counter attack. But the marshy ground worked against him, preventing his men from advancing in order. Lawers now

115

had the support of Lothian's regiment to his right, which threatened to turn MacColla's flank. Faced with this new threat he was forced once again to give ground, fighting his way back to the yards and dikes. The Highland chief's courage was legendary;

> He was ever in the frount, and his strenth, his curage, and dexterittie let his enemies sie, even with terror, wonderful feats of armes for his fellowes to imitate, his strong arme cutting asunder whatsoever or whosoever did him resist. He brack two swords; and when they had fastened a number of pikes in his tairge, wherwith they could have born thre or four ordinarie men to the ground, they could not make him to shrink, or bow so much as an kne to the ground; but with a blow of his sword the strenth of his vallorous arme cute all the pikes asunder that stuck in his target, whill non durst approach within the lenth of his weappon.

The fierce determination of MacColla and his men was giving valuable time to the rest of the army; but it was increasingly obvious that he could not hold out for much longer. Aboyne had now managed to organise part of the Gordon cavalry. To prevent his comrades going under, he at once charged the Covenanter right wing, where the danger was greatest. Ruthven describes the Covenanters' attempt to beat off this sudden threat;

> ...they receive his charge with such a conteinuell giveing of fyre, as he semed, by the thick smok throw which he went, to asalt a terrible cloud of thunder and lightening...

At this critical point in the battle the Covenanters made a fatal mistake. Lawers was supported on his southern flank by the Moray horse, commanded by Captain Drummond. Instead of wheeling right to counter Aboyne, they wheeled left into their own infantry, adding to the general confusion. The Gordons came on, crashing into the rear of the Covenanters and driving the Moray horse from the field. Montrose had now managed to assemble the rest of his infantry, advancing to support the beleaguered MacColla on the left. Patrick Gordon of Ruthven, who provides by far the best account of the Battle of Auldearn, does not make it clear how this support was given; but it would appear that Montrose inclined slightly to the south of the village, covering MacColla's flank with an extended line. At the same time the rest of the cavalry under Lord Gordon attacked Hurry's left from the northern side of the village, charging with drawn swords straight into their opponents, driving Hurry, Seaforth and Sutherland from the field, before wheeling round to attack the infantry in the centre. All of the Covenanter cavalry and the Highland militia to the rear had now been chased off, exposing the professional infantry regiments in the middle of the field. In the battle of annihilation that followed, Lawers and most of his regiment were killed. Many more died in the inevitable pursuit, including the Frasers of Lord Lovat, a leading Covenanter clan.

Two things robbed Hurry of victory at Auldearn: his own impetuosity and the quick thinking of Alisdair MacColla. But for him it is almost certain that the royal army would have been overwhelmed. His triumph was celebrated in verse by Ian Lom;

> Health and joy to the valiant Alasdair who won the battle of
> Auldearn with his army;
> You were not a feeble poltroon engaging in crossing of swords
> When you were in the enclosure alone.
> Helmeted men with pikes in their hands were attacking you with all
> their might until you were relieved by Montrose.

Montrose makes no mention of the Highlander's vital role in his own battle report. What is worse, when his pastor, George Wishart, wrote his *Memoirs of Montrose* a few years later, MacColla was caricatured as a brave but stupid man, who almost robbed the Marquis of his victory. Auldearn is by far the most confused of Montrose's battles, in no way resembling the bloodless chess game described by Wishart. Unfortunately, Wishart has become the basis of the modern hagiography of Montrose, causing John Buchan to make the absurd claim that Auldearn was a prototype for Napoleon's victory at Austerlitz.

Auldearn had a surprising sequel: a few weeks after the battle the rebels were joined by none other than Sir John Hurry. He had managed to escape the carnage at Auldearn, riding through the enemy lines with only one hundred of his cavalry. But soon after he rejoined Baillie he left the army, pretending to be sick, only to end up offering his services to Montrose. The reasons for this latest switch are unknown. Baillie's dislike of him was doubtless deepened by his defeat; but it seems more likely that, once again, he thought he was backing the winner. Given his record, it is quite likely that he would have switched back, as circumstances altered. Sadly for him, the Covenanters soon made it clear that Hurry, like Montrose, was beyond the pale.

News of Auldearn caused a fresh alarm in Leven's army. Fearing the long promised link up between Montrose and the King, he moved into Westmorland. He was now receiving virtually no help at all from Parliament, forcing him to make exactions from the local population. At Westminster the Scots' Commissioners complained at his treatment, and raised objections to a new plan of campaign proposed by the Committee of Both Kingdoms. Leven was expected to act as the hammer, rushing south to smash the King on the anvil of the New Model Army. But unlike Leven's men, Fairfax's troops were receiving regular pay. Rupert was aware of the problems, and urged an attack on the Scots, the weakest link in the Parliamentary chain; but Charles bowed to the advice of Lord George Digby, a skilled courtier and military ignoramus, and decided to attack Fairfax instead. Thus began the decisive campaign of the English Civil War which ended on 14 June 1645 at the Battle of Naseby, the first and greatest victory of the New Model Army.

Naseby took some of the pressure off Leven, who enjoyed his own small success when Carlisle finally fell in late June. With the western Border now secure, and little danger that the King had sufficient strength to join Montrose, Leven finally agreed to march south. He returned to Yorkshire, and by 20 June was at Mansfield, entering Nottingham two days later. With the Scots in the Midlands, the Committee of Both Kingdoms decided to send the New Model Army to the south west, where George Goring commanded the last royalist field army. To support this move Leven was ordered to advance to Worcester, to pin down Charles in the west. There was some anxiety that this would lead to direct conflict with the King for the first time since 1639; but the advance continued. While Charles was distracted by Leven, Fairfax won another victory on 10 July at the Battle of Langport. After Langport the English Civil War became little more than a grand mopping up operation.

For Charles the situation was fairly desperate. But Naseby and Langport worried some of the Scots lords that the war was going to end in a complete victory for the Independents. They sent messages to the King hinting at a possible union against the sectaries in the New Model. Charles was encouraged by this and began to dream of an impossible alliance between the Covenanters, Montrose and the Catholic Confederation against his rebel English subjects. In this he lost all grip of political reality. However, his general confidence was kept up by news of two further remarkable victories in Scotland.

Throughout May and June Baillie and Montrose played cat and mouse games in northern Scotland. Tiring of this, the Committee of Estates wrote to their general, criticising his 'slow prosecution of the warre.' Baillie, in frustration, offered to resign. This was not accepted; for while the government was full of strategists in the mode of Argyll, some of whom were even willing to bring their armchairs to the army, there was no one skilled enough to take over from the harassed commander. There was still a tendency, despite all that had gone before, to dismiss Montrose's battle hardened soldiers as 'scum', best engaged at the earliest opportunity. To make matters worse, Baillie was deprived of 1000 of his most experienced men, who were sent on a pointless march into Atholl, while he was given only 400 green recruits to replace them.

Montrose now had news of Naseby, and realised how desperate the King's affairs were in England. The time had come to force another battle. He found the enemy in a strong defensive position on a hilltop at Keith. Some skirmishing followed, which failed to provoke Baillie out of his strongpoint. To Montrose's invitation to fight in the open, the Covenanter replied that he would 'fight when it pleased himself.' With nothing further to be gained, Montrose drew off to the south to Pitlurg and then Druminnor. Baillie by this time had learned that Alasdair MacColla was absent in the west on another recruiting expedition, and quickly decided that the time had come to please himself. He set off after his quarry and found it on 2 July at the Howe of Alford, just south of the River Don.

Montrose had crossed the Don by the ford at Boat of Forbes, and placed his army on Gallow Hill, a good position overlooking the ford with a clear view of the approach road from the north. It is sometimes suggested that Baillie marched straight across the Boat of Forbes, in the mistaken belief that the enemy was in full retreat. But he was too good a soldier for that. The ground along the banks of the Don was boggy; and to cross here while the enemy held the high ground a short distance to the south would have been military suicide. Instead he swung his army to the east, crossing the Don at Montgarrie, a mile from Boat of Forbes. Once across he deployed in safety, hoping to outflank Montrose.

For the first time in the campaign the two armies were evenly matched. With almost 2,000 men, Montrose enjoyed a slight superiority in infantry. Baillie had more horsemen than his opponent, but only just. The royalists were drawn up on a six hundred yard front across Gallow Hill. As usual the cavalry were placed on both wings of the main infantry body, Lord Gordon commanded the right with the assistance of Nathaniel Gordon, and Aboyne the left. Both cavalry wings were backed up by some of the Irish musketeers. Is not clear who commanded the infantry in the centre, mostly Highlanders; but it is thought to have been Angus MacDonald, chief of Glengarry. There was also a small reserve behind the brow of the hill, commanded by the Master of Napier. All that can be said with certainty about Baillie's own dispositions is that the cavalry on the left was commanded by Alexander Lindsay, Earl of Balcarres.

The Battle of Alford began when Lord Gordon led a downhill charge against Balcarres. So furious was the onslaught that the Covenanter cavalry was quickly disorganised. Balcarres managed to rally his men, fighting back with great determination. Both sides were now locked together in a grim melee, swords slashing and pistols firing in all directions. Gordon had been followed by the Irish musketeers, who stood on the fringe of the fight, unable to fire their weapons in the confusion. Nathaniel Gordon called on them to stab or hamstring the horses with their dirks. Without hesitation they advanced amongst the screaming and kicking horses to begin work. They had lamed about ten or twelve before the rest fled.

Battle had now been engaged all along the line. Aboyne broke through the cavalry on the right, allowing the Irish under Colonel O'Cahan and James McDonnell to complete the fight. With the cavalry wings gone, the royalists turned on the rear of the Covenanter infantry, already closely engaged with the High-landers to their front. Under this pressure the outcome was inevitable: they broke and ran. But, as always, there was no safety in flight. At Feight Faulds, to the west of the village of Alford, many were cut down; still more at Bloody Faulds, four miles to the east. Buckie Burn is said to have turned red with blood. Riding off in a panic, one of Baillie's troopers was sucked down into a bog together with his horse, to be discovered one hundred years later by a peat digger. Altogether the Covenanters lost seven hundred dead. Montrose's casualties are said to have been light. However, these included Lord Gordon, killed at the height of his cavalry battle.

With southern Scotland now in the grips of an outbreak of plague, news of this latest catastrophe had a profoundly depressing effect on Robert Baillie;

> We pray the Lord to discover the cause of his great wrath manifested by the continuel heavy judgements of pestilence and sword, and why our forces there (in Scotland) have received defeat upon defeat even these five times from a despicable and inconsiderable enemy, while the forces of this nation (England) obtain victory upon victory by weak meanes against considerable and strong armyes.

Once again Montrose had won another fine victory; yet he was no closer to coming out of the mountains. No matter how welcome the news of the Battle of Alford, it did little to ease the pressure on the King in England. Most frustrating of all, it did nothing to weaken the resolve of the Covenanters. The Earl of Crawford-Lindsay was still in the field with an army that stood between Montrose and England. With Edinburgh beset by the plague, Parliament met at Stirling, and immediately ordered the raising of yet another army, to assemble at Perth on 24 July.

Baillie once again offered to resign, and was once again refused. Forced to retain his command, he was also burdened with a travelling committee of noblemen, who were to supervise the operations of the army. Argyll was there, as were Burleigh, Tullibardine, Balcarres and Elcho, failed soldiers all. The only reassurance Baillie received was that the new committee would only concern itself with the general direction of the war, leaving operational matters to him. Nevertheless, he seems to have been profoundly depressed both by his defeat at Alford and by the growing political interference in the army. He also recognised that yet another trawl of levies was not enough to beat the Irish and the Highlanders. Filled with foreboding, he appeared to lose the will to win.

If Montrose was ever to break into the Lowlands he needed more cavalry. Aboyne was sent home on another recruiting drive. In his absence, MacColla reappeared in the camp at Fordoun in the Mearns with a fine reinforcement of 1400 men, bringing his infantry up to about 3,000 in all. With this, Montrose decided to put some pressure on the Covenanter government, now at Perth uneasily lodged between the royalists in the north and disease in the south. Crossing the Tay at Dunkeld, the rebels advanced to Methven Wood, close to the old battlefield of Tippermuir. His movements caused some panic in the town, which expected to be attacked at any time. But, without cavalry support, Montrose was taking a huge risk; and when no attack came, the Covenanter horsemen emerged from Perth, forcing the royalists to retreat back towards Dunkeld. Some of the female camp followers were left behind in the rapid withdrawal, and were promptly murdered by the vengeful Covenanters.

Once back at Dunkeld, Montrose was heartened by the arrival of Aboyne with 800 Gordon infantry and 300–400 horse, followed by nearly 100 Ogilvie horsemen. He now had close on 5,000 infantry and 500 cavalry, the strongest his army had ever been. Here, perhaps, was the core of the proud army he had promised King Charles. It was now time for a march into the low country.

Once again Montrose headed south, past Perth towards Kinross. For a time it looked as if he was about to enter Fife, a Covenanter heartland, where fresh troops were being raised to fight against him. Not wishing to be trapped here, he turned instead to the west, plundering the parishes of Muckhart and Dollar, closely observed by the garrison of Castle Campbell, Argyll's Lowland stronghold. The destructive sweep continued on through Alloa. While here, Montrose accepted an invitation to dine with the Earl of Mar at Alloa Castle, taking off the cavalry. MacColla marched on with the infantry, hardly a prudent move, considering this was enemy country; but the Covenanters, surprised by the royalists' movements, were too far off to take advantage of this act of negligence. While with Mar, Montrose received news that Baillie was on the march. He immediately rejoined the infantry, and the whole army crossed the Forth above Stirling, on towards Kilsyth, half way to Glasgow, where they camped on the evening of 14 August.

Baillie, meanwhile, stopped at Stirling, where he was joined by the regiments from Fife, yet another batch of half trained levies. Now thoroughly dispirited by the interference of Argyll and the other amateur soldiers on the travelling committee, he resolved only to act as directed, with disastrous consequences. The army marched from Stirling to Bridge of Denny, on to Hollandbush, a farm five miles to the east of Kilsyth. Baillie's best option was to wait for further forces being raised in Clydesdale by the Earl of Lanark, a large party of whom were only twelve miles away. But Argyll and the travelling committee were in favour of intercepting the enemy at once, before they slipped away. So, on the morning of 15 August, Baillie's whole force of 6,000 infantry and 800 horse left the main road and climbed over the Campsie hills, across ground so rough that it was impossible to preserve a proper marching order. They eventually caught sight of their enemy across Banton Burn, in a hollow around the village of Kilsyth. Baillie placed Balcarres' regiment on his right, with Lauderdale's next to it, followed by Home's and then Loudoun's. Crawford's regiment was behind Lauderdale's and Home's in the centre, and behind it the levies from Fife.

Although Montrose was some two hundred and fifty feet below Baillie, the terrain favoured his lightly clad Highlanders rather than the Covenanters, especially the pikemen, struggling across ground badly broken by scrub and boulders. The Gordons were placed on the left under Nathaniel Gordon, backed up by Aboyne. Between the two armies were some cottages and enclosures providing some good defensive cover, just beyond the Banton Burn. One of these enclosures was occupied by Ewan MacLean of Tresnish, with one hundred of his clansmen. The main body of the royalist infantry was in the centre under the command of MacColla; and, although there is no information on this, it seems likely that the Earl of Airlie was on the right wing with the rest of the cavalry, in accordance with conventional military thinking.

To the north of the Covenanters the ground started to rise, peaking in a five hundred foot hill. Baillie advised against any attempt to take this position, which would mean an advance across the enemy front. Supported only by Balcarres, he was overruled by the rest of the travelling committee. The army turned to the right and marched in column towards the new position, with their flank towards the enemy. The spearhead was led by Major Haldane, who was ordered to take a party of musketeers forward to occupy an enclosure on the hill. Lauderdale's and Balcarres' regiments followed on in support with the horse, the rest of the infantry coming on behind.

Baillie hoped to screen this dangerous manoeuvre behind the slope leading down to the royalist army. Riding to the crest of the slope with Crawford and Burleigh, he was horrified to see Haldane leading his musketeers into an attack on the enclosure held by the MacLeans. He failed to break off, even when ordered to do so. Soon after, the rebel army began to advance in strength. Baillie returned to the rest of the army, ordering them to wheel round and form a battle line, well short of their planned objectives. He attempted to organise his regiments at the foot of the hill, but Home's regiment broke ranks, advancing to the dikes in the west, followed soon after by Loudoun's. Volley after volley was vainly poured on the MacLeans, secure behind the walls of their enclosure. Soon the Covenanters were confronted by the rest of the Irish and Highland infantry, closing up to support their embattled comrades.

While the infantry battle was underway in the centre, Nathaniel Gordon rode forward to attack the leading Covenanter regiments, despite being heavily outnumbered. Getting into difficulties, he had to be supported by Aboyne and the reserve cavalry, who in turn had to be supported by Airlie. Crawford's regiment soon gave way under the combined pressure of the enemy horse. In the centre Baillie's musketeers continued to fire wildly, in a desperate attempt to stop the surge of the Highland army, who cleared the last dike with their heads held down, before charging in amongst their frightened opponents with drawn swords. In a final attempt to stabilise the line, Baillie rode off to bring up the Fife reserves, only to find them in full flight, before a shot had been fired or a blow struck. With his army failing all along the line, the Battle of Kilsyth had reached its bloody climax. The fighting had been so fierce that the ground where Home's and Loudoun's troops made their desperate stand is still known as Slaughter Howe.

Kilsyth marks the nadir of the Covenant; a time, as an Edinburgh memorial stone still relates, 'when judgements did this land surround.' On receiving news of the battle, Lanark's troops dispersed, leaving no other army to face the royalists. Argyll's flight from the battlefield took him all the way to Berwick, where he was joined by Lanark. From here he sent to the army in England for help. At Westminster, Loudoun, in tears, appealed for assistance, a sad reversal of the position a mere two years before. In an attempt to preserve their influence in England and Ireland, the Covenanters had lost Scotland. Baillie expressed his own doubts about God's purpose for Scotland;

> I confess I am amazed, and cannot see to my mind's satisfaction, the reasons for the Lord's dealing with that land. The sins of all ranks there I know to be great, and the late mercies of God, spirituall and temporall, towards them have been many; but what means the Lord, so farr against the expectation of the most clear sighted, to humble us so low, and by his own immediate hand, I confess I know not.

Montrose was now at the peak of his career. With Edinburgh still ravaged by the plague, he made Glasgow his capital. It was from here, three days after Kilsyth, that he issued a summons for a new Parliament, to meet on 20 October. With the backing of the whole nation, he intended to raise the proud army he had promised Charles after Inverlochy and march on England. There appears to have been not the least doubt in his mind that he would have been able to sweep away Leven and then Fairfax's triumphant New Model Army.

The news also caused great excitement at the royal court in Oxford. With their territory in England diminishing by the week, Montrose offered a lifeline to the failing royal cause. In writing to Charles, Prince of Wales, Lord George Digby announced;

> These are things rather like dreams than truths, but all most certain, wherin God is pleased to point out the way by which he will bring upon the rebellion of both kingdoms the judgements that are due unto it, having already brought so heavy a vengeance upon that which hath been the original of all our miseries.

The King himself decided the time had come to meet his most successful general. Riding north, he reached Doncaster on 18 August, the same day that Montrose entered Glasgow. Leven, now besieging the royalist garrison at Hereford, and not yet aware of the latest crisis at home, sent David Leslie and the cavalry off in pursuit. But Doncaster was the nearest Charles ever got to Scotland. To the north, a Parliamentary army, commanded by Major General Sydnam Poyntz, was advancing on him from Scarborough; and with Leslie fast approaching from the rear, he withdrew to Huntingdon. Leslie did not bother to resume the chase; for he now had definite word from Loudoun that Montrose was in control of Scotland. He wrote to General Leven from Nottingham on 26 August;

> I did acquaint you formerly with my resolution to go to Scotland with four regiments of horse, and a regiment of dragoons, and leave the rest under the command of General Major Middleton; but I have been forced to alter that resolution, for the sad news of the last defeat of our army near Kilsyth, and the enemy being master of the field at home being noised abroad amongst the common soldiers, they all openly professed that none of them would stay, but all go for the relief of their native country.

125

At Hereford Leven's position was precarious. With Leslie gone he had no cavalry screen. Supplies were, as always, a huge problem, seriously affecting the morale of the army. The King decided to take advantage of this opportunity, making a rapid advance from Huntingdon to relieve Hereford. He arrived by 4 September; but by this time the Scots had retreated to Gloucester. Charles' spirits were boosted by this minor triumph, an echo of the Battle of Kilsyth. The ever optimistic George Digby wrote that if Leslie dared to approach Scotland he would be devoured by Montrose. As fate would have it, it was Montrose who was devoured, not Leslie.

For Montrose, Kilsyth created more problems than it solved. If he was to have any prospect of raising a national army at his planned Parliament, he could not afford to alienate the Covenanting south any more than he already had. But his victorious troops were, in the main, Highland irregulars, whom he had never been able to pay. All were eager to begin plundering the despised Lowlanders. Montrose's refusal to allow this was the cause of considerable discontent. To remove them from temptation, the army was marched out of Glasgow to a new camp at Bothwell. Here Montrose received encouraging promises of support from some of the southern nobility, including the Marquis of Douglas, and the Earls of Home, Roxburgh and Traquair. Although these men were all royalist in sympathy, they had, up to now, done very little to further the King's cause in Scotland. Both MacColla and Aboyne were irritated by the favourable treatment given to these people, seemingly at their own expense. Soon an even more profound cause of resentment arose between Montrose and MacColla.

It had always been Montrose's intention to march to the aid of the King, whenever circumstances allowed. With this prospect now becoming a reality, a clear chasm opened up between the Marquis and his greatest follower. MacColla had little interest in the fate of the King; his own war had always been against Clan Campbell. Already angered by the refusal to allow the plunder of Glasgow, he resolved to take no part in Montrose's planned march to the Borders. Instead, he insisted on returning to Argyllshire, to recover the ancient lands of Clan Ian Mor, where he expected to be joined by the Earl of Antrim with reinforclements from Ireland. Although he left Montrose with 500 of his Irish musketeers, almost all the clansmen followed him back to the north. MacColla promised to rejoin the Marquis as soon as he could; but the two men had parted for the last time.

Soon after the Highlanders left, Montrose received another serious setback. Aboyne, too, wished to return home. He excused himself, saying that had been summoned by his father, alarmed by the aggressive intentions of the northern Covenanters. However, he had been deeply wounded when Montrose, with a complete lack of tact, named the Earl of Crawford as his General of Horse. All 500 of his men went with him. Only Nathaniel Gordon remained. With his army now severely reduced in size, Montrose went off on 4 September to rendezvous with his new allies in the south. His march took him straight into the jaws of the wolf.

By early September Leslie, with some 6,000 horsemen, was at Berwick. From here John Middleton was sent on with an advance party to arrest the Earls of Home and Roxburgh. Both men, now thoroughly alarmed by their imprudent commitments to Montrose, were willing captives, who could appear to be loyal without having to take any risks. Leslie's plan was to advance up the east coast, past Edinburgh and on to Stirling, with the intention of preventing the rebels escaping back into the Highlands. But by the time he reached Haddington, he discovered that Montrose was in the Borders with a very modest army. He at once changed his strategy, deciding on a direct attack.

Montrose's march to the Border was a major disappointment. The Marquis of Douglas had managed to muster some troops at Galashiels; but most had deserted by the time the rest of the army arrived. Traquair sent his son, Lord Linton, to join Montrose; only to recall him a few days later. By the time the royalists reached Kelso they had, in addition to the Irish regulars, only 1200 horsemen, a force of indifferent quality drawn from the local gentry. This was staunch Covenanter territory, and the ordinary people were deeply hostile to Montrose. With almost all hope gone, the army marched on to Jedburgh, as close as they ever got to England. Now aware that Leslie was to his rear, Montrose returned up the valley of the River Yarrow, reaching Selkirk on Friday 12 September. The army camped on a plain known as Philiphaugh, were the Yarrow joins with the Ettrick. After ordering the infantry to dig a defensive ditch beside a wood at the foot of Harehead Hill, Montrose abandoned the rigours of the camp for the comforts of Selkirk. Once again, as at Auldearn, there was no proper attention given to gathering intelligence, even though this was enemy country; and MacColla was not present to correct Montrose's fatal mistakes.

As he settled down for the night, Montrose believed Leslie was still some distance to the north. Instead he had advanced rapidly down by the Gala Water, reaching the small village of Sunderland, where the Ettrick meets the Tweed, only three miles from Selkirk. On the following morning, riding through a thick mist, the Covenanters moved for the kill. Montrose was wakened to the news that Leslie was only a mile away, and closing fast. Riding to the camp at Philiphaugh, he discovered a scene of complete confusion. Most of the Border horse was already in flight, leaving him only a small force with Airlie and Nathaniel Gordon. Apart from these men, only the Irish musketeers, with nowhere to run, stood awaiting the Marquis' orders. They were placed on the left, behind the ditch, their flank protected by Harehead Hill.

No sooner had these dispositions been made than the Covenanters were upon them. One wing of Leslie's army attacked in the front, while the other crossed the Ettrick and attacked in the rear. The cavalry managed to withstand two assaults, only to be overwhelmed by sheer force of numbers. With desperate courage, Montrose and some others managed to fight their way free, some escaping to the north, others to the west. The Irish infantry had no choice but to fight on. Some two hundred had been killed behind the ditch, when the remainder, tiring of this pointless slaughter, were allowed to surrender, after being promised that their lives would be spared. But only the officers survived the death march to Edinburgh: the rest were murdered on the way. Hot for vengeance against the Catholic 'savages', the Covenanters also fell on the women and children left behind with the baggage train. The scenes that followed were unbelievably grim;

> With the whole baggage and stufe...there remained now but boyes, cooks, and a rabble of rascalles, and women with there children in there armes, all those without commisseration ware cutte in pieces: whereof there ware three hundred woemen, that being natives of Ireland, ware the maryed wyfes of the Irishes; there ware many bigge with child, yet none of them ware spared, but all were cutte in pieces

with such savage and inhumane crueltie, as nether Turke nor Scithen was ever hard to have done the lyke. For they ript up the bellies of the woeman with there swords, till the fruit of there wombe, some in the embrion, some perfectly formed, some crouleing for lyfe, and some ready for birth, fall doune upon the ground, waltering in the gorie blood of there mangled motheres.

It was the exact anniversary of the Battle of Aberdeen; the year of miracles was over.

CHAPTER 8
The Engagement

Reports of the Battle of Philiphaugh were carried far and wide. Argyll, perhaps with more reason than most to be grateful, said 'the Lord hath this day here at Philiphaugh appeared gloriously for his people.' Montrose had managed to escape back to the north, where he set about raising a new army; but the magic had now gone from his name. Huntly appears to have taken some perverse delight at the downfall of his hated rival, emerging from his tent in the style of Achilles, ready to challenge him for the leadership of a battered cause. Montrose successfully summoned Aboyne, who joined him at Drumminor in October, close to the battlefield of Alford, with 1500 foot and 300 horse. He was followed shortly afterwards by his brother, Lord Lewis, with additional reinforcements; but both were almost immediately recalled by Huntly, once again alarmed by the advance of the Covenanters. It was soon clear that neither man was willing to yield to the other, both fighting for the role of the King's chief officer in Scotland.

Leslie followed up his success in the battlefield by marching on to St Andrews. From here he sent a force under John Middleton on to Aberdeen. Montrose, robbed of the prospect of another southern march by the withdrawal of the Gordons, opened negotiations with Huntly, to no purpose. He also sent out messengers, asking for news of Alisdair MacColla. No reply came. Mustering all his available forces, the survivors of Philiphaugh together with some fresh Highland levies, he ordered a general rendezvous at Dunkeld, where he received the welcome news that the King was sending a cavalry force under Lord George Digby to join him.

The mood of elation caused in the King's camp by the relief of Hereford was quickly destroyed when the New Model Army captured the vital port of Bristol from Prince Rupert, three days before the Battle of Philiphaugh. With his cause in England failing everywhere, only Montrose seemed to offer any kind of hope. Rumours had spread from the north that the victorious general had already entered England, carrying all before him. He was even reported to be at Penrith, and then Kendal. From South Wales, the King set out with his remaining cavalry to join him. Charles made it as far as Chester, the only important port remaining in royal hands, only to see his men hammered by Sydnam Poyntz and the Parliamentarians of the north. He at once retreated to Denbigh, and tried to encourage his dispirited troops with a rumour that Montrose had defeated Leslie and would soon join them. But by now the ever hopeful despatches from Scotland had dried up; and before the end of September Charles received the dreadful news that his saviour had been cast into the dust.

Charles turned to George Digby, the master of the great illusion, ever hopeful of an impossible alliance between the Irish Catholics and the Covenanters. An approach was made to General Leven, who simply reported the matter to Parliament. Desperate for solutions, Charles called a Council of War at Welbeck on 13 October. Digby urged an immediate march to Scotland to find Montrose. He was supported in this by Marmaduke Langdale, commander of the Northern Horse, and the best soldier left to Charles after the disgrace of Rupert at Bristol. Receiving a false report that Montrose had retaken Glasgow, Digby and Langdale managed to ride through the north west of England, before crossing the Border and advancing as far as Dumfries on 22 October. This was an alarming development for the government in Edinburgh. Parliament had been urging that Leven be sent south to lay siege to Newark, to which the Committee of Estates replied on 25 October;

> ...wee have just now receaved certane information that the Lord Digby and Sir Marmaduck Langdale, with a considerable body of horse and dragounes, have invaded this kingdome towards Carleill, that thair numbers do much increase by the addition of the disaffected on both sides of the border, and that James Grahame and Alisdair McDonald with all they can mak were joyning in Monteith, with the intention, if they can, to march to those that are come into this kingdome...

The position in Scotland was more dangerous than the royalists had believed. Although Montrose had come to Lennox, within striking distance of Glasgow, he did not have the strength to advance any further. Unwilling to take the risk of fighting their way through the Covenanter Lowlands, Digby and Langdale recrossed the Border. They were soon abandoned by almost all their men, and Digby crossed to the Isle of Man, hoping to make contact with the Irish Confederates.

Now firmly back in control, the Covenanter government began to dispose of the surviving prisoners taken at Philiphaugh. Magnus O' Cahan and Major O' Lachan were hanged in Edinburgh. Others soon followed, including Sir William Rollo, executed in Glasgow. The Kirk was especially vehement in its demands for retribution against the enemies of the Covenant, urging on the government in the name of 'Him who must judge the quick and the dead, to hear the voice of your Brethren's blood.' Lord Ogilvie only avoided this judgement by escaping from prison, after he had exchanged clothes with his sister. Some of the captives tried to avoid their inevitable fate by pleading that they had only agreed to surrender after Leslie had promised that their lives would be spared. When this argument looked close to prevailing at the St Andrews tribunal, Warriston was quick to intervene;

> ...the massacre of Kilsyth was never to be forgotten and that God, who was the best judge of the world, would not but judge righteously and keep in remembrance that sea of innocent blood which lay before his throne crying for vengeance on those bloodthirsty rebels, the butchers of so many innocent souls.

In January 1646 the *Maiden*, an early Scottish guillotine, arrived at St Andrews from Edinburgh. Nathaniel Gordon was the first to die. He was followed to the scaffold by Sir Robert Spottiswood, a son of the former Archbishop of St Andrews, the King's Secretary of State for Scotland, and a distinguished lawyer. Spottiswood's principle crime was that he had carried the King's commission to Montrose. It is noted in the prefix to the 1706 edition of his book, *The Practicks of the Law of Scotland*, that

> Though many liked not his party, they liked his person, which made him many friends even among the Covenanters, insomuch that after his sentence was read, some of the nobility spoke in his behalf, and entreated the house to consider the quality and parts of that excellent gentleman and most just judge, whom they had condemned, and begged earnestly that his life might be spared. But an eminent knowledge and esteem which, in other cases, might be a motive to save a criminal, was here only the cause of taking an innocent man's life...the gentlemen who spoke were told that the authority of the established government was not secure while Sir Robert's life was

spared. Whereupon the noblemen who presided at the meeting of the estates at Glasgow, and in the parliament at St Andrews, openly declared, when they signed the respective sentences, that they did sign as preses, and in obedience to the estates, but not as to their particular judgement.

Sir Robert's head was cut off on 20 January. Robert Baillie, far less fanatical than Warriston, recorded his own unease at these proceedings in Scotland, observing in his Journal that no royalist in England had been executed for taking arms against Parliament.

On 31 October, with Digby gone and the immediate threat to Glasgow lifted, Leslie was ordered to take the bulk of his troops back to England. Middleton was left behind with barely adequate forces to contain the royalists in the Highlands. All of this seemed to imply a dangerous degree of overconfidence, especially as Montrose and Huntly were still active in the north and MacColla in the west. That they still packed a punch was demonstrated on 13 February 1646, when 700 Athollmen under Patrick Graham of Inchbrackie and George Drummond of Balloch routed 1200 Campbells near Callander. But, luckily for the Covenanters, the royalists were too fragmented to make an effective stand. Besides, it was felt that Leslie had to make an early return to join Leven in the south, in an attempt to restore some of the Covenanters battered credibility.

Philiphaugh had come far too late to do much good for the Presbyterian cause in England. The Civil War had been all but won by the New Model Army. All that was left was to reduce a few strongholds. The Scots had come to England in 1644 with a mission; now the men with the mission were serving under Cromwell and Fairfax. In the Westminster Assembly the Independents were still a minority. That, however, made little practical difference; for, as Cromwell and his colleagues were soon to show, real power in religion and politics came from the barrel of a gun. In the Commons, criticism of the Scottish auxiliaries grew ever more trenchant, climaxing in a resolution passed on 13 October, which condemned their behaviour in the north and demanded that all garrison towns be handed over to English forces. A full breach was prevented by the diplomatic intervention of the Lords; but the damage done to relations between the two allies was almost beyond repair. The Scots also had other concerns at this time, as Samuel Gardiner, the great nineteenth century historian of the Civil War, points out;

> ...there was no need for a Scotsman to be a bigot to make him anxious to see presbyterianism established in England. The Scottish nobility and gentry did not so much dread either Episcopacy or Independency, in so far as they were ecclesiastical institutions, as they feared the establishment of a military organisation by their powerful neighbour under influences hostile to themselves. They believed, rightly or wrongly, that a negotiation was a foot between the King and the Independents, and the prospect of a junction between Royalty, Independency and the New Model Army naturally filled them with dread.

For some time after abandoning the siege of Hereford, Leven and his unpaid and demoralised army had been left with no definite role. He remained in the north for some weeks before and after the Battle of Philiphaugh, increasingly angry at the neglect of his soldiers. Finally, in November, after receiving assurances that his troops would receive one month's pay and a sufficient supply of ammunition, he at last agreed to move south to lay siege to the royalist stronghold of Newark. After a brief fight with enemy forces at Muskham Bridge on 27 November, he proceeded to invest the town from the north, while the siege lines were completed to the south by the forces of General Poyntz. But most of the fight had now gone out of the old commander. Once again, promises of pay and supplies were broken. Starved of pay, the army in rags, and with no prospect of a Presbyterian settlement in England, it was inevitable that the Scots would seek to do their own deal with the King.

In Paris Cardinal Mazarin, the chief minister of the young Louis XIV, believed he could settle the problem in Britain by calling on the traditional links between Scotland and France, and by appealing to the self interest of all the parties concerned. He was wrong on both counts. A man of Machiavellian outlook, who subordinated all higher considerations to the interests of the state, he saw little difference between various shades of heresy, and completely underestimated the determination with which all would cling to entrenched ideals. He sent Jean de Montreuil, a career diplomat, to open discussions with the Scots, with a view to forging an alliance between them and the King against the English rebels. Montreuil arrived in London at a time of acute bad feeling between the Covenanters and Parliament. He immediately opened discussions with Lord Balmerino and the Earl of Loudoun. But while the Scots were responsive, the continuing execution of Montrose's supporters in Scotland showed the true strength of their feeling. As well as killing off the King's chief supporters in Scotland, Parliament passed an Act of Classes on 8 January 1646, forbidding all who had followed Montrose from holding offices of public trust. If Charles wanted to do a deal, he would have to abandon Montrose and embrace Presbyterianism.

If the Covenanters would not compromise easily, then neither would Charles. Montreuil came to see him in early January at Oxford, now a dismal place with an ever diminishing royalist hinterland. Charles would neither abandon Episcopacy nor Montrose, whom he professed to view as one of his own children. Although he was making no progress at all, Montreuil found, on his return to London, that news of these secret discussions had leaked out, causing an even deeper rift between the Covenanters and Parliament. What was worse, this came about at a time when details of the secret negotiations between the King and the Irish Confederates became public.

The Earl of Antrim had every reason to be pleased with the conduct of his troops in Scotland. They had won six remarkable victories, and come close to bringing the Campbells and the Covenanters to their knees. To keep up the pressure, he urged that reinforcements be sent to Scotland. But the Kilkenny government measured success only in results; and so far MacColla's expedition had failed in its primary purpose of drawing the Scots out of Ulster. Plans had been made to pull what remained of Monro's army out after Kilsyth; but Philiphaugh followed soon after. Antrim's continuing appeals were ignored, as the Confederates preferred to concentrate their military resources at home.

This was to change, however, with the arrival in Ireland in October 1645 of Giovanni Battista Rinnuccini, appointed Papal Nuncio and sent to Kilkenny as the representative of Pope Innocent X. Rinnuccini came with a clear mission: to remove the scourge of Protestantism from Ireland. He was to prevent any deal between the King and the Confederates that was not based on a full restoration of the Catholic Church. Rinnuccini did not only arrive with an evangelical purpose; he also came bristling with all kinds of armaments – 2,000 muskets and cartridge boxes; 4,000 swords; 2,000 pikeheads, as well as gunpowder and other military supplies. As far as he was concerned, the top military priority was the defeat of the Scots. The beneficiaries of this new strategy were to be Antrim and Owen Roe O' Neil, the commander of the Confederate forces in Ulster.

While the King's cause was crumbling away to nothing in England, Montrose continued with his own desperate ventures in the north of Scotland. Continual efforts were made to interest Huntly in joint operations, with only limited success. Montrose's principal military objective was to take Inverness. Once this important base was in his hands, he reasoned, then Seaforth would be forced to make terms. He depended on the Gordons to ensure that Middleton made no attempt to take him in the rear while the siege was underway. But Huntly and his son, Lord Lewis Gordon, did little more than engage in some pointless plundering in the north east. Although Montrose was able to win over the ever vacillating Seaforth, this was only of limited value. Middleton advanced rapidly from Aberdeen at the end of April, forcing Montrose to abandon his operations at Inverness. Having achieved nothing of any real value since Philiphaugh, he made one last attempt to reach agreement with Huntly in late May. Huntly, on learning of his approach, ran away. Montrose rode off in disgust. It was obvious that without the hard core of professional soldiers provided by Antrim, the northerners were, at best, shifting and uncertain allies. Once again, Hamilton's prediction had proved correct.

Unlike Montrose, MacColla had enjoyed some limited success in his continuing war against the Campbells. Although the details are sketchy, he seems to have spent most of late 1645 and 1646 attempting to capture enemy castles in Argyllshire. In December 1645 the people of Arran and Bute were so terrified that he might land on the islands, that they fled in hundreds to Ayrshire. Establishing a base at Dunnaverty Castle on the Mull of Kintyre, he proceeded to reclaim the rest of the Kintyre peninsula for Clan Ian Mor. For Clan Campbell the agony seemed to be endless. Under the leadership of Donald Campbell of Lochnell and John Campbell of Bragleen they managed to raise another small army, only to be broken in battle at Lagganmore in Glen Euchar. MacColla herded all the captives into a barn, together with the local women and children. All were burned to death after the barn was set alight. The site of this grim atrocity was ever afterwards known as *Sabhal nan Cnàmh* – the Barn of Bones.

Atrocities, however, were not the preserve of one side only. Campbell anger was particularly hot against the Lamonts of Cowal, their one time allies. In the middle of May 1646, a large Campbell force landed in the Cowal Peninsula from Ayrshire, headed by James Campbell of Ardkinglas. The Lamonts quickly retired to the castles of Towad and Ascoy. Both castles were bombarded into surrender. All the Lamont prisoners were then taken to Dunoon, where over one hundred were massacred. Thirty six of them were hanged. Some of these men were cut down before they were dead, and then buried alive, so it was later claimed.

Antrim himself came over to Kintyre in late May or early June 1646 with a reinforcement of between 500 and 800 men. His return to the ancestral lands of Clan Ian Mor was warmly welcomed by the balladeers;

Welcome to the Earl with a fanfare, to himself and
his army, as he comes to Scotland, to the land of
his ancestors, a masterful kingly folk: Clan Donald
from Isla, rulers of the Islands of the warriors; they
held sway over land and sea, a splendid company with banners.

He was not fated to remain for long.

Throughout the winter Montreuil continued to try to win Charles over to a deal with the Covenanters. Wearied of all other hopes, including the longed for Catholic Irish regiments, Charles began to crumble. He agreed to listen to their arguments on religion, provided he was not forced to agree to anything against his conscience. Montrose was to be sent abroad in honourable exile as ambassador to France. Finally, the King agreed to order the garrison at Newark to surrender to Leven. In return, Montreuil promised to ensure that he was received by the Scots army with safety and honour. He then left Oxford on 2 April, promising to send word to Charles as soon as it was safe for him to come.

No sooner had he left than Charles began to dream of his own impossible schemes for a grand alliance between the Covenanters, Montrose and the Irish Confederates. He seems to have had absolutely no conception of the damage the great Marquis had done to the royal cause in Scotland, or the deep loathing the Protestant Scots felt for the Catholic Irish. Secure in his own dogged principles and convictions, he had little understanding that others might hold to their own beliefs with equal strength. With no sense of political reality he wrote to Montrose, making the absurd suggestion that he should come to the Covenanter headquarters in England and 'take them by the hand.' But when word finally came from Montreuil on 21 April it was far from optimistic. The Scots at Newark would give no definite guarantees if the King appeared in their camp and were insisting that he accept Presbyterianism without reservation. It was also made clear that Montrose was beyond all pardon. Having failed in all essentials, Montreuil advised the King strongly against going to Newark.

After making one last futile attempt to do a deal with the Independents, Charles left Oxford in disguise on 26 April 1646, accompanied by only two companions. Three days later his flight was reported in Parliament, raising the political temperature by several degrees. One side began to accuse the other of indulging in elaborate conspiracies and the tension mounted. For a time it was even believed that he was hiding somewhere in London. Not until 5 May was the mystery finally solved, when he rode into the Scots camp at Newark, apparently having accepted Montreuil's latest assurance, that while they would accept nothing in writing, the Scots would receive him with safety and honour. Nevertheless, he came without definite terms; and whatever protestations of loyalty were made towards him, it was soon apparent that he was a prisoner, not a guest.

Charles' unexpected appearance at Newark was a cause of some embarrassment to the Scots, seemingly confirming all the conspiracy stories that had been rife throughout the winter. Fearful of the consequences of the King's actions, they wrote to Westminster the following day;

> ...we do persuade ourselves, that none will so misconstrue us, as that we intended to make use of this seeming Advantage, for promoting any other Ends than are express'd in the Covenant, and have been hitherto pursued by us with no less Conscience than Cause. And yet for further satisfaction, we do ingeniously declare, That there hath been no Treaty nor Capitulation betwixt his Majesty and us, nor any in our Names; and that we leave the Ways and Means of Peace, unto the Power and Wisdom of the Parliaments of both Kingdoms.

Charles' entry into Leven's camp was the first clear admission that he had lost the war; but, in his own mind, the way was still open to winning the peace. Apart from a small republican minority, all sides still professed loyalty to the King. In the game that was about to be played, there could be no solution without him. It was only a matter of time before the victors fell out and then the King would come into his own again. The victors did indeed fall out; but Charles was not to be the beneficiary of their quarrel.

Charles at Newark increased the vulnerability of the Scots. For a time it even looked that it might force them into a direct clash with Fairfax and the New Model Army. Baillie noted

> ...there was great appearance of surrounding our armie at Newark with all the forces they had, at least with twenty thousand well-armed men, to take the King from us to prison, or to cast us off. This made us, after the ending of the capitulation from Newark, to retire with speed. We are now out of their danger in haste.

Leven's ragged army could not possibly face the New Model in combat without English allies; nor could it remain in its present exposed position in central England. At the command of the King the garrison at Newark surrendered, after which the Scots made off with their royal prisoner to the relative safety of Newcastle. With Montrose and other royalist forces still under arms, there could be no question of taking the King across the Border, even assuming the Parliamentary forces would have allowed such a move. On 19 May, four days after the Scots arrived at Newcastle, the Commons passed a resolution, declaring that they had no further use for their inconvenient allies. But the Scots held on in England, determined to rescue all the broken promises of the Solemn League and Covenant, and thus win by persuasion that which they could not win by arms. Control of the King seemed to give them a decisive edge over their enemies in the New Model Army. It was written at the time;

> All men's eyes are upon them, to see what course they will take; for that is the hinge upon which all turns: if they stand firm with the parliament, as is not to be doubted they will, we shall have peace and presbytery. The Independents is exceeding crestfallen, and, if the Scots continue their fair correspondence, is like to lose all; for the parliament will concur with the presbyteries; and though the other

party desire more to fight the Scots, yet they will need the name of the parliament to give countenance to the action.

While the King was taking up residence at Newcastle, where he was to remain for the next six months, the war in the north smouldered on. Huntly and Aboyne attacked Aberdeen on 14 May. Their first two assaults were repelled, but the town fell after a third attempt. As always, Huntly then stood and dithered, with absolutely no idea of how to exploit his success. At the approach of a fresh force of Covenanters, he withdrew back to the Gordon heartlands.

Soon after, Charles issued instructions from Newcastle, ordering all the royalist forces in Scotland to disband. This was variously received. Never happy in the role of a soldier, Huntly obeyed with alacrity, sending his own men home in early June. Montrose, who was in Badenoch with what was left of his army after the abortive siege of Inverness, was immediately suspicious, believing that the King had issued these orders under pressure. He outwardly offered to comply, while sending secret messages to Charles that he would remain under arms, until he received further instructions. Antrim and MacColla, fighting their own private war in the west, refused to obey.

The fate of Montrose was one of the chief obstacles in the talks between the King and the Covenanters. Charles continually refused to repudiate his Scottish lieutenant. It was eventually agreed that he should be allowed to go into exile, if he obeyed the order to disband. As always, there was an element of theatrical posturing in Montrose's attempts to hold off for as long as possible; for even if Charles had ordered him back into battle, he had insufficient force to accomplish anything meaningful, without the support of Antrim and Huntly, neither of whom showed the least inclination to join him. Finally, he agreed to meet John Middleton on 22 July on the Water of Isla to discuss terms. He was told the he, Sir John Hurry and the Earl of Crawford were all exempt from a general pardon. All they would be allowed would be a safe passage overseas, provided they left before 1 September. Eight days later the Marquis took leave of his guerrilla band at Rattray near Blairgowrie, finally sailing into exile from the port of Montrose. Most of his countrymen were glad to see him go.

Montrose was of small consequence when it came to the main

issue at Newcastle – Charles' continuing refusal to sign the Covenant. Every effort was made to win over the stubborn King. Alexander Henderson and four other ministers came to persuade him. But neither arguments, nor written appeals, nor tearful pleas could induce him to change his mind. Henderson eventually realised that further debate was futile, and retired to Edinburgh. This was to be is last service for the Covenanters. He died on 19 August of a broken heart, according to his friend Robert Baillie, and was buried in Greyfriars churchyard, where his nephew eventually raised a monument to his memory. A gentle man with none of the self righteous fanaticism of Warriston, his co-architect of the National Covenant, he tried to embrace an impossible contradiction, exhorting his countrymen to the end to remain loyal to both the King and the Covenant.

Angered by the continuing browbeating he received from his hosts, the King began to look around elsewhere for friends. Returning his thoughts to the summer of 1643, he even sent for the Duke of Hamilton, in the hope of building a new royalist party in Scotland. Hamilton was released from his prison in Cornwall by the arrival of Parliamentary troops at the end of April 1646. Considering he had been held there for over two years without trial, on no more than a supposition of disloyalty, he had little reason to love the King. But he came at his master's bidding. The first meeting between the two men was awkward, but Charles finally managed to win Hamilton over. However the message he received from his ill-used servant was not a welcome one: Hamilton added his voice to that of Henderson in attempting to get Charles to accept the Covenant.

Surprisingly, he also received similar advice from his Catholic Queen, Henrietta Maria, writing to him from exile in France. She seems to have had an even weaker grip of political reality than her husband. If Charles accepted Presbyterianism, she reasoned, he would be able to unite the Covenanters, the Irish and Montrose in a grand alliance against Parliament. As an alternative, he might reject the Covenanters, and unite with the Independents, the Irish and the Highlanders! Secure in her own faith, she saw little difference between heretics, whether they be Anglicans or Anabaptists; and it mattered not what oaths one swore with Protestants, for they could always be broken.

For a time the discussions at Newcastle were interrupted by serious news from Ulster. Owen Roe O' Neil had made excellent use of the weapons brought to Ireland by Rinnuccini. He had used them to train his men to Continental standards of warfare, and by the early summer of 1646 his army – now 5,000 strong – was ready to emerge from its long hibernation. It was the time for action. Not only was his army fully equipped and ready to fight, but Monro's Scots were no longer the force they had been. Starved of both pay and supplies, they had also lost up to a third of their strength in men sent back to Scotland to fight Montrose. Yet they remained contemptuous of their opponents, who, in the past, had simply fled back into the interior when faced with a serious challenge. Supplemented by four regiments of Ulster Protestants, Monro moved his force of 6,000 men out of winter quarters in Antrim and Down in May, ready for the new season's campaign.

Monro reached Poyntz Pass, north of Newry, in early June. From here he intended to move on to Glaslough, to the west of Armagh, to join with a second group of Protestant settlers, moving south from Coleraine, under the leadership of his son-in-law, Colonel George Monro. An even stronger force of Ulstermen was advancing towards him from the Foyle valley. Once all three had combined, it was planned to strike into the centre of the country, perhaps even as far south as Kilkenny. This was changed when Monro received reports that O'Neil and his Irish army were on the move. Crossing Cavan and Monaghan, O' Neil had reached Glaslough on 3 June. His march resumed the following day into the valley of the River Blackwater, where he camped on the north bank at Benburb. He now stood at the cross roads of the enemy forces, advancing on him from three different directions.

Since the Scots arrived in Ireland in 1642, the Confederates had been careful to avoid the risk of a full scale battle, preferring more limited guerrilla operations. O'Neil now took a deliberate risk. He reckoned that Monro could not ignore this challenge, and would be anxious to close with the Irish before they slipped back to their fortified base at Charlemont. Using the river as a shield, he intended to force his opponent, advancing breathlessly towards him, into a precipitate engagement. Monro fell willingly into the trap.

On the morning of 5 June O'Neil placed his troops on the high ground at Benburb, close to the ruins of an old castle, once the property of his Ulster ancestors, the Earls of Tyrone. It was now impossible for the enemy to cross to the north bank of the Blackwater at this dangerous point. Monro at once moved on to Caledon, the only other ford, some five miles upstream from Benburb. With the cavalry to the fore, the army then marched on to confront O'Neil. As the main enemy force approached, O'Neil detached part of his army to intercept the second detachment led by Colonel George Monro, while he moved the rest of his men on to a new position on the hill of Drumflugh, a mile to the west of Benburb. Some of the cavalry and a good part of the infantry were then sent south across the smaller River Oona, which joins the Blackwater slightly to the north of the hill of Knocknaclog. Monro's scouts were immediately thrown back by this advanced party, which then took up a position across the track from Caledon, protected by some bogs on the one side, and rising ground on the other.

The first Scots' units to make contact with the enemy were headed by Viscount Montgomery of Ards. Montgomery was halted for a time, but managed to break through, forcing the passage of the Oona, and fighting on across the rising ground at Derrycreevy, where he caught site of the main Irish force at Drumflugh. Monro with the rest of the army had now caught up with Montgomery. Preparing for battle, Monro deployed his regiments in conventional fashion. He was faced, however, with a serious problem. The ground before Drumflugh was too restricted to allow him to make best use of his superior strength. His front line stood virtually shoulder to shoulder, with insufficient space between the regiments to allow the second line to move forward, should this prove necessary. With the second line similarly spaced, the front would not be able to pull back without causing major disorder. The cavalry had to be positioned to the rear, ready to charge through the narrow passages between the foot. Arranged like this the army might just be able to carry off the offensive; but if for any reason it was forced on to the defensive, then disaster was likely to follow.

Still believing the enemy was intent on slipping away, Monro made an attempt to turn O'Neil's left, intending to get between him and the river, and the safety of Charlemont beyond. Montgomery advanced forward, only to be forced back by a cavalry charge. Faced with this unexpected repulse, Monro was put on the defensive. Soon after both sides saw a party of horsemen, riding hard from the north. Monro's spirits were at once raised, for he believed this to be the men from Coleraine. Sadly for him, it was the cavalry of Brian Roe O' Neil's detachment, with news that George Monro had been intercepted near Dungannon and had promptly run away, believing he was being attacked by the main Irish army.

With these troops now added to his army, O'Neil ordered a general advance. Monro's cavalry tried to break up the enemy with a charge, only to be beaten back once more. As the Irish infantry closed on their opponents for the inevitable push of pike, the Scots made the unhappy discovery that the enemy's weapons were longer than theirs. Nevertheless, the front ranks fought back with determination. After an hour of punishing struggle, they began to give way. Unable to bring his second line forward in support, Monro's whole army began to collapse into confusion. Montgomery was sent back into the attack, with no more success than before. O'Neil then managed to turn the enemy left and force their whole line back towards the Blackwater. The cavalry rode off leaving the infantry to face disaster on its own. Monro himself managed to escape, leaving his coat and wig behind. Many who were not killed in the fighting were drowned in the Blackwater and some others died of simple exhaustion. This defeat is best summoned up in the words of one of the soldiers who said 'Too much confidence makes security, and security makes carelessness: and so it happened this day.'

The Battle of Benburb was the most significant victory ever enjoyed by the Confederate Irish. In Kilkenny the Nuncio ordered a *Te Deum* to be sung in celebration, and pompously proclaimed that this was the worst Scottish defeat since William Wallace was overwhelmed at the Battle of Falkirk in 1298. The situation, though, was serious enough without this exaggeration. A determined push by O'Neil might have forced the battered remains of the Scots' army out of Ulster; but it was not to be. Rinnuccini had been challenged by a more moderate faction at Kilkenny, who, alarmed by the success of the puritans in England, wanted to make peace with the Earl of Ormonde and come to the aid of the King. However, the Nuncio would accept no arrangement that did not allow the full restoration of the Catholic Church in Ireland. O'Neil and his army were called south to intimidate his opponents, and the opportunity in Ulster passed, never to return. Except for isolated raids, the province remained quiet until 1648, giving the Scots time to make a slow recovery.

Benburb briefly closed the ever widening gulf between the Covenanters and Parliament. Fresh supplies were at once sent to the Ulster army, whose neglect over the past few years had made a strong contribution to their defeat. Now that the war in England was over, Parliament also began to make arrangements for recruiting its own volunteers for the Irish war.

For a time the old brotherhood of puritans was remembered, and Argyll was well received on his visit to London, a few weeks after the Battle of Benburb. Argyll's visit showed him at his most statesmanlike. In a speech to the House of Lords on 25 June he attempted to heal some of the wounds, tackling the vexed question of religion head on;

> Upon the one part we would take heed not to settle lawless liberty in religion, whereby instead of uniformity, we should set up a thousand heresies and schisms which is directly contrary and destructive of our Covenant. Upon the other part we are to look that we persecute not piety, and peaceable men who cannot, through scruple of conscience come up in all things to the common rule; but they may have such forbearance as may be according to the word of God, may consist with the Covenant, and not be destructive of the rule itself, nor the peace of church and kingdom.

Argyll went on to accept the peace propositions formulated at Westminster, although there were aspects – especially the clause allowing Parliament long term control of the armed forces – that caused the Scots some unease. But in their alliance the two nations had achieved much and this was no time to delay the conclusion of peace. As for the Scots taking the King's part, Argyll continued, it was true that Scotland, after a long line of kings, had a natural affection for monarchy which made them wish that Charles may be 'rather reformed than ruined' and the institution may be 'rather regulated than destroyed.' All this from a man whose enemies, not many years before, had claimed that he planned to depose the King and set himself up as dictator.

Charles resisted the new peace propositions, just as strongly as he resisted signing the Covenant. Frustrated by his intransigence, in late July the Earl of Loudoun threatened to hand him over to the English, the first time this had been raised as a possibility. Charles simply refused to believe this, viewing it as no more than a bluff to make him take the Covenant. But, in the end, this is exactly what they had to do. It was simply too dangerous to take Charles to Scotland with nothing definite decided. Not only would this encourage the Scots' royalists, still troublesome in the north, but it would most likely end in a war with England. Montreuil recognised their dilemma in a letter he wrote to Mazarin in October 1646;

> What embarrasses most the Scots is to see themselves burdened with the person of their king, which they can neither deliver up to the English, nor put in prison without perjury and infamy, and are not able to preserve without danger and without drawing down upon them all the armies at present in England.

The danger he represented was shown when the unpredictable Huntly raised the standard of rebellion in December, after he received a message that the King intended to escape from his Presbyterian tormentors. The escape attempt failed; and although Huntly seized Banff, he was able to do little more, remaining there in splendid isolation throughout the winter. Only a short time before this latest rising by the Gordons, the Estates in Edinburgh had considered whether or not the King should be allowed to cross the Border. Hamilton and his brother Lanark had been in favour of this, but large majority voted against. Hamilton had also argued against withdrawing the army from England; but there was little more to be achieved by keeping it there.

All that now remained was to finalise the details with Parliament. Scotland had been impoverished by the role she had played under the banner of the Solemn League and Covenant. There could, therefore, be no withdrawal from England until some of the outstanding bills had been settled. The Scots estimated the total cost of their services at £600,000. Parliament responded by offering £100,000. After some detailed bargaining the figure was set at £400,000, to be paid in four instalments, the first to be handed over when the Scots army left England. The treaty for the hand over of the King to the Commissioners of Parliament was subject to separate negotiations; but it was inevitable that the two transactions were confused, leading many to conclude that the Covenanters had 'sold' their King. The Scots asked for guarantees for Charles' safety, though nothing definite was concluded.

On 28 January 1647 the Scots finally marched out of Newcastle for the last time, and a Parliamentary force under

Philip Skippon moved in. Under the custody of Parliament, the King was taken to Holmby House in Northamptonshire. Two days later the first instalment of the agreed expenses was paid, followed by the second soon after. No more was ever received. The Scots had come to England in 1644 as allies, who expected to have a voice in the final settlement; they left as mercenaries. The ever perceptive Jean de Montreuil expressed his own feelings to Mazarin;

> I do not know what will be the result of the bargain that the English have just concluded with the Scots, but it seems to me that they have not separated very satisfied with each other...it will be very difficult for the enmity that is between these peoples to remain long without breaking out.

While these dramatic events were taking place, the Westminster Assembly continued on its weary course. Bit by bit it managed to produce a new set of standards – the Directory of Public Worship, the Confession of Faith, a Longer and Shorter Catechism, a Form of Church Government and the metrical version of the Psalms. The Westminster Confession was duly accepted by Kirk and Parliament in Scotland, which thus abandoned the older standards practised since the Reformation. In England, however, opinion was too divided, and the Independents too strong in the army and Parliament, for these uniform standards to be adopted as the basis for a new national church. Discussion over some of the finer points continued until the summer of 1648; but unity of church government, the illusive promise of the Solemn League and Covenant, was never achieved.

While the Civil War was over in England and Wales, it was still smouldering away in northern Scotland. Hamilton wanted to retain the whole army under arms; but Argyll and his supporters felt that he really intended it to be used against the English, rather than in a campaign against the rebels in Scotland. Instead, on Argyll's suggestion, Parliament in Edinburgh agreed to form its own 'New Model Army.' The old army was slimmed down to a professional force of 5,000 foot and 1200 horse. Leven was given supreme command. However, the old general was now considered to be well past his best, so for all practical purposes the real chief was David Leslie, a strong supporter of Argyll.

The first task of the new force was to deal with Huntly, as well as the Irish and Highland rebels in Argyllshire. Antrim had left Scotland in January, but Alisdair MacColla was still very active.

Leslie made his first moves against Huntly, advancing to the north east in March. Banff was evacuated, as the Gordons fled back into the hills. By the end of the month almost all of Huntly's castles had fallen. Any Irish soldiers found in the garrisons were immediately put to death. Never one for a fight, Huntly fled with his bodyguard into the mountains of Lochaber. Here he remained in hiding until November, when he was captured by Middleton and taken to Edinburgh as a prisoner for the second time in his life. He was never to return to his beloved Strathbogie. Aboyne managed to escape to France.

Having disposed of Huntly, Leslie moved quickly to deal with the MacDonalds. Leaving Middleton to hold the north east, he moved south to Dunblane, and then on to Argyllshire. In the company of Argyll he entered Kintyre on 24 May. MacColla and 1200 of his men were caught in the open at Rhunahaorine Point and routed in a cavalry charge. MacColla and the Irish managed to escape to Gigha and then Islay on the few boats available, leaving his Highland allies to face the anger of their countrymen. These men promptly fled south, where three hundred shut themselves up in Dunnaverty Castle for safety. Unable to hold out, they surrendered on promise of quarter, only to be massacred to a man. The killing is said to have been entrusted to the relatives of the women and children burnt to death at Lagganmore.

In late June Leslie crossed to Islay, landing close to Dunyveg Castle, the ancient stronghold of Clan Ian Mor. By this time MacColla had returned to Ireland, leaving the castle in the keeping of his father, Coll Ciotach, who had been released in a prisoner exchange some time before. Dunyveg was taken, and Coll Coitach was once again a prisoner of the Campbells. This time Argyll, taking no more chances, had the old man hanged. After Islay, Leslie continued his island hopping campaign, advancing from Jura to Mull, the home of the MacLeans. Duart Castle was surrendered by Sir Lachlan MacLean. This time the garrison were spared, with the exception of fourteen Irishmen, who were all hanged. North of Mull the islanders under the leadership of MacDonald of Clanranald continued to hold out, and small scale mopping up operations continued into 1648. As for Alisdair MacColla, perhaps the greatest of all the Highland warriors, he did not survive long after his flight from Islay, dying in the continuing wars in Ireland. Ian Lom recorded his passing with deep sorrow;

I got news from Dungannon that has dimmed my sight, my utter
woe that Alasdair was dead:
And the truth from the harper when he landed at Port Patrick my
mind made no glad response to his music.
Sad to me is the dispersing of the men of Islay and the noblemen of
Kintyre...

With the end of Alisdair MacColla and Coll Coitach, Clan Ian
Mor finally sank into the mists of time. Antrim, now fully engaged
in the Irish troubles was never to return to Kintyre. But the
ravaging of Argyllshire in the period between 1644 and 1647
considerably weakened the military power of Archibald Campbell.
Although a committed Presbyterian and Covenanter, Argyll was
never an extremist. But his political position at the head of the
Covenanter movement was more than ever dependent on the
support of the clergy and the middle classes; men like Warriston,
for whom the pure principle of the Covenant came before all other
practical considerations.

By the time Leslie returned from the north there had been a
steady shift in the Scottish political climate. Many men were
worried by the increasingly alarming situation in England. There
was still no solution to the constitutional problem. What is worse,
Parliament had lost control of the New Model Army. To increase
their power, Cromwell and the other leaders sent a body of
troopers under a young officer, Cornet George Joyce, to bring the
King from Holmby House to Hampton Court, closer to London,
where they could keep him under their direct control. The
Presbyterians in the Commons and the Lords were placed on the
defensive, and the Independents were becoming ever more
influential. If the religious radicalism of the sects was bad, the
political radicalism of Levellers and even more extreme minorities
was even worse. For a time even the conservative grandees, like
Fairfax and Cromwell, looked like losing control. The great army
debates at Putney raised ideas that threatened to immerse
England in a social and political revolution. In desperation, the
English Presbyterians turned to the Scots for help.

Even Argyll was worried enough by June 1647 to offer the King
the aid of a Scottish army. Charles rejected this offer, fearing that
the Presbyterian price tag would be too high. By the end of the
summer Argyll had, in any case, gone off the idea. In early August
he was warning the Committee of Estates against a rupture with

England, soon after telling Montreuil that no action would be taken unless Charles took the Covenant. But the seizure of the King by the army had caused a major shift in his favour amongst the Scottish nobility, who increasingly took the lead of the Duke of Hamilton. Gradually, a moderate royalist party began to take shape, probably delayed for some years by Montrose's murderous adventure. Even the Earl of Loudoun, hitherto one of Argyll's strongest supporters, was won over. Hamilton and his friends decided that the time had come, once more, to attempt to do a deal with the King.

On October 22 Lauderdale, Lanark and Loudoun all came to see Charles at Hampton Court. Of all three, the case of John Maitland, Earl of Lauderdale, is perhaps the most interesting. A member of the Committee of Both Kingdoms, he had acquired a close knowledge of English affairs since coming to London in 1644. He took part in the abortive Treaty of Uxbridge, and was frustrated by the failure to reach agreement with the duplicitous Charles. Although a committed Presbyterian, he was largely indifferent to the religious views of the Independents; but their political radicalism was quite another matter. Compromise was now the only way to serve both the King and the Covenant.

During the discussions the Scottish Commissioners attempted to persuade Charles to make concessions on the religious question, in return for Scottish support. At first, Charles was no keener than he had been at Uxbridge or Newcastle to consider this as an option. But both sides were essentially working towards a political deal in the guise of a religious bond, much like the Solemn League and Covenant. On the urging of Lanark and Lauderdale, Charles decided to escape from Hampton Court. It was thought he would come to Berwick; instead he ended up at Carisbroke Castle on the Isle of Wight. From here he kept up his fruitless public negotiations with Parliament, and his secret talks with the Scots. These concluded with a treaty signed on 26 December. Although he would not take the Covenant himself, Charles agreed to establish Presbyterianism in England for a trial period of three years and to suppress all of the sects, including the Independents. In return, Lauderdale, Lanark and Loudoun promised him an army. This bargain, known as the Engagement, was to bring about the Second Civil War in England and to tear the Covenanter movement in two. For the King himself, it opened the path to the scaffold in Whitehall.

CHAPTER 9
Preston and the Whiggamore Raid

For Hamilton and his party, the Engagement was a major gamble. Unlike the Solemn League and Covenant, it had neither been approved by Parliament nor by the General Assembly of the Kirk. In a sense, it was an attempt by the aristocracy as a whole to regain control of Scottish politics, which they had been steadily losing since 1643. Much depended on the success in getting the other estates, especially the clergy, to accept a treaty which fell well short of the Covenanting ideal.

As soon as they returned to Scotland, Lauderdale and the other Commissioners set about winning support for the treaty. Their conduct was quickly approved by the Committee of Estates, now dominated by the Hamilton party. But even before Parliament met in March 1648, opposition to the Engagement was on the increase. The Commission of the Kirk, the permanent executive of the General Assembly, openly declared that the King's concessions on religion were destructive to the Covenant. They were also concerned about giving church agreement to a treaty that would inevitably lead to a war with England. Lauderdale at once sensed the danger and wrote to Charles, asking him to yield a little further on this vital issue. He refused. As the year progressed it became more apparent that the Engagement had brought about the first split between church and state since 1638.

Early on Argyll made his own position plain. When commissioners arrived from the English Parliament in late February to protest against the Engagement, they were well received by the Marquis. But, for once, he found himself in the minority. When Parliament met in March Hamilton's party dominated the proceedings. Of the fifty noblemen who attended, less than ten supported Argyll, including the Earls of Eglinton, Cassillis and Balcarres, and Lord Balmerino. Argyll had also lost considerable support amongst the representatives of the shires and burghs, hitherto solidly behind him. Against this the Kirk Commissioners ordered a declaration to be read from every pulpit in the land, denouncing the Engagement. One minister, carried away by his passion, predicted that Hamilton would bring the curse of God down upon himself and all his posterity.

Hamilton was alarmed by the increasingly bitter dispute with the church. He remained, in most essentials, the same man he had been in 1638, looking for compromise where none was to be found, seeking to satisfy all, only to end by satisfying none. With the backing of Parliament, political power was his, even more completely than it had been Argyll's in the summer of 1643. Even so, he was anxious not to alienate the Kirk or Argyll any more than was necessary. He made no attempt to intervene on behalf of the imprisoned Huntly, despite appeals from the King to do so. But, in the end, he was unable to master the opposition raised against him in the country at large; and even before he crossed the Border to save the King, the Engagement was already close to ruin.

Towards the end of April the chief officers of the Engagement army were appointed. Hamilton was named as commander-in-chief. Considering his conduct as a soldier, both during his brief intervention in the Thirty Years War, and, more recently, in the First Bishops' war, this was hardly a choice to inspire much confidence. Ruthven made his own biting comment on this appointment;

> But, O Maloure! there began our miserie. The Devyne Majestie was not content with us; we must be better humbled; and, therefore, God suffered them to err in this, that they made choise of the greatest man of the kingdome, and thought to be the wysest man, the most profound man, the greatest steatsman and deipest politiciane, not onlie of the thrie kingdomes, but of all Christendome: in this only was he defectiue, that he had never practised the airt militarie. He was fitter for a cabinet counsell nor (not) for a counsell of warre; he could haue bein precedent in the grauest senat that euer sat in the Vaticane, yet he knew not what belonged to the leadinge of ane armie.

His greatest need was for a good professional soldier to assist him in the task of command. But neither Leslie nor Leven – assuming that anyone seriously considered him for the role – was willing to serve in the army of the Engagement. Only the Earl of Callendar, who led the second Scots' army into England in 1644, was really fitted. The problem was that Callendar clearly thought he was a better man than his chief, who, if not actually frightened of his second in command, invariably gave way to him in military matters, with disastrous consequences. William Baillie, twice beaten by Montrose, was pulled out of retirement and given command of the infantry. John Middleton was appointed to lead the cavalry.

The case of John Middleton is as interesting as that of Lauderdale. These two men, destined one day to be the greatest of political enemies, both started life as firm supporters of the Covenant. Like Lauderdale, Middleton now realised the importance of compromise. But he began a journey that was to take him, at the end, far away from the ideals of the Covenanters. He was, above all, a soldier, with a soldier's simple view of complex problems. Increasingly angered by the Kirk's attempt to interfere in secular affairs, he was eventually to try and tame it by bringing the bishops back to Scotland.

The army had its generals: now it needed soldiers. In early May a proclamation was issued calling the country to arms. It was hoped that 30,000 men would join the colours before the end of the month, even more than had crossed the Border with Leven in January 1644. Hamilton also arranged for the recall of a large part of the army in Ulster – 1,200 horse and 2,100 foot under Sir George Monro, to provide a hard professional core to an army made up of untried men. But the Kirk had done its work well: recruiting officers were met with strong resistance, especially in the south west of Scotland, now emerging as one of the main heartlands of the Covenant. Before long, Hamilton's timetable was suffering from serious delays. This was particularly bad for England was now rising against the New Model Army. The Second Civil War was underway.

Hamilton's brother, Lanark, had been in close touch with the royalist underground in England since the close of 1647. He was told by both Lord Byron and Sir Philip Musgrave that a Scots invasion would receive wide support in the north of England. However, much depended on the timing of this invasion. Unlike 1642 there would be no royalist army in England, so the Scots would have to support local risings with organised military force. Clearly, it would make good strategic sense if these risings coincided with a Scottish invasion, perhaps stretching the New Model to breaking point. Unfortunately, the upheavals began, quite spontaneously, when John Poyner, the governor of Pembroke Castle in South Wales, declared for the King in March, even before the Scottish Parliament had met. Soon afterwards the rebellion spread throughout the neighbourhood. In Yorkshire Pontefract Castle was taken by a group of royalists, and the garrison at Scarborough Castle joined the rebellion. The insurrection spread to Cornwall, Northamptonshire, Surrey and Kent, dangerously close to London, where local Presbyterian feeling was strongly against the New Model. A party of royalists led by the Earl of Norwich even managed to take Colchester in Essex, right in the heart of the Eastern Association.

Hamilton was able to do little about this; the English and Welsh royalists would have to manage as best they could until he was ready to march. However, large parties of English Cavaliers had been allowed to gather on Scottish soil, seemingly only under the loosest supervision by the government. On 28 April a group of these men, led by Sir Marmaduke Langdale, managed to capture Berwick. Carlisle fell the following day to another force under Sir Philip Musgrave and Langdale rode across country to join him. Together, with a combined force of about 3,000 horse, they began to fan out across the north west. Fairfax sent John Lambert north to contain the royalists, and act as a first line of defence against any supporting Scottish invasion. Lambert only had 5,000 men to guard the whole of the Border; but these included three crack formations – Robert Lilburne's, Thomas Harrison's cavalry regiments, as well as part of Cromwell's.

Lambert quickly moved to the offensive, intercepting Langdale's forces in Cumberland and Westmorland to prevent him joining up with the garrison at Pontefract. Appleby and four other captured castles were retaken, as Langdale was forced back to the safety of Carlisle in June. It was inevitable that the northern royalists would be forced to give in unless relieved quickly by the Scots. Even before Hamilton crossed the Border, Lambert had been able to seize the strategic initiative.

Early in July Hamilton had a conference with his senior commanders. Callendar and Middleton were joined at this meeting by James Turner, who had returned from the army in Ireland. All three expressed concern over the military crisis caused by the premature march of Musgrave and Langdale. The levy had met with considerable resistance, and the army, which was supposed to be ready by the end of May, was only partially under arms. Yet Langdale and the garrison at Carlisle could not be expected to hold out much longer. Turner explained his own feelings in his *Memoirs;*

To marche to his reliefe, were to leave the halfe of our forces in Scotland unlevied, and ane enemie behind our hand, ourselves in a very bad condition, without money, meale, artillerie, or ammunition; to suffer him to perish was against honour, conscience, and the reason both of state and warre. It wold have given our enemies occasion to insult; wold have brought the Dukes honor (rudlie enough delt with by some before) to an everlasting losse, and wold have given such just apprehensions of jealousies to the royalists in England, that never one of them wold have joynd with us, or ound us.

Langdale's precipitate and ill advised invasion had also brought about an even greater dilemma. Once the army was ready, it would be forced to cross the Border into north west England, rather than the easier eastern route taken by Leven in 1640 and 1644. A march through Cumberland, Westmorland and on into Lancashire would be over restricted territory, hemmed in between the Pennines and the Irish Sea, with the ever present danger of a flank attack from the east. It was, of course, open to Hamilton, once Langdale had been relieved, to strike across the Pennines at the first convenient pass, to link up with the garrison at Pontefract and allow his army to deploy in the open country of Yorkshire. Everything depended on the commander-in-chief's determination and strategic sense, qualities with which he was not greatly endowed.

While Langdale and Lambert were already fighting in Cumberland, the Engagers were raising their army with great difficulty. Even some six hundred of Hamilton's own tenants in Lesmahago and Avondale rose against him. In Glasgow the burgh magistrates refused to co-operate with the draft. To avoid being called up, many men from Ayrshire and Galloway fled to the Presbyterian communities in Ulster. There was even resistance in the conservative north east. The area had not yet recovered from the upheavals between 1644 and 1647, and was suspicious both of Hamilton's moderate Covenanter views and the continuing imprisonment of Huntly.

Desperate for soldiers, Hamilton even welcomed home the irrepressible Sir John Hurry. No consideration was given to the return of Montrose. A few months before the Engagement was signed, his pastor, George Wishart, published in Holland a work in Latin entitled *De Rebus*, the first biography of the Marquis.

155

Wishart's book – which appeared anonymously – did much to feed Montrose's sense of self esteem, but it angered almost everyone in Scotland, royalist and Covenanter alike, causing Patrick Gordon of Ruthven to take up his own pen in defence of Huntly. Even the future Charles II ordered Montrose to suppress *De Rebus*, because it contained some injudicious accusations against senior figures in Scotland, an echo of those made against Hamilton in the early 1640's.

The government was forced to take severe measures to end resistance to the draft. Turner was sent to Glasgow with an infantry regiment to force the magistrates into changing their minds. His technique was simple, but effective;

> ...I found my worke not very difficill; for I shortlie learnd to know, that the quartering tuo or three troopers and halfe a dozen musketeers was ane argument strong enough, in two or three nights time, to make the hardest headed Covenanter in the toune to forsake the Kirk and side with Parliament.

Many gave in when faced with the expense and inconvenience of keeping soldiers. News of this new approach reached the nearby communities; so when Turner moved on to Paisley, the magistrates there were quick to submit. Hamilton, in the meantime, was forcibly raising men in Lanarkshire, while Callendar moved west to support him. Hundreds of men, many of the mounted and armed, fled over the county boundary into Ayrshire, where opposition to the Engagement was particularly acute.

By early June some 2,000 or 3,000 militant Covenanters had gathered at Loudoun Hill, near Kilmarnock. But what they possessed in will, they lacked in leadership. Appeals were sent to both the Earl of Eglinton and David Leslie to come and join them. Both men prudently decided to ignore the invitation. Disappointed by this failure, the gathering began to break up. Enough of them remained together, including the refugees from Lanarkshire, to attend the celebration of the Lord's Supper at Mauchline on Sunday 11 June. With many people arriving from nearby parishes, the preaching and prayers continued on to the following day.

While at Paisley Turner learned that there was a dangerous gathering in Ayrshire, although he had no information on its exact location. A report was immediately sent to Hamilton, who ordered Callendar and Middleton to join him. On 12 June both men met at Stewarton, mustering a total force of 1,600 cavalry and 2,000 foot. By now Callendar knew that the Covenanters were at Mauchline. One regiment was sent on to Irvine, while Turner and Middleton advanced with six troops of horse to confront the rebels. Callendar followed on with the remainder of the force, intending to rest at Kilmarnock. However, he now received further reports that the anti-Engagers – originally estimated at 600 men – were some 2,000 strong, including 1200 horsemen. At once he sent on reinforcements to join his forward units.

Middleton now faced the Covenanters, drawn up on Mauchline Muir, with 600 troopers, including Callendar's reinforcements. After failing to get the dissidents to disperse, Middleton ordered part of his force forward. These men were immediately repelled, after which the rest of the Engager force went forward to battle. Callendar, who clearly misjudged the seriousness of the situation, arrived just in time to prevent Middleton being overwhelmed by force of numbers. Faced with this additional government force, the rebels fled the field. Few men were killed on either side, but a large number were wounded, including Middleton and Sir John Hurry. There was no pursuit, and many of the insurgents escaped into the relative safety of Galloway, another Covenanter stronghold.

This small engagement hardly justifies the grand title of the Battle of Mauchline Muir; but it had important repercussions. Hamilton and the rest of the Engager government were alarmed that the country was on the brink of civil war. An attempt to subdue the west would have meant further delays in the proposed invasion of England. Believing that success in England would be a more effective answer to the discontent in the west than direct confrontation, the government decided not to force the issue. Far fewer forces were therefore raised in the south west than was estimated. For the Covenanters, dispersed but not destroyed, Mauchline Muir was unfinished business. Secure in their stronghold, they watched and waited. Robert Baillie, now back in Scotland, saw the danger;

> There is indeed in our people a great animositie put in them, both by our preaching and discourse; also by the extream great oppression of the sojours; so that it fears me, if Lambert be come to Carlisle with

157

fresh men...so soon as our army shall be intangled with the English, many of our people will rise on their backs.

Time was moving on and it was now past mid summer. In England, many of the risings were already failing. There could be no further delay. But the augers could not be worse: the army was under strength, badly equipped and poorly trained. Supplies and transport were both serious problems, and there was no artillery. Moreover, Monro's troops from Ireland had not yet come. In his book, *The Memoirs of the Dukes of Hamilton*, Gilbert Burnet details the problems;

> The regiments were not full, many of them scarce exceeded half their number, and not a fifth man could handle pike or musket. The horse men were the best mounted ever Scotland set out, yet most of the troopers were raw and undisciplined. They had no artillery – not so much as a field piece – very little ammunition, and very few horses to carry it; for want of which the Duke stayed often in the rear of the whole army till the countrymen brought in horses and then conveyed it with his own guard of horse.

Fearing the worst, Lanark urged that the opposition in Scotland be crushed before the Border was crossed. This would also give more time for fresh supplies of arms and ammunition to arrive from Holland. Lauderdale, one of the chief architects of the Engagement, opposed this, saying the rebellions in England would be crushed one by one unless the Scots arrived in time. Hamilton bowed to this, ordering a general rendezvous of the army on 4 July at Annan. Four days later he crossed the Border with 10,500 men, only a third of the force he had expected. That same day he joined up with Langdale and the English cavaliers at Carlisle with a welcome reinforcement of 3,000 men. Lambert withdrew before them.

In London the newspaper *Mercurius Britannicus* tried to whip up anger against the Scots' invasion, accusing them of 'bringing their lice and their Presbytery amongst us.' Yet it was not certain how the Engagement army would be received. Hamilton, with the assurances of Musgrave and Byron to support him, clearly felt that it was only necessary to kick in the door for the whole house to fall down. But he made certain that any welcome he received was soon dissipated by the nature of the force he had brought with him. Leven had been careful in both his invasions of

England to see that nothing was done to alienate the local people. Hamilton, in contrast, coming without money, food or transport, could not afford to be so fastidious. The ill discipline of his raw army added to the general resentment caused by the forcible seizure of fresh supplies;

> That the Scots play at sweepstake, take all, moveables, cows, sheep, and all household stuff to the very pothooks; that they take children, and make their parents pay ransoms for them, and force women before their friends' faces.

Once over the Border Hamilton's progress southwards was painfully slow. With no sense of urgency, he spent six days at Carlisle, before advancing on to Penrith, and then another three days before continuing on the few miles to Kirkby Thorne, where the army remained until the end of July. Matters were made worse by the weather, which was atrocious, raining virtually the whole time Hamilton was in England. The halt at Kirkby Thorne is described by Turner;

> The Duke is necessitated to stay ten or twelve days at Kirkbie-thorne, to receave those regiments marching from Scotland, which did not exceed the halfe of their numbers they should have beene, all neulie levid, raw and undisciplined; and that summer was so excessivle raine and wet, that I may say it was not possible for us to keepe one musket of ten fixed, all the time we were in a bodie in England.

Lambert's task was to try to read Hamilton's mind, never an easy thing. Still not convinced that the enemy intended to keep on the southern route, he expected Hamilton either to make for Newcastle, or to head across the passes of the Pennines to link up with the royalists at Pontefract. Attempting to delay the enemy's progress, he left a garrison at Appleby Castle, while stationing his main force at Barnard Castle, intending to hold the Stainmore Pass against any Scots' advance into Yorkshire. He also prepared himself to strike in the flank, should the Engagers continue on into Lancashire. While waiting for Hamilton's next move, he received the welcome news that Cromwell had taken Pembroke Castle on 11 July, thus ending the revolt in South Wales, and was on his way to join him.

Even after Hamilton had crossed the Border, the struggle against the Engagement continued in Scotland. The General Assembly met in Edinburgh on 12 July, and denounced the

159

treaty with the King as 'sinful and censurable'. All ministers supporting the agreement were to be deposed, which included the veteran Andrew Ramsay, who had taken a leading part in the riots of 1637. On 1 August a declaration was issued to 'their brethren of England,' saying that the well affected were opposed to 'so unlawful a war.' Argyll, in temporary retirement at Inveraray, waited patiently for the outcome of Hamilton's adventure.

At the end of July the lumbering Scottish war machine cranked back into action. Lambert, who now had about 9,000 men under his command, kept a close watch on the Scots as they moved through Appleby and on to Kendal, arriving there on 2 August. Here Hamilton was joined at last by Monro's troops from Ulster. Unable to make a direct landing on the coast of Lancashire, Monro had dodged the Parliamentary warships in the Irish Sea by crossing in small vessels at night, landing on the coast of Galloway. From here he and his men marched on to join the main army, berated by the local country people, firm in their support for the Covenant.

Hamilton's combined force now amounted to some 18,000 horse and foot. But, almost at once, a serious quarrel broke out. Monro refused to serve under Callendar, and Callendar saw no reason why Monro should be allowed an independent command. Unable to reconcile the two men, Hamilton opted for the worst possible solution. The battle hardened Ulster troops were to be left behind at Kirkby Lonsdale with the regiments of Sir Philip Musgrave and Sir Thomas Tyldesley, to wait for the artillery from Scotland, while the rest of the army continued on to Hornby. Here Hamilton settled down for another week, having made the first in a series of catastrophic decisions.

A council of war was held at Hornby to decide whether to continue the advance south through Lancashire, or to cross into Yorkshire. Both Middleton and Turner were for Yorkshire. Turner recorded a view, which made good strategic sense;

When my opinion was asked, I was for Yorkshire, and for this reason onlie, that I understood Lancashire was a close countrey, full of ditches and hedges, which was a great advantage the English would have over our raw and undisciplined musketeers; the Parliaments armie consisting of experienced and well trained sojors and excellent firemen; on the other hand, Yorkshire being a more open countrey,

160

and full of heaths, where we both might make use of our horse, and come sooner to push of pike.

For once, Callendar had no view. Hamilton, supported by Langdale and Baillie, was for the onward march, hoping to link up with royalists in the south of the county and Lord Byron from North Wales. So, the weary trek continued onwards on 14 August towards Lancaster and then Preston. Langdale and the English cavaliers were placed some distance to the east of the main body of the Scots' army, protecting the flank and charged with gathering intelligence on enemy movements across the Pennines.

While Hamilton was limping through Lancashire, Cromwell had made remarkable progress since leaving Pembroke. His troops needed boots; so, avoiding the direct route through the mountainous country of North Wales, he marched on a circular path through the Midlands. This had the double advantage of allowing the army to pick up footwear and other essential supplies, as well as placing himself between Hamilton and the direct route to London. He finally joined Lambert between Wetherby and Knaresborough on 13 August, having covered 287 miles in 13 days. Contrast this with Hamilton, who, by the time he reached Preston two days later, had taken 39 days to travel 94 miles. The combined Parliamentary force now amounted to 14,000 cavalry and infantry, weaker than their opponents, but stronger than Cromwell subsequently reported. With Fairfax and the rest of the New Model still busy mopping up the royalists in the south east of England, Cromwell was about to enter battle for the first time in full command.

Hamilton still had no idea of the danger that was beginning to take shape on his eastern flank. Still suffering from supply and accommodation problems, he allowed Middleton and the cavalry to ride south of Preston, across the River Ribble and on towards Wigan on a foraging expedition. On 16 August, the eve of the Battle of Preston, the Engager army was like a snake, strung out over an incredible distance of almost fifty miles: Monro and the tail was still at Kirkby Lonsdale to the north; Hamilton and the main body was in the neighbourhood of Preston; while Middleton and the head was south at Wigan. Langdale and his separate force of English royalists had, in the meantime, marched south from Settle through Ribblesdale, approaching Preston from the north east.

Cromwell at Wetherby had no precise information on Hamilton's whereabouts. The conventional thing to do was to fall back southwards to cover the approach to London, while cavalry probes were sent westwards to locate the enemy. But Cromwell, who realised the importance of securing a quick decision, decided on a brilliant gamble. Rather than move south, he decided to cross the Pennines into Lancashire on a seek and destroy mission. From Otley on to Skipton, his army then descended into the Ribble Valley, camping at Gisburn on 15 August. Here Cromwell received news from his scouts that Hamilton was approaching Preston from Lancaster.

The following day the Parliamentary army continued south westwards to Clitheroe. Just outside the town, at the bridge over the River Hodder, a tributary of the Ribble, a vital war conference was held. The decision was whether to advance along the north bank of the Ribble, and so attack Hamilton directly at Preston, or to continue along the south bank towards Whalley, and thus block his further progress towards the Midlands. Once again, the conventional text book move was to adopt the latter choice; but Cromwell decided on a direct attack to prevent Monro closing with Hamilton. This was a risky move, for the Engagers were thought to be stronger than the Parliamentary army; but the number of their troops in no way made up for Hamilton's incapacity as a general when set against the genius of Cromwell. His army was now poised, like a spear, ready to be thrust into the side of the snake.

On the night of 16 August the soldiers of the New Model camped at Stonyhurst Hall, north of the Ribble, a mere seven miles from Preston, and only three miles from Marmaduke Langdale and the English royalists, camped at Longridge on Ribbleton Moor, west of the main army. Thomas Carlyle describes the scene on the eve of the battle;

On the night of Wednesday, 16th August, my Lord Duke has got to Preston with the main body of his foot, his horse lying very wide ahead of him at Wigan, ahead of him one knows not where, he himself hardly knows where, Sir Marmaduke guards him on the left, on Preston Moor, about Longridge Chapel, some four miles up the Ribble, and knows not in the least what storm is coming. For Cromwell, that same night, has got across the hills at Clitheroe and further.. and to-morrow morning they will have news of Cromwell.

162

All too late, Langdale was wakening to the danger. He told Hamilton and Callendar that he believed that Cromwell was now poised to attack; but they did not take his warning seriously. Early the following morning, Langdale's fears were confirmed. Still, his men held a good position, astride the main road between Preston and Skipton, little more than a deep, narrow lane, now saturated with rain water. On either side they were protected by the hedges of a small enclosed field, which guarded them against a cavalry attack. If they were able to hold off the New Model for long enough, reinforcements from the main army might be enough to swing the battle in their favour. Cromwell sent an advance party of 200 horse and 400 foot to force a passage through the lane. Soon after they were reinforced by Captain John Hodgson, whose *Memoirs* tell of the opening scenes of the Battle of Preston;

> And at Longridge Chapel our Horse came upon Sir Marmaduke drawn up very formidably...And here being drawn up by the Moorside (a mere scantling of us, as yet, not half the number we should have been) the General comes to us, orders us to march. We not having half our men come up, desired a little patience; he gives out the word 'March!'

Bit by bit the royalists were forced back over the rain sodden ground, fighting fiercely from hedge to hedge, with the musketeers firing off at short range, and the pikemen pushing in on each other. While the battle was underway, Langdale rode off to warn Hamilton that he was subject not to a probe, but a full scale attack. He found him with Baillie, preparing to move the infantry across the Ribble at Preston Bridge. Hamilton countermanded the order, telling Baillie to remain on the north side in support of Langdale, and sent off a message to Middleton and the cavalry to hurry back from Wigan. But Callendar objected that the infantry would be destroyed without immediate cavalry support. Once reunited with the cavalry, Callendar maintained, the army would have the advantage of fighting with the Ribble in front, rather than behind. No consideration seems to have been given to the thought that it would be completely cut off from Monro and Scotland. As for Langdale, he was exaggerating the scale of the enemy attack, and in any case he could always fight his way back through Preston and join the Scots south of the Ribble Bridge. Hamilton gave way, reverting to his original plan. The only help he sent to Langdale's hard pressed troops was a small force of lancers. Mistake was now piled on mistake.

Langdale's fight at the hedges and ditches of Ribbelton Moor had now gone on for over four hours. Unable to envelop the enemy in a cavalry attack, Cromwell continued to fight his way slowly forward in a bloody frontal assault. Eventually, with the enemy infantry cleared from the hedges, he sent two cavalry regiments down the lane, which chased the panicking royalists back towards the town. Langdale managed to join Baillie; but almost all the infantry which survived the fight was taken prisoner, while his cavalry galloped north to join Monro. Hamilton himself had come to the aid of Langdale with his own life-guards. However, his personal courage in battle in no way made up for his deficiencies as a commander.

South of the river, Baillie drew up his infantry on Church Brow Hill, overlooking the Ribble Bridge. Cromwell's men advanced on this vital crossing from the high bank to the north, their approach covered by a body of musketeers. The battle for Ribble Bridge continued for another two hours, 'a very hot dispute', in Cromwell's own words. With evening now falling, the Scots were finally driven back by a charge of pikemen under Colonels Thomas Pride and Richard Dean. With Baillie falling backwards, the fight continued ever southward across the bridge on the Darwen, a small tributary of the Ribble, causing the poet John Milton to write of 'Darwen's stream with blood of Scots imbued.' Only night brought the savagery to an end.

Darkness came as a welcome relief to both armies, soaked, tired and hungry. But the Parliamentary soldiers at least had the scent of victory in their noses. Cromwell's flank attack had succeeded brilliantly: Hamilton's army had been cut in two, and he was now separated from Scotland, with no line of retreat. By the end of the first day's fighting the Engagers had lost, in Cromwell's own estimate, 1,000 killed and 4,000 captured. Their army was still powerful, but it soon lost all confidence in the competence of its commanders.

There was to be no rest for the exhausted Scottish soldiers. At midnight, with the rain pouring down interminably, Hamilton held a gloomy council of war. Callendar urged a night march to meet Middleton and the cavalry coming up from the south. Both Baillie and Turner argued against this, pointing out the difficulties of moving a tired army along muddy roads on a dark wet night; but, as usual, Callendar prevailed. As the army had no means of transport, the musketeers were only permitted to take as much gunpowder as they could carry. All the rest was left behind, to be blown up by a slow burning fuse. This, like all of Callendar's schemes, came to nought; for no order was given to light the fuse, and all the powder was taken by Cromwell's men the following morning. With no drum beating, and all musket fuses extinguished, the demoralised soldiers slipped into the night.

This was an army where if anything could go wrong it would go wrong; and so it happened on this unhappy march. While Middleton was riding north from Wigan through Chorley, Hamilton was marching south through Standish, some distance to the west, so both forces passed each other in the night. The first Middleton knew of this was when he came across not his own infantry, as he had expected, but two regiments of Ironsides under Colonel Francis Thornhaugh, whom Cromwell had sent off in pursuit of Hamilton. In the engagement that followed, Thornhaugh was killed, but his men pressed Middleton hard all the way back to the south. Facing round again and again to fight off his pursuers, Middleton lost many men killed and captured, including Sir John Hurry, who was slightly wounded. He afterwards managed to escape, eventually rejoining Montrose on the Continent.

Hamilton had already travelled three miles from Preston before Cromwell discovered he was gone. After sending Thornhaugh off, he followed with the rest of the army, leaving Colonel Ralph Ashton and the Lancashire levies to hold Preston against a forward march by Monro, with orders to kill all of Langdale's captured men if the enemy attacked. He need not have worried; for, in spite of the pleas by Sir Philip Musgrave, Monro refused to budge from Kirkby Lonsdale.

With the rain pouring down night and day, the Scots' infantry was sodden and half starved by the morning of 18 August. On Standish Moor near Wigan they were finally rejoined by the cavalry. This was a good position on which to make a stand, as the ground was intersected with enclosures. Unfortunately, the rain had destroyed the small supply of powder available, and, as there was no more to be had, the weary march continued on to Wigan, where the wretched inhabitants were plundered 'almost to their skins' by the desperate soldiers, now on the verge of panic. The army was close to disintegration, as Turner explains;

As I marched with the last brigad of foot through the toune of Wiggam, I was alarmed that our horse behind me were beaten, and runne severall ways, and that the enemie was in my reare. I faced about with the brigad, and in the market place ferrd the pikes together, shoulder to shoulder, to kepe up any sould charge, and sent orders to the rest of the brigads before to continue their march and follow Lieutenant General Baillie, who was before them. It was then night, bot the moone shone bright. A regiment of horse of oure oune appeared first, riding very disorderlie. I got them to stop, till I commanded my pikes to open, and give way for them to ride or runne away, since they wold not stay. Bot my pikemen being demented (as I thinke we were all) wold not heare me, and tuo of them runne full tilt at me. One of their pikes, which was intended for my bellie, I griped with my left hand; the other run me neere tuo inches in the innerside of my right thigh; all of them crying, that all of us were Cromwells men...I rode to our horse and desired them to charge through these foot. They, feering the hazard of the pikes stood, I then made a cry come from behind them, that the enemie was upon them. This encouraged them to charge my foot so fiercelie, that the pikemen threw dounne their pikes and got into houses. All of the horse gallopd away; and I was told afterwards rode not through, bot over our whole foot, treading them doune...

From Wigan the retreating army ploughed through the mud on to Warrington, closely pursued by Cromwell. On the morning of 19 August the Scots turned on their tormentors at a place called Winwick, three miles north of Warrington. Cromwell described the fight in his despatch to Parliament;

We held them in some dispute till our army came up, they maintaining the pass with great resolution for many hours; ours and theirs coming to push of pike and very close charges, and forced us to give ground; but our men, by the blessing of God, quickly recovered it, and charging very hard upon them, beat them from their standing, where we killed about a thousand, and took (as we believe) about two-thousand prisoners.

The fight had taken place in a narrow lane on the road from Newton. All Cromwell's attacks were beaten back, until the local people showed him a way through the fields, outflanking the Scots position. Thereupon, they were pushed back by Colonel Pride's regiment to the village green on the south side of Winwick

166

Church, where their resistance was finally broken. The refugees made their way towards Warrington, where the rest of the army was busy barricading the bridge across the River Mersey. Even after the victory at Winwick, Cromwell would have had a hard time pursuing the Scots south of the Mersey, where they had built up a strong bridgehead. But even though Hamilton still had most of his horse and 4,000 infantry, this was a beaten army; and no one was more beaten than the general himself. Callendar, who had led him by the nose almost all the way, now persuaded him to instruct Baillie to order the, by now, useless infantry to surrender, while the cavalry attempted to join up either with Byron in Wales or other royalist forces still in arms. Baillie, shocked by the treachery of his fellow officers, refused to obey. He gave orders to defend the bridge, an honourable but completely unrealistic decision. Most of his musketeers had thrown away their useless weapons. Those who retained them had neither shot nor powder, and the pikemen were close to collapse. When the order was given only 250 men rose to obey. Baillie duly surrendered; and Cromwell, anxious to secure the bridge at Warrington, granted him generous terms. By the end of the running battle from Preston to Warrington 3,000 men had been killed and 10,000 taken prisoner.

Riding off with no clear sense of direction, Hamilton and the cavalry eventually ended up at Uttoxeter in Staffordshire on 22 August. Here he finally managed to muster enough spirit to blame the whole debacle on Callendar. Turner, who witnessed the quarrel, wrote;

> The Duke and Calander fell out, and were at very hie words at supper, where I was; each blameing the other for the misfortune and miscarriage of our affaires; in which contest I thought the Duke had the better of it. And heere, indeed, I will say, that my Lord Dukes great fault was in giveing E. Calander too much of his pouer all along; for I have often heard him bid him doe what he pleased, promiseing to be therwith well contented. And therfor Calander was doublie to be blamd, first for his bad conduct (for that was inexcusable) and nixt for reproaching the Duke with that wherof himselfe was guiltie.

This seems rather generous in the circumstances; for while Callendar's conduct had been bad, Hamilton's had been disastrous, amounting to a complete dereliction of his duty as a commander. Compromise may be an admirable quality in a politician; but in a soldier it only leads to doubt, confusion and uncertainty. From his inability to ride the storm in Scotland, to his failure to set clear objectives for his army, Hamilton led the Engagement to disaster. He was never a traitor, as Montrose and his supporters had argued; he was simply the wrong man for the times.

Ordered to continue their pointless ride on from Uttoxeter, the cavalry mutinied. Many deserted, including Langdale. Some others eventually rode off with Callendar, who finally managed to make good his escape to Holland. Hamilton had no alternative but to open negotiations with the enemy, finally surrendering to John Lambert, whom Cromwell had sent off in pursuit from Warrington, after his safety and that of his officers had been guaranteed. But it was not to be. Under his English title of Earl of Cambridge, he was tried and executed for treason in March 1649, only a few weeks after the death of the master he had given so much to serve.

News of Hamilton's defeat started a revolution in Scotland. In Ayrshire a group of the Earl of Eglinton's tenants led by his son, Robert Montgomery, attacked and dispersed a troop of cavalry that had been quartered amongst them. With this signal the whole of the south west rose in revolt. This time there was no lack of leadership. Loudoun, who had long since abandoned the Engagement, Eglinton, Leven and David Leslie placed themselves at the head of several thousand men from Ayrshire and Clydesdale. From Galloway, the Earl of Cassillis joined with still more. The insurrection spread from the Solway to the Firth of Clyde, as the local ministers urged their flocks to join. By 28 August the Committee of Estates had received word that the western army was advancing on Edinburgh. This was the beginning of the Whiggamore Raid.

The term Whiggamore is of obscure origin. According to Bishop Burnet, it comes from the term 'Whiggam', which the country people of the south west are said to have used to urge on their horses, although the word 'whigg' appears to have been in use in the north west of England to denote a country bumpkin. Whatever the origin, the label was to be a lasting one, eventually abbreviated to Whig to describe, first of all, the extreme Covenanters, and afterwards, as a term of abuse for an English political alliance that grew up in the Restoration to oppose the policies of Charles II.

With insufficient force to meet the threat from the west, the government, headed in the absence of Hamilton by his brother Lanark, was dependent for support on Monro and the remnants of the Engager army, making their way back from England. Rather than risk capture by the Whiggamores, Lanark and his colleagues left Edinburgh, making their way towards the Border in search of their army. The gates of the capital were opened and the western Covenanters received with joy in early September. All attached special significance to the fact that the Battle of Preston had opened on 17 August, the fifth anniversary of the signing of the Solemn League and Covenant, now known as 'St Covenant's day.' No thought seems to have been spared for their wretched countrymen, lying dead in the mud of Lancashire. Although supported by a section of the nobility and most of the clergy, the Whiggamore Raid was little more than a *putsch* by a zealous minority in the nation as a whole, the Bolshevik section of the Covenanter party.

Monro managed to make it back to Scotland through Durham, with Cromwell on his tail. But with the New Model Army pausing on the Border to recover Berwick and Carlisle, there was no immediate pursuit. To make absolutely sure of this, Monro refused to allow the English royalists to accompany him. Once joined by the Committee of Estates, he made his way past the Whiggamores in Edinburgh, seizing Linlithgow. Argyll was now marching to the west of Stirling with a force of Campbells, on his way to join his colleagues in Edinburgh. Anxious not to be cut off from their potential support in the north, the Engagers moved forward on 12 September. Argyll's men were intercepted and scattered with heavy losses, as their leader rode away, taking ship at North Queensferry for Edinburgh.

Monro's army gave the Engagers a decisive edge over their Whig opponents. Both Lanark and Monro were for continuing resistance against their opponents; but with Cromwell poised to cross the Border, their colleagues thought it best to open negotiations. Neither side wished for civil war in the face of an English invasion. While discussing terms with the Committee of Estates at Stirling, the Whigs sent Sir Andrew Ker and Major Archibald Strachan to see Cromwell. Strachan, in particular, was so extreme in his anti Engager views that he had even fought with the New Model at Preston; so Cromwell could take some comfort from his assurance that the only treaty he and his party would

169

conclude with their opponents would be on the basis of a complete surrender of power. But he knew that with a superior military force behind them, the Engagers were unlikely to give way very readily. So, to make absolutely sure, he crossed the Border with his whole army on 21 September, advancing north to Edinburgh, to offer fraternal aid to the 'honest party.'

Faced with this threat, the game was over for the Engagers at Stirling. Five days later they handed over all their power to Argyll and his party. It was agreed that Monro and his men should be allowed to return to Ulster to join their comrades there; but it was too late for this. Since the end of the First Civil War, Parliamentary troops had been sent to Ireland in increasing numbers. After Benburb and the departure of Sir George Monro for Scotland, the Scots' army in Ulster was a shadow of its former strength. Taking advantage of this opportunity, English troops under George Monk, who had agreed to take up service for Parliament, attacked and captured the main Scottish base at Carrickfergus Castle. Monk was assisted in this by troops from Glencairn's regiment, who had opposed the Engagement. Soon after Coleraine surrendered and the Scots army in Ulster finally ceased to exist. With nowhere else to go, Monro left for Holland, forbidden to return to Scotland.

Now camped just outside Edinburgh at Seaton, Cromwell was invited into the city for talks by Argyll. He rode through the gates on 4 October, and was lodged in the house of the Countess of Moray in the Canongate. That night, he was entertained at the Castle by Argyll and Warriston. Over the next few days Argyll, whose government as yet had no legal standing, and Cromwell established a mutual understanding. All Engagers were to be systematically excluded from political and military office, and the Scottish army was to be disbanded, save for a small force of 1,500 men under Leven's command. It was also suggested that Argyll had agreed with Cromwell that the King should be tried for his life; but there is absolutely no evidence to support this, and subsequent events indicated that there was no such undertaking.

It seems that Cromwell believed that the Kirk Party – as Argyll and his allies were generally known – would continue to be dependent on English military support, and neglected to conclude a more permanent settlement. But this alliance between Covenanter and Independent, both natural enemies, was too unstable to last. The only fruit it bore was a second Act of Classes passed by a new Parliament summoned by Argyll in January 1649. By this all prominent Engagers, as well as those who had fought with Montrose, were disqualified for life from holding public office. In addition, there was a sliding scale of exclusion, ranging from ten years to one, for those guilty of lesser offences. All readmission was to be subject to the approval of the Kirk, which thus acquired a decisive role in public life. When the showdown finally came between the Covenanters and the Independents, the Act of Classes was to be of major benefit to Cromwell.

Cromwell, satisfied by his meeting with Argyll, left Edinburgh on 7 October, returning to England to settle some unfinished business. Lambert was left in Scotland for another four weeks with a number of regiments, to ensure that the new regime was able to tighten its grip. Whatever the political views of individual Scots, the presence of English troops in the country was far from popular, as Lambert himself testified;

> Divers of our soldiers have lately had particular Injuries offered to them, by being set upon in the High-way, and other Places, by some loose and desperate Persons in this kingdom; many of their horses have been taken away, stolen...and other things: And truly there is such watching and waylaying of us, that we dare not stir without cokt and prim'd, and resolute to meet with some Encounter before we come to our Journeys end...

In England events moved quickly towards a tragic conclusion. Angered by the Second Civil War, and the perceived faithlessness of the King, Cromwell and a faction within the army decided on a permanent solution to the continuing constitutional deadlock. The Engagement, 'intended for the Kings relief and restoration,' James Turner wrote, 'posted him to his grave.' Charles was moved from the Isle of Wight and taken to a more secure prison at Hurst Castle on 1 December. Soon after the army took control of London, and some of the soldiers led by Colonel Thomas Pride expelled the Presbyterians from Parliament; all, that is, who still wished to negotiate with the King. The remainder, known as the Rump, agreed that a court be appointed to try Charles Stewart, the 'man of blood.'

In early January 1649 the Covenanter Parliament met in Edinburgh, basking in the glory of the Whiggamore Raid. The

Engagement was condemned, and all Acts of the previous Parliament repealed. Parliament also declared that the rising at Mauchline Muir was 'not only lawful but a zealous and loyal testimony to the truth of the Covenant.' Sensing danger, Lauderdale, Lanark and other prominent Engagers slipped into exile. Parliament proceeded to debate the Act of Classes; but it was also deeply concerned by events in London. The Committee of Estates wrote to the English Parliament in early January, urging that no action be taken against the King without the consent of its Scottish counterpart. Scots' commissioners arrived in London, and on three separate occasions denounced the proceedings against Charles. A last minute written appeal was sent to Thomas Fairfax on 29 January;

> ...entreat that you will take into serious consideration that the Kingdome of Scotland hath undoubted interest in his Majesty's person, and how hard a thing it is to proceed against there King, not only without but against their advice and consent. That his person was intrusted by that Kingdome to the honorable Houses of Parliament, and how much it will reflect upon the honour of Scotland and the faith of England to take away his life.

But nothing availed. On 30 January Charles was beheaded in Whitehall, a process that was little better than an act of judicial murder. The brief alliance between Argyll and Cromwell was over.

Charles Stewart was transfigured in death; but this could not wipe out the stain of his reign. Quite simply, he was one of the worst rulers ever to sit on the throne of Great Britain. Nurtured in the doctrine of divine right, he did not have the skill, the patience, or the intelligence to deal with the complex problems that beset his reign. His faults, if anything, were magnified in captivity, when his double dealings and intrigues reached new peaks. He both encouraged and undermined those who worked for him, whether it be Hamilton in Scotland or Ormonde in Ireland. His support of adventurers like Montrose and Antrim lost him the assistance of more moderate men, who might have saved him from his worst mistakes. It has been written of him that he was a man who mistook dissembling for cleverness, and a King who mistook crooked dealing for statesmanship. Single handedly he brought about a revolution and his own ruin. Nevertheless, he faced death with great courage, reaching for a martyr's crown to replace the earthly one which had led him to disaster.

CHAPTER 10
Dunbar

News of the King's murder reached Edinburgh on 4 February 1649. With it came the announcement that the English Parliament, what was left of it, had threatened death to anyone who proclaimed his successor. Without hesitation, Chancellor Loudoun, dressed in a black velvet gown, stood at the market cross of Edinburgh the following day, and declared that Charles II was now King of Great Britain and Ireland. 'One act of our lamentable Tragedy being ended,' Baillie wrote, 'we are entering again upon the scene.'

In killing the King, Parliament had given no thought to the forty-six year old regal Union with Scotland, which was now effectively dissolved. While England became a republic under the title of the Commonwealth, the government in Edinburgh had every right to declare Prince Charles to be King of Scots; but in giving him a British title the Covenanters deliberately provoked the new regime in London. However, there was no immediate showdown between the two countries. After the defeat of the Engagement, the Scots, for the present, were no risk to the Commonwealth, which was more concerned with repressing the revolt in Ireland; and the Covenanters had yet to decide on the terms for inviting Charles to Scotland from his Dutch exile.

The execution of the old King completely upset all of Argyll's political calculations, which had been based not on a personal arrangement between himself and Cromwell, but on a close alliance between the Parliaments of Scotland and England. He failed to appreciate that Cromwell's power base was in the New Model Army and not Parliament; and, when the real issues were being decided, Cromwell was quite prepared to betray his Scottish ally. Although Argyll remained the dominant figure in Scotland for some time afterwards, from this point forward his influence began to decline steadily. His style of pragmatic politics no longer suited the times, as the Kirk Party found the extreme views of Warriston more in keeping with its mood. Years later, while awaiting his own execution, he wrote the following words, in a small book intended for the eyes of his son;

By that confusion my thoughts became distracted and myself encountered so many difficulties in the way, that all remedies that were applied had quite the contrary operation; whatever, therefore, hath been said by me or others in this matter, you must repute and accept them as from a distracted man of a distracted subject in a distracted time wherin I lived.

When Montrose heard of the King's death he cut himself off for two days, during which time he expressed his own thoughts in verse form;

Great, Good, and Just, could I but rate
My grief with thy too rigid fate
I'd weep the world in such a strain
As it should deluge once again.
But since thy loud-tongued blood demands supplies
More from Briareus' hands than Argus' eyes,
I'll sing thine obsequies with trumpet sounds,
And write thine epitaph with blood and wounds.

Bloody retribution was to be inflicted on Argyll and the Covenanters, as well as Cromwell and the New Model Army, both of whom, in Montrose's eyes, shared responsibility for the regicide. His particular hatred, however, seems to have been reserved for his own countrymen, who, in handing the late King over to the English in 1647, had been directly responsible for his fate. Although the chief Engagers had now appeared at the court of Charles II in The Hague, there was to be no reconciliation between them and Montrose. Lauderdale made a point of telling the King that Scotland would never forgive Montrose for his barbarities in the field, and refused to stay in the same room as him. Ignoring this, on 22 February Charles appointed the bloodthirsty Marquis to be Lieutenant-Governor of Scotland and Captain General of all his forces there. Although the King was about to receive a deputation from the government in Edinburgh, he was prepared to listen to Montrose's more militant advice, especially as there were already some stirrings against the Covenanters in northern Scotland.

It was a matter of constant regret to the Scots that Charles I had been so adamant in his refusal to take the Covenant. They were all the more determined, therefore, that his son would not escape. Charles II would be welcome in Scotland, but only as a

Covenanted King. He would have to sign not only the National Covenant but the Solemn League and Covenant, and remove Montrose from his presence for ever. The need for the additional security this would provide was demonstrated by the first royalist rising in the north for over two years.

The execution of the King was a cause of considerable unrest in the north east, restive under the yoke of the Covenant. In early February the magistrates of Inverness told Parliament that the burgh was in immanent danger of attack by a group of royalist noblemen. Lord Lewis Gordon – now the heir of Huntly after the death abroad of Aboyne – Sir Thomas Urquhart of Cromerty, Sir Thomas Mackenzie of Pluscardine, Seaforth's brother, and Mackenzie of Redcastle were all summoned to Edinburgh to sign guarantees of loyalty.

Perhaps fearing they would not be allowed to return, all of them rose in revolt a few days after receiving this summons. On 22 February Inverness was seized by 700 horsemen, mainly Mackenzies led by Pluscardine. General Leslie was at once sent to the north. At his approach the royalists withdrew into Ross. He was about to set off in pursuit when he received intelligence of a new crisis further south: the men of Atholl had taken up arms under Lord Ogilvie and John Middleton, who had managed to escape from his prison in England. Unable to deal with both emergencies, and with his men suffering from exposure in the mountains, Leslie offered terms to the northerners. Some accepted, but Pluscardine and the Mackenzies refused. Leaving three troops of horse in Ross to keep them bottled up in the mountains, Leslie took the rest of his small force south to prevent Ogilvie and Middleton advancing into the Lowlands. But the Atholl rising was more bluster than substance. At the approach of the Covenanters, the rebels submitted, while Ogilvie and Middleton went into hiding.

The chief victim of these new troubles was the Marquis of Huntly, who was beheaded in Edinburgh on 22 March, only two weeks after the death of Hamilton in London. This is also said to have served as a signal to the young King, showing the determination of the Covenanters to eliminate their enemies. His fellow nobles had made appeals for clemency on his behalf; but with the Kirk strongly in favour of his death, they were overruled, an interesting sign of the shift in the balance of power. The power of the Kirk was further enhanced in March with the abolition by

Parliament of lay patronage – the right hitherto of the nobles and gentry to appoint ministers to livings under their control.

In the north, the royalist rising, which went underground for a time, emerged back onto the surface in mid April. Pluscardine was joined by Ogilvie and Middleton, as well as Lord Reay. Together they marched into Badenoch, where they met up with some Gordons under Lord Lewis, now the new Marquis of Huntly. With about 1,000 men the rebels made camp at Balvenie near Dufftown. Leslie responded quickly, moving north from Atholl with his own men. With their eyes fixed to the south, the royalists had forgotten the three troops of horse under Colonel Gilbert Ker and Lieutenant Colonels Halket and Strachan stationed in Ross earlier in the season. These men, although heavily outnumbered, surprised the rebels at Balvenie on 8 May, killing sixty or eighty and capturing 800, including Lord Reay. This episode, known as the 'Bourd of Balvenie,' convinced Strachan and the more extreme Covenanters that all that was needed to disperse the mighty was a small band of righteous men, after the example of Gideon in the Book of Judges. The Gideonites were fated to bring ruin on Scotland.

The activities of the royalists in the north were as nothing compared to the threat to Scotland that was taking shape elsewhere in the British Isles. Towards the end of March, Cromwell addressed a meeting of the officers of the New Model Army. Having beaten the King, he said, they now had to turn their attention against their old enemies in Scotland and Ireland. In other words, the war between King and Parliament was about to be transformed into a war to establish English supremacy throughout the British Isles. There could never be any kind of co-operation between the Catholic Irish and the Protestant Scots. The irony in this was that it was the Celts, whether Presbyterian or Papist, who were soon fighting and dying for the King. For Cromwell, Ireland was the greater danger. Rinnuccini and Owen Roe O'Neil were gone, and Ormonde had signed a second peace with the Confederates, now willing to fight for the King. After a summer of preparations, Cromwell landed at Ringsend near Dublin on 15 August, ready to begin a war of conquest and atrocity.

The Commissioners from Scotland finally arrived at The Hague on Monday 26 March 1649. The following day, dressed in mourning as a mark of respect for the late King, they had their first meeting with his successor. The Earl of Cassillis spoke for Parliament, and Robert Baillie for the Kirk. Charles was offered the crown of Scotland, but only if certain essential conditions were observed. In the first place, Charles was required to banish from his presence that 'that cursed man, James Graham.' That this should be raised before all other causes is a reflection of the deep loathing of Montrose in Scotland. Lauderdale understood this, as did the Earl of Lanark, now second Duke of Hamilton following the recent execution of his brother, who at once supported the Commissioners, even though he was exiled from Scotland as a 'malignant.'

Next, the King was required to subscribe to both Covenants, establish Presbyterianism in all three of his kingdoms, agree to the Westminster Confession and submit all civil affairs to Parliament and all ecclesiastical affairs to General Assemblies. It was some weeks before the King gave his answer. When the matter was debated in council, Lauderdale, Hamilton and Callendar were in favour of a marriage of convenience with Argyll and the Kirk Party. After all, once the King was established in Scotland, he would easily be able to set his rivals aside. In contrast, Montrose and some of his English advisors urged him to go to Ireland to join with Ormonde and the Catholic Irish, a better route to the Restoration, in their view, than that offered by the Covenanters. Montrose also suggested another armed descent on Scotland, and promised to lead it; although the King might, in the meantime, accept the National Covenant out of expediency, while rejecting the Solemn League. It was this view that the King favoured.

On 29 May Charles told the Commissioners that he would accept the National Covenant, the Confession of Faith and Presbyterian government in Scotland, but that he would give no assurances about church government in England and Ireland until he had consulted with the Parliaments of those countries. While reasonable enough in itself, it was less than the King's father had promised under the Engagement; and the Scots could hardly be expected to fight and die for no better reason than to place Charles on the English throne. In deep disappointment, the Commissioners left The Hague, arriving back in Scotland on 6 June. Charles remained their King, but in name only. Before they left he renewed Montrose's commission as Commander-in-Chief of the royalist forces in Scotland, and appointed him

Ambassador-Extraordinary with powers to seek aid from foreign states for an invasion of his native land. Ever eager, Montrose set out to prove himself in 'blood and wounds.' Hamilton tried to warn the King against any imprudent course of action by the Marquis. He pointed out that the influence of the clergy was strong amongst the ordinary people. As for Montrose himself, he was, in George Wishart's recollections;

> ...represented as a headstrong, reckless, self-seeking adventurer too eager for civil wars, and ready to promise more than he could perform.

While disappointed by the failure of The Hague negotiations, the Scottish Parliament still refused to consider any compromise with the English regicides. To an English proposal for a treaty of friendship, the Scots said that they would agree to no such arrangement until Parliament at Westminster disowned the execution of the King and the abolition of monarchy and the House of Lords. The General Assembly, meeting in Edinburgh in July 1649, made its own feelings quite clear;

> That prevailing party of Sectaries in England, who have broken the Covenant, and despised the Oath of God, corrupted the truth, subverted the fundamental Government by King and Parliament, and taken away the King's life, look upon us with an evill eye, as upon those who stand in the way of their monstrous and new fangled devices in Religion and Government...

But, for the present, the most immediate fear was of royalist attacks, especially by Montrose, so orders were given to speed up the construction of new fortifications at Leith and Burntisland.

Despite the dangers besetting Scotland from both royalists and republicans, the Kirk and its supporters, greatly encouraged by the Bourd of Balvenie, were as eager as ever for a purge of the ungodly elements from the army. Parliament bowed to this pressure, ordering a fresh search on 21 June for any who had taken part in past royalist risings or the Engagement. This process inevitably rid the army of professional soldiers, especially in the officer class, forcing an ever greater reliance on a green but Godly peasantry.

Montrose had been busy using his Ambassador's commission, attempting to raise troops and money in the German state of

Brandenburg, as well as in Sweden and Denmark. This met with only limited success; but by September 1649 he had managed to raise and equip a small force of 80 officers and 100 Danish soldiers. Under the leadership of the Earl of Kinnoul these men were sent as an advance party to occupy the islands of Orkney, charged with recruiting local forces, while Montrose remained on the Continent employing more professional troops. Orkney was a good base; for the islanders had little enthusiasm for the Covenant, and the government had no navy with which to dislodge the royalists. Leslie came north with all the troops at his disposal to guard the Pentland Firth. However, he could not keep his men in arms throughout the winter season, and retired back to Edinburgh in late November, leaving a few garrisons behind to keep a watch on the Isles.

The Covenanters also faced a fresh danger from the west at this time. Sir George Monro had returned to Ulster and had managed to raise troops from amongst the Protestant settlers, forcing Leslie to watch the western approaches as well as the north. Monro remained a threat, until dispersed by Cromwell at the end of the year.

Charles was too pragmatic to place all his hopes on Montrose's wild schemes. Even after the failure of The Hague talks, he kept up some contact with Argyll. These had been encouraging enough for him to propose to Parliament in August 1649 that a fresh approach be made to the King. Although Argyll had chosen his timing carefully, raising the suggestion when some of the most intransigent of his colleagues were absent, Parliament only agreed that new talks would have to be conducted on the basis of the terms rejected in May. The initial approach was entrusted to George Wynrame of Liberton. Wynrame took some time to make contact with the King, only arriving at his base on Jersey in the Channel Islands in December. By this time his prospects in Ireland were disappearing in the wake of Cromwell's bloody progress round the island. With no dissenting voices, the royal council decided to reopen formal negotiations with the Covenanters at the Dutch town of Breda in March 1650.

For Charles, Scotland now represented the last prospect of a successful Restoration by armed force. But he was no more anxious than he had been at The Hague to accept the full Covenanter package. While welcoming the new negotiations, he continued to encourage Montrose, less because he believed that his planned invasion had any real chance of success, and more in the hope that it would cause the Covenanters to moderate their demands.

Not all in Scotland were happy about the new negotiations. Some, including the irreconcilable Warriston and the Earl of Cassillis, who clearly had enough of Charles from his contacts with him at The Hague, were opposed. The Commissioners who were eventually sent to Breda represented a balance between the moderate and more extreme sections of the Covenanter movement; but it was quickly apparent that the extremists – Cassllis, Alexander Brodie and Alexander Jaffray – were more dominant than their milder colleagues. No sooner had the discussions opened in early April than Charles saw that there was little room for compromise. He was required to recall Montrose, confirm all Acts of the Scottish Parliament since 1641, sign the Covenants and declare that they applied to all three of his kingdoms, leave behind any of his supporters considered to be malignants, disown Ormonde's treaty with the native Irish and introduce new measures against Catholics. Even in his own household, Charles was to permit no other form of worship, which would mean denying liberty of conscience even to his own mother. If anything, these proposals were worse than those rejected in May 1649.

During the negotiations at Breda, Charles was open in professing his own personal preference for Episcopacy. But the Covenanters, especially George Wynrame amongst the moderates, deluded themselves into believing that once away from the malignant influences of the exiled court, and breathing the pure air of Covenanted Scotland, he could be moulded into a new shape. Charles, increasingly desperate to claim his rights as a King and to avenge the murder of his father, was almost bound, sooner or later, to accept any conditions to achieve his fundamental goal. The Covenanters were equally prepared to use his desires without any scruple of conscience. It was not the King who was at fault here: bad faith was present on both sides. Charles gave in to almost all the demands, and would swear the Oath of the Covenant, which his father had always refused; but he could neither bring himself to accept Presbyterianism for England, nor to abandon Ormonde and the Catholic Irish treaty.

Montrose was becoming more of a problem for Charles. His attempt to use him to obtain some concessions from the

Covenanters was clearly not working, and he would soon give in to pressure to have him recalled. Montrose himself cared little for the manoeuvring at Breda; he was anxious to embark on a new campaign of violence before any agreement between Charles and the Estates put a stop to his plans. He came to Kirkwall in March 1650 with some more foreign mercenaries to join with his advance party and the Orcadian levies. Amongst his officers was Sir John Hurry, his old opponent at Auldearn, still carrying the scars of the wound he had received during the retreat from Preston. Altogether he had 40 horse, 500 foreign mercenaries and 700 Orcadians, completely unskilled in the arts of war. On board his ship, the *Herderinnan*, anchored in Scapa Flow, Montrose issued his orders to Hurry at a conference on 9 April. Hurry was instructed to cross to Caithness that same evening with part of the little army and advance to Ord of Caithness, a high hill overhanging the sea just north of Kildonan. Montrose crossed with the rest of his force a few days later. This time there was no Alisdair MacColla to meet him.

In Edinburgh the Committee of Estates was now aware that the rebels had crossed from Orkney. Leslie was instructed to take his troops north to prevent this incursion developing into a general rising. A rendezvous was held at Brechin on 25 April, from where Archibald Strachan was sent ahead to gather the cavalry that had wintered in the north. He now had five troops of horse under his command, including the three that had fought at Balvenie, the very cream of the Gideonites. God had shown what could be accomplished by a small righteous company at Balvenie, and Strachan rode on into Ross, convinced that the victory was already his.

Montrose joined with Hurry at the Ord of Caithness. From here their combined force advanced along the coast towards Dunrobin Castle, garrisoned for the Covenant by the tenants of the Earl of Sutherland, as were some smaller fortresses at Skelbo, Skibo and Dornoch. Avoiding these obstacles, the royalists turned aside, marching up Strathfleet on towards Strathoykell. The Oykel was forded just to the west of its junction with the Cassley, and the treck continued along the southern bank. Montrose had counted on the support of the Mackenzies, but Seaforth was in exile, and even his brother Pluscardine, who led the rising the previous year, remained quiet. With no support in the hills, the rebels continued back towards the coastal plain, halting at Carbisdale on the southern side of the Kyle of Sutherland on 27 April. That same day, Strachan was at Tain conferring with the Earl of Sutherland. Learning of Montrose's whereabouts, he decided on an immediate surprise attack.

Montrose's army was in a narrow glen, where the Culrain Burn flows into the Kyle of Sutherland. To his rear the ground rose up to the wooded hill of Creag a' Choineachan. With a good view of the surrounding countryside, Montrose would be able to deploy his men on the hill if subject to a sudden attack. Yet, believing that there was only a small body of enemy horse in the area, he failed to carry out a thorough reconnaissance, thus making the same mistake that led to disaster at Philiphaugh.

Strachan had now reached Wester Fearn to the south east of Carbisdale. On his onward march he still had the River Carron to cross by a ford which left him some miles short of the enemy position. A direct approach would only alert the enemy to his presence. Fortunately much of the way was covered by thick broom, which only ended just before the Culrain Burn was reached. Close to the Burn, Strachan concealed his men in a gully overshadowed by broom, allowing only a single troop to emerge into the open. Montrose sent forward his cavalry under Major John Lisle to investigate, while his infantry made ready to take cover in the woods of Creag a' Choineachan. Before this exercise was complete, Strachan's whole force emerged and charged. Lisle was immediately overwhelmed as the Covenanters rode on towards the infantry. Hurry and some of the Danish and German musketeers attempted to make a stand, but the Orcadians crumbled in panic. Two hundred of them drowned trying to escape across the waters of the Kyle of Sutherland. In a matter of minutes the whole affair was over. Carbisdale was not a battle; it was a rout. The defeated soldiers were hunted over the slopes of Creag a' Choineachan for two hours. Montrose had promised blood and wounds; unfortunately for him, the wounds were his and the blood that of his own men. Four hundred of them were killed, and over four hundred and fifty taken prisoner, including Sir John Hurry, whose amazing career as a soldier was shortly about to end.

Despite his wounds, Montrose managed to escape the debacle at Carbisdale. For some days he managed to avoid capture, disguised as a shepherd, until he finally fell captive to Neil MacLeod of Assynt, an ally of the Earl of Sutherland. He was taken to Edinburgh, and heard his fate read out by Warriston at Parliament House. He was to be hanged at the Cross of Edinburgh with a copy of Wishart's *De Rebus* round his neck. He was to swing on the scaffold for three hours, after which time he would be taken down, his head cut off and his body divided in four quarters. The head would be displayed on a spike on the wall of the Tolbooth prison, while his arms and legs would be sent for similar display to Glasgow, Perth, Stirling and Aberdeen. Only his trunk was shown any mercy: for, if he repented his crimes, it would be buried in consecrated ground at Greyfriars; otherwise it would be deposited in a common grave outside the city on the nearby Burgh Muir. Needless to say, he would concede nothing to his enemies. Sentence was carried out on 21 May. He accepted his fate with courage, and, like the King before him, was transfigured in death. Hurry followed soon after.

The day that Montrose entered Edinburgh, Parliament considered and rejected the Treaty of Breda. It had to be all, or nothing. Fresh instructions were sent to the Commissioners in Holland, who were told to insist on all of the original terms. They were received shortly before the whole party sailed with the King for Scotland. A decision was taken, on the suggestion of the moderates, to conceal Parliament's decision from the King, on the assumption that, once underway, it would be more difficult for him to refuse. When the ship anchored at the island of Heligoland in the North Sea, to await a favourable wind for Scotland, Charles was effectively presented with an ultimatum. Understandably angry at this calculated breach of faith, he held out for some days; but as it was now a choice between agreeing to these dictated terms or facing a humiliating return Holland, he surrendered. He agreed both to sign the Covenants and to disavow the Ormonde treaty. Sadly for Charles, the Treaty of Heligoland was not the end but only the beginning of a bitter journey.

On 23 June the royal flotilla anchored off Garmouth in the Moray Firth. Not able to delay signing the Covenants any longer, Charles tried to insist that the laws of England took precedence over them. The Commissioners refused to allow this caveat, and added another clause to the Solemn League, committing the King to accept all future Acts of Parliament embodying the ideals of the text. Scotland now had the pretence of a Covenanted King; for pretence it was. Charles had been deliberately manipulated into a position where he could do nothing but swallow all that was given to him. There was no real sincerity behind any of this; both sides clearly understood that the whole thing was a sham. If the King was cynical in taking an oath which was clearly contrary to his own conscience, the Covenanters were equally cynical in forcing him to do so. Even Alexander Jaffray had the sense to recognise this when he noted in his Diary;

> We did both sinfully entangle and engage the nation ourselves and that poor, young Prince to whom we were sent, making him sign and swear a Covenant which we knew from clear and demonstrable reasons that he hated in his heart.

Soon Charles found himself housed in Falkland Palace, with all regal state; but, for all practical purposes, he was still King in name only. The pleasures of his Dutch exile, limited as they were, quickly faded into memory as the King was subjected to the Spartan rigours of Covenanting Scotland. According to Clarendon, he was made to observe the Sabbath with more rigour than the Jews. Gilbert Burnet, himself a cleric, describes his ordeal with some sympathy;

> He wrought himself into as grave a deportment as he could: he heard many prayers and sermons, some of a great length. I remember in one fast day there were six sermons preached without intermission. I was there myself and not a little weary of so tedious a service. The King was not allowed so much as to walk abroad on Sundays; and if at any time there had been any gaiety at court, such as dancing or playing at cards, he was severely reproved for it. This was managed with so much rigour, and so little discretion, that it contributed not a little to beget in him an aversion to all sort of strictness in religion.

While the arrival of Charles in Scotland was a clear provocation to the Commonwealth, there was no real evidence, beyond rumour and supposition, that Argyll and the Kirk Party were prepared to invade England on his behalf. There were too many political problems and internal difficulties for an attack on England to be carried out with any degree of unanimity. Only the most extreme royalists, moreover, can have looked forward with any enthusiasm to a showdown with the New Model Army. It had now been continuously under arms for five years, had proved its superb fighting qualities in two Civil Wars, and now in the conquest of Ireland. Scotland had only recently suffered a serious defeat and had been largely demilitarised as a consequence. Any new levy of troops was bound to cause problems because of the Act of Classes and the rigours of the Kirk Party. David Leslie was the best soldier Scotland had; but he was no Cromwell. Recognising the weaknesses of his own troops when compared to the chilly professionalism of the New Model Army, it is unlikely that he would readily agree to an ill considered military adventure.

In England the Council of State, the executive body of the Commonwealth, was not prepared to await events. Cromwell had been summoned back from Ireland in the spring, leaving the remaining military operations on the island to his son-in-law, Henry Ireton. No sooner had Charles set foot in Scotland than it was decided to launch a pre-emptive military strike. The question was, who would lead the invasion? Sir Thomas Fairfax was still the commander-in-chief of the army; but since the death of the King, in which he had taken no part, he had quietly distanced himself from his former comrades in arms. When offered command of the Scottish expedition, he refused, saying;

> I think it is doubtful whether we have a just cause to make an invasion upon Scotland. We are joined with the Scots in the National League and Covenant, and for us, contrary thereunto, and without sufficient cause given us by them, to enter their country and make war upon them, is that which I cannot see the justice of.

In his place, Cromwell was named as 'General of the Forces of the Commonwealth of England', a clumsy appellation, which he was allowed to shorten to Lord-General. This was the decisive point in his career, which, in a few years, was to make him the first military dictator of the British Isles.

Before the end of June English troops had started to gather on the eastern Border. Cromwell himself left London on the 28th, and joined the rest of the army at Newcastle on 10 July. He had at his disposal a superb striking force of 16,000 men, made up of the best formations of the New Model Army. The eight cavalry regiments were Cromwell's own, Lambert's own, Edward Whalley's, Francis Hacker's, Robert Lilburne's, Charles Fleetwood's, Philip Twistleton's, and John Oakey's dragoons. The infantry comprised Cromwell's own, Thomas Pride's, Maulevereer's, Charles Fairfax's, Coxe's, Daniel's, Overton's and John Bright's. Cromwell appointed Lieutenant-General Charles

Fleetwood as his second-in-command and Major General John Lambert was put in charge of the infantry, as well as being appointed Chief of Staff. He also brought with him Colonel George Monk, whose military expertise had impressed the Lord-General when he was campaigning in Ireland. Monk, as yet, had no command of his own. When John Bright, who had no more enthusiasm for the Scottish enterprise than Fairfax, resigned his commission, Cromwell at once proposed Monk as a replacement. But Bright's men, who had fought against Monk at the Battle of Nantwich, refused to have him, selecting John Lambert instead. To compensate him, Cromwell pulled together a scratch force made up from the garrisons of Newcastle and Berwick. In time, this formation, which had such an inauspicious birth, was to become the Coldstream Guards, the only regiment of the New Model Army to survive the Restoration.

Parliament had declared war on Scotland in June, shortly after Charles' landing. The Covenanters were at once faced with the need to raise a new national army as quickly as possible. Amazingly, even in the midst of this crisis, there was opposition in Parliament to a levy of troops, because it was felt that the army would tend to favour the King, and it would be impossible to ensure that, in a rapid trawl, all men would come up to the required moral standard. The Kirk was also suspicious in case any 'malignants', who were more prepared to fight for King and Country, than Covenant and King, slipped in to the ranks. To push the draft through, its supporters were obliged to agree that a new commission for purging the army be appointed, even before a single troop had been raised. David Leslie was appointed to lead, though still under the nominal headship of Leven, now something of a military fossil.

By the time Cromwell crossed the Border, Leslie had about 20,000 men in arms. Given the speed with which this force had been raised, most of the them had received only the most elementary training. To compensate for his obvious weaknesses, Leslie decided to pursue a strategy used by Scottish commanders for ages past. Supplies were bound to be a problem for the English; so, copying the tactics of Wallace and Bruce, Leslie had the south east systematically stripped of all available sources. To defend the capital he constructed a huge defensive line running from Leith in the north to Canongate in the south, behind which he placed his men and guns. The southern flanks were protected by outposts on Arthur's Seat and St Leonard's Hill. Leith was further protected by a massive boom placed across the harbour mouth. Other key points along the Firth of Forth were similarly guarded: Burntisland was fortified, and gun emplacements constructed on the island of Inchgarvie. This was a good strategy; but there was one key weakness – the English had command of the sea. The presence throughout the campaign of a powerful supply fleet was to help Cromwell overcome many of his problems, both before and after the Battle of Dunbar.

Cromwell finally crossed the Tweed on 22 July 1650, taking the same route that Protector Somerset had in 1547 on his way to the Battle of Pinkie. Leslie had done his best to ensure that the country before him was empty. Even if he had not, the reputation that the soldiers of the New Model Army had acquired in Ireland, especially after the massacres at Drogheda and Wexford, was enough to ensure that few would stay to welcome them. Stories were also spread about by the ministers that the English intended to slice the throats of all men, cut off the sword hands of the young and sear women's breasts with hot irons. But Cromwell came to fight a different kind of war in Scotland; the Scots, after all, were only misguided Protestants, not Papist savages. His campaign was to be a war of words as well as of bullets. Proclamation after proclamation was issued from his headquarters, intended to enlighten the Scots and persuade them to abandon a 'malignant' King.

Captain John Hodgson, a company commander in Lambert's regiment of horse, was to publish a valuable account of the invasion of Scotland some thirty years later, in which he recorded many of his impressions. Of the first stage of his journey he records the following;

> In the march between Mordington and Coppersmith (Cockburns-path), we saw not any Scotchmen in Eyeton, and other places that we passed through; but the streets were full of Scotch women, pitiful sorry creatures, cloathed in white flannel, in a very homely manner. Very many of them much bemoaned their husbands, who, they said, were enforced by the lairds of the town to gange to the muster. All the men in this town (Dunbar), as in other places of this day's march, were fled; and not any to be seen above seven, or under seventy years old, but only some few decrepid ones.

News of the English invasion had a mixed reaction. John Spreul, the Town Clark of Glasgow, recorded his horror at the evils of religious toleration, which the Independents and the other English sects represented. A more common reaction was one of simple fear, as John Nicoll noted in his Diary;

> At the approaching of this Englische airmy mony peipill heir in the eist pairtes and south wer overtakin with great feares...Mony also in Edinburgh, Leith, Linlithgow, Falkirk and other pairtes about, wer put in great perplexitie, quha removd thair best guidis over to the north syde of Forth.

By 28 July the English were at Haddington, where they made their first contact with Scots troops. These men were immediately pursued by the English cavalry, and there was some light skirmishing near Musselburgh. On its advance up the east coast, the army had been accompanied by the fleet, which based itself at Dunbar, the best port before Leith. A forward base was also established at Musselburgh; but the mud flats here made the landing of stores difficult.

The following day Cromwell took up a position at Restalrig and Jock's Lodge, where he had his first full sight of the strength of Leslie's entrenchments. Determined to hold on to the vital port of Leith, Leslie had made the north the toughest part of the line, placing thirty-seven of his field guns here, all mounted on platforms. A direct assault on this little Maginot Line would have subjected the English to a murderous cross fire, and Cromwell was not the kind of soldier to squander his men in useless battles of attrition. Leslie's southern flank, however, was slightly more vulnerable; so it was here that Cromwell decided to begin a probing attack. In the north a squadron of English warships under Admiral Hall began to bombard Leith, while Cromwell sent part of his force to occupy Arthur's Seat. Once the Scots were driven from this position, two cannons were brought into position to fire on Leslie's right. A counter attack was mounted by the regiment of James Campbell of Lawers, which pushed the English back. He captured their guns for a brief time, before they were retaken in a second assault. Beyond that, nothing happened for Leslie refused to be drawn out of his fortifications.

The summer of 1650 was little better than that of 1648. With his troops lacking shelter, short of provisions and drenched by the incessant rain, Cromwell ordered his army to fall back on Musselburgh the following day. Taking advantage of this, some of the Scots' cavalry emerged from the defences and fell on the English rearguard at Restalrig, putting them in some disorder for a time, before reinforcements drove them back. In a brief but intense fight, John Lambert was wounded in the shoulder and thigh by the Scottish lancers, and was taken prisoner for a short period. Meanwhile, the vanguard approached Musselburgh, only to face yet another fight. While the army was before Edinburgh, five hundred country people had entered the town and barricaded themselves in, until they were dislodged by Fleetwood's regiment. With the weary English troops settled down for the night in whatever shelter they could find, the Scots' cavalry attempted a further surprise attack at 3 o'clock on the morning of 31 July. After enjoying some initial success, they were driven back for a second time by Lambert's musketeers. Following this repulse, Leslie allowed no further adventures.

For the Scots' army, the highlight of the first day's fighting was a morale boosting visit from the King, who came to Leith on 29 July at the invitation of the Earl of Eglinton and some other officers. Warriston, who was already beginning to interfere with Leslie's operational decisions, and the other zealots in the Kirk party were immediately alarmed. Charles, in their view, was a threat to the Godly purity of the army, as Warriston noted in his Diary;

> At night the enemy cam to Restalrig and the King to Leyth. The airmy's exclamation and carnal courage at his prescence mor than the Lord's was ominous in my thought that, at the best wee get a mixed dispensation...

On 2 August the King was forced to return to Dunfermline, as the purging committee cranked into action. In a space of three days no fewer than 80 officers and 3,000 men were sent home, although Argyll and Leslie did their best to moderate some of the worst excesses of the purgers. Warriston had not the least interest or concern about what this would do to the morale and fighting ability of the army. Strachan and the Gideonites had shown at Balvenie and Carbisdale what a few good men could accomplish against the multitude, with the help of God. While weakening the army, Warriston also entered into a treasonable correspondence with Cromwell, expressing his concern that he might be in alliance with malignants. To try to placate fanatics like Warriston and Strachan, Charles was forced into ever deeper humiliations, signing a declaration on 16 August expressing regret for the crimes of his father and the idolatry of his mother. Even Argyll was moved to tell the King that 'when he came into England he might be more free, but for the present it was necessary to please these madmen.'

Unable to break Leslie's line in battle, Cromwell tried to break it with words. From the camp at Musselburgh he addressed his most famous appeal to the General Assembly;

> Your own guilt is too much for you to bear: bring not therefore upon yourselves the blood of innocent men, deceived with pretences of King and Covenant, from whose eyes you hide a better knowledge. I am persuaded that divers of you, who lead the people, have laboured to build in yourselves in these things wherin you have censured others, and established yourselves upon the Word of God. Is it therefore infallibly agreeable to the Word of God, all that you say? I beseech you, in the bowels of Christ, think it possible you may be mistaken.

The Assembly replied by asking him if he would have them be sceptics in their religion, and reminding him, no doubt to his annoyance, that he was breaching the Solemn League and Covenant to which he was sworn.

Unable to maintain his exposed position at Musselburgh, Cromwell retired back to Dunbar for fresh supplies. Disappointed in his attempt to force a battle, he decided to try to manoeuvre round Edinburgh to the south and west. The obvious danger in this was that his lines of communication would be greatly extended, and he might be cut off from the base at Dunbar. But it would have the advantage of threatening Leslie's own supply lines, and perhaps drawing him out of his fortified position into open country.

On the evening of 13 August the English occupied the Braid Hills, with an outpost on the nearby Blackford Hill, just to the south of the city. But almost at once Cromwell was forced to withdraw because of supply problems. He returned five days later. On each occasion Leslie mirrored Cromwell's moves in a complex game of tactical chess. When Cromwell attempted to move to the north west of Edinburgh, to cut the city's links with Queensferry and Stirling, Leslie moved his whole army to the west, taking up a strong position on the rising ground at Corstorphine, with his front protected by the two small lochs of Gogar and Corstorphine (long since drained away) and some marshes further to the west. Although Cromwell managed to capture the fortified house of Redhall on 24 August, which allowed him to move his army north over the Water of Leith, Leslie refused to budge. When Cromwell attempted to by-pass the lochs to the west, Leslie at once made his own compensating move to the right, occupying a new position on the rising ground at Gogar on 27 August. The English moved forward, eager for battle; but the ground was far too boggy to allow the cavalry to deploy. Both sides exchanged cannon fire for the rest of the afternoon, though nothing more was attempted. Losing the war of manoeuvre, Cromwell retreated back to Braid; and with many of his men now falling sick of dysentery and other exposure related diseases, he continued the retreat all the way back to Dunbar, which he reached on 1 September.

So far Leslie, fighting with one hand tied behind his back, had behaved faultlessly, continually getting the better of his old comrade from Marston Moor. Lucas Philips has written of this, that Cromwell;

> ...for the first time in his career he was faced with a general of real ability, a general accomplished in Fabian tactics, and was being outpointed. Leslie knew his Cromwell. Oliver wanted a swift rough-and-tumble, but Leslie forced him into the harder trial of chess.

But he was now about to make a fatal error. With so many of the English soldiers falling sick, the retreat to Dunbar looked as if Cromwell was on the run. Leslie promptly abandoned his defences at Edinburgh and set off in pursuit, extending his own lines of communication, while Cromwell was shortening his. But while Cromwell was entering a secure base at Dunbar, Leslie, who had his own supply problems at Edinburgh, was advancing across territory already ravaged by the passing of armies. Abandoning the main road from Edinburgh, he took up a position on Doon Hill, on the northernmost edge of the Lammermuirs, overlooking Dunbar from the south west. This was a good situation, too high to be assaulted from below, and with a clear view of the enemy dispositions; but it was also very exposed, and the weather was no kinder to the Scottish soldiers than it had been to the English at Braid. It was Leslie, rather than Cromwell, who was now looking for a quick solution.

Rising in the Lammermuirs, the Brock or Spott Burn flows in a north easterly direction past the foot of Doon Hill, before turning sharply to the north, continuing over the coastal plain, before meeting the sea to the east of Dunbar. While of no great significance in itself, it runs through a deep ravine, with sides too steep to allow infantry to cross in formation. As the burn continues on its northern course, over the main road to Berwick and past Broxmouth House on its way to the sea, the banks flatten out, allowing an easy passage for both horse and foot. Cromwell's army occupied a position on the west of Brock Burn around Dunbar. With Leslie poised on its flank, another Scots' force was sent ahead to block the dangerous pass at Cockburnspath, which the Lord-General, surprisingly, had neglected to secure. The army was effectively cut off from England by land, although the fleet ensured that the sea routes were kept open. This was a dangerous position to be in, as Cromwell recognised himself in a letter he wrote to Arthur Hazlerigg, the Governor of Newcastle;

> We are upon an Engagement very difficult. The enemy hath blocked-up our way at the Pass at Copper's path, through which we cannot get without almost a miracle. He lieth upon the Hills that we know not how to come that way without great difficulty; and our lying here daily consumeth our men who fall sick beyond imagination... whatever becomes of us, it will be well for you to get what forces you can together; and the south to help what they can...If your forces had been on readiness to have fallen upon the back of Copper's path, it might have occasioned supplies to have come to us...do you get together what forces you can against them. Send to the friends in the south to help with more...

It's worth noting that there is absolutely no suggestion of a retreat here, either by sea or land. Cromwell's concern about reinforcements is understandable enough; for he had lost up to a third of his original strength through illness, giving him no more than about 11,000 effective troops. Compare this with Leslie, who, despite the purges, had over 20,000 men poised on Doon Hill.

Keeping a close eye on his enemy from the vantage point of Doon on Monday 2 September, Leslie was able to observe large parties of English troops being ferried out to the fleet. Cromwell was doing no more than sending his sick soldiers to the relative comfort and safety of the ships; but to Leslie it looked as if he was planning to ship his army away by sea. Believing he now had the New Model Army in the palm of his hand, the Scottish general was frustrated by the limitations of his defensive position. He could not fire on the English because their camp was beyond the range of his artillery; he could not launch a direct attack because the Brock Burn would have interfered with the passage of his army. To be ready for the expected kill, he decided to move the bulk of his cavalry regiments to his right, and descend gradually down the hill, with the right wing fanning out over the coastal plain towards the sea. Throughout the campaign, Leslie had read Cromwell's mind with faultless precision. Now, in his eagerness for victory, he forgot an essential lesson: that Cromwell was always at his best in a crisis, a point well made by a Scottish preacher after the battle, who said of the English general that he was;

> ...worse than the Devil, for the scripture sais, Resist the Devil and he will flie from you, but resist Oliver, sais he, and he will flie in your face.

Based at Broxmouth House north of the Berwick road on the west bank of the Brock Burn, Cromwell was alert to any movement on the hill. As the Scots' army began to deploy downwards, roughly in line with the burn, he compensated by moving his own regiments out of the camp on the Dunbar peninsula, with his right close to the ravine at the foot of Doon Hill and the left close to the sea at Broxmouth House. With the Scots moving ever closer towards the coastal plain, Cromwell immediately spotted a serious weakness in Leslie's line. His left was pinned in between Doon Hill and the ravine of the Brock Burn. This meant that if the right got into trouble, the regiments on the left could not be called to its assistance. Here, in miniature, was the Battle of Preston: an army, superior in strength, could be defeated in detail by a weaker foe concentrated at a crucial point. After consulting with Lambert and Monk, Cromwell decided to launch what was, in effect, a powerful left hook across the Brock Burn smashing into Leslie's exposed right wing and rolling up his whole army from the right to the left.

It was clear from Leslie's new position that it was he who expected to do the attacking, not the enemy. Much was to be gained, therefore, by assaulting the Scots when they least expected it. The decision was taken to begin the offensive in the early hours of September 3, while it was still dark. At a council of war the other regimental officers initially favoured shipping away the infantry and attempting to break through the Scots with the cavalry – the very thing that Leslie anticipated – but, after an intervention by Lambert, all accepted Cromwell's plan.

Shrouded by the dark of a stormy night, the English got into position. The artillery, which Leslie was convinced had already been shipped away, was brought into the centre of the field to pin down the Scots on the left while the right was under attack. Lambert and Fleetwood were to lead the main thrust across the burn with six cavalry regiments, backed up by Monk further to their left with three and a half regiments of foot. The remaining infantry regiments under Colonels Pride and Overton and the last two cavalry regiments, were to follow in support and protect the guns in the centre, while, on the right, Oakey's dragoons were to open fire on the Scots' left, cramped between Doon Hill and the ravine. As the final dispositions were being made in the dark, Cromwell rode amongst his troops on a little Scottish nag, biting his lip hard and so preoccupied that he failed to notice the blood running down his chin.

The Scots, completely unaware of what was going on below them, settled for the night as best they could on the soaking fields. Many of the officers, tiring of these hardships, sloped off from their regiments to find shelter in local farmhouses, after ordering most of their musketeers to extinguish their match, lest it betray their position to the enemy. In wet and windy weather these would be almost impossible to relight in a hurry, which perhaps explains why so few of the musketeers made a stand the following morning. This order, which appears to have been made contrary to Leslie's own instructions, was a quite astonishing piece of negligence in the face of the enemy, and highlights the fatal confidence of the Scots' army.

At 4 o'clock in the morning the English spearhead formed up to the north of Broxmouth House awaiting the signal. No sooner had they crossed the burn than the leading Scots' cavalry units fell back in complete surprise. By now the alarm had spread across the field, as the Scots' soldiers struggled into battle order in the dark, many, presumably, still without their officers. By now Cromwell had established a bridgehead on Leslie's side of the burn, and was pressing the attack on the left. Leslie, from above, would still have no clear idea of what form the offensive was taking. Recovering from the initial shock, the Scottish cavalry on the right began to make a determined stand against the Ironsides. Lambert was repulsed by a charge of the lancers. The pikemen also managed to make a resolute counter attack, even pushing Monk's infantry back towards the burn. At this critical point Cromwell sent in his reserves, ordering them to incline to the left to turn the exposed Scottish flank. At the same time Lambert managed to rally his own troopers and renewed the forward pressure. Unsupported, and attacked in both front and flank, the cavalry charged off the field, leaving the infantry fully exposed to the full force of the enemy. Dawn was now breaking, and John Hodgson described the scene that followed in his *Memoirs*;

> ...and one of the Scots brigade of foot would not yield, though at push of pike and butt end of musket, until a troop of our horse charged from one end to another of them, and so left them at the mercy of the foot. The General himself comes to the rear of our regiment, and commands to incline to the left; that was, to take more ground, to be clear of the bodies. And we did so, and horse and foot were engaged all over the field; and the Scots all in confusion: And, the sun appearing upon the sea, I heard Nol (Cromwell) say 'Now let God arise, and his enemies be scattered;' and he, following us as we slowly marched, I heard him say, 'I profess they run!' and there was the Scots army all in disorder and running, both right wing, and left, and main battle.

With almost breathtaking speed the army was destroyed. As the English army wheeled round to the right, the Scots troops on the left, who had not been engaged at all, fled across the ravine to Dunbar, where many were surrounded and taken. Others were pursued all the way to Haddington. In all some 2,000 Scots are thought to have been killed at the Battle of Dunbar and the pursuit that followed, with a further 10,000 falling prisoner. The rest managed to escape and a rump of 4,000 men made it to the safety of Stirling with Leslie. Ever mindful of the importance of winning the political war in Scotland, Cromwell picked out the most starved, the sick and the wounded from amongst the prisoners and allowed them to go home. The rest – about 3,000 men – were sent south to Berwick. Although Cromwell had asked that they be well treated, the English state did not have the capacity for dealing with such large numbers of prisoners of war, and most died of starvation, disease or neglect.

Leslie lost the battle to a combination of his own negligence and Cromwell's genius. All advantage the Scots had in numbers – if not in quality – was lost by a concentration of the enemy force at a decisive part of the field. If he had had any sense of history, Leslie might not have chosen this field on which to make a fight; for it was here, in 1296, that the Scots lost the first great battle of the Wars of Independence. For many, tired of the arrogance and incompetence of the Kirk Party, a new struggle for independence was about to begin.

CHAPTER 11

Worcester and the End of the First Covenanter War

Cromwell was quick to take advantage of his victory. Moving forward from Dunbar, he took possession of Leith and the rest of Leslie's old defensive line. Edinburgh was also occupied, although the castle managed to hold out for some months afterwards under the leadership of Walter Dundas.

With his army still suffering from the after-effects of the previous campaign over the Braid Hills, Cromwell did not have the strength to push on in pursuit of Leslie and the shattered remnants of the Scottish army. This gave the Scottish general time to dig himself into a new defensive position close to Stirling. The English finally moved forward on 12 September, over roads so saturated with rain water that they would not carry the heavy guns. It took three days for them to reach Falkirk. Failing to persuade the Scots at Stirling to surrender, Cromwell returned to Edinburgh, establishing an advance base at Linlithgow on the way. Once back in the capital he settled down to await reinforcements.

News of Dunbar was warmly welcomed in London. Parliament ordered a campaign medal to be struck, with a depiction of Westminster on one side and a bust of Cromwell on the other. Inserted above the image of the Lord-General was the inscription 'Lord of Hosts', the battle cry of the army, taken from the 46th Psalm. For the first time the medal was to be awarded to all ranks, a practice not repeated until the Battle of Waterloo.

For the Scots, the period after the battle was a time for serious reflection; but not all reached the same conclusion. Archibald Strachan and the Gideonites believed that Dunbar only proved that the army had not been Godly enough. At Stirling, Strachan and his colleague, Colonel Gilbert Ker and Lieutenant-Colonel Robert Halket, had no hesitation in laying all the blame on Leslie. He was, in their view, an incompetent, graceless man, to whom God would give no success. These men were no ordinary soldiers; for they represented the Western Association, a union of the strongest of the Whig counties, modelled on the English Eastern Association. Originally set up in the wake of the Whiggamore Raid, the Western Association was revived earlier in the summer, to serve both as a recruiting ground and as the conscience of the Revolution. Causing too much dissension in Stirling, Strachan and his fellow Whigs were sent home to raise fresh forces. But the political divisions they raised were to have a far greater impact than their army.

In contrast to the Whigs, there were others who took a view, perhaps best summarised by John Nicoll;

> ...befoir this airmy wes routtit, thair wes much bussiness maid anent the purging of the Scottis airmy of malignantis be the space of many dayis...evin the nycht befoir the feght, our Scottis leaders wer in purging the Scottis airmy, as gif thair haid bene no danger!

As things turned out, Dunbar was the beginning of the end for the Kirk Party and the pretence that the war was between Presbyterians and Independents. Patriotism, never entirely absent, began to revive, unifying Scots of all shades of opinion in an effort to rid themselves of an ancient enemy. Even the western Whigs, with one or two exceptions, were not willing to consider a peace with the English, so long as their troops remained on Scottish soil, thus frustrating all Cromwell's efforts to build up a puritan fifth column.

To balance the Whigs in the south west, the royalists in the north east began to make their own recovery, under the leadership of Atholl, Huntly, Seaforth and John Middleton. So, by October 1650, there were four armies in Scotland: Leslie at Stirling, Strachan and the Whigs at Dumfries, Cromwell at Edinburgh and the royalists in Angus and Atholl. If the Scots were to have any hope of resisting the further advance of Cromwell, then it was vital that all parties unite; but the Act of Classes and the zealotry of the westerners made this a difficult prospect.

For Charles, still an important but powerless figure, there were some alarming features to these developments. Shortly after Dunbar he had been told by Robert Douglas, a moderator of the General Assembly, that the defeat had been due to the anger of God at the royal family. This was bad enough; but he was now seriously afraid that he might fall captive to the Strachan faction, who by early October had managed to gather a sizeable force of

4,000 men, at least equal to the 'official' army at Stirling. Fearing that these extremists intended to advance on his headquarters at Perth, with a view to handing him over to Cromwell, Charles made arrangements to join the northern royalists. On 4 October he rode out of Perth with a small bodyguard, pretending to go on a hunting trip. As soon as he was clear of the town he hurried westwards towards Dundee, hoping to link up with the Earl of Airlie and his son Lord Ogilvie, the old companions of Montrose. But the whole scheme went wildly wrong; and after an uncomfortable night in a filthy hut in the Grampians, Charles was only too pleased to be escorted back to Perth by two officers who managed to catch up with him.

This comic opera incident, known as 'The Start', had important political repercussions, leading directly to the eclipse of the Kirk Party and, in time, to the first serious split within the Covenanter Church. Argyll and some of his more moderate colleagues were seriously alarmed by the implications of a union between Charles and the northern opposition. To prevent any repetition, they decided to let the King have a taste of real power by inviting him to attend meetings of the Committee of Estates. Arrangements were also made for his coronation, scheduled to take place on 1 January 1651.

Reports of Charles' attempted flight greatly increased the Western Association's suspicions of the 'Covenanted' King. Even before The Start, Strachan, with the aid of Patrick Gillespie, a minister, had written a Remonstrance, saying the insincerity of the King and his preference for the company of malignants had brought God's judgement down on Scotland. On 17 October a second Remonstrance was drawn up at Dumfries with the assistance of Warriston, even more critical of both King and Parliament. In both of these documents, addressed to the Committee of Estates, the Westerners declared that they would not fight for the King until such time as they were convinced of his commitment to the Covenant. They made a further declaration, presumably intended for the ears of Cromwell, that they would not take part in any attempt to impose Charles on the English, although they remained implacably hostile to sectaries, as well as malignants. The Remonstrance, in effect, was a kind of declaration of independence by the Whigs.

Ever since the Engagement, a majority of the nobility had opposed the more extreme Covenanters, who had maintained their hold on power by an axis between an aristocratic rump headed by Argyll and the Covenanter middle classes, most typically represented by Warriston. The Western Remonstrance broke this axis. Argyll was furious at this evidence of desertion in the face of a great national danger. In spite of opposition from Warriston, his erstwhile ally, and some of the less compromising ministers, headed by James Guthrie, he succeeded in having the Remonstrance condemned by the Committee of Estates and, even more significantly, by the Commission of the General Assembly. This first division in the Covenanter church was shortly to harden into a schism.

Charles' botched escape attempt did little to weaken the resolve of the northern royalists. In obvious contrast to the Whigs, they adopted a purely patriotic stance. At Forfar on 26 October they drew up bond, a copy of which was sent to David Leslie. In this the signatories referred to;

> ...a deepe sense of the sade condition this our native kingdome of Scotland is in, by a prewailling armey of sectaries, quho having murthered our lait king, and overturned religione and govuerniment in our nighboure kingdomes of England and Ireland, hath invaded this kingdome, and are in a way...to reduce the quoll to a province...

The signatories of the Forfar Bond were placing commitment to the nation above commitment to the Covenant, a position hardly likely to appeal to Warriston, Guthrie and Strachan. But they were also quite prepared to resort to hard knocks, as well as soft words. A few days before the Forfar Bond was concluded, Sir David Ogilvie, a younger son of Airlie, launched a surprise night attack against the government regiment of Sir John Brown at Newtyle, killing four and taking twenty prisoner. Leslie sent off a stronger force in pursuit; but, after the intervention of Charles, the Committee of Estates, opening up itself to the need for unity, issued a promise of pardon and indemnity for the northerners. These terms were accepted at a meeting with Leslie in Strathbogie on 4 November. With the troubles in the north now settled, the position of the rebel Western Association became ever more vital.

Cromwell kept a close watch on all of these developments. So far, and despite his magnificent victory at Dunbar, the war in Scotland had been a disappointment. He had come to Scotland, so says Robert Baillie, believing he would have a quicker conquest than any of the English Kings. But the country had not collapsed, and it looked as if the war was going to drag on into the new year. His army, despite reinforcement, was seriously overstretched. Edinburgh Castle was an awkward problem, defying the best efforts of all Cromwell's gunners and military engineers. Still worse, from October bands of royalist partisans began to appear in the area occupied by the English in the south east. These men, know as Moss Troopers or Tories – a term borrowed from the wars in Ireland, supplying the second great political label of British history – were soon a serious threat to English security in Scotland. Operating in small bands from old medieval castles like Borthwick, Tantallon and Dirleton, they fell on stragglers, ambushed messengers, threatened communications and gathered military intelligence. The most effective groups were led by a German mercenary by the name of Captain Augustine Hoffman, who by November 1650 was based in the area of the Soutra and Pentland Hills, and by the Scotsman, Sandy Ker. Faced with this novel threat, Cromwell, like many military commanders since, issued warnings of dire reprisals against all who assisted the partisans.

For Cromwell, the key to this complex situation lay in the south west. Not only did the Whigs of the Western Association occupy a vital strategic position across his flank, but they also offered the best prospect of political collaboration. On the one hand he took precautions to treat the Association as a military threat, while on the other opening up a friendly correspondence with Strachan and some of the others. Troops under Whalley and Hacker were concentrated at Carlisle, while Cromwell made a progress across towards Glasgow in mid October. To create a good impression amongst the Westerners, his troops were instructed to be on their best behaviour. But neither the correspondence nor his good intentions produced the desired results, beyond the defection of Archibald Strachan. Now under the military leadership of Gilbert Ker, the Western Association remained defiant. With insufficient strength to hold Glasgow, Cromwell marched back to Edinburgh, still hoping until mid November for some accommodation with his 'natural allies' in Scotland.

Back in the east, the English army began a series of operations to reduce the strongholds used by the Moss Troopers. Newbattle Abbey was taken by 21 October, and Dalkeith Castle a week later.

George Monk, fast acquiring a reputation as an artillery expert, was sent to attack Dirleton Castle, held by a band commanded by one Captain Watt; but his artillery shells merely bounced off the thick medieval walls. He returned again in November, this time armed with two mortars, just recently arrived from Hull. Monk was now able to lob his shells over the walls into the soft interior of the castle. Against this the Moss Troopers had no answer; so, after the forth mortar shot, they surrendered. Surprisingly, in view of their unconventional form of warfare, these men were all spared, with the exception of Captain Watt, who was placed in front of a firing squad. One by one other strongholds fell, until Tantallon Castle, standing in defiant majesty on the East Lothian coast, held out alone.

By now the government in Perth had reached the end of its patience with the obstinate Western Association. So far the 4,000 troops at Ker's disposal had accomplished nothing of any military value, compared with the partisans operating in the east. When Cromwell himself moved to take Borthwick Castle, Ker was ordered to hurry to its relief. He refused to move, claiming he had not the strength, and Borthwick duly fell to the English on 22 November, increasing their hold on the Lothians. In frustration the Committee of Estates at once dispatched Colonel Robert Montgomery with 3,000 men to take over command of the western army from Ker. Montgomery was a good choice for the task. Coming from a family with impeccable Covenanter associations, it was he who had sparked off the Whiggamore Raid in August 1648. Now of a more moderate outlook, he could, as the son of the Earl of Eglinton, still expect to command much support in the area. But Cromwell had made his own plans to deal with the threat in the west; and Ker, anxious to preserve some of his credibility, walked, as if blindfolded, right into a trap.

Cromwell had decided to end the stalemate in the west by military force. Ker was at Rutherglen with a large party of cavalry and dragoons. Cromwell left Edinburgh on 27 November with eight regiments of cavalry, while Lambert, with an additional force, approached the Clyde Valley from the south east. The following day the soldiers from Edinburgh came across the Whigs, on the opposite bank of the Clyde at Bothwell Brig. Ker had taken the precaution of fortifying the old bridge against attack. Cromwell immediately saw that the enemy position was too strong to be forced, and the river too swollen to be forded elsewhere. As Lambert had not yet arrived, he decided the prudent thing to do was to retire back to the east. Lambert, in the meantime, advancing quickly from the south, had managed to ford the Clyde by its more manageable upper reaches, and then across an unguarded bridge on the Avon Water, taking possession of the town of Hamilton on 30 November.

It was vital that this bridgehead should be destroyed before the English consolidated their hold on the western counties. Ker hoped for a quick success, like Balvenie or Carbisdale, which would increase the bargaining power of the Western Association before Montgomery arrived, and remove some of the odium it had incurred by separating itself from the rest of the King's army. In the mistaken belief that Lambert had only a modest sized force, Ker decided to dislodge him from Hamilton in a surprise night attack. Unfortunately for him, the night of 30 November/1 December was bright with moonlight and the ground hardened by frost. At midnight the English pickets picked up the distant rumble made by the hoofs of the approaching Scottish horsemen. Forewarned, Lambert withdrew his guards from the moor outside the town, and prepared to draw the enemy into a trap. Ker's advance units under Colonel William Ralston were allowed to ride into Hamilton unopposed. Once amongst the streets, with their ability to manoeuvre greatly restricted, the Scots were attacked by a party of English soldiers near the Tolbooth. The Moon had now set, and the confused street battle that followed was punctuated only by pistol light. Bit by bit, the Scots managed to master the situation, forcing the enemy to take cover in the houses. Ralston now believed, mistakenly, that he was in control of the town.

While the street battle was underway, Ker had arrived on the outskirts of Hamilton with his remaining regiments on the western bank of the Cadzow Burn. After some initial reluctance to commit his troops to a battle amongst the houses, he was encouraged to move forward by reports of Ralston's success. As the Scots' horse splashed through the waters of the burn, and then up the eastern bank, they were surprised in a sudden attack by a large party of Ironside cavalry, emerging out of the darkness. Ker, expecting to create a trap, had ridden right into one. He and his men did their best to fight back; but, caught off balance by superior forces, they gave way. The regiment commanded by Robert Halket was routed, but Ker fought a fierce rearguard action until many of his men were killed or wounded. Ker himself had his horse shot from under him, and was taken prisoner, with his hand almost severed from his wrist. The fugitives from the battle were pursued as far as Ayr.

Ralston, meanwhile, realising just how illusory his victory had been, was faced with a renewed attack. In desperation, he and his men tried to cut their way out. Lord Sommerville described the fight;

> Most of the men's fyre being spent in the night service, they were necessitat now to dispute it with ther swords, which they did very gallantlie...but to ther great losse, being felled with the enemies shott, and cutt doune with the multitude of ther swords, which in a manner surrounded them, ther was the greatest slaughter imaginable...

Almost sixty men were killed as the rest, broken in the struggle, fled out of the town. After the Battle of Hamilton the Western Association ceased to exist. Ker's defeat greatly improved Cromwell's strategic position in southern Scotland; but it also had the paradoxical effect of improving the political position of the Scottish government. With the western Whigs out of the reckoning, there was nothing in the way of a general reconciliation, now desired by most Scots. Certainly, James Turner made no secret of his own pleasure at the defeat of the extreme Covenanters;

> ...if Lambert had not, by good fortune to us all, beaten Colonell Ker at Hammiltoun, I beleeve the King had beene just as safe at St Johnston (Perth), as his father was at Westminster.

But the ideals could not be so easily dispelled; and the Western Association, albeit in a shadowy form, was a cause of much trouble for Turner after the Restoration.

If the passing of the Whigs was a matter of no great regret in Perth, it was followed soon after by a more serious setback. For as long as Edinburgh Castle held out, Cromwell could not devote his full attention to prosecuting the war in the north. Government concern for the stronghold was the occasion for one of Captain Hoffman's most daring exploits. Crossing in secret from Fife with 120 horsemen, he bluffed his way into the city at Canongate. Galloping up the High Street, he cut through the English troops, bringing reinforcements and fresh supplies to the beleaguered garrison. With the enemy still reeling from this totally unexpected incursion, Hoffman astonished them still further by riding back out again with equal ease half an hour later, taking five prisoners on the way. Eighty of Cromwell's men were left lying dead behind him. In fury the Lord-General wrote to Leslie, complaining of 'barbarism and inhuman acts', and demanding action against Hoffman. Leslie responded by promoting him to the rank of colonel. But even while the heroic Hoffman was engaged on his morale boosting raid, the Governor of the Castle, Walter Dundas, was negotiating surrender terms.

All the usual methods used to take the castle had failed: cannon shot made no impression against its formidable defences; incendiary shells lobed in by the mortars had been extinguished by the garrison; and even the miners, brought from the east of Scotland and Derbyshire, had been unable to cut their way through the rock. During the Marian civil wars in the previous century, the then governor, Sir William Kirkcaldy of Grange, had managed to hold out for three years. It's unlikely Dundas would have been able to resist for quite so long; but he had plenty of fresh water, ammunition and several months supply of food. Unfortunately, what he did not have was the will to fight. Politically, he was very much in the same mould as Archibald Strachan, more concerned by the presence of 'malignants' around the King, than with the defence of his country. It has been suggested that Strachan, who was now in Cromwell's camp, may have helped to persuade him to surrender. This is not impossible, but the evidence is not conclusive. What is certainly true is that he opened the gates to the enemy on 24 December, with no pressing military reason for doing so. For this betrayal of the trust placed in him, Dundas was declared to be a traitor by Parliament and excommunicated by the Kirk. Cromwell was delighted; for this removed the last significant obstacle in southern Scotland. All of the Castle ordnance fell into his hands, including 'The great Iron Murderer called Muckle Megg.'

Just over a week later the leading figures in church and state gathered for the coronation of Charles II at Scone, a site rich in history, where his ancestors had been similarly honoured in ages past. Argyll, as the senior Scottish nobleman, placed the crown on the King's head, in what was to be his last significant political act. It's quite likely that the general mood was more sombre than an occasion like this would normally have warranted. Robert Baillie noted his own gloomy observation of the times;

I cannot be denyed but our miseries and dangers of ruine are greater nor for many ages have been; a potent victorious enemy master of our seas, and for some good time of the best part of our land; our standing forces against this immanent invasion, few weak, inconsiderable; our Kirk, State, Armie, full of divisions and jealousies; the body of our people be-south Forth spoyled, and near starveing; they be-north Forth extreamlie ill used by a handful of our owne; many inclyning to treat and agree with Cromwell, without care either of King or Covenant; none of our neighbours called upon by us are willing to give us any help, though called. What the end shall be, the Lord knows. Many are ready to faint with discouragement and despaire...

What most people would agree on was the need for a new national army. Leslie had recovered well from Dunbar, and was entrenched almost as strongly at Stirling as he had been at Edinburgh the previous summer. Nevertheless, he was seriously short of men, and could be expected to do little beyond minimal defensive operations. But the Act of Classes was a major obstacle to the raising of a fresh force, especially in the Highlands and the north east, the last major recruiting grounds and the home of many royalists and former Engagers. Even the Kirk was aware of this. On 14 December 1650, the Commission of Assembly, under pressure from the government, passed an important resolution;

We cannot be against the raising of all fensible persons in the land, and permitting them to fight against this enemy for the defence of the Kingdom, except such as are excommunicated, forfaulted, notoriously profane, or flagitious...

This first Resolution was a significant breach in the Act of Classes; it was also a beginning of a major breach in the Church of Scotland itself. Those sympathetic to the Whig Remonstrance of October immediately protested against a measure, which would allow malignants and other ungodly elements into the army. The ministers who accepted the Resolution were in a clear majority; but the 'Protesters', headed by men like James Guthrie and Patrick Gillespie, formed an active and troublesome minority, eventually destroying the unity of the Kirk. The Covenanter movement, so impressive in 1638, was steadily disintegrating.

Soon after the first resolution was passed over twenty former Engagers, one of whom was John Middleton, applied to rejoin the army. His request was granted; but only after he dressed himself in sackcloth and made public repentance of his sins at Dundee. For this humiliation, Middleton was one day to exact his own slow revenge.

A second resolution was passed by the Commission in March 1651; and the following June Parliament finally repealed the Act of Classes. Perhaps no one worked towards this goal more than Argyll, even though it meant the end of his political influence. Ever since The Start and the Remonstrance, he had been steadily separating himself from the Whiggamore extremists. Distrusted by most of his fellow peers, he was now resented by many of his former middle class allies. In a last attempt to preserve his declining influence, he tried to persuade Charles to marry his daughter, Lady Ann Campbell, with no success. By July it was written of him that he 'is gone down the winde; nobody takes any notice of him.' After warning against the planned invasion of England, he retired back to Inverary, more hated by the King than he ever realised.

For Cromwell, the coronation of Charles and the passing of the Resolutions, marked an important change in the character of the war. The enemy were ceasing to argue over fine points of doctrine and were making it 'not a religious war, but a national quarrel.' Unable to push past Leslie's defences at Stirling, or to risk an advance into the uncertain interior far away from his supply bases, it was clear to the Englishman that Fife was now the key to the campaign. Once across the Forth, the English would be able to march on Perth and cut the Scots' lines of communication with the northern hinterland, now essential for both supplies and recruits. On 18 January 1651 an attempted crossing was made by a party under the leadership of George Monk, intending to capture the port of Burntisland. But before he could land, the expedition was spotted and the men of Fife summoned to the defence of their shores by warning beacons. Faced with an effective enemy bombardment, coupled with choppy seas, Monk had to abandon the enterprise. Nothing further was attempted after Cromwell, returning from another abortive probe into central Scotland, fell seriously ill from the effects of exposure in early February.

While Cromwell lay inactive at Edinburgh, the Moss Troopers

became ever more troublesome. Under the direction of Colonel Robert Montgomery, the partisans penetrated far into Clydesdale, assisted by the local people. Soon the English were beginning to lose their precarious hold over large parts of the south west. Both Dumfries and Hamilton had to be abandoned by the early summer. In the east, however, the position improved steadily. Hume Castle was taken in February, from a governor who had defied the English in the old spirit of the Border wars. Soon after, Monk moved for a final reckoning with Tantallon. After a sustained combination of cannon and mortar fire, as well as a bombardment from nearby English warships, the Moss Troopers surrendered on 21 February. This was followed a few days later by the capture of Fast Castle, further down the Berwickshire coast. Next month he also took Blackness Castle, on the shores of the Forth to the west of Edinburgh, an important preliminary to the planned landing in Fife. Monk's use of artillery was so skilful that he was appointed Lieutenant-General of Ordnance on 6 May.

Cromwell did not fully recover from his illness until June. By this time, Leslie had pushed steadily from the north, retaking Falkirk and fortifying Callander House. Colonel Hoffman even managed to push as far as the western Border, only to be defeated by a party of English troops. On 28 June the whole of the Scots army moved forward to a new position just south of Stirling at Torwood. In response, Cromwell moved to his old camp in the Braid Hills, and then on to Linlithgow, hoping to draw the enemy into battle. Leslie, however, had still not recovered from the shock of Dunbar, and held to his old Fabian tactics. Falling back to Edinburgh, Cromwell then attempted another flanking probe to the west. Passing through Shotts and the village of Shettelston, he occupied Glasgow once more. Newark castle on the opposite side of the Clyde estuary from Dumbarton was taken, and Lambert sent off on a reconnaissance to the west of Leslie's position; but with the enemy making no counter move, all of this simply emphasised the importance of crossing over to Fife. On the way back east the army stormed Callander House, still failing to draw the Scots from their armoured shell.

A seaborne invasion of Fife was a tricky operation. Early in the year the Council of State in England had ordered the construction of special flat bottomed boats, which arrived at Leith in April. While this would enable men and horses to be ferried in close to the northern shore, it would take time for the army to land in sufficient strength to fight off a counter attack. Leslie could easily move sufficient forces from Torwood to throw the invaders back into the sea. Or, alternatively, he could wait for enough of the Englishmen to cross to Fife before falling on the weakened remnant at Edinburgh, and then sweep south towards England. This was a considerable risk; but the only alternative was another indecisive winter of war, which neither the Lord-General nor his men can have viewed with any enthusiasm.

The Firth was to be crossed at the narrowest point, between North and South Queensferry, spanned today by the road and rail bridges. A landing here offered another advantage, besides speed: North Queensferry stands on a narrow peninsula, which offered good prospects of building up a defensive bridgehead against an enemy attack. After the local defences were softened up by a bombardment of the forts at Inchgarvie, Burntisland and Ferryhill, Colonel Overton led an assault party across on the night of 16/17 July, landing on the eastern side of the Ferry Peninsula at Inverkeithing Bay. By the morning almost 2,000 troops were on the northern shore of the Forth, and Overton at once set about constructing entrenchments. Reinforcements were sent across with Lambert two days later, bringing the New Model Army's strength up to about 4,500 men by the morning of 20 July.

No sooner had the Scots heard of the landing than a force of about 4,000 was detached from the main army to counter the threat. This detachment was placed under the command of Sir John Brown of Fordell and Lieutenant-General Holburne. While most of these troops had little military experience, there was a hard core of professional soldiers, including some Borderers under Walter Scott, parties led by Colonel Augustine Hoffman and Colonel Colin Pitscottie, and the regiments of Lord Balcarres and Lord Brechin. They were ordered to do no more than prevent the English breaking out of their bridgehead into the heart of Fife.

It's possible that Cromwell at first saw the Fife operation as no more than a diversion, intended to unlock the Scots' position at Stirling. While the landings were taking place he approached Torwood with the rest of the army. Seeing Leslie march off in support of Brown, he then moved quickly across the hills, through Bannockburn and on to the vacated camp. A little to the north the Lord-General found his further progress blocked by the enemy, now occupying a strong position in the King's Park. Unable to make any headway, Cromwell withdrew by nightfall, allowing the Scots back into Torwood. It was now up to Lambert.

The Ferry Peninsula is separated from the rest of Fife by a narrow isthmus, about a quarter of a mile wide. From the low-lying land of the isthmus and the surrounding shore, the centre is dominated by the Ferry Hills, rising to two hundred and forty feet above sea level. Beyond the Peninsula, to the north west, the ground rises up again to Castland Hill and its neighbour Meickle Hill, between which the road runs inland through a narrow valley to Dunfermline. These two hills also command the coastal route to Rosyth and the road running eastwards from the village of Inverkeithing. If the Scots occupied this position it would be impossible for the English to make any forward move. The Scots' army advanced through these hills on the 20th; but for reasons that are not entirely clear, Brown and Holburne were attracted down from the heights on to the lower ground close to the isthmus, looking across to the English entrenchments on the Ferry Hills.

Realising the danger they had placed themselves in, the Scots began to wheel as if to move back slightly on to the higher ground. Lambert at once sent John Oakey and his dragoons forward to attack their rear. Faced with this threat, Brown and Holburne had no choice but to form a line of battle on the Whins, three eminences rolling outwards from Castland and Meickle towards Inverkeithing Bay, and across the valley in the direction of Rosyth Castle. Lambert made his own battle dispositions. The ground on the left was difficult and rocky, so he concentrated his greatest strength on the right: his own cavalry regiment, two troops of dragoons and two troops of Lydcot's horse, all under the command of John Oakey. His own infantry were placed in the centre, and Colonel Daniel's infantry regiment on the left, with the remaining four troops of Oakey's dragoons and two of Lydcot's, all commanded by the latter. The remainder of the infantry formed a reserve line on the broken ground to the rear under Robert Overton.

Lambert waited, expecting to be attacked at any moment; but for an hour and a half nothing happened. By now he received news that Cromwell had fallen back on Linlithgow, and that the enemy might at any time receive reinforcements. This was the moment to act. His army moved forward, keeping formation as it squeezed through the bottleneck of the isthmus. The Scots' lancers in the valley swept downwards towards Lydcot's wing, cutting through the thin ranks with ease. Seeing the danger, Lambert responded by swinging round his infantry reserve, supported by a troop of horse, which thrust into the flank of the advancing Scots before they were able to change front. Against the fire of the musketeers and the long reach of the English pikemen, the lancers had no chance. Within a quarter of an hour the fight on this side of the field was over.

Lambert was now free to concentrate on attacking the main part of the Scottish army around the Whins. Against the ferocious discipline of the New Model Army, the green Scottish recruits had little chance. General Holburne was one of the first to run. The infantry reserves and portion of the cavalry fled with him, leaving Brown to face the onslaught of the enemy right with only 200 horse and two battalions of infantry. He was completely overwhelmed. Lambert's men occupied the heights, and the Scots were driven back to the level ground between Hillfield and Pitreavie. Here, in one of the most heroic episodes of the Battle of Inverkeithing, the MacLeans of Mull, surrounded by superior enemy forces, fought to the death in defence of their chief. They began the battle with 500 men; only 40 survived. In all 2,000 men died at Inverkeithing and the pursuit that followed, and 1,400 were taken prisoner. Only 1,000 made it back to Stirling. Four days later, Cromwell crossed to Fife in person. For him, the victory was 'an unspeakable mercy.'

Although far smaller than Dunbar, the Battle of Inverkeithing was the decisive encounter of Cromwell's Scottish war. It ended a long strategic deadlock, giving the English command of the plains of Fife and the north east. With his supply lines now threatened, Leslie's second defensive campaign was at an end. If the English managed to take Perth, the position at Stirling would no longer be tenable. For Leslie the choice was now starkly simple: he had to run or fight. Some attempt was made to recover the situation before it deteriorated any further. After receiving news of the disaster, the army began the slow move over Stirling Bridge towards Lambert. Cromwell at once edged forward from Linlithgow. Rather than risk being caught in the open between two enemy armies, Leslie retreated backwards, having gone no more than five or six miles. No sooner had he reached his original lines than he found Cromwell at Bannockburn, offering battle. Leslie declined. No Scot would ever wish for a rematch on that historic field. As for Holburne, he was tried for desertion, but acquitted. However, feeling against him was so strong that he was forced to resign his command.

Cromwell was quick to exploit the advantage opened up by Lambert. He returned from Linlithgow. Soon the bulk of his army crossed to Fife. On 29 July Burntisland fell, and the army moved rapidly across country to Perth, the headquarters of the Scottish government. Leslie was completely outmanoeuvred. By shifting the thrust of his offensive to the northern shore of the Forth, Cromwell deliberately dropped his guard in southern Scotland. He reckoned that Charles could not resist the lure of a march into England; and once into the open the enemy could be destroyed.

The royal council obliged the Lord-General by walking right into his trap. Leslie was not keen to abandon Scotland while she was occupied by English troops; but, with Charles now firmly in the ascent, he was a figure of decreasing importance. The King's English counsellors, headed by the Duke of Buckingham, were all confident that he would be able to rouse the old Cavalier party once across the Border. Besides, with the bulk of the New Model in Scotland, the army would only have to face county militias and newly raised regiments. Charles, tired of the rigours of Scotland, responded eagerly. With Cromwell poised to take Perth, the army moved southwards from Stirling on 31 July; by 6 August it crossed the Border at Carlisle. Charles was proclaimed King of England, and soon after renewed his commitment to the Covenants. He was also effective commander of his own army; for while Leslie accompanied him, he had no real enthusiasm for the endeavour.

Cromwell was fully prepared. Instructions had been sent to Major General Thomas Harrison to gather all available forces and shadow the enemy. After the surrender of Perth on 2 August, Lambert was sent on with the cavalry to join Harrison, while Cromwell followed with the rest of the army. At Leith on 4 August he wrote to steady the courage of the Council of State in London, understandably nervous at the descent of a Scottish army into England;

I do appreciate that if he goes for England, being some few days march before us, it will trouble some men's thoughts, and may occasion some inconveniences; of which I hope we are deeply sensible, and have, and I trust shall be, as diligent to prevent as any; and indeed this is our comfort, that in simplicity of heart as to God, we have done to the best of our judgements, knowing that if some issue were not put to this business, it would occasion another winter's war, to the ruin of your soldiery, for whom the Scots are too hard in respect of enduring the winter difficulties of this country, and been under the endless expense of the treasury of England in prosecuting this war. It may be supposed we might have kept the enemy from this, by interposing between him and England; which I truly believe we might; but how to remove him out of this place, without doing what we have now done, unless we had a commanding army on both sides of the river of Forth, is not clear to us...

The invasion of 1651 was far better organised than that of 1648. No plundering was allowed, and the army moved quickly to stop it becoming too great a burden on the local people. But there was a notable lack of enthusiasm for the royal cause, backed up by what was perceived to be a foreign army. Official propaganda did its best to play up anti-Scottish feeling. *Mercurius Politicus*, the official newspaper, detailed the history of Scottish invasions of England, going right back to that of Malcolm III in 1071. It said that anyone so un-English as to join Charles, who it only ever described as King of Scots, should be stoned. Many responded to the appeal to arms, including Sir Thomas Fairfax, who came out of retirement to gather the Yorkshire militia. Charles Fleetwood prepared to defend London. The Duke of Hamilton, perhaps inspired by the gloomy fate of his brother who took the same route through Lancashire, noted his feelings on the ill judged enterprise at Penrith on 8 August;

...we are all now laughing at the ridiculousness of our situation. We have quit Scotland, being scarce able to hold it; and yet we grasp at all, and nothing but all will satisfy us, or to lose all. I confess I cannot tell you whether our hopes or fears are greatest; but we have one stout argument, despair; for we must either stoutly fight it, or die.

By 15 August Charles was at Wigan, with advance parties riding ahead towards the bridge over the Mersey at Warrington, where Baillie had made his futile stand in 1648. By now Lambert and Harrison had joined up, and rode to assist Colonel Birch and the Cheshire militia, who were attempting to bar further Scots progress to the south. With 6,000 cavalry and 3,000 foot, the Commonwealth forces on the southern bank of the Mersey were not much weaker than their opponents; but the proportion of foot was too low in comparison with horse, and Cromwell had made it clear that no battle was to be risked without more infantry. Besides, the country south of Warrington Bridge was heavily enclosed, and therefore not suited to cavalry. Only one company of foot was left on the bridge. When Charles attacked the following day he managed to force the passage. The royal cavalry then set off in pursuit of the enemy, only to be checked two or three times in the narrow lanes by Colonel Rich, commanding the rear guard. Lambert and Harrison withdrew through Knutsford Heath to Coventry, where they remained, poised on the enemy flank, awaiting the arrival of Cromwell.

On the day of the fight at Warrington, Cromwell and the infantry reached Catterick in Yorkshire, having averaged a march of twenty miles a day. He had left George Monk behind with four regiments of horse and three of foot to complete the conquest of Scotland. In view of the task he had before him, Monk was also left with most of the artillery. Cromwell's understanding of his subordinates was acute. Lambert, his second-in-command, would normally have been expected to remain behind in Scotland to take charge of the English forces. But Lambert was essentially a field campaigner, a cavalry general of dash and brilliance. Monk, on the other hand. was deliberate and cautious; a skilled technician and artilleryman, with a slightly heavier touch than his younger colleague, best left to deal with the engineering problems of reducing castles and fortified towns. Both men combined aspects of Cromwell's own personality as a soldier; and both, in their own individual ways, were to make important contributions to the Lord-General's victory.

For Charles, the march into England was a bitter disappointment, much as it was to his grandnephew and namesake, who was to follow the same path almost a hundred years later. Buckingham's optimistic forecasts were wrong: few recruits came to join the army; and those who did were poorly armed. The only significant addition was the Earl of Derby, who was left behind to recruit in Lancashire, while the rest of the army crossed the Mersey. Cromwell, advancing rapidly through

214

Yorkshire, sent orders for Colonel Robert Lilburne, who was with Lambert and Harrison, to return with his regiment to Lancashire to prevent Derby using the county as a recruiting base.

Still hoping for recruits from the old loyalist heartlands of western England and Wales, Charles continued on a straight southern route, rather than making an attempt on London. But the frustrations continued. The governor of Shrewsbury not only refused to surrender, but offensively addressed his reply to Charles not as King, or even as Prince of Wales, but only as the commander-in-chief of the Scottish army. It was with no high hopes that the army entered the town of Worcester on 22 August, where the exhausted troops were finally allowed to rest. Charles now had 16,000 men, mostly Scots. The day after the arrival at Worcester a summons was sent out for all loyal subjects between the ages of sixteen and sixty to come and join the King: scarcely a man responded. From Worcester there was nowhere else to go. Charles dug in to await the inevitable onslaught.

Two days after Charles reached Worcester, Cromwell joined Lambert and Harrison at Warwick. Three days later, their combined forces met with Fleetwood's, advancing westwards from London. They now had 30,000 troops, almost twice the number of their opponents, with more recruits arriving all the time. Perhaps for the first time in his career, Cromwell had the strength and time to deal with his opponents at leisure. Like some huge cat, the army of the Commonwealth made its way towards the royalist mouse trapped at Worcester.

Charles used his time wisely, securing his position at Worcester. The River Severn runs through the town, providing a defensive barrier to the north and south. But most of Worcester lay on the east bank of the river, the direction of the enemy approach. To improve the situation, the crumbling fortifications were hurriedly repaired. New earthworks were thrown up outside the walls, and the vulnerable city gates were strengthened. The north or Foregate was blocked up, leaving St Martin's Gate as the only exit here. Opposite the wooded slope of Red Hill, overlooking the walls from the south east, a large star fortress by the name of Fort Royal was constructed, connected to the other defences by an earthen rampart, close to the Sidbury Gate on the south side of the town.

Attempts were also made to improve the security of Worcester by blocking any approach from the south and north by the west

215

bank of the Severn. Two miles to the south of the city, the Severn is joined from the west by the River Teame, a swift flowing river some ten yards wide with very steep banks. It can only be crossed by the bridges at Powick and Bransford, both of which were destroyed, as was the bridge over the Severn at Bewdley, fifteen miles to the north of the city, and the bridge at Upton, six miles to the south. Just how necessary all of this was, was underlined when Derby arrived at Worcester with news that the Lancashire royalists had been defeated by Lilburne at Wigan on 25 August. Only the Scots stood between Charles and disaster.

Charles had divided the army into two main parts: the largest was kept at Worcester to defend the walls and fortifications, while the smaller was positioned in the meadows on the arc of land formed by the junction of the Severn and the Teame, to defend the southern flank. A smaller body was left at the bridge of Upton to keep a watch for the enemy. Unfortunately, for the eventual fate of the whole army, this party was negligent in two respects: they failed to keep an adequate watch, and they left a single plank across the ruined arches of the bridge. Never slow to spot a weakness, Cromwell sent Lambert on 28 August to attempt to force the southern passage across to the west bank of the Severn.

Lambert arrived at Upton before dawn on 29 August. No look out had been posted by the Scots, apparently in the mistaken belief that there were no enemy forces in the neighbourhood. Lambert picked a small shock part to make their way across the plank, suspended precariously above the deep waters of the Severn. Loaded down with their equipment, the men began to walk in slow single file with the sound of the river rushing in their ears from the gloomy light below. Overtaken by the fear of falling, all sat down and shuffled across on their backsides, a comic scene, as Lambert himself noted;

> They mounted it as though it was their wooden Pegasus, and so scrambled across to the opposite bank.

Once across, all made it safely to Upton; but now the hard part began. They barricaded themselves into the local church, where they were at once attacked by greatly superior enemy forces. Keeping up their fire on the enemy through the windows of the church, this small party provided a diversion, while the remainder of Lambert's horse crossed the Severn, partly by fording and partly by swimming. They formed up on the opposite bank, charging the Scots in the rear. Despite the surprise of this sudden attack, the Scots responded well, killing several enemy dragoons before giving way to a fresh assault. Back in their entrenchments they continued to hold the enemy off. But by now additional planks had been placed over the gap in the bridge, and Lambert's men were crossing in ever increasing numbers. Subject to ever more intense attacks, the royalists were badly discouraged when their commander, Edward Massey, an Englishman who held Gloucester for Parliament during the First Civil War, was badly wounded. After this the survivors retreated back to Worcester, leaving their baggage and wounded behind. Anxious to secure the position, Lambert did not order a pursuit. Word of the success was sent to Charles Fleetwood at Evesham, who at once sent reinforcements. Cromwell now commanded both banks of the Severn. The only obstacle to his onward march to Worcester was the River Teame.

The day after the fight at Upton there were 12,000 Commonwealth troops on the western bank of the Severn, with advance parties pushing northwards to Powick. With the jaws about to close the Council of State wrote to Monk in Scotland:

> The Scottish King's army with their King is now in Worcester, the Lord General with his army on one side of the river, and Lieutenant-General Fleetwood with another army on the other side of the river, ready to march from Upton (which bridge we have) towards the enemy.

The question now was how to cross the Teame and to ensure communications between both wings of the army on opposite banks of the Severn. On 29 August, on the hill overlooking Worcester, a war conference was held, where it was decided to construct boat bridges across both rivers. Once these were in place, Fleetwood would press his attack northwards towards St John's, a western suburb of Worcester, while Cromwell attacked Fort Royal and the town itself from the east. Forces could be transferred to either bank as the situation developed. To prevent any break out to the north, Lilburne took up a position at Bewdley. The trap was now set and ready to spring.

Lambert was detached to scour the river as far south as Gloucester for boats, and bring to the mouth of the Teame all he could find. To distract the Scots while this operation was underway, Cromwell's guns, under the cover of Perry Wood on

Red Hill, opened fire on Worcester. In an attempt to end this, the defenders launched a surprise night attack led by one Major Knox. But the enemy, forewarned by a spy in the town, were ready, and Knox met with an unexpectedly hot reception. Attempting to urge his men on, he leapt over a hedge, only to land on a stand of pikes, which killed him instantly. After this the royalists gave way, fleeing back to the town, having suffered heavy losses in the abortive attack.

By September 2 the bridge of boats was ready. Cromwell then gave orders for the general attack to begin the next day, the exact anniversary of the Battle of Dunbar, his lucky day. Fleetwood was to command the left, from where the main thrust was planned to come, and the Lord General the right. Cromwell would keep an eye on the city, and reinforce his left across the larger bridge of boats on the Severn: one was to be the sword and the other the shield.

Fleetwood decided to launch a two pronged attack: the first by Richard Dean against the Scots guarding the passage at Powick, where the river was fordable; and the second by Lambert across the smaller of the two boat bridges, positioned close to the mouth of the Teame. It was vital for the Scots to hold both of these attacks; for if either succeeded the position would be generally untenable. Powick was held by a detachment led by Robert Montgomery, and the second, consisting mostly of Highlanders under Colin Pittscottie, was placed on the meadows towards the Severn. Another force was held in reserve close to St, Johns, under command of Tam Dalyell of the Binns, a crusty old soldier who had served with Monro in Ireland. Hamilton was in command at Fort Royal, where the main body of the Scots was placed. Yet another detachment was at Castle Mound with Lord Rothes. Leslie and the bulk of the cavalry were at Pitchcroft, well away from the main fighting, ready to exploit any advantage.

Lambert got across the bridge, but his attack was soon bogged down in a ferocious fight with Pittscottie's Highlanders, who used the defensive cover of the thick hedges. Similarly, at Powick the Scots fought from hedge to hedge, with great determination. Charles watched their tough resistance from the vantage point of Worcester's cathedral tower. He came to Powick to encourage the troops there to hold on at all costs. With the Scots continuing to resist the attacks by both Dean and Lambert, Cromwell, on the opposite bank of the Severn, saw that the crisis had come.

Unless Fleetwood received assistance the battle might be lost. He decided to weaken his right wing on Red Hill to reinforce the left, leading three brigades over the bridge of boats, to take the Highlanders in the flank. Still fighting yard by yard, Pittscottie's men began to fall back to the north. Sensing that they were beginning to weaken, Lambert pressed even harder. The fighting retreat quickly degenerated into a rout, isolating the forces still fighting north of Powick. Here, too, Scots' resistance began to collapse, as the front units fell back in disorder on Dalyell's reserve. Panic spread as both men and horses raced back to St John's. Dalyell tried in vain to steady the line, as the retreat continued back to the illusory safety of Worcester.

From the Cathedral tower, Charles had kept up his watch on Cromwell. Seeing the enemy right on Red Hill being weakened in support of the left, he decided that his final opportunity had come. With Montgomery and Pittscottie fighting their defensive battle in the ground between the Teame and the Severn, he decided to lead an attack on Red Hill in person. With the support of Hamilton from Fort Royal, he charged out of the Sidbury Gate, catching the Commonwealth forces off balance, forcing them back from the hill. But the attack was not supported by Leslie, whose cavalry remained immobile at Pitchcroft. Word was brought to Cromwell, who returned back across the Severn. His arrival inspired the men on the right with renewed confidence, and they began a vigorous counter attack. In Perry Wood, Hamilton was running low on ammunition, as the enemy troops surged forward. After he fell mortally wounded, his column collapsed, fleeing back to the fort. This led to a general retreat all along the line. Pressing hard into the backs of their enemy, Cromwell's troops poured into the entrenchments around the city. The Essex militia took possession of Fort Royal, turning the guns on Worcester.

Now, from both the eastern and western banks of the Severn, the city streets filled with men from the beaten army. There was hopeless confusion at Sidbury Gate, where the passage was quickly choked with fugitives. Those who turned to fight off the pursuit were cut down. Some of the cavalry managed to rally in the High Street, only to be taken in the rear by Fleetwood, entering Worcester from St John's. Charles managed to escape out of the city, taking the route north out of St Martin's Gate, the last possible exit. Leslie had already ridden off, so the only resistance now was offered by the Earl of Rothes, Sir William Hammond and Colonel Drummond, who fought off repeated attacks at the Castle Mound, until offered surrender terms by Cromwell. By nightfall the Battle of Worcester was over. Over 3,000 men had been killed, and the rest were either prisoners or fugitives. The last great Covenanter army had been annihilated, and Cromwell had his supreme victory, his 'crowning mercy.'

After many adventures, and several close escapes, Charles made it back to the Continent, where he lived as an exile for almost nine years. His companions were not so lucky. Leslie and Lauderdale were both taken prisoner. So, too, was John Middleton, who eventually managed to escape, rejoining the King in Paris. Few made it back to Scotland; and even those who did, found that all organised resistance was almost at an end.

While the campaign in England had been underway, Monk went steadily about his work in Scotland. Assisted by Joachim Hane, a German engineer, his mortars had brought about the surrender of Stirling Castle on 13 August. On 25 August he crossed the Tay, making for Dundee, now crowded with refugees from Edinburgh and Stirling. The governor, Robert Lumsden, elated by false reports of a Scottish victory in England refused to surrender. On 1 September, just as Cromwell was closing in on Worcester, Monk's troops managed to breach the defences, killing 800, soldiers and civilians in the process, many in cold blood.

A few days before the Battle of Worcester, Colonel Alured captured most of the Committee of Estates and the Commission of the Assembly at Alyth in Perthshire; so the country lost its government and then its army. The captives included the old Earl of Leven, perhaps comparing present misfortunes with the vanished glories of 1640. Some places, notably Dunnotar Castle where the crown jewels had been taken for safety, held out to the spring of 1652; but for all practical purposes the first Covenanter war was over.

CHAPTER 12
Rullion Green – The Agony of the Covenant

Scotland was more completely conquered than at any time since the days of Edward I. But this time there was no William Wallace to come and save the pride of the nation. After seven years of almost continual warfare, the country was politically and economically exhausted. English military occupation was to be more complete than ever before, with large forts built at Inverness, Inverlochy, Perth, Leith and Ayr, as well as twenty smaller ones. At the beginning of 1652 the country was forcibly incorporated with England into a single republican Commonwealth. Of this it was written;

> As for the embodying of Scotland with England it will be as when the poor bird is embodied into the hawk that hath eaten it up.

The whole basis of a unified Presbyterian church was undermined when the Commonwealth authorities proclaimed a general policy of religious toleration for all; all that is, apart from Episcopalians and Catholics. For many of the nobility, sickened by the political arrogance of the Covenanter Kirk, this was not an unwelcome development. In the north, the old royalist party issued its own declaration against the 'bloodie and barbarous inconvenientis quhich hath alwayis accompanied the presbiteriall government.' When the Presbytery of Aberdeen tried to discipline Sir Alexander Irving of Drum, he simply appealed to Colonel Overton, the local military commander, who disallowed the proceedings.

With no Parliament to sanction the decisions of the General Assembly, the divisions in the Kirk between the Resolutioner majority and the Protester minority grew ever more bitter. It was the Protesters who kept alive the uncompromising spirit of 1638 and the Whiggamore Raid, refusing to accept the authority of the General Assemblies from 1651 onwards because they were dominated by the moderate majority. When, in July 1653, the Resolutioners and Protesters held rival Assemblies in Edinburgh, both were sent packing by Lieutenant-Colonel Cotterell and a party of English musketeers. No Assembly was to meet for the next thirty seven years.

Scotland was too weak and divided to offer any effective opposition to the Commonwealth; but the country did not readily submit to her subject status. In Kirkcudbrightshire, the Declaration of Union was rejected on the grounds that the execution of Charles I and the abolition of monarchy was contrary to the terms of the Solemn League and Covenant: brave words which made little practical difference. But the Highlands continued to be a source of trouble for Cromwell, as they had been for the Covenanters.

The Highlands were not completely subdued by the time the Anglo Dutch war broke out in 1652. Monk, who left Scotland in February because of illness, was appointed to a naval command, leaving Richard Dean to pacify the western Highlands, with forces barely adequate for the task. By June 1652, Charles had received news that a rising was planned in the Highlands. He appointed his fellow exile John Middleton to take charge of the loyalists; but Middleton fell ill, and temporary command passed to the Earl of Glencairn. This was hardly an inspiring choice, as Glencairn was a man with limited military experience, and with even less charisma. But he at least knew the country; and, as a Lowlander, he was expected raise the chiefs above their petty personal rivalries.

By the summer of 1653 the so called Glencairn Rising began in earnest, after the royal standard was raised at Killin on 27 July. The following month Glencairn arrived in person, and managed to recruit about 5,000 men, chiefly from the clans of Atholl and Lochaber. Even the Kirk showed signs of warming to this purely royalist endeavour, provoking the Commonwealth authorities into banning all prayers for the King. Argyll's son, Archibald Campbell, Lord Lorne, joined the rising, although he himself held aloof. Glencairn was no Montrose, and the rising failed to achieve anything of any substance; but hostility to the English was so widespread that parties of Moss Troopers were able to raid deep into the Lowlands, setting off small disturbances here and there. By November 1653 the gates of Edinburgh had to be closed at night, to prevent insurgents slipping into the town. The following month the troubles had spread even further south. Parties of armed men penetrated into Dumfriesshire and

Galloway, and within four miles of Berwick. Robert Lilburne, the military commander in Scotland, wrote to Cromwell in increasingly desperate terms, pleading for reinforcements.

Encouraging reports on the success of the rising reached Charles on the Continent. Middleton, who had recovered from his illness, landed in Sutherland in February 1654, ready to take charge from Glencairn. But things did not go as planned. Glencairn, rather than mastering the rivalries between the Highlanders, seems to have made them worse. Supplies were either low or non existent. There was no clear agreement on the strategy to be pursued. Still worse, the Dutch war ended in the spring, leaving Monk free to devote all his attentions to the north. Like a relentless bloodhound, Monk began a steady pursuit of Middleton and Glencairn. Systematically destroying the property of the rebel chiefs, he sweept the country with cavalry and carefully sited garrisons to cut the Highlands off from the Lowlands; the kind of methodical campaign that might so easily have brought Montrose to his knees. He also secured the support of Argyll, for which the Marquis was later to pay with his life. Finally, in July, some of Monk's forward units under Colonel Thomas Morgan surprised and routed Middleton's little force at Lochgarry, just south of Dalnaspidal. Able to do little more, Middleton escaped back to the Continent, and the rising steadily petered out. Monk was left as the effective ruler of Scotland, and was to remain as such until the fateful year of 1660.

If the Commonwealth was a military success, it was also a political failure. The constitutional issue remained unresolved. In 1653 Cromwell dismissed the Rump of the Long Parliament and soon after had himself proclaimed Lord Protector. He tried from time to time to establish his rule on a firm legal basis, but the Protectorate was never more than a military dictatorship, always dependant on the will of one man. When the Lord Protector died on 3 September 1658, his 'lucky' day, the title passed to Richard Cromwell, who had no better claim than that he was the son of his father. 'Tumbledown Dick', as he was fated to be known, had not the personality to dominate men like John Lambert and Charles Fleetwood, who felt they had a better claim to his position. In an attempt to strengthen his civil authority Richard summoned a Parliament. To his cost, he found he could neither master Parliament nor the Army. He exited the stage in the spring of 1659, as meekly as he had come.

In Scotland, Monk, who enjoyed complete authority over his own section of the New Model Army, waited and watched as the power struggle in England became ever more confused. The Rump was conjured back into life, only to be dismissed once again. For a time, John Lambert rose to the top, determined to preserve the Republic; but opinion was moving strongly in favour of the old constitutional order. Monk, whose loyalty had been to Cromwell rather than the Commonwealth, decided the time had come for him to act. Declaring for a free Parliament, he crossed the Tweed with his army in January 1660. Lambert's own forces melted away before him and Monk entered London unopposed. A new Parliament was elected, strongly royalist in feeling. Events now moved steadily towards the Restoration of the monarchy.

The Restoration was very much an English affair. There was no Parliament or General Assembly to represent the interests of Scotland. The Church itself was still divided between Protesters and Resolutioners, whose quarrel had become more bitter as the years passed. Charles was to be restored with no adequate guarantees of Scottish political and religious liberties. Much depended on the advice he received from individual Scots, like his fellow exile John Middleton, or the Earl of Lauderdale, who had been a prisoner in England since the Battle of Worcester. For advice on church matters, Charles was also able to turn to James Sharp, the minister of Crail in Fife, and a prominent Resolutioner, who came to visit the King at Breda in Holland.

James Sharp was destined to become one of the great villains of Covenanter mythology; but in reality he was a very small player in a very big game. Clearly a talented individual, he was well known to Cromwell and Monk, who summoned him to London in February 1660 to make use of his pronounced skills as a diplomat and negotiator. The Resolutioners had remained consistently loyal to the King throughout the Commonwealth period, and hoped to benefit as a result. Sharp was charged with two things: to remind Charles of his commitment to the Covenants, and to blame the humiliations of 1650 on the Protesters. But he soon realised that there was no chance of a general Presbyterian settlement in the British Isles as a whole, because opinion in England and Ireland was strongly against the Covenants. All that remained was to try to safeguard Presbyterianism in Scotland itself, although when this was raised with Charles his response was, at best, ambiguous. For Sharp, the real problem was that the majority of the Scottish nobility, reacting strongly against the politics of the late 1640's and early 1650's, did not want to see the old Kirk Party restored in any shape. Sharp was not a knave, as some have alleged; but he was an opportunist; and, in the end, seeing the inevitable drift in the affairs of state, he went with the current. As for the King's own true feelings, these are best expressed in some remarks reported to Burnet by Lauderdale;

> The Earl of Lauderdale at his first coming to the king stood firm to presbytery. He told me, the king spoke to him to let that go, for it was not a religion for gentlemen.

When Charles finally came home in May 1660 he did so at the invitation of his former enemies in England. In large measure, this determined the early character of the Restoration. Those who were penalised for the sins of the Commonwealth were carefully restricted: only the surviving regicides were arrested, as well as a few republican die-hards, like Sir Harry Vane and John Lambert.

Most Scots welcomed the Restoration with great enthusiasm. But there were some, chiefly amongst the Protesters, who had little reason to celebrate the return of their 'Covenanted' King. John Livingstone noted his own misgivings in his Memoirs;

> When in Summer 1660 the word came of the King's being called home, I clearly foresaw there would ensue an overturning of the whole work of reformation, and a trial to all who would adhere thereunto.

Despite the general policy of clemency, men like Archibald Johnston of Warriston could expect no mercy from the King. Alarmed by the prospect of his immanent arrest, Warriston fled to the Continent. But Argyll, expected no ill design against himself and, despite the warnings of Sharp and others, came to see the King at Whitehall in July. Charles refused to receive him. Instead, he was arrested and sent to the Tower, sailing back to Scotland in December to face a charge of treason.

Having disposed of the old order, Charles set about constructing the new. The Cromwellian Union was dissolved, as Scotland's ancient Parliament prepared to revive to give a legal basis to the restored royal government. In London, John, now Earl of Middleton, was named as the Royal Commissioner to Parliament, the most powerful political office in Scotland. Lauderdale was appointed Secretary of State for Scotland, and as such remained in London for some years to advise Charles on affairs in his northern kingdom. Middleton and Lauderdale, once allies in the Engagement, were to become the bitterest of rivals; and, to a large extent, it was the rivalry between them that was to determine the character of early Restoration Scotland. Other appointments included the Earl of Rothes, the son of the great Covenanter, as President of the Council; and the Earls of Glencairn and Crawford as Chancellor and Treasurer respectively. In Scotland, the old Committee of Estates, captured by the English at Alyth in August 1651, was summoned back to life to form a provisional government until such time as Parliament assembled.

On 23 August 1660, the same day the Committee of Estates reassembled, a group of Protesters met in Edinburgh. It might have been more prudent for these men to remain out of the King's sight; instead, they drew up a petition congratulating Charles on his Restoration, going on to remind him of his obligation to enforce the Covenants in all three of his kingdoms. All, including James Guthrie, were immediately arrested and imprisoned in Edinburgh Castle. The Committee followed this up by banning all unlawful assemblies and seditious petitions.

With the Scottish Parliament due to open in January 1661, the Royal Council in London met in December to consider the instructions to be given to Middleton as the King's Commissioner. Middleton, who had converted to Anglicanism during his exile, was a protégé of Charles' chief minister, Edward Hyde, Earl of Clarendon. With Clarendon set to restore the old Episcopal order in England, Middleton conceived a similar project for Scotland. The alliance between these two men is interesting. Clarendon, who had little time for most Scots, had conceived a particular hatred for Covenanters and Presbyterians, believing them to be responsible for the betrayal of Charles I. Middleton's motives were somewhat baser: he was determined to humble a Kirk that had been responsible for his own personal humiliation in 1651. As far as these men were concerned, there was no better time to restore the old Episcopalian order in Scotland. The nobility, impoverished by years of war, were anxious for state employment and pensions. Besides, most of them were now heartily sick of the ministers, whose domination during the high noon of the Covenant had been far more irksome than the bishops ever were. Clarendon also insisted on retaining the English garrisons at

Inverness, Ayr, Leith and Perth, with the support of Monk, now resplendent in the title of Duke of Albermarle. These men would be able to suppress any attempt at armed resistance, and their future withdrawal could be made conditional on the acceptance of Episcopacy.

Lauderdale, in contrast, still hoping himself for a moderate Presbyterian settlement, urged caution. He was convinced that a rapid restoration of Episcopacy would be the source of future trouble. Sadly for him, this prediction proved all too accurate, but with the added irony that he himself was to be the author of much of the trouble. It should be emphasised that the whole question of church government in Scotland was determined in political terms alone. No consideration was given to theological issues, and no churchman was present at the London meeting. James Sharp, far from being the architect of the new Episcopal order that was shortly to descend on Scotland, was merely the tool of others. But how far his own thinking had gone down the Erastian road is indicated by a letter he wrote in December;

> I remember I sayed to the king whyl my Lord Lauderdaill was by, that now his majesty had the opportunity to secure his interests in the Church of Scotland, and if it were not done I was not to be blamed; the king did then smyle, saying to me you will be counted a malignant when you come home; I have since my return professed to the brethren with whom I had occasion to speak of these matters that I see no way for the Church of Scotland to redeem themselves and ther doctrine and practices from the imputations which lye upon them, and to secure the order of this church, but to disown whatever hath been preejudiciall to the kings interest; and make it appear that his authority may be as much found in this church as in any other of his dominions, for I saw evidently that for us ministers in Scotland ther is no reserve but in the kings favor and countenancy of us.

On New Year's day 1661 Parliament gathered in Edinburgh, for the first time in over ten years. As a first and symbolic act, all progressed to the Boroughmuir several days later, where the trunk of Montrose was disinterred. It was taken back to Edinburgh and reunited with his head, taken down from the spike on the Tolbooth, where it had been for the past ten years, grinning down on the citizens of Edinburgh. His coffin was then taken to Holyrood Abbey. After remaining here for some months, Montrose was given a state funeral on 11 May, when his remains were interred in a splendid new tomb built to receive them in one of the side chapels of St Giles. The thoughts of Middleton, whose own father had been cut down unarmed by Montrose's men and who fought against him at Philiphaugh, are unrecorded. But the view of James Kirkton, expressed in his *History of the Church of Scotland*, can perhaps be made to serve for contemporary Covenanter opinion;

> This man, after he hade most cruelly destroyed his own nation, employing for his souldiers the barbarous Irish papists, who had cruelly murdered two hundred thousand innocent protestants some years before...

The spike, vacated by Montrose, was shortly to receive a new tenant. Argyll, who had been tried before Parliament, as a scapegoat for the Covenant, was sentenced to death on 25 May. Two days later his head was taken off by the *Maiden*, and fixed on the Tolbooth wall, while the rest of his remains were taken to Argyllshire for burial. On the scaffold he had counselled his audience to adhere to God and the Covenants in the 'sinning and suffering time to come.' Lord Lorne was eventually allowed to succeed his father to the earldom, but Archibald Campbell was to be the first and only Marquis of Argyll. As for the reasons for his execution, John Willcock wrote;

> The overthrow of the Covenant and of Presbyterianism in Scotland, and a reversal of the measure of political liberty which the struggle for religious liberty had brought with it, had been decided on by the Government of the Restoration, and they were likely to find in Argyll one who would foil their schemes.

This is an inflated estimate of his power and influence; for the Argyll of the 1660's was not the same as the Argyll of the 1640's. Nevertheless, he was still an awkward symbol of past disorders, and of a precocious spirit of national freedom; and, as such, he had to be eliminated. History has not been kind to Archibald Campbell, whose reputation has suffered in comparison with the mercurial Montrose. He deserves better. Ambitious he may have been, yet he never abused his power, and at no time attempted to make himself dictator of Scotland, as his enemies alleged. He did his best, often in difficult circumstances, to defend the interests of his country and his religion; but never to the exclusion of common sense and good judgement. His willingness to break with his more fanatical allies, like Warriston, did much to bring about his political ruin. With good reason, and unlike Montrose, he was not prepared to trust Charles I. It would be wrong to call Argyll a democrat. However, again unlike Montrose, he did at least have his eyes on the future.

Proceedings were also taken against prominent members of the old Protestor faction. Warriston was declared to be a fugitive and a traitor, and condemned to death in his absence. On the Saturday following the death of Argyll, James Guthrie was hanged, after which his head was severed and fixed on the Netherbow Port. He was joined in death by Lieutenant William Govan, a Gideonite who had deserted with Strachan to Cromwell in 1650, and now stood proxy for his long dead superior. Samuel Rutherford was also summoned to appear before Parliament, but, by now mortally ill, he made a defiant reply to the official herald;

Tell them that sent you that I have got summons already before a Superior Judge and Judicatory, and I behove to answer to my first summons, and ere your day come, I will be where few kings and great folk come.

He died on 29 March 1661. His fellow minister, Patrick Gillespie, one of the authors of the Western Remonstrance, was not the stuff of martyrs. On appearing before the bar of Parliament he managed to put an acceptable interpretation on his past conduct, and was duly released, much to the surprise of the King.

Parliament, which continued in session from January through to July, was meeting all of Middleton's expectations. In his opening speech, he had exhorted the members to sweep aside all the measures approved by the Covenanters and to restore the King's prerogative power. As if anxious to wipe out memories of the past, Parliament agreed an oath recognising the King's superiority in all civil and ecclesiastical matters. The Solemn League and Covenant was condemned, and all forbidden to renew any Covenant or Oath without royal Warrant. These measures were too much for the rump of the old Covenanter party, headed by the Earl of Cassillis and Lord Balmerino, who now left the stage. Charles regained the right to appoint the chief officers of state, a right taken away from his father in 1641. For the moment, the question of church government was left deliberately vague – it was to be secured 'as the king finds most consistent with scripture, monarchy and peace.' There was enough in this to cause alarm to those hoping for some form of Presbyterian settlement, even assuming they were not taking the hints Sharp was giving in his letters from London. But the centre piece of this first Parliament of the Restoration – sometimes known as the 'drunken' Parliament – was the Act Recissory.

This Act, passed on 28 March, essentially wiped the statute books clean of all legislation going right back to the Parliament of 1633, with the exception of the Parliaments of 1650–51, even though this included the Engager Parliament of 1648 and the Parliament of 1641, both of which had been approved by the King's father. At a stroke, all of the measures that underpinned the Covenanter Revolution in Scotland were wiped out, as was the abolition of lay patronage. Now all the Kirk depended on for a fair and final settlement was the goodwill of the King.

Middleton's haste was determined in part by a desire to gain a quick political victory over his great rival Lauderdale. Even Charles, always a pragmatist, was alarmed by his eagerness, urging caution. When the Act Recissory ran into opposition headed by William Douglas, now third Duke of Hamilton in right of his marriage to the first Duke's eldest daughter, this seemed to confirm the risks created by Middleton's imprudent conduct; but the triumph of Episcopacy in England greatly eased his position.

The counter-revolution of 1661–1662 was very much the work of Middleton. It was driven less by the need for a peaceful settlement of the Scottish Church, and much more by personal ambition, liberally seasoned with petty spite. If more time had been taken, it might have been possible for Charles to secure the restoration of a modified Episcopacy, with considerably less trouble than Middleton's hurricane was to cause. After all, the Kirk, still bitterly divided between Resolutioners and Protesters, was not able to speak with a unified voice. There were many, moreover, like Sharp, followers of the old conservative Aberdeen school, who would have accepted the gradual return of the bishops. James VI, with far greater skill, had taken the time to recreate a broadly acceptable Episcopacy within the Kirk. Middleton used his own power, against the advice of Lauderdale and others, not simply to control but to humiliate the Presbyterian party, a cause of considerable resentment and much future trouble.

When Parliament rose in July, the government of Scotland was placed in the hands of a restored Privy Council. On 5 September it received a letter from the King, saying that he intended to reintroduce Episcopacy in the Scottish Church. The following day a declaration was made at the Cross of Edinburgh, announcing the abolition of Presbyterianism because of its 'unsuitableness thereof to his Majesty's monarchical estate.' Bishops were to be restored, all clerical courts banned and magistrates ordered to send all nonconformists to prison. Naked coercion was soon to become an essential part of the new policy.

Lauderdale, not so committed to Presbyterianism that he would risk his political career, quickly accepted the new realities, as did James Sharp. Sharp, never really more than a spectator when it came to the real decision making, had long since given up even on the moderate Presbyterianism desired by his Resolutioner colleagues. Aware of the strength of the Episcopalian wind blowing from London, he decided to allow himself to be carried along, all to his greater glory and personal profit. In December he was consecrated as Archbishop of St Andrews at Westminster Abbey, the first man to occupy this office since the death of John Spottiswood in 1639. Perhaps in anticipation of this final outcome, he had written, some time before, that;

> ...in spyte of malice I shall be found faythfull to the king and my countrey and to my Lord Lauderdaill. I will not give two pence what others say of me.

Both Lauderdale and Sharp had hoped that the other prominent Resolutioners would accept the remaining vacant bishoprics; but none were prepared to follow their former colleague down this particular road. Instead, Thomas Sydserf, one of the most despised figures in the troubles of 1637, and the only surviving prelate of the days before the revolution, was trundled out of retirement and given the bishopric of Orkney. The other bishoprics were offered to prominent opponents of the Covenanters, or to men of the second rank. Andrew Fairfoul was named as Archbishop of Glasgow, James Hamilton as Bishop of Galloway and Robert Leighton as Bishop of Dunblane. Although he had signed the Covenant, Leighton now confessed that he had always been opposed to it in his heart, and that 'The Couenant was rashli enterd in, and is now to be repented for.' In the new year, the other vacancies were gradually filled, including the bishopric of Edinburgh, which was taken by George Wishart, the biographer of Montrose.

When Parliament met again in May 1662 to give legal sanction to the new arrangements, the bishops were invited to attend to assist in finalising the details of the church settlement. The 'ancient and sacred order of episcopacy' was restored, and both Covenants declared unlawful, as was the General Assembly of 1638. It was made treasonable to preach against the King's prerogative and supremacy in church questions, or against Episcopalian government. All ministers appointed since the abolition of lay patronage in 1649, were to be presented by a lawful patron before they were allowed to collect their stipends; and they were also to seek collation – confirmation of their office – from the bishop of their diocese. All who did not obtain presentation and collation by 20 September 1662 were to be deprived of their livings. Synods, Kirk Sessions and Presbyteries were not to meet without the authority of the bishops. But of particular significance for the future, conventicles – the informal gathering of the faithful either in private houses or in the open air – were also forbidden.

Middleton was happily laying other traps for the hated Presbyterians. May 29, the King's birthday and the date of the Restoration, was declared to be a public holiday, even though he knew very well that there were many in the Kirk would accept no holy day apart from the Sabbath. There were many who shared his pleasure in the downfall of the Covenanters. On Restoration Day 1662 the common hangman in Edinburgh tore up the Covenants; and in Linlithgow a banner was displayed with the following inscription;

> From covenanters with uplifted hands,
> From remontstrators with associate bands,
> From such committees as governed this nation,
> From kirk commissions and their protestations.
> Good Lord deliver us.

Others were less joyful. Robert Baillie, a moderate all of his life, concludes his voluminous correspondence with the following sad note;

> Our Kirk, all the English tymes, had been very faithfull to our King, and so instrumental as we could for his restoration. We had lost

much blood at Dunbar, Worcester and elsewhere, and at last our libertie, in his cause. We did firmly expect, at his Restitution, a comfortable subsistence to ourselves, and all our Presbyterian brethren, in all his dominions; and believed the King's intention was no other; but by divine permission, other counsells thereafter prevailed, and now carry all.

He died in August 1662, reputedly of a broken heart.

It should be noted, that while diocesan Episcopacy was restored in the form it had before 1638, this was purely an organisational change. The innovations in worship and the liturgy which lead to the riots of 1637, were all absent. Charles was careful, moreover, to see that the new bishops were not set up as rivals to the nobility, as they had been in his father's day. The general mood of anti-clericalism amongst the ruling elites of the Restoration was to ensure that both bishops and ministers were firmly subordinated to the state. Sharp and his colleagues were, for the most part, not figures of any great spiritual authority – this was no Laudian settlement – but little more than glorified civil servants. This was an Erastian solution to the government of the Kirk; and, as such, all the more repugnant to the committed Presbyterians.

Middleton, in his contempt for the Scottish churchmen, seems to have expected no real resistance to the acts of presentation and collation, beyond ridding the Kirk of a few Protesters. On 1 October the Privy Council declared that all ministers who had not observed the statute, as well as all those who had not observed the Restoration holiday, were to leave their parishes by 1 November. It was soon apparent that Middleton was going to have a major problem: far from there being only a few irreconcilables, most of the ministers in the western Whig heartlands either walked out or simply ignored the order. Middleton was shocked by the unexpected reaction of 'these mad fellows.' Faced with the political embarrassment of having so many parishes vacant at one time, the deadline for presentation and collation was extended to 1 February 1663; but in the end more than 300 ministers either resigned or were deposed, about a third of the total Scottish establishment. If this had been evenly spread across the whole of the Scottish ministry it would have been bad. What made it far worse was the geographical concentration of the resignations. In the Synod of Galloway only

3 out of 37 ministers were left; and in the Synod of Glasgow and Ayr, the largest in the church, only 35 out of 130 ministers remained in their parishes. In Dumfries just over half the ministers were deprived of their livings. Deprivations in Lothian, Fife and the south east were also high; but it was clear that it was the old lands of the Western Association that were set to cause the most trouble. Burnet noted the implications of this purge;

> The people were much troubled when so many of their ministers were turned out. Their ministers had, for some months before they were thus silenced, been infusing this into our people, both in public and private, that all that was designed in the change of church government was to delay the power of godliness, and to give an impunity to vice; that prelacy was a tyranny in the church, set up by ambitious and covetous men...

Middleton's rush to reimpose Episcopacy was the cause of almost three decades of upheaval and unrest in the south. The church question was thus destined to remain at the centre of national politics, just as it had in the 1630's. From time to time the discontent caused was to spill over into outright rebellion; and, in the end, when the ancient Stewart monarchy finally crumbled, it had virtually no support in southern Scotland.

The outed ministers were replaced with men barely adequate for the task. Burnet, no enemy of Episcopacy, called them the 'dregs and refuse of the northern parts.' Local people simply dismissed them with contempt as the 'curates.' Some of these men could only take up their new charges when provided by a military escort. At Irongray in Dumfriesshire, the unfortunate curate was greeted by the local women with showers of stones, which sent him hurrying off in fear of his life. Another had ants placed in his boots to torment him during the service. Troops had to be sent to stop the spread of disorder.

It was one thing getting these men into their new churches, and quite another to get people to come and hear them. Men, women and children, first in hundreds and then in thousands, drifted off to hear their old ministers preach in the fields. Men like John Welsh, Donald Cargill, John Blackadder and Alexander Peden – the Prophet Peden – acquired an almost legendary reputation. Hunted across Scotland as outlaws, they appeared from place to place, often in disguise, like so many clerical Robin

Hoods, to preach at large open air conventicles. During 1663 the number of these illegal meetings had grown alarmingly, causing the Council to send James Turner, recently knighted by the King, with a party of troops to the south west in September, charged with hunting down the conventiclers. But the forces he was allowed were just enough to cause anger, not enough to deal with the results.

For a time, Middleton ruled Scotland as a virtual dictator. Those who crossed him could expect serious trouble. For opposing the death sentence in the case of James Guthrie, John Hay, the Earl of Tweeddale, was accused of treason and placed under house arrest, only to be set at liberty after the intervention of Lauderdale. Lord Lorne also fell foul of the King's Commissioner, who hoped to lay his hands on his patrimony, and was condemned to death on a spurious charge of treason. He, too, was rescued by Lauderdale. But Middleton took a step too far when he finally tried to bring down his great rival by a manoeuvre in Parliament. Lauderdale was quick to tell the King of the Commissioner's arrogance and Charles recalled him in fury. Rothes, an ally of the Secretary, replaced Middleton as Commissioner, and Lauderdale moved to the centre of the Scottish political stage, a position he was to occupy for the next sixteen years.

It was Lauderdale's misfortune that to dispel any lingering suspicions of his former Presbyterian sympathies, he had to carry out Middleton's policies with even greater rigour than before. When he and Rothes arrived in Edinburgh in June 1663 for the new session of Parliament, the measures against the illegal conventicles began to intensify. As a first step, the Lords of the Articles was restored on the old basis before the changes of the early 1640's, which gave the King complete legislative control of Parliament. On 10 July an act was passed ratifying all the ecclesiastical legislation of the previous sessions, and allowing for a system of fines against all those who refused to attend their local parish churches. For those who would not, or could not pay, seizure of goods was authorised, no matter how poor the individual. Ministers were to send the names of all non attenders to the Privy Council for further action. The following month the Twenty Mile Act was passed, preventing dissident ministers from coming any closer than that to their former cures. In September, authorisation was given to raise 20,000 foot and

2,000 horse, as a safeguard against invasion or rebellion anywhere in the British Isles. Only a small part of this proposed force was ever assembled; but that which was, was soon to find employment in Scotland itself.

This Parliament also presided over the destruction of one of the leading figures of the Covenanter Revolution. Archibald Johnston of Warriston had been tracked down in Rouen by English spies and subsequently extradited by the French authorities. All his former courage and certainty had deserted him, and when he appeared before the bar of Parliament on 8 July to hear sentence of death pronounced against him, he ran up and down on his knees begging for mercy. Lauderdale noted his own impressions on Warriston's wretched demeanour;

> I have often heard of a man feared out of his wits, but never saw it before; yet what he said was good sense enough, but he roared and cried and expressed more fear than ever I saw.

In pleading for a delay of execution, he said that his memory was gone, and that he remembered 'neither matter of law, nor fact, nor a word of the bible.' Lauderdale, whatever pity he may have felt in his heart for his old colleague in the Covenant, was anxious to have the whole business concluded as quickly as possible, for if the Marquis of Argyll was hated by the King, Warriston was loathed. He was hanged on 22 July, after recovering some of his composure. After death, his head was cut off and fixed beside that of Guthrie on the Netherbow Port.

The legislation of 1663 had almost no effect on the steady growth of the field assemblies. In Galloway and the south west in general, the position was particularly bad, because many Presbyterian ministers from Ulster had taken refuge there, after the restoration of Episcopacy in Ireland. Turner was ordered to hunt them down, as well as increasing repressive measures against the Scottish dissenters. Military intervention was growing from a temporary expedient into a permanent feature of government policy. It was to be associated in the period leading up to the Pentland Rising of 1666 with the name of Alexander Burnet, formerly Bishop of Aberdeen, who replaced Fairfoul as Archbishop of Glasgow, following his death in November 1663. Sharp still preferred a slightly less militant approach, using a new Court of High Commission, established on his initiative in early 1664, to punish nonconformity.

The outbreak of the second Anglo Dutch War in 1664, was the occasion for a new drive against the Covenanters. Scotland had close religious and commercial contacts with Holland, and had been pulled into this conflict against her own interests. Many of the ministers ousted in the purges of 1662–63 had taken refuge there, telling their fellow Dutch Calvinists of the extent of the persecution in Scotland. Hoping to benefit from these troubles, the States-General, the Parliament of the Netherlands, passed a secret resolution to help the Scots' rebels with arms and money, as soon as they had taken possession of any fortified places. The assumption was that the underground in Scotland was organised and ready to act; but this was far from being the case. Field conventicles were expressions of spontaneous religious zeal, not organised conspiracies. But Archbishop Burnet had absolutely no hesitation in making rigorous use of conspiracy scares to prompt the Privy Council into ever more drastic action against the Whigs. Over the next two years those who attended illegal gatherings were steadily transformed from religious dissidents into enemies of the state. This was the beginning of a new Covenanter War.

With Lauderdale back in London, Rothes was left to manage the measures against the dissidents. Fines were imposed with ever greater rigour on those who would not take the Oath of Loyalty and make a declaration against the Covenants. Sir James Turner was sent to the west with 140 horse and foot guards, a dangerously understrength force, to gather fines and quarter troops on the recalcitrant, much as he had done before the Mauchline Muir rising in 1648. He was subsequently told by his enemies that he was the 'greatest persecuter of Christians, than any who were ever mentioned in historie.' A number of prominent individuals thought to be sympathetic to the rebels were arrested, including Major-General Robert Montgomery, the man who started the Whiggamore Raid. Yet another act was passed in December 1665, declaring conventicles to be 'seminaries of separation and rebellion,' and all who attended them were declared to be traitors. New declarations were made demanding the appearance of eleven leading field preachers before the Privy Council, including the terrible trio of Welsh, Blackadder and Peden. Nothing seemed to work. In frustration, Rothes wrote to Lauderdale in late November 1665, blaming the field preachers for stirring up the women especially;

...thes rouges stirs up the uimin so they are uors than deivils, yay I dear say if it uear not for the uimin uie should have litill trubell with conventickles or such caynd of stuff, bot ther ar sucj a ffulith jenerasione of pipil in this countrie uhu ar so influensied uith ther fanatick uayffs as I thinck uill bring reuin upon them.

The government was even more incensed by the publication abroad of a book entitled *An Apologetic Narration* by John Brown, the former minister of Wamphray near Lochmaben, now living in exile. Brown defended the actions of the Covenanters and their right to defend themselves against the oppressions of the authorities. His book was at once declared to be seditious, and a copy was burnt by the public hangman. Sharp described it as 'a damned book' which had fired the west against the Crown. Any Scot found in possession of it was to be fined £2,000, a prodigious sum for the day, beyond the means of all but the very rich. But each act of repression was followed by more acts of resistance – an angry reaction, rather than a preconceived plan. The military build up, which continued into 1666 when new forces were raised from the fines of nonconformists, provoked the very thing it was intended to avoid.

In February 1666 the Scots' bishops, meeting in convocation, sent an alarming report to the King;

If the warre with frrance (a temporary ally of the Dutch) and Holland goe on it will be necessary to provide for the peace and security of this kingdome, for at present we may possibly prevent domestike disorder and insurrections, but the least commotion in England or Ireland, or encouragement from forraigners, would certainly engage us in a new rebellion.

In March Turner was again sent westwards, this time with only 120 footguards. Additional troops were now being mustered by Sir William Drummond and Tam Dalyell of the Binns, who since escaping from the Battle of Worcester had served for many years in the service of the Tsar of Russia. But the forces in the west were badly overstretched. Sensing the hostility of the local people, Turner's nervous soldiers tended to react with even greater brutality. Even the Bishop of Galloway was moved to complain about some of their excesses, with no result. The west was now a powder keg; it only needed a spark to set off an explosion. It came at the small village of Dalry, in the valley of the River Ken, on Tuesday 13 November 1666.

Sir John Maclellan of Barscob and three other fugitives of conscience, had come down from their hiding place in the hills of Kirkcudbrightshire looking for warmth and refreshment in the village. Three of Turner's soldiers, headed by one Corporal George Deanes, were collecting fines in the area. At the local inn, Barscob and his comrades heard that Deanes had arrested a local farmer, an elderly man named Grier, and planned to strip him naked and set him on a hot grid iron because he could not afford to pay his fines for refusing to attend his local church. Incensed, they at once set off to rescue the man. In a comic touch, Barscob, for want of a bullet, rammed his tobacco pipe into his pistol, fired and hit Deanes with sufficient force to knock him to the ground at the feet of his intended victim. After a brief sword fight, the rest of the soldiers surrendered. From such small beginnings the Pentland Rising was born.

For the previous two years the government had been expecting the Whigs to rise in revolt. Now that this had happened they found themselves not only taken by complete surprise, but absurdly ill prepared. Since March, Turner had lost almost half his force, including all his cavalry, as men were sent off to the Dutch War. He now had about 70 in all, 12 or 13 in Dumfries and the rest scattered across the countryside. News of the scuffle at Dalry reached Balmaclellan the following day, where a conventicle was in progress. Immediately breaking off their devotions, the men gathered what weapons they could, setting upon the local garrison, killing one man and capturing the rest. Turner, aware of what was going on, sent urgent word for all his men to join him at Dumfries. It was already too late. Barscob had issued his own call to arms at Irongray, the old parish of John Welsh, and was quickly joined by 50 horse and 200 foot. The insurgents then swept into Dumfries and took Turner prisoner. He only narrowly escaped being shot. There is absolutely no suggestion in any of these events of a preconceived plan or foreign intervention; it was simply a spontaneous outpouring of frustration and anger, which, in the end, was to have tragic consequences.

Eager not to be perceived as rebels, the small Whig army declared its loyalty to King and Covenant in Dumfries town square, clearly not aware of the contradiction between the one and the other, saying that their sole quarrel was with the bishops. All available arms were seized and distributed to the infantry. With rain now falling in torrents, which continued throughout the campaign, the Whigs set off aimlessly in search of recruits or inspiration, under the leadership of Andrew Grey, one of the most mysterious figures of the whole Pentland Rising, who disappeared almost as suddenly as he came.

When news of the rebellion in the south west reached Edinburgh, the Privy Council, in the absence of Rothes, who was in London on business, ordered Tam Dalyell to take all his available troops to Glasgow, and set out from there in pursuit. While he mustered his forces, the rebels entered Tarbolton on 19 November, with Turner in tow. Here they were joined by recruits from Ayrshire and Clydesdale, including 50 horsemen from Cunningham. The march then continued through the rain, south west to Ayr. At the Brig o' Doon they were joined by Colonel James Wallace, their most important recruit. Wallace was an experienced soldier, who had served with the army in Ireland and had fought for the Covenanters at the battles of Kilsyth and Dunbar, where he was taken prisoner. Grey had now left the scene, so it was natural for Wallace to take command. He at once introduced some much needed military discipline into the rag taggle army. Officers of horse and foot were appointed, and the men organised into proper formations. At Ochiltree the force was further enlarged when the irrepressible John Welsh appeared with 300 foot and 15 horse from Galloway. All, however, were very badly armed.

Dalyell finally left Glasgow on 23 November, looking for the trail of the Whigs. In a steady pursuit, he sought to wear down the resolve of the rebels. With still no news from the west, the Council in Edinburgh was close to panic, issuing proclamations against the 'insurgents at Dumfries and the western shyres,' and authorising fresh mobilisations in various parts of Scotland. Cannons were brought down from the castle and placed at the city gates. Wallace was aware that Dalyell was close behind, and, not yet ready to risk an engagement with professional troops, he continued his march, setting off for Cumnock the day the government soldiers entered Kilmarnock. The plight of these wretched men is described by James Kirkton;

> ...in the most tempestuous rainy evening they sett foreward toward Moorkirk of Kyle, through a miserable deep moore, so that they came not to their quarters till two houres within night. The poor souldiers

were drouckt with rain as if they hade been dragged through a river;
their foot were forced, wet as they were, to lodge in a church without
any meat, and very little fire to drie them.

Wallace entered Lanark on 26 November, where his army grew
to 1100 men, the greatest strength it ever attained. Thereafter, it
was weakened by desertions, as men steadily left for home,
defeated by the weather. At Lanark, the Whigs paused to renew
the Covenants. Hoping to put pressure on the Council to make
concessions and to attract more recruits in the Lothians, Wallace
and his colleagues decided to continue their march towards
Edinburgh, in a tragic repeat of the Whiggamore Raid. Kirkton
describes the army as 'rather like dyeing men than soldiers going
to conquer.' Hoping to stop them before they got too far, Dalyell
rode ahead with his cavalry. Wallace turned to fight; but with
darkness beginning to fall, and the rough ground on the moors
to the east of Lanark not suitable for cavalry, Dalyell decided not
to risk defeat in an encounter that would breath new life into a
cause so clearly on the point of exhaustion. As the rebels made
their escape through two mosses, Dalyell returned to Lanark to
wait for his infantry and to rest there for the night.

With the enemy now poised across his line of retreat, Wallace
had no choice but to continue to go forward. He halted at
Bathgate on the night of the 26th and resolved to march on
Edinburgh the following day. But conditions for his tired army
were even worse on this dreadful night, as William Veitch
explains;

> Night came on, and as no quarters could be had for such a number,
> they were forced to stand with their arms without in the field. And a
> great snow coming like to discourage the company, some of the
> officers, thinking it was better to be marching than standing in such
> a posture, gave a false alarm that the enemy was approaching.

Newbridge was reached the following morning. There was no
sign of new recruits, and no word from their friends in the
capital. Still the desultory march continued, onwards towards
Colinton. On the morning of 28 November the insurgents were
attacked near Colinton churchyard by a party of the Edinburgh
Fencibles, who had ridden out from Canongate. They were
quickly driven off after they had killed one man, the first Whig to
die in the rising. Wallace now faced the risk of being caught

between Dalyell and the hostile capital. Rather than continue on a hopeless eastern march, he decided to pull off to the south, hoping to escape back to Ayrshire through the Pentland Hills. Crossing the Braid Burn and passing by Dreghorn Castle, where Dalyell had planned to intercept them, the rebels continued east for a time in the direction of Dalkeith, turning south on the Linton road towards Biggar. Crossing the Glencorse Burn at Flotterstone, Wallace then halted for a rest on the southern side of the Pentlands at a place called Rullion Green, the site of an ancient market. It was now about noon.

Dalyell had reached Currie the same morning, where he crossed the Water of Leith. By now he had discovered that the rebels were retreating through the Pentlands. At Currie he was well placed to cut off their retreat. Following the valley of the Kenleith Burn, he hurried to the south east, entering the Pentlands between Bell's Hill and Harbour Hill, continuing on south of Castlelaw Hill towards Rullion Green. His advance party led by the brother of the Earl of Airlie caught sight of the Whigs at noon, now reduced to about 900 men. A contemporary writer described the equipment of Wallace's motley army in verse;

> Some had halberds, some had durks,
> Some had crooked swords like Turks;
> Some had slings and some had flails
> Knit with eels and oxen tails.
> Some had spears and some had pikes,
> Some had spades which delvy and dykes;
> Some had guns with rusty ratches,
> Some had fiery peats for matches.
> Some had bows but wanted arrows,
> Some had pistils without marrows;
> Some the coulter of a plough,
> Some had syths such for to hough;
> And some with a Lochaber exe
> Resolvd to gi'e Dalziel his packs.

With his experienced soldier's eye, Wallace arranged his men to fight in a defensive position on the lower reaches of nearby Turnhouse Hill, opposite Castlelaw Hill, north west of the low lying ground at Rullion Green. This was a good place to make a stand, forcing the enemy to make a steep ascent to reach him. On the southern shoulder of the hill he placed his right wing, a body of Galloway horse under Barscob. The remainder of the horse was placed on the left on the northern shoulder under Joseph Learmont, while he himself commanded the infantry in the centre. With the main body of the army still some distance away, Ogilvie and his troopers were uncertain what to do. Wallace's army was so well posted that any approach was bound to be risky. After a time he decided to send a party cross the valley and probe Learmont's wing. Wallace detached a force of equal size from the left to meet the threatened attack. After a volley of gunfire, the two sides closed with swords. Although the rebels suffered some losses, the government forces were beaten back. Ogilvie now realised that this was no rabble, but an army prepared to fight with courage and discipline.

Reports of the skirmish were carried back to Dalyell, approaching with the remainder of the army. More of his cavalry hurried forward in support with Lieutenant-General William Drummond, joining Ogilvie on the high ground to the west of Glencorse Burn. Drummond decided to attempt nothing further until Dalyell arrived with the infantry. By the time he arrived at 4 o'clock in the afternoon it was already starting to get dark. Not wishing to waste any more time, Dalyell ordered his whole force across the burn, and drew them up at the foot of Turnhouse Hill. On the right he placed the Life Guards, Rothes troop of horse as well as Drummond's. On the left were his own, as well as Hamilton's, Atholl's and Airlie's troops. The infantry were in the centre. Altogether he had 2,000 foot and 600 horse, far superior in every way to the desperate Whig rebels. To encourage the men, John Welsh and his fellow preacher Gabriel Semple cried out 'The great God of Jacob, The Great God of Jacob, See the Lord of Hosts is fighting for us!' The doomed army joined in, raising their voices to sing the 71st and 78th Psalms, as Dalyell's troops closed in on them.

Dalyell began by detaching a body of his horse with infantry support to attack Learmont. As before, Wallace sent forward a similar party to meet them. The two sides met in a furious hand to hand clash. But as the slope of the hill favoured the rebels, the government soldiers were forced to give way. Dalyell continued to attack from his right, intending to force the rebels down towards the low ground, and then finish them with his left. A second attack was therefore launched against Learmont, with no greater success. Dalyell immediately ordered a third assault, which this time succeeded in beating back both Learmont and Wallace. Wallace tried to strengthen his left by detaching some of the troops from the right; but Dalyell immediately took advantage of this by ordering a general advance. His left, so far unengaged, threw itself on Wallace's weakened right. Unable to make a stand the Whigs collapsed, protected from pursuit by the thickening darkness of a winter night. Fifty men were left dead on the field, and many more were lost in the Pentland Bogs.

One severely wounded Whig managed to run twelve miles from the battlefield, and was finally given refuge by one Adam Sanderson of Blackhill, who hid him the following day from Dalyell's dragoons. On the point of death he made Sanderson promise to bury him high on the slope of the Black Law, close to Cairn Knowe, where he could rest forever within sight of the hills of Ayrshire.

CHAPTER 13
Drumclog and Bothwell Bridge

As soon as the reports of the outcome of the Battle of Rullion Green reached Edinburgh, the guns of the castle were fired in celebration. Turner was liberated without harm, as the Whig prisoners were herded into the 'Haddock's Hole', part of the High Church of Edinburgh, or the Tolbooth. Sharp had been in the grip of terror as the rebels approached the capital, suggesting that the Privy Council take refuge in the Castle. He now wrote to the King in delight, saying that only nightfall had prevented the extermination of his enemies. Lord Lorne, who by now had been allowed to assume the title of ninth Earl of Argyll, wrote to Lauderdale, his benefactor, saying that the ministers who had encouraged the rising deserved to be tortured. Wallace, more fortunate than many of his comrades, managed to escape to Holland. The Dutch government resisted all attempts to extradite him. He died in 1678, a respected member of the exiled community and an elder of the Scottish Church in Rotterdam.

The day after the battle, a proclamation was issued by the Council making it treason to harbour any of the fifty-seven named ringleaders of the rising, thus ushering in a brief reign of terror. Torture was liberally used to extract confessions. Ten of the leading prisoners were hanged in Edinburgh in early December, after which their severed heads were sent to various parts of the country as an example to others. Further executions were ordered in Glasgow, Ayr, Dumfries and Irvine. Strength of feeling in the west was shown when the official hangmen at Irvine and Ayr refused to execute the victims. At Ayr the problem was only solved when one of the condemned was reprieved after promising to hang the others. Altogether, thirty-six men were hanged, and a further fifty-six sentenced to death in their absence.

To prevent any repetition of the Pentland Rising, Dalyell was sent to the west, as James Kirkton explains, to;

...improve his victory and destroy his enemies; and here he carried himself as if he had been in Muscovia. The souldiers take free quarters and doe what they will; the whole substance of the countrey is consumed. Himself takes up his quarters at Kilmarnock, and there upon private examination of any whom he suspected either to have been in armes, or to harbour any of them, he not only threatened, but cruelly tortured whom he pleased.

The policy of repression continued until the summer of 1667. But when the three year war with Holland ended, official anxiety began to subside. Lauderdale, whose principle concern was peace and order in Scotland, began to consider an alternative way of dealing the Covenanter opposition. Middleton's over hasty reintroduction of Episcopacy had the effect of pushing some of the Resolutioners into taking sides with the Protesters against the government. But what if the moderates and extremists could, once again, be separated from one another, as they had after Dunbar? Lauderdale would clearly have liked to have worked within a moderate Presbyterian settlement; but Episcopacy was now the settled will of the King. However, he managed to persuade Charles, that the continuing policy of military repression was forcing peaceful non-conformists into the arms of their less compromising brethren, and that much would be gained by a limited policy of toleration. Episcopacy was retained as the government of the Church of Scotland, and conventiclers were to be punished with all the force of the law; but, under the system proposed by Lauderdale, moderate dissenters were to receive some form of official recognition. This was to be the basis of the First Indulgence.

Lauderdale could only introduce this new policy by first forcing through some changes in church and government. As a preliminary step he began to look more deeply into the causes of the Pentland Rising. Sir Robert Moray, his under secretary, was sent to Scotland to carry out an investigation. Moray reported that the gathering of fines from non-conformists by the military had been accompanied by excesses and corruption. Turner, vulnerable enough to be singled out as a scapegoat, was dismissed from the service. In August 1667 the army was disbanded, except for two troops of lifeguards and eight companies of foot. Archbishop Burnet of Glasgow, a firm supporter of continuing military repression, was opposed to this; but it was obvious that his opinion and that of Sharp counted for very little.

Lauderdale already had a group of political allies in Scotland, willing to implement a change in policy. These men, who included the Earls of Argyll, Tweeddale and Kincardine, were all labelled as the 'Presbyterians' by Sharp, although it would perhaps be more accurate to describe them as anti-clerical instead. They were certainly opposed to the political arrogance of the bishops. Sharp may have cared little for these men; but, unfortunately for him, he had also made the mistake of crossing Lauderdale. Despite his seniority in the Scottish Church, he soon found he had little more influence than Sir James Turner, and ended up sharing the blame with him for the Pentland Rising. Sharp's fall from power was rapid and humiliating. When he finally rose again, he was only allowed to do so as Lauderdale's poodle.

Rothes, too, felt the limits of his own power. Closely associated with the discredited policies of the past, Lauderdale decided he had to be moved to a position where he could cause less damage. He was too close to the King to be broken like Middleton or Sharp. Instead, he was forced to resign as Royal Commissioner to Parliament and created Lord Chancellor instead. The position of Commissioner was left vacant for two years, until Lauderdale came north to assume the title himself.

The centrepiece of the new policy was the First Indulgence, granted in July 1669. Under this, some ministers were allowed to return to their old parishes, or another vacant charge, provided they restricted their activities to their own churches. Although required to attend church courts, and to pay lip service to the Episcopal authorities, they did not have to obtain collation from a bishop. A number of the more moderate ministers accepted this meek form of Presbyterianism. By March 1670 forty-three had taken the Indulgence, seventeen of them being restored to their former parishes.

A Second Indulgence was passed in September 1672, which further increased the number of Presbyterian parishes; the policy, however, was a failure, at least in the way that Lauderdale conceived it. He expected it to produce a major split amongst the dissidents; instead only a minority ever accepted the Indulgences. Many of the outed ministers refused to agree to any restriction on their activity, or to accept what, for them, was simply another Erastian solution to the church problem, and a breach of the Covenant. Nevertheless, Lauderdale had succeeded in ways to subtle for him to appreciate. Amongst the non-conformists, bitterness began to grow against those prepared to take the Indulgences, so much so that the seeds were sown that were to destroy the Whig rising of 1679 from within.

If the more extreme Covenanters were unhappy at finding a place within an Erastian Church, there were some on the other side outraged by the intrusion of a Presbyterian wedge; none more so than Archbishop Burnet. According to Kirkton, he is said to have remarked that 'the gospel was banished out of his diocese the day the army was disbanded.' He was especially angry by the passing of the First Indulgence, which would allow 'rebels' to be supported from church funds. Showing a singular lack of judgement, he decided to protest in the worst possible way by sending a formal Remonstrance to the King, the first for many years. For Charles, the Glasgow Remonstrance immediately awakened some unpleasant memories, and he is said to have remarked;

> ...this damned paper shewes Bishops and Episcopall people are as bad in this chapter as the most arrant Presbyter or Remonstrator.

Charles replied by commanding Lauderdale to rid him of the turbulent priest. But Lauderdale did not need swords to accomplish the task; he simply told Burnet, in his own direct and brutal fashion, that it was 'the King's will and pleasure that ye be no more Archbishop of Glasgow.' Burnet was sent packing like a disgraced civil servant, rather than a mighty Prince of the Church. He was replaced by Robert Leighton, the former Bishop of Dunblane, who accepted his new charge with some considerable reluctance. A much more conciliatory figure than Burnet, he was to spend his time at Glasgow seeking some accommodation between Presbyterians and Episcopalians.

Lauderdale finally arrived back in Scotland in October 1669, to attend Parliament in his new role of High Commissioner. The first important measure he saw through was the Supremacy Act, which gave the monarch complete control over all church affairs. The western Covenanters at once denounced this measure, which they said was setting Charles up as a kind of Pope on the throne of Christ. But Lauderdale, now aware of the limited impact of the First Indulgence, followed this up with measures specifically directed against the extremists. In the summer session of 1670, Parliament passed the so called Clanking Act against conventicles, a far more severe measure than anything yet considered by the government. Heavy fines were fixed for all those listening to unlicensed preachers; and the death penalty was decreed for ministers calling field assemblies. Only the Earl of Cassillis, remembering his Covenanter past, had the courage to vote against this drastic measure. Lauderdale was effectively offering the Covenanters a stark choice: the olive branch of the Indulgence, or the club of the Clanking Act.

Despite all of the Commissioner's efforts, field conventicles became ever more popular, as the Earl of Kincardine reported to Lauderdale in March 1669;

> ...wee are allarum'd from the west of the dayly encrease of Conventicles, and withdrawing from the church, that it is groune to that height that those who were lookt upon formerly as sober persons have now broke out into these disorders, that not only upon Sundayes, but all the dayes of the weeke, they have avowed conventicles through most of that dissafected part of the contrie.

People attended in their thousands. What is worse, many of the men came with arms, giving these assemblies the appearance of little armies. They were especially numerous in the Whig heartlands of Ayrshire and Galloway; but they also made an appearance in Fife and the east. In June 1670 John Blackadder preached to a multitude on the Hill of Beath Hill near Dunfermline, protected by an armed troop from Galloway, led by John Maclellan of Barscob, who had managed to escape detection after the Battle of Rullion Green. Some of those who attended this meeting were later seized and transported to Virginia. Nevertheless the problem began to grow throughout the 1670's. One conventicle held in 1677 at East Nisbet in Berwickshire went on for three days. Immense gatherings were held in Teviotdale and at Maybole and Girvan in Ayrshire. House conventicles, popular with the more well to do, even spread into Edinburgh, where Margaret Johnston, the daughter of Warriston, was arrested and expelled from the city in November 1674 for attending one. At Skeoch Hill near Dumfries 14,000 people gathered to hear Blackadder, Welsh and others in the summer of 1678. Outlaw ministers were hunted down with great vigour, many, including Alexander Peden, being sent to the state prison on the Bass Rock, off the coast of East Lothian. All Robert Leighton's attempts at conciliation failed. He resigned from the See of Glasgow in 1674. In his place the hard-line Alexander Burnet was restored, signalling a new departure in policy.

For Lauderdale, increasingly arrogant in his exercise of power, this was no longer a struggle against a few religious dissidents; it was a full scale war. To prevent any further erosion in the security of the state, he returned to a policy abandoned after the Pentland Rising. In July 1677 the Privy Council passed an act establishing thirteen new garrisons in the south and south west. The practice of fining and quartering was pursued with ever greater vigour. Always looking for new ways of putting pressure on the Whigs, the Council decided to enforce a decree making landlords responsible for the actions of their tenants. Concerned by the implications of this, the gentry of Ayrshire met, under the chairmanship of the Earl of Loudoun, the son of the Covenanting nobleman, and rejected the measure as impractical, recommending a general policy of toleration instead. But there was little desire for this. A shooting incident at Kinloch in October caused much concern in Edinburgh, greatly heightened by alarming reports from the Earl of Nithsdale and others on conditions in the west, as the Duke of Hamilton reported;

> Ther wes a great allarum att Edinburgh that the West was aboutt rysing in arms. The bishops bleu the coill, and Earl Nithsdale wes cheaff informer, for he sed ther wer conventickels keapt consisting of over 3000, wherof 1000 wes weall mounted and armed as any in the nation to his certen knowledg, Some others told that some gentlemens houses were provyded with arms far abov the condition of pryvett familes; that in some wer 20 pair of pistols, 20 carbyns, besyd mussquetts and fyerlocks. Bott the principall poynt wes moir considerable, which is that with this year or thereby 7000 horses ar transported from Ireland; hitherto non can geit account of them bott that they ar in the hands of disaffected persons in the western and southern shyrs.

The defiance of Loudoun and his fellow landowners gave Lauderdale the excuse to take the most drastic action of all against the dissidents of the west: the whole area was to be treated like an enemy country and occupied by an alien army. Convincing Charles that rebellion was about to break out by a faction favouring republicanism, and that the local gentry had lost control, he obtained the King's approval to raise an extra-ordinary army – the Highland Host. Scotland was placed under martial law, and Lauderdale wrote to the Earls of Huntly, Perth and Airlie to assemble their men for a march on the south west.

Arrangements were also made to assemble forces in Ulster for a possible landing in Ayrshire, and English troops were mustered at Newcastle. At the beginning of January 1678, the Host assembled at Stirling. There were 750 horse and over 7,000 foot, mostly Highland irregulars, but also a large party of regular troops and Lowland militia. Robert Woodrow describes their appearance;

> They had no small store of ammunition with them, four field pieces, vast numbers of spades, shovels, mattocks, as if they had been to have attacked great fortifications. They had a good store of iron shackles, as if they were to lead back vast numbers of slaves; and thumblocks, as they call them, to make their examinations and trials with. The musketeers had their daggers so made, if need were, to fasten upon the mouth of their pieces, and maul horses, like our bayonets, not yet brought to perfection. In this posture they came to the West.

For the northerners, the expedition to the west was little more than a grand plundering raid, for once carried out with the approval of the law. Advancing through Glasgow to Ayr, the Host had orders to seize all weapons, and live free at the expense of the unfortunate Whigs. Landlords were required to sign a bond, promising to ensure that their tenants kept the peace; otherwise they risked a visit from the Host. But it was the ordinary people of Ayrshire and Galloway who suffered most from their attentions. Everything was taken, from livestock to pots and pans. Although they only stayed a few weeks, they left Ayrshire, according to Kirkton, as if they had been at the sack of a besieged city. One contemporary account of their conduct reads as follows;

> I hear not yet of any killed by them, but several are grievously wounded and beaten; and in effect, the poor people's lives, goods, and chastites, are exposed to the crueltie of these strange locusts. The other day I heard, that of the burying of a child, the burial party was assaulted by some of these ruffians, and, after a great scuffle, the mortcloth was robbed off the coffine, and that notwithstanding all that their officers could do to hinder or recover it. They tell me also, that some of these savages, not knowing what the coffine meaned, as being a thing to them not usual, would have broken it open and searched it if not restrained by their neighbours.

As a political tactic the Highland Host was a failure. No sooner had it left than the westerners began to rearm themselves, and

251

field conventicles continued as vigorously as before. In a fit of bad temper, Lauderdale had sought a short term solution to a long term problem, that did little more than demonstrate the military incapacity of his government. It also created a lasting bitterness in the western Lowlands against both the Highlanders and the Stewart monarchy itself, which, in time to come, was to make the area the most staunchly anti Jacobite in Scotland. A seventeen year old poet by the name of William Cleland, a student from St Andrews University and the future commander of the Cameronian Regiment, wrote a satire on the exploits of the Highland Host;

> ...more savage far than those were,
> who with Kollkittoch and Montrose were,
> And sixtie times worse they're worse than they
> Whom Turner led in Galloway,
> They durk our Tennents, shames our Wives,
> And were in hazard of our lives,
> They plunder horse, and them they loaden
> With Coverings, Blankets, Sheets and Pladin'
> With Hooding gray, and worsted stuff,
> They sell our Tongs for locks of snuff,
> They take our Cultors and our soaks,
> And from our door they pull the locks,
> They leave us neither shoals nor spaids,
> And takes away our Iron in laids,
> They break our pleughs, ev'n when they're working,
> We dare not hinder them for durking...

The passion for field and house conventicles showed no sign of abating. One held near Whitekirk in East Lothian on 5 May 1678 was attacked by some troops from the garrison on the Bass Rock, who were driven off, leaving one of their number dead. James Learmont, one of those who attended the conventicle, was later tried and executed, although he had no part in the death of the soldier. He was simply charged with accession to murder, a dangerous precedent which could be used against anyone who attended illegal assembles where there was an armed encounter. Before long the prospect of a serious clash between the Covenanters and the army became ever more likely.

After the Highland Host, the Privy Council returned to more conventional military methods. An extra two companies of dragoons were raised in May, as well as a further regiment of foot. In addition to this, three independent troops of horse were raised on the orders of the King. The Earl of Airlie was to command one, and the Earl of Home the other. Command of the third was given on the personal recommendation of the King's brother, James Duke of York and Albany, to a young captain by the name of John Graham of Claverhouse, a distant relative of Montrose. Claverhouse, after Sharp, was to become the second great demon of Covenanter mythology; but he was simply a cold blooded professional soldier, very much in the same manner as Sir James Turner, for whom the principle of obeying orders was the highest moral duty. He took up his duties at Dumfries in late December 1678, charged with dispersing conventicles, and arresting outlawed preachers and other rebels.

By the beginning of 1679 the attitude of the Covenanter underground was becoming ever more threatening. In one particularly notorious case a group of twenty armed dissidents attacked Major Johnston, one of the officers of the Edinburgh city guard, and threatened to kill him if he took any further action against conventicles. He refused, and was badly wounded. But by far the most serious incident occurred on Sunday 30 March at Lesmahagow in Clydesdale. A party of dragoons under the command of Lieutenant Dalziel heard that a large assembly was being held in the area and set off, hoping to surprise the Whigs. When they arrived they found that the rebels had organised themselves with military precision. They had three companies of foot, each 100 strong, as well as a troop of 60 horse. Up to a third of the foot had muskets, and the rest were armed with swords, halberds and pitchforks. The horsemen were well mounted, each man armed with a pistol or carbine. Not willing to risk a clash, Dalziel hung on the margins, seizing stragglers. News of his presence reached the main body, which promptly attacked and surrounded the soldiers. Although hopelessly outnumbered, Dalziel bravely called on the Whigs to disperse in the name of the King;

> ...wherupon the comander of the Whiggs horse ansuered disdainefully, Farts in the kings teath, and the Counsells, and all that hes sent you, for wee appear here for the King of Heaven.

In the scuffle that followed, Dalzell was wounded and seven of his men captured, while the rest made off. As the Lieutenant lay bleeding on the ground, the Covenant was read out to him, no doubt increasing his suffering still more. One of the commanders of the rebel foot was the same William Cleland who parodied the Highland Host, and the commander of the horse was Robert Hamilton, who, by mid-summer, was to lead his comrades to disaster.

The incident at Lesmahagow was followed by the murder of two soldiers at Newmilns in Ayrshire on 20 April. The following day, Claverhouse wrote to Lord Linlithgow, reporting that John Welsh was busy organising an armed rebellion, and that the local peasants had seized the arms of the militia. However, there was very little evidence of any preconceived plan for rebellion. The situation, rather, was very much like that in 1666. Discontent in the west was, once again, reaching a peak; and government forces were badly overstretched. To patrol the whole of the south west from Glasgow to the Solway Firth, Claverhouse and his colleague Lord Ross had only 500 troopers between them. Two incidents, one following hard upon the other, were soon to cause the greatest Whig rebellion of the Restoration.

For many of the Covenanters, Archbishop Sharp was a living symbol of all the sufferings of the Restoration. He had already been the target of one assassination attempt in 1668, when James Mitchell shot at his coach and missed, wounding Bishop Honeyman of Orkney instead. Mitchell was executed for this ten years later, although the only evidence against him was his own confession, obtained after he had received a promise from the Privy Council that his life would be spared. Sharp is said to have opposed any reprieve, because this would only encourage further assassination attempts, although this only increased the general resentment against him. But when his end finally came, it was by accident rather than design: sadly for him, he found himself in the right place at the wrong time.

To extinguish dissent, the Council had appointed a number of sheriff-deputes, with power to hold weekly courts. Claverhouse received such an appointment, combining legal and military functions in his attempts to eliminate the Whig underground. In Fife, the sheriff-depute was William Carmichael of Easter Thurston, who was accused of torture and other outrages against the local people. By April a plan was taking shape to murder both him and Sharp. Twelve men were involved, headed by John Balfour of Burleigh and David Hackston of Rathilet, who seemed to have combined the high ideals and low resentments that led a similar group of Fifemen to murder David Beaton, the Cardinal Archbishop of St Andrews, over a century before.

On Friday 2 May 1679 the conspirators met on the moor near Gilston, and from thence went to Baldinny to spend the night. Early the next morning, they set off intending to ambush Sheriff Carmichael, who was supposed to be on a hunting expedition; but, having received a warning that some action was planned against him, he abandoned his plans and returned to Cupar. Uncertain how to proceed, the conspirators then received news that Archbishop Sharp's coach had been spotted on the road to St Andrews. 'God,' they are said to have exclaimed 'hath delivered him into our hands.'

Sharp was on his way back from a Privy Council meeting in Edinburgh in the company of his daughter, Isabella. Considering the temper of the times, and that one attempt had already been made to kill him, it is surprising that he came with only five of his own servants and no military escort. As his coach entered the road through Magus Muir, close enough to St Andrews to allow a clear view of the cathedral towers, a party of horsemen were seen hurrying to catch up, pistols in hand. Fearing for his life, the Archbishop urged his coachman to drive faster; but it was too late. Burleigh and his companions overtook the coach, forcing Sharp to get out. This was no martyrdom; for James Sharp did not die well. He was cut down, pleading for his life, under the eyes of his daughter, who was wounded trying to come between her father and the swords of his murderers. He was later buried in the parish church of St Andrews, where a marble monument was later erected in his memory, the victim, like so many others, of an intolerant age.

By the time the news of the Archbishop's murder reached Edinburgh, some of his assassins were already making their way to the west. The Council at once issued a Hue and Cry, with the names of the perpetrators printed in red. A reward of 10,000 merks was offered for their apprehension, and the deed was associated with conventiclers, although there was no evidence for this. But it is certainly true that a new mood of fanaticism was growing amongst some of the lay Covenanters, although, as yet, it had little support from the ministry. Sir Robert Hamilton, a nephew of Gilbert Burnet, was the most prominent amongst the zealots, who believed, amongst other things, that the assassination of apostates like Sharp was justified. Blackadder had little time for him or his political schemes, and Burnet described him as 'a crack brained enthusiast, and under the show of a hero was an ignominious coward.' But the union of Hamilton with Hackston and Burleigh towards the end of May was the signal for a new rebellion.

All three men came to Glasgow to meet Donald Cargill, one of the more extreme ministers, to agree a new manifesto. On 29 May, Restoration Day, a party of Covenanters rode into Rutherglen and extinguished the celebratory bonfires. They then forced the magistrates to accompany them to the market cross, where Hamilton read out the manifesto, which denounced the setting up of Episcopacy, the rejection of the Covenants, the outing of the ministers, the imposition of Restoration Day, royal supremacy and the Indulgences. The document was then fixed to the cross, and copies of all the official statutes thrown into a fire.

For the Council, still hunting for the murderers of Sharp, the Rutherglen Manifesto was little more than a declaration of war. Expecting further trouble, Claverhouse was ordered to join Lord Ross in Glasgow. Yet, despite all the warnings, the threat was still seriously underestimated. On 31 May Claverhouse rode out of Glasgow in pursuit of Hamilton and the others with only 150 troopers, leaving the rest in the city with Ross. He advanced to Rutherglen, and then on to the town of Hamilton, where he captured John King, one of the more militant field preachers, and another fourteen Whigs. Early on the morning of 1 June he was at Strathaven, where he received reports that a large conventicle was due to take place that day near Loudoun Hill, close to Darvel in Ayrshire. The dispersal of field meetings was a routine task for his men; so they expected no real trouble when they rode to a the top of a hill at a place called Drumclog. There, half a mile or so to the north, were the Whigs, drawn up for a battle rather than a service. The scene was a marshy moorland, under the shadow of Loudoun Hill, where Robert Bruce had won his first important battle against the English in 1307.

As Claverhouse approached Drumclog, the congregation was being addressed by the minister, James Douglas. He was reaching the conclusion of his sermon, when a watchman on a neighbouring hill fired his rifle as a warning that the enemy was near. Douglas finished, saying;

I have done. You have got the theory – now for the practice; you know your duty; self-defence is always lawful.

As the women and children were sent to the rear, the men moved forward. Under the command of Hamilton, there were about 50 men of horseback, and 200 foot. Some had swords and firearms; the rest had home-made pikes, halberds or pitchforks. Balfour and Hackston were there, acting as officers, as was William Cleland, who was given a command in the foot. Their ground was well chosen, more by accident than design. Between them and the dragoons was a small piece of marshy ground a few yards wide, covered with a sward of green herbage. Although the Covenanters knew the way through, the bog was generally too soft to support the weight of horses, and Claverhouse seems not to have been aware of this obstacle. It was to be the chief reason for his defeat.

Leaving King and the other prisoner under escort at the farm of North Drumclog, Claverhouse attempted to negotiate with the rebels. His overtures were rejected, as all voices were raised to sing the triumphant 76th Psalm;

There arrows of the bow he brake,
   the shield, the sword, the war.
More glorious thou than hills of prey,
   more excellent art far.

Those that were stout of heart are
   spoil'd,
And none of those their hands did find
   that were the men of might.

Rather than await reinforcements from Glasgow, Claverhouse decided to risk an engagement, even though he was unfamiliar with the terrain. His confidence that his men were dealing with no more than a badly armed rabble, clearly outweighed his judgement. He sent a skirmishing party out towards the moss. In response, the Whigs sent forward a party of equal size under Cleland, which advanced to within pistol shot of the enemy. As the government soldiers raised their carbines to fire, the rebels immediately prostrated themselves on the suggestion of Burleigh, with the exception of one John Morton, who, taking a rather strict view of predestination, refused to stoop, and was killed instantly. Rather than risk another volley, the Whigs fell back, whereupon Claverhouse ordered a general advance.

At this point, a cavalry charge might easily have dispersed the rebels, but his troops were immediately entangled in the waterlogged marsh. This was the opportunity for the Whigs, who had not enough guns to match Claverhouse in a firefight. With a cry of 'ow'r the bog and on them lads' they moved forward to engage in close quarter combat with halberds and pitchforks. Cleland led his own men across the marsh towards Claverhouse's left flank, while the main body moved through the centre, taking paths hidden to the enemy. Unable to form proper ranks, the dragoons now found themselves in serious difficulties. Claverhouse's horse was gored in the belly by a pitchfork, and, badly wounded as it was, carried him right off the field. Most of his men followed, leaving Lieutenant Robert Graham, Cornet John Arnot and thirty-four others dead in the field. A further twelve were killed in the pursuit through Strathaven. As the Covenanters surged forward the prisoners at High Drumclog were liberated, and King called out to Claverhouse to stay for the afternoon service.

Once back in Glasgow, Claverhouse wrote his own report on the encounter;

> ...with a pitch fork they made such an opening in my sorre horses belly, that his guts hung out half an elle; and yet he carried me af an myl. Which so disincoraged our men, that they sustained not the shok, but fell into disorder. Their horse took the occasion of this and persued us so hotly that we got no tym to raly...What these rogues will do next I knou not, but the country was floking to them from all hands. This may be counted the beginning of the rebellion in my opinion.

Drumclog was more of a large scale skirmish than a battle; but it electrified the west. Here was the sign of Divine favour that so many had waited for so long. Soon hundreds were on the march from all over the region to join the victorious rebels, far more than had come to Wallace in 1666. News of Drumclog reached Edinburgh the following day, and the Privy Council immediately decided to concentrate all the available troops, now scattered across southern Scotland.

As soon as Claverhouse arrived in Glasgow with news of his defeat, Lord Ross immediately made preparations to defend the city. Barricades were placed across the streets and lined with all his available musketeers and dragoons. All was ready by the time the Whigs appeared before the city on 2 June. Dividing their forces in two, one party tried to storm the Gallowgate, while the other attempted an entry close to the Cathedral. But they had no artillery to break the barricades, and the concentrated firepower of the government troops was simply too great. They were repulsed with heavy losses and fell back on Hamilton by way of Tollcross Moor. However, as their numbers were growing by the day, the Earl of Linlithgow, commander-in-chief of the government forces in Scotland, decided not to risk a second assault. He ordered Ross and Claverhouse to evacuate Glasgow and join a general rendezvous of the army at Stirling. No sooner had they left than the Whigs entered, setting fire to the mansions of Lauderdale and the Archbishop. Thereafter, the army moved to a new camp at Bothwell Bridge on the west bank of the Clyde, where, by 7 June, over 7,000 Whigs had gathered. On the march the men of Ayrshire removed the heads of those executed in 1666 from the Tolbooth spikes in Ayr, Irvine, Kilmarnock and Glasgow.

Although Linlithgow now had command of 1,800 professional troops in central Scotland, far better armed than the Covenanters, he seems to have lost all control of the situation. He confined himself to writing alarming reports;

> ...the numbers which flock to thses rouges doe incress dayly, to the end his Majestie may send down such of his English forces as he shall think fitt, and to make use of such other meanes for extinguishing this flam of rebellion as in his princly wisdome he shall judge convenient.

England was currently in the grip of a sustained bout of anti-Catholic hysteria, known as the Popish Plot. Charles was thrown on the defensive by a powerful opposition party – known as the Whigs by their enemies – headed by the Earl of Shaftesbury. His own brother James was a known Catholic; and, as Charles had no legitimate offspring, he was also heir to the three kingdoms. Attempts were being made by Shaftesbury and his allies to have James excluded from the throne, forcing Charles to send him into temporary exile. Although they had no part in its outbreak, the Covenanter rising in Scotland provided useful leverage for the English Whigs. For them it was a further indication that the government of men like Lauderdale was moving the whole country slowly towards absolutism, and they were determined that the Scottish rebels would not be as roughly handled as they had been after the Pentland Rising. To placate them, Charles appointed his own illegitimate son James, Duke of Monmouth in the English peerage and Buccleuch in the Scottish, to take charge of his forces in the north. Monmouth had the advantage of being both a staunch Protestant and a political ally of Shaftesbury. He was instructed to treat the insurgents with as much leniency as the circumstances would allow. Although Dalyell, the terror of 1666, was appointed as his Lieutenant-General, his commission came too late for him to play any part in the action that followed.

Things were not going well at Bothwell. There was no experienced officer like Wallace to bring discipline and organisation; for Hamilton was proving himself to be more of an amateur theologian rather than a good commander. In the weeks after Drumclog the Whig camp degenerated, with breathtaking incompetence, into some kind of mad General Assembly. As fruitless debates continued between moderates and extremists, indulged and non-indulged, Resolutioners and Protestors, absolutely no attempt was made to see that the men were either properly trained or armed. Robert Woodrow, the great eighteenth century chronicler of the Church of Scotland during the Restoration, says of this;

> ...they were not only broken in their affections, but the common soldiers were under no kind of discipline; their confusion increased, and numbers lessened much, before the king's army came up; and...they wanted skilled officers; their arms were out of case; they had very little ammunition, their rising being without any prior concert; and they were in melancholy circumstances.

With the Whigs still static at Bothwell, the government began to regain its confidence. At Edinburgh forces had built up steadily, so that by 15 June they were strong enough to take the offensive. Around the hard core of professional troops, the militias of Fife, the Lothians, Berwickshire, Angus and Perthshire had all assembled. Moving slowly towards the west, Linlithgow was joined by the more distant shire levies at Blackburn on 18 June, bringing his total strength up to 5,000 men. Monmouth arrived in Edinburgh on the same day, and left to join the army the following morning.

As the enemy closed in, the debates at Bothwell continued as intensely as before. Many tired and discouraged, simply drifted away. The Hamilton faction, now dominant, was blind to all appeals to military necessity, preferring days of humiliation to reflect on the sins of the land and the defects of the church since 1648. In desperation, James Ure of Shargarton appealed for some sanity;

> We intreated them...to let us go on against our enemy, and let all debates alone till a free parliament and a general assembly. They told us, we were for the indulged, and they would sheath their swords as soon in those who owned it as they would do in many of the malignants.

John Welsh arrived at Bothwell on 20 June, with 1,000 recruits from Galloway; but this was only an occasion for fresh disputes over the selection of officers, and whether the Indulged should be accepted or not; and so it stood as Monmouth approached from the east. On 21 June the Whig outpost at the ford east of Hamilton was attacked. News of this was carried to Bothwell; still the desperate attempt to create a Godly army continued with as much fire as before. This would have been a comedy, save for the bloody and tragic conclusion.

Monmouth, true to the terms of his mission, made it known that he had the power to pardon all, except those already forfeited and the murderers of James Sharp. Some negotiation took place; but before he would agree to final terms, Monmouth required the rebels to lay down their arms. Although Hamilton promptly refused, he did nothing to ensure that his men were ready for battle; for, as Gilbert Burnet says, 'they had neither the grace to submit, nor the sense to march away, nor the courage to fight it out.'

By 7 o'clock on the morning of Sunday 22 June, the government army was poised on the north side of the Clyde before Bothwell Bridge, approximately where Cromwell had faced the Western Association in 1648. The Whig forces, now reduced to about 4,000 men, had been divided in two: the main body was drawn up on some rising ground on the edge of a moorland, close to the town of Hamilton, while a smaller party of 300 men from Kippen and Galloway under Hackston and Shargarton prepared to defend the Bridge itself. It is not clear who made these dispositions, or if the party by the Bridge simply represented a hard core of those who recognised that it was necessary to make a stand. As well as their muskets, these men had one small brass cannon to hold the passage of Bothwell Bridge.

Monmouth's own guns were brought down to pound the barricades erected by the enemy; but the single Whig cannon and the musketeers opened up with such effect, that the timid artillerymen abandoned their weapons. For a brief period the rebels had a chance to spike the enemy guns. However, the opportunity was allowed to slip, and the government soldiers composed themselves enough to return to their posts. For two hours the battle continued, with the defenders running low on ammunition, sending messages for reinforcements and more powder. None ever came. It has been written of this;

> Hamilton's friends say, that he had no ammunition to send to his men. This must have been owing to gross mismanagement. Why was no ammunition provided? Did Mr Hamilton and Mr Cargill, his Chief priest, expect that the King's army was to be blown off the field by paper Declarations...?

As Monmouth's cannons kept up a steady fire, a party of dragoons under Major Oglethorp made ready to exploit any breach. With the Whigs running short of ammunition they charged into action, and, after a brief struggle, managed to gain possession of the Bridge. This was the critical point in the battle; for once Monmouth's whole force was across the Clyde, it was unlikely that the disorganised army would have been able to make a stand; but neither was a counter attack ordered nor was the Bridge mined. All that Hamilton did was to order his forward party to rejoin the main army. He then stood back while Monmouth crossed in unbroken order and formed up on the other side of the Clyde. All hope was now gone.

Both armies were now only a short distance apart. To strengthen his vulnerable right wing, Monmouth moved his artillery forward, as well as posting a body of the Atholl Highlanders, supported by five troops of English dragoons, in some hollow ground. He was still busy forming his left when the Highlanders came under attack; but the pressure was immediately taken off them when the artillery fired on the cavalry on the Whig left. After only a few rounds, the horses started to panic, stampeding from the field, followed soon after by those on the right. Oglethorpe and Claverhouse were then ordered forward in pursuit, while Monmouth followed with the infantry. It was now 10 o'clock. The Whig foot, abandoned by the cavalry, was at the mercy of the enemy. About 400 were killed and 1,200 taken prisoner. As for their commander, the last word to be said about him is best left to Reverend Blackadder;

Hamilton behaved not worthily that day, showing neither courage, conduct nor resolution; but at best as a man damned or demented, and also among the foremost that fled.

Monmouth ended the slaughter as quickly as he could, and prevented any attempt to kill the prisoners. Tidings of the outcome of the Battle of Bothwell Bridge were carried to Edinburgh and London, as Monmouth continued his advance into the south west. By 24 June he was near Strathaven. He sent out parties to scour the area around Douglas and Newmilns, to confirm that the rebels were making no attempt to rally, after which he returned to Edinburgh. The last great Whig rising was over.

CHAPTER 14

The Cameronians
and the Killing Time

While Monmouth was still in the west, the prisoners taken after the Battle of Bothwell Bridge were brought to Edinburgh, roped together in pairs. They were met by a jeering mob, who cried 'Where's your God? Where's your God?' The Tolbooth was not large enough to host such a multitude, so many were held in a vacant, walled in part of Greyfriars Churchyard, a place heavy with memories of the National Covenant. Charles gave the Council leave to torture any of them who might be in possession of valuable information. Not slow to take action, the Council issued a proclamation on 26 June, declaring sixty-five of the leaders still at liberty to be guilty of treason, and all who helped them, even in the smallest way, were declared to be accessories.

Alongside this harshness, the policy of conciliation was continued when, largely under the influence of Monmouth, a Third Indulgence was announced on 29 June. Great emphasis was placed on the need to suppress illegal field conventicles, and officiating ministers were threatened with death; but, in a surprising departure from past policy, house conventicles were allowed under certain conditions. They were permitted in any part of Scotland south of the Tay, except Edinburgh and certain other places. But it was perfectly clear that this new measure was little more than a sop to Shaftesbury and his party. The King had no real interest in a more tolerant regime; nor had the Scottish Privy Council. After Monmouth left Scotland on 6 July, little attempt was made to implement the Indulgence.

In general, the treatment of the Whig prisoners was less ferocious than it had been after the Battle of Rullion Green. An Act of Indemnity was passed, allowing for the release of those who took a bond, promising not to rise in arms again. If they continued to attend conventicles, then the pardon was revoked. A few were hanged, including the Reverend John King, and some were transported; but most either escaped or were set at liberty after taking the bond. Some of the most obdurate were taken to the spot on Magus Muir where Archbishop Sharp had been butchered, and hanged in chains by order of the King. These men, who had no part in the crime, were judged to be accessories because they would not denounce it as murder. Clearly, both King and Council, frustrated by their continuing inability to track down the real perpetrators, had to make an example of somebody. Over 200 Covenanters, on their way to the penal colony on Barbados, were drowned when their ship went down off the coast of Orkney in November,

There was one other victim of the 1679 rising; it brought the long reign of King Lauderdale to an end. His enemies, headed by the Duke of Hamilton, and including some of his former friends, like Tweeddale, complained of his arbitrary government in Scotland. Charles continued to defend his minister; but when he sent his brother James to Scotland in November to replace Lauderdale as High Commissioner, this marked the beginning of the end of the old regime. Lauderdale was allowed to retain the Secretaryship for a time; but with his health in decline he lost most of his remaining offices in 1682. He died in August of that year at Tunbridge Wells, and was brought home to Scotland for burial. Thus ended the career of one of the most remarkable figures of seventeenth century Scottish politics. More than any other man, he defined the character of the Restoration regime. It was his tragedy that he had been left to defend a church policy of which he had never approved, forcing him into ever more oppressive measures in his elusive search for order. But repression simply produced even greater disorder. If all political careers end in failure, Lauderdale's was one of the greatest failures of all.

Shortly before York arrived in Edinburgh, another man came to Scotland, who, in almost every way conceivable, was his direct opposite. His name was Richard Cameron. Cameron, who had been ordained at the Scots Church in Rotterdam, was far more extreme than the old style of preacher like Blackadder, Welsh and Peden. These men had always retained some residual respect for the person of the King; but for Cameron there could be no hollow pretence of loyalty to Charles, who was the enemy of God and one of the most vile adulterers that ever lived. He lost his right to the throne, Cameron believed, when he caused the Covenants to be burnt; and as for those who placed him there;

I think that never was a generation of more worldly men about an evil deed, than the bringing home that abominable person from Breda in Holland, to be again set up in Scotland. They have set up Kings, but not for me. The land was not with them in an approving way when they did this.

Although his immoderate ways were rejected by some of the older field preachers, like Welsh, he at least managed to attract the support of the veteran Donald Cargill. Together they formed the Cameronian party. If the Whigs were the extreme section of the Covenanters, the Cameronians were the extreme section of the Whigs. Never more than a tiny minority of the Scottish Church, the Cameronians refused to accept Indulgence or any other form of compromise with the Erastian state. They saw themselves as God's vanguard, unstained by any form of compromise with earthly authorities.

By the time Cameron returned to Scotland, field conventicles had all but ceased in the aftermath of Bothwell Bridge. Blackadder and a few others kept house assemblies going, but in general the whole Covenanter movement was at the lowest ebb of its history. Cameron came to breath new life, in such a way that made not only him but all Presbyterians enemies of the state. In April 1680 both he and Cargill held a meeting at Darmead, Cambusnethan, at which prayers were said for the sins of a land that had received the Catholic Duke of York, 'a sworn vassal of Antichrist.' As yet the authorities were probably not fully aware of this new, more dangerous strain in the Presbyterian underground. However they were already beginning to tighten up. House conventicles were declared illegal in May, marking a definite end to the Third Indulgence. Pressure for this move came from the bishops, especially Alexander Burnet, who had succeeded Sharp as Archbishop of St, Andrews. Even those authorised under the first two Indulgences were no longer secure, as action began to be taken to restrict their activities. Before mid-summer, the Privy Council was in possession of a document that seemed to underline all of its deepest fears.

On 3 June one Henry Hall arrived at Bo'ness to meet with Donald Cargill. Cargill was recognised by the local minister, who promptly told the captain of nearby Blackness Castle. The two outlaws were then tracked down to an inn at Queensferry. Cargill was wounded in the scuffle that followed, although he managed to escape. Hall, too, managed to get away; but, more seriously injured than his friend, he was not able to go far. General Dalyell had been alerted to the situation, and his men found Hall, now close to death. In his pocket they discovered a paper, which turned out to be a new Covenant, subsequently called the Queensferry Paper. Amongst other things the Queensferry Paper bound all signatories to uphold the Presbyterian Church and reject all forms of Erastianism, a restatement of the position taken in the earlier Covenants. But in a dangerous new departure it proposed to discard the royal family and set up a republic. Signatories were also pledged to defend their worship and liberties, and to treat all assaults upon them as declarations of war. It was legitimate, in other words, to take up arms in defence of personal freedom.

The Queensferry Paper seems to have been part of a process at work in the Presbyterian underground to define a more aggressive posture to be taken against the state. It was confirmed on 22 June, the anniversary of the Battle of Bothwell Bridge, when Cameron and a group of twenty followers rode into Sanquhar in Dumfriesshire with drawn swords and pistols in their hands and fixed a new Declaration to the town cross. In ringing terms it announced that the persecuted party in Scotland;

...disown Charles Stuart, who hath been reigning (or rather tyrannizing we may say) on the throne of Britain these years bygone, as having any right, title to, or interest in, the said Crown of Scotland for government, as forfeited several years since, by his perjury and breach of covenant both to God and His Kirk...For which reason, we declare, that several years since he should have been denuded of being king, ruler, or magistrate, or having any power to act, or to be obeyed as such. As also, we, being under the Standard of our Lord Jesus Christ, Captain of Salvation, we do declare a war with such a tyrant and usurper, and all the men of his practices, as enemies to our Lord Jesus Christ, His Cause and Covenants...and against all such as...have acknowledged him...

York was also denounced as a professed papist, and Cameron declared that theirs was a 'standard that shall overthrow the throne of Britain.'

The Sanquhar Declaration was little more than an empty act of boldness by a group of desperate men; but the government took it seriously enough. Six days later it offered a reward of 5,000 merks for Cameron dead or alive; 3,000 merks each for his brother Michael, Cargill and Thomas Douglas, another Cameronian field preacher; and 1,000 each for their followers, all dead or alive. A vigorous man hunt was also put under way throughout the south west. On learning of the whereabouts of Cameron and his colleagues a month later, Dalyell at once sent a strong body of mounted troops under Captain Bruce of Earlshall to intercept them.

On Thursday 22 July Cameron and his little band of guerrillas, no more than sixty men in all, were on their way up the valley of the River Ayr, making for the wilds of Muirkirk. They only got as far as Airds Moss, when they spotted Earlshall and his troopers bearing down on them. His soldiers made ready for battle, as Cameron uttered his brief, memorable prayer 'Lord spare the green and take the ripe.' Command of the Cameronians was in the hands of David Hackston of Rathillet, who had fought at Bothwell Bridge. With his infantry in the centre, he divided his small party of horse, eight on the right, and fifteen on the left. Bruce sent forward a probing party of twenty of his own horsemen, who were thrown back by a volley from the Cameronian guns, whose horses were at once thrown into a panic by the noise.

Now beset by superior numbers, the rebels fought on with courage. Hackston managed to cut his way through the enemy ranks, before his horse got stuck in a bog, whereupon he was taken prisoner. At some point in the fight Richard Cameron himself fell dead, and his infantry fled from the scene, using the safety of a swamp against pursuit. Cameron was joined in death by his brother Michael and seven of their comrades. Besides Hackston, another three men were taken prisoner. To claim their reward, Bruce and David Ramsay, a fellow officer, cut off the head and hands of Richard Cameron. These grim relics were laid before the Privy Council, with the words 'See, there, the head and hands of a man who lived praying and preaching, and died praying and fighting.'

If the Council were grateful for the head of Cameron, they were even more grateful for the body of Hackston. Here, at last, was one of the company responsible for the death of James Sharp. On 30 July he was put on trial for his part in the murder, as well as his involvement in Bothwell Bridge, the Queensferry Paper, the Sanquhar Declaration and the skirmish at Airds Moss. He refused to plead, denying the authority of the court. His judges then announced the death sentence, to be carried out that same afternoon at the scaffold between St Giles and the town cross, with a savagery not usual in Scottish justice. First, his right hand was cut off, followed, after an interval by his left. Then his body was drawn up a pulley to the top of the gallows and dropped alive. After this his heart was cut out, followed by his entrails, which were burnt on a fire by the scaffold. His head was removed and his body quartered, the pieces sent to St Andrews, Cupar, Glasgow, Leith and Burntisland for public display.

With the death of Cameron, Donald Cargill was the only figure of note left among the field preachers. Defiant as ever, he held a great conventicle at Torwood near Stirling in September 1680. Declaring that all his actions were approved by Heaven, Cargill proceeded to excommunicate and deliver up to Satan, Charles II and the Duke of York, as well as the Dukes of Rothes, Monmouth and Lauderdale, Sir George Mackenzie of Rosehaugh – the Lord Advocate – and General Dalyell. The reward for the capture of Cargill was now upped to 5,000 merks. Despite this he remained elusive, although some of his colleagues were caught and executed. In the spring of 1681 the more moderate Blackadder was taken prisoner in Edinburgh and sent to the prison on the Bass Rock, where he died four years later. Cargill remained at liberty until July 1681, when he was captured by a party of dragoons at Covington Mill and brought to Edinburgh for execution. After death his head was cut off and placed beside that of Richard Cameron on the Netherbow Port.

On 28 July, the day after Cargill's execution, the Duke of York opened a new session of the Scottish Parliament in his role as Royal Commissioner. Two acts were passed, which had an important bearing on the future course of the Covenanter struggle: the Succession Act and the Test Act. The Succession Act secured James' right to inherit the throne, despite the fact that he was a Catholic; and the Test Act required all office holders to recognise the monarch as the supreme arbiter in all matters, temporal or spiritual. Taken together, these measures involved the acceptance that a Catholic sovereign would one day be ultimate judge of all issues concerning the government, doctrine and practices of the Church of Scotland. It wasn't only the Cameronians who balked at this. Many moderates, who hitherto had collaborated with the authorities, were alarmed by the new measures. Some of the orthodox clergy were to be deprived of their livings for refusing to take the Test. Objections were even raised by some members of the Privy Council, including the Lord President, Sir James Dalrymple and the Earl of Argyll.

The Test Act is arguably one of the ludicrous and contradictory laws ever placed on the Scottish statute book. It required all to swear to uphold the true Protestant religion, contained in the Confession of Faith, ratified by the first Parliament of King James VI in 1567, besides requiring a recognition of the King's authority in spiritual and temporal matters. But the two elements of this oath simply did not hang together. York was clearly unaware that the Confession of Faith not only condemned Catholicism, but it affirmed that Jesus Christ was the only Head and Lawgiver of the Church, and that it was blasphemous for any man to intrude on this position. This simply could not be reconciled with an assertion of royal supremacy; and the conservatives, who thought that Episcopacy was divinely ordained, found themselves faced with an oath that allowed the King to choose whatever form of church government he pleased. Dalrymple's son John pointed out how absurd the whole thing was;

> It inferred an obligation upon those who took it, to conform to any religion the King pleased, and yet to adhere to the Presbyterian religion; to oppose prelacy and yet to maintain the present constitution of the church, which was prelacy; and to renounce and yet affirm the doctrine of non-resistance.

James Dalrymple, not willing to face the consequences of his refusal to take the Test, joined the Presbyterian exiles at Rotterdam, under the protection of William of Orange. Argyll tried to save both his person and his conscience by adding a caveat to the oath, which he would take 'only so far as it was consistent with itself and the Protestant religion.' When he refused to commit himself without reservation, he was deprived of his seat on the Privy Council. Soon after he was arrested on a charge of treason. When the case came to trial the jury was packed with the political enemies of the Campbells, including the second Marquis of Montrose, the Earl of Airlie and James Graham of Claverhouse. All defence was useless; and when Montrose announced a guilty verdict, Argyll decided to escape. On 20 December he made his way out of Edinburgh Castle in disguise, fleeing to Holland to join Dalrymple. In his absence, he was condemned to death, and the house of Argyll wiped out for a second time in a generation.

This blatantly biased trial involving the ridiculous Test Act, greatly reduced the credibility of York and the Scottish Privy Council. The boys of George Heriot's Hospital in Edinburgh covered a copy of the hated act in butter and offered it to a dog, which was hanged for treason after licking off the butter and refusing to swallow the Test whole. During the Christmas celebrations, the students of the University carried an effigy of the Pope to the Market Cross, and burned it with a copy of the Test in one of its hands. Government policy, in alienating Presbyterian opinion at large, allowed the rare Cameronian orchid, which would have been killed off in a more temperate climate, to survive in the hothouse atmosphere engendered in the declining years of Stewart Scotland.

Alarmed by recent developments, and now seriously short of spiritual leaders, the scattered Covenanter groups banded together in a Union of Correspondence Societies. Their first meeting was held at Lesmahagow in December, during which they decided to publish a Declaration at Lanark in January 1682. On the appointed day forty horsemen, including a young man by the name of James Renwick, and twenty men on foot gathered round the Cross of Lanark and affixed a new manifesto, repeating most of the previous accusations against the King and rejecting the Test and the other statutes passed in the Parliament presided over by his brother. For failing to clear the town of these 'desperate villains', the Privy Council later fined the magistrates of Lanark 6,000 merks. In addition they ordered the town council of Edinburgh to assemble at the Cross on 18 January to witness the Covenants being put to the torch once more, along with the Lanark Declaration and other Cameronian documents. In the same month, Claverhouse was granted the Heritable Sheriffdom of Wigtoun and the Heritable Regality of Tongland near Kirkcudbright. This added considerably to his powers, and gave him the right to summon anyone suspected of attending conventicles.

Claverhouse obtained these new appointments because the previous holders refused to take the Test. A number of other heritable offices reverted to the crown because the incumbents would not subscribe to the Oath. Numbered amongst these were some of the most powerful figures in the land, including the Duke of Hamilton, and the Earls of Haddington, Nithsdale, Galloway, Cassillis, Sutherland and Kenmure. The interesting thing about the Test Act is that it could unite a Catholic like Nithsdale and Covenanter like Cassillis in opposition to the government.

After the departure of York for London in May 1682, the policy of repression continued as intense as before, especially in the south west. Claverhouse organised sweeps of the area, targeting those who refused to attend their local parish church, and looking out for field assemblies. Rather than subject themselves to the attentions of his troopers, most people hurried back to church, although resistance still remained strong in Lanarkshire and Ayrshire. Inevitably, this coercion was accompanied by some brutality, although a large number of the atrocities alleged against Claverhouse cannot be proved one way or the other. But in one notorious case a party of his dragoons brutally beat up two boys aged ten and fourteen to make them reveal the whereabouts of their father. Claverhouse's more usual tactic was to appear, like a stern headmaster, at Sunday services to take a register, as he reports on 17 April;

> We ar nou com to read lists every Sonday afrer sermon of men and weomen, and we fynd feu absent...I examined every man in the shyr, and almost all the Steuartry of Galouy, and fixt such a guilt upon them, that they ar absolutly in the King's reverence...Did the King and the Deuk knou what those rebellious villans, which they call minesters, put in the heads of the people, they would think it necessary to keep them out. The poor people of Menegaff confess upon oath that they wer made reneu the Covenant, and believe the King was a Papist...

For dissidents, quartering and fining continued to be the main tools of oppression. Realising the limited impact of these measures, the Council considered ever more repressive acts. In April 1683 it was declared that all persons suspected of harbouring rebels, even if they did not know them to be such, were to be called upon to answer for their behaviour. This was followed by an offer of indemnity to all prepared to take the Test before 1 August 1683. As a warning to all non-conformists, the number of those executed began to increase steadily. The continuation of a strong line against all dissidents was indicated when Claverhouse was appointed as a Privy Councillor in May 1683.

Despite all of this the Covenanter underground continued to function, rather like a bush fire, stamped out in one place, only to appear in another. But most of the old field preachers were now either dead or in prison. A new unifying force was needed. This was provided when James Renwick, a disciple of Richard Cameron, returned to Scotland in September 1683 as an ordained minister, having completed his studies abroad. He had been present at the execution of Cargill in 1681, and was determined to take over the leadership of the various Cameronian societies, known as the Remnant. Field conventicling, sometimes flickering on the threshold of extinction, began to revive under his guidance. Alert to this new wave of dissent, the government applied ever more stringent tests of loyalty. Three Whigs were hanged in December for refusing to say 'God save the King' without reservation. A further twelve, some of whom had been in prison for years, were executed in the first few months of 1684, including the veteran Captain John Paton, who had fought at Marston Moor, Kilsyth, Dunbar, Worcester, Rullion Green and Bothwell Bridge. He was eighty years old.

Despite the efforts of Claverhouse and others, Renwick and the Cameronians evaded all attempts at capture. It was felt that their activities were the nursery of a new rebellion, and the general situation resembled that just before the uprising of 1679. This appeared to receive confirmation when a party of thirty dragoons escorting Whig prisoners from Dumfries to Edinburgh, were ambushed at Enterkin Pass near Sanquhar on 29 July 1684. Determined to rescue the prisoners, a group of Covenanters had been gathering for several days in upper Nithsdale. A trooper was killed in the ensuing encounter, and several of the prisoners escaped, as the soldiers fled back down the Pass. Six of the rescuers were later arrested by Claverhouse near Dumfries on 9 August. They were taken to Edinburgh and condemned for being in arms against the King, the executions following hard upon the verdict. The Killing Times had begun.

In September the Privy Council increased the political temperature by several degrees, by establishing circuit justiciary courts by order of the King. The instructions issued to the judges allowed for a whole range of powers to be used against dissenters. Amongst other things, all who refused the oath of allegiance were to be banished. Ships' captains were instructed to offer the oath to all passengers, and travellers were not allowed to go any further than three miles from their homes without the authority of a magistrate. Later in the month Renwick was declared to be a traitor, rebel and outlaw. Failing to distinguish between the Cameronians and more moderate shades of opinion, the Council adopted a harsher policy towards all Presbyterians, and some of the Indulged ministers were outed for the second time in their careers.

Frustrated by their continuing inability to track down Renwick, the authorities were outraged when a new manifesto was posted on several Mercat Crosses on 8 November 1684. This *Apologetic Declaration* was yet another statement of Cameronian principle. It restated all former resolutions to defend the Covenants, and disowned the authority of Charles Stewart. More than this, it announced the right of the persecuted to defend themselves against the state;

> ...to pursue the ends of our Covenants...we...declare...that whosoever stretch forth their hands against us (justiciary, military, assenting gentlemen, viperous and malicious clergy, intelligencers, delators, raisers of hue and cry), all and every one of such shall be reputed by us enemies to God and the Covenanted Work of Reformation, and punished as such, according to our power and the degree of their offence.

Two weeks later two soldiers were shot dead at Swyne Abbey in West Lothian, in what was considered to be a direct result of the Cameronian declaration. In responding to these provocations, the authorities decided on the most drastic action yet taken. After seeking the advice of the Law Lords, the Privy Council decreed that all who refused to disown the *Apologetic Declaration*, whether in arms or not, might be shot without trial, provided two witnesses were present.

The Council was quick to make an example. A number of Whigs were still being held in the prisons of Edinburgh, including John Semple, whose father had died at Rullion Green, John Watt from Kilbride and Gabriel Thomson, of whom nothing is known, apart from his name. All three were brought to trial on 24 November. Semple freely admitted that he approved of the Declaration, and the other two simply refused to disown it. For this, all three were sentenced to die that afternoon. In the crowds that gathered to watch them die, there were many moved by the plight of these unfortunate men, which resulted in a black farce being played out after they were cut down from the gallows. It was now night, and the public hangman and his companions were about to follow the normal practice of striping and burying the victims at the place of execution. Before they were able to complete the task, a large party of students drove them off, whereupon the dead men were placed in coffins by a group of women, who immediately rushed off to bury them in the consecrated ground of Greyfriars Churchyard. When they arrived, they found the entrance blocked by the guard. The corpses had to be abandoned, and they lay all night in the open, before being taken back to the gallows. In a fit of pique, the Council ordered the coffin maker to be prosecuted.

As the winter of 1684 approached, the trouble grew in intensity. Guerrilla bands were operating over large areas of the south west. In Nithsdale, the castle of the Depute-Sheriff of Kirkcudbright was attacked; and on 16 November a large group of armed Cameronians broke into the prison at Kirkcudbright, killed a sentry and released all the inmates. Peter Pierson, the orthodox minister of Carspharin in Kirkcudbrightshire, was shot dead by some extreme Cameronians, an act not approved by Renwick and the rest of their comrades. On 27 November the Council extended the conflict to all Presbyterians, regardless of their opinions, by ordering all Indulged ministers to quit their charges. Those who refused to go were to be sent to the Bass or the local Tolbooth.

From this point forward, no distinction was made between straightforward non-conformity and outright rebellion, giving the Cameronians a far greater importance than their numbers justified. Lieutenant-General Drummond was ordered to take a thousand foot and horse, including Claverhouse's companies, to the west and south in early December. He was given the authority to quarter troops where he chose and to kill all rebels and those who abetted them. The Council concluded the year by publishing another proclamation against Renwick's Declaration, commanding all living south of the Tay to take an oath rejecting all its principles. Early in January 1685 burgh magistrates were commissioned to enforce what was known as the Abjuration Oath. Soon, the number of field executions increased: the Killing Time was now approaching its most intense phase.

On 6 February 1685 King Charles II died. He was succeeded by his brother, now James VII of Scotland and II of England, the first openly Catholic monarch to rule in the British Isles since the days of the two Maries – Mary Queen of Scots, his great grandmother, and Mary Tudor. James' succession was widely acclaimed, both in Scotland and England. In the last years of the previous reign there had been a steady reaction against the excesses of the Popish Plot. Shaftesbury had died an exile in Holland, and the Whig opposition in England was broken and discredited. James, Duke of Monmouth, also a Dutch exile, immediately set himself up as the Protestant alternative to his Catholic uncle; but few were willing to support an illegitimate pretender against the lawful King, whatever his personal beliefs happened to be. Nevertheless, Monmouth determined to attempt to raise the standard of rebellion in England. It was vital for the success of his scheme that Argyll, his fellow exile, should make a similar attempt in Scotland.

Argyll had kept a steady watch on events in Scotland since he had left in 1681. He considered making an armed descent as early as 1684. But the government sent a large armed force into Argyllshire under the Marquis of Atholl, to ensure that no landing could be attempted in the country of the Campbells. Atholl arrested all those suspected of treasonable correspondence with Argyll, and imprisoned a number of local Indulged ministers. Neil Campbell, Argyll's brother, was only allowed to remain at liberty after he pledged himself to remain loyal and ensure that his fellow clansmen followed his example.

With the county now garrisoned, Argyll was unable to count on the support of his tenants and kinsmen. However, he hoped, as the son of the great Covenanter Marquis, that he might be able to get help from the Whigs in the Lowlands. He found some encouragement in this from the presence in his camp of William Cleland, who had escaped to the Continent after Bothwell Bridge. Cleland attended a meeting in Amsterdam in April 1685, where the final details of Argyll's planned invasion were discussed. He was then sent on ahead to Scotland to prepare the ground in the Lowlands. But the Cameronians remembered Argyll as the ally of Lauderdale, rather than as the son of his father. Besides, years of persecution had made them unwilling to trust anyone beyond their rather select ranks. When Argyll eventually came, he was to receive no support in either his own Highlands or the Covenanter Lowlands.

In the same month as the Amsterdam meeting, the first Parliament of James VII opened in Edinburgh. William, Duke of

Queensberry, acting in his capacity as Commissioner, demanded fresh legislation to destroy the Covenanters. His speech was followed by that of that of the Earl of Perth, the Chancellor, who launched a bitter tirade against the Cameronians;

> ...we have a new sect sprung up among us from the dunghill, the very dreggs of the people who kill by pretended inspiration...whose idoll is that accursed paper the Covenant...These monsters bring a publick reproach upon the nation in the eyes of all our nighbours abroad... they bring reproach upon our religion, and are our great plague.

Parliament went on to confirm Episcopacy as the settled form of government of the Kirk of Scotland. It was declared treasonable to take or defend the Covenants of 1638 or 1643, and the death penalty was decreed for all who attended field conventicles. In response, the Cameronians held their own field parliament on the Moss of Blackgannoch, between Muirkirk and Sanquhar, late the following month, and agreed a Protestation against the accession of James, who, in their opinion was a murderer, idolater and a subject of Anti-Christ. This was fixed, once again, to the Market Cross at Sanquhar. The Cameronians were now faced with their ultimate nightmare – a Catholic King who was the supreme arbiter in all civil and religious matters, about as far away from the Covenanter ideal as it is possible to get.

In the period following the accession of James, the greatest fear of the authorities was that the Cameronians would make common cause with Argyll, which explains why the policy of repression reached such a pitch of intensity. Field executions peaked in the two months of April and May 1685, as Argyll was making his final preparations to return from exile; and it was during this time that most of those were killed whose fate is still recalled by monuments liberally scattered across southern Scotland. One such was John Brown of Priesthill, who was murdered at his home in front of his wife on the orders of Claverhouse. At Wigtown on 2 May two women – Margaret Maclauchlan and Margaret Wilson – were tied to stakes and drowned by the incoming tide for failing to take the Abjuration Oath. On the same day Argyll finally sailed for Scotland. With many prisons now full to overflowing, the government decided to transfer some of the most stubborn Whigs from Edinburgh to Dunnotar Castle in the north east. There were over 150 in all, women as well as men, in various states of health, as may be gathered from the notes of Major John Wedderburne;

277

John Broun ane old decrept creature; Thomas Peticrew...old age...being paralitick; Nicolas McNight, a dyeing woman; Michael Smyth a lame and decryped man; John Williamson mad and furious; Jean Stodhart, big of child and in hazard of dying if forced to travell.

At Dunnotar, the prisoners were packed into two small vaults, 110 men and women in one alone. A number were tortured after an abortive escape attempt, reputedly with burning match. For all, the Whig Vaults still stand at Dunnotar, a silent echo of their suffering.

Argyll finally reached Campbeltown on 20 May with small force of 300 men; an odd company, including one Richard Rumbold, a former Cromwellian officer, who had fought at Dunbar and Worcester; and John Balfour of Burleigh and George Fleming, both of whom had played a part in the murder of Archbishop Sharp. No sooner had he landed than Argyll published a declaration against 'the hellish mystery of antichristian iniquity and arbitrary tyranny...of James, Duke of York, a notorious apostate and bigot Papist.' But most of Argyllshire was too firmly under the heel of the Marquis of Atholl for many to answer the call to arms.

Still hoping that the rest of Presbyterian Scotland would rise to greet him, Argyll sent emissaries across to Ayrshire and Galloway. Encouraging news was received from one of them, a minister by the name of George Barclay, who said that the country was eager for his coming, that the enemy were panic stricken, and 1000 Whig horse could easily be raised within a short space of time. But Argyll neither established a hold on the Highlands, nor did he strike decisively at the Lowlands. Renwick and the Cameronians, moreover, showed no enthusiasm for Argyll, who, while perfectly willing to use the Covenanters, was clearly no Covenanter himself. With his force dwindling away in a pointless march, he crossed the Clyde at Kilpatrick in early June, hoping to make for the friendly county of Ayrshire; but he was captured near Paisley on the 18th. He was taken to Edinburgh to be kissed by the *Maiden*, as his father had been a quarter of a century before. Monmouth's expedition to England fared no better. Starting later than Argyll, his army of west country peasants was defeated at the Battle of Sedgemoor on 6 July. Monmouth was captured and executed a short time after. Aside from the rantings of a handful of Cameronians, James was more secure than ever on his throne. The Counter Revolution was triumphant.

CHAPTER 15

Dunkeld and the End of the Covenanter Wars

By the summer of 1685 the government had virtually won the war against the Covenanters. Most people had been forced back into the established church by the policy of systematic repression. The irreconcilables had been hanged, shot, transported, or had died from natural causes. After the death of the legendary Peden in early 1686, only Renwick and a desperate minority remained, running from place to place in search of refuge. The authorities began to relax, and the regular martyrdoms, a feature of the Killing Times, began to decline. Only one field execution, that of David Steel of Nether Skellyhill, took place in the whole of 1686. It is possible that, in time, Scotland would have come to accept Episcopacy, as the old Covenanter tradition died away. But fate had decreed another course, which was to lead directly to the re-establishment of the Presbyterian Church and the end of the Stewart dynasty.

James VII was not at all like Charles II, for whom self-interest was a guiding principle, and survival an overriding objective. The new King was in every sense a 'man of principle', very much in the same mould as his father, King Charles I. He had a clear sense of duty, and a desire to do what his conscience dictated, regardless of the political cost. As a man, he had many admirable qualities; but intelligence and good sense were not among them. As the principle target of Shaftesbury and the Whigs during the Popish Plot, he had felt the distant lash of persecution, under which his Catholic subjects had suffered for many years. There is absolutely no evidence that he planned to re-establish Catholicism as the state religion, but he was determined to lift the legal restrictions which prevented the Catholic minority from enjoying full liberty of conscience, even if this meant clashing with established interests. In ending the persecution of Catholics, he also had to end the persecution of the Presbyterians and the other Protestant sects. His aims may have been admirable; his timing was disastrously wrong. In France, Louis

XIV had revoked the Edict of Nantes, under which the French Protestants, known as the Huguenots, had enjoyed a measure of tolerance. James rushed into his new policy at the same time as Louis was beginning the wholesale persecution of the Huguenots, using many of the methods perfected by Turner and Claverhouse in Scotland. With French refugees arriving in England in ever increasing numbers, fear of James' intentions began to rise. Here, now, was the true test of the Restoration, the Stewart dynasty and the Divine Right of Kings.

Parliament assembled at Edinburgh on April 29 1686 to consider the King's desire to secure toleration for Catholics. But the members were already suspicious. Leading Catholic noblemen had been exempted from the obligation to take the Test Act the previous November. Queensberry, a committed Protestant, had been replaced as Commissioner to Parliament by the Earl of Moray, whom many suspected was a secret Catholic. The Earl of Perth, Chancellor of Scotland, and his brother, Lord Melfort, were both opportunist converts to Catholicism. Edinburgh Castle, the most powerful fortress in the land, was put in the charge of the Duke of Gordon, also a follower of the King's religion. To allow for their worship, the nave of Holyrood Abbey had been consecrated as a chapel. Against this background, Parliament, little more than a rubber stamp since the Restoration, discovered an ancient spirit of self determination, replying that it would only go as far as its conscience allowed 'not doubting that your Majesty will be careful to secure the Protestant Religion established by law.' The message was cautious, polite, but unmistakable: Parliament had defied the will of the King. Soon after it was adjourned, and then dissolved. James now looked to other methods.

In the absence of Parliamentary approval, James proceeded to establish toleration by use of the royal prerogative alone. In August he wrote to the Privy Council, announcing his decision to allow freedom of worship to Roman Catholics in private households; and in February 1687 he followed this up with a new Indulgence, embracing moderate Presbyterians and Quakers, as well as Catholics. A second and even more comprehensive Indulgence was proclaimed in June, in which all were allowed 'to meet and serve God after their own way, be it in private houses, chapels, or places purposely hired or built for that use.'

Almost at once, the whole structure of Restoration

ecclesiastical policy came crashing down. To secure freedom for his fellow Catholics, James, had pulled the Episcopal temple down around his ears. Presbyterianism, almost on the point of death, came back to life. Ministers began to return from exile. With the removal of compulsion, many abandoned the official church, to attend their own meeting houses, especially in the south west. In the most extreme case, a curate saw his congregation sink to one person, the local laird, who also tired of his ministrations. Although still strong in the north, the Episcopal church was effectively disestablished across much of southern Scotland. Presbyterianism had been granted, albeit in a limited form, by a Catholic King acting as the supreme arbiter in ecclesiastical matters, the purest expression of Erastianism imaginable; but most dissenters were too relieved to consider this philosophical point. In July 1687 a number of Presbyterian ministers met in Edinburgh and wrote to the King expressing their gratitude, all thoughts of the Covenants forgotten.

There was one important exception to the new policy. Field conventicles were still banned, and the Council was urged to 'root them out with all the severity of the law.' In any case, Renwick and his associates were more irreconcilable than ever, remaining true to the ideals of the Covenant and refusing to accept any concessions from the state. But the second Indulgence had exposed them as a tiny and unimportant minority, as well as showing how foolish official policy had been since the days of Middleton. For most people, the struggles of the past were over, and few took the Cameronian *Testimony against Toleration* seriously when it was published in January 1688. Almost as a desperate act of provocation, Renwick continued to preach at field conventicles, even holding one on the Braid Hills, dangerously close to the capital. Soon after he was captured on a secret visit to Edinburgh, and executed on 17 February, the last great martyr of the Covenant.

The death of Renwick was officially reported to a meeting of the Societies, held on 7 March at Blackgannoch. Like so many minorities throughout history, the Cameronian movement was like a hydra: no sooner had one head been cut off than it was replaced by another. Thomas Lining was appointed to take the place of Renwick, although he was never to acquire the same stature. Despite this, the sect was now too weak to maintain its struggle against the state. In their last aggressive action of the reign, they attacked a party of soldiers escorting David Houston, a colleague of Renwick's, on the road to Edinburgh at Crichton Path, three miles from Old Cumnock on 20 June. Houston was rescued, although badly wounded in the battle, and a number of the soldiers were killed. In the military sweep that followed one George Wood was shot dead, in what was probably the last of the field executions. In the final crisis of James VII's brief rule, the Cameronians played no part; nor, for that matter, did most Scots.

Ten days before the clash at Crichton Path, Mary of Modena, wife of King James, gave birth to a male heir, also named James, fated to pass into history as the Old Pretender. Prior to this the heir to the throne had been Mary, James' eldest daughter by his first wife, Anne Hyde. Mary was not only a staunch Protestant, but she was also the wife of the Dutch Prince, William of Orange. For William, now engaged in his great struggle with Louis XIV, the prospect of a permanent Catholic dynasty in the British Isles was a serious threat to his security. William was fortunate that James' arbitrary actions in England, which included the arrest of a number of senior churchmen, had created a powerful coalition against him, some Tories as well as Whigs, headed by the Earls of Danby and Devonshire. Many believed, or pretended to believe, that Prince James was not the son of Mary of Modena, but had been smuggled into St James's Palace in a warming pan. This was little more than a ludicrous myth; but it served a purpose. On a rising wave of anti-Papist hysteria, which found popular expression in the song *Lilliburlero*, William was invited by the opposition to intervene in the affairs of England. This was the beginning of the Glorious Revolution.

William also realised the importance of winning over Scottish opinion. For many years Scots, both humble and great, had sought refuge in Calvinist Holland. Lord Lorne, son of the executed ninth Earl of Argyll, had joined William, along with Gilbert Burnet, the historian, Sir James Dalrymple, and the Whig, William Cleland, who left Scotland for a second time after the failure of the Argyll rising. He also had a brigade of Scottish soldiers, under the command of Hugh Mackay of Scourie. Mindful of these men, William issued a proclamation on 10 October from The Hague, addressed to the people of Scotland, saying that he was coming in defence of Protestantism and the laws and liberties of the northern kingdom. The Privy Council did its best to prevent circulation of this document; but its contents were soon widely known. It was openly proclaimed in several towns, Glasgow amongst them. Amongst other things, William condemned the persecution of Presbyterians since the Restoration, although his picture of the true situation was somewhat narrowed by the advice he received from the exiles. In desperation, King James, looking for support against his son-in-law in all quarters, sent out feelers to the leading Presbyterians in Scotland to test the measure of the gratitude expressed towards him the previous summer. The reply he received was equivocal at best: he was told that they would act as God inspired them.

It might be thought that the Cameronians would look favourably on Dutch William; but, moulded into a spirit of self-righteous arrogance by years of persecution, they were cool to all who were not of their own party. For them the Dutch were 'a promiscuous conjunction of reformed Lutherans, Malignants and Sectaries.' At a meeting held at Wanlockhead on 24 October 1688, they agreed to make defensive preparations and to ally themselves with unadulterated Covenanters only. William's proclamation was too lame and defective, because it ignored the 'Covenanted Work of Reformation.' William Cleland later appeared back in Scotland, ready to introduce a note of realism into the deliberations of his colleagues.

On November 5 William landed with his army, Mackay and the Scots amongst them, at Torbay. Two days before the Scots' bishops had met in Edinburgh and drafted a letter to King James, calling him the 'darling of Heaven,' praying to God to give him victory with 'the hearts of your subjects and the necks of your enemies.' This inability to distance themselves from James was to lead to the ruin of their cause. With a greater sense of the dangers of the time, and an eye to the possible outcome, the Privy Council ordered the heads of all those executed during the repressions of the previous years were to be removed from the Tolbooth spikes across Scotland.

While events were being played out in the south of England, Scotland remained quiet. James had built up a powerful army in the north, well placed to ensure that there was no rising on behalf of William. But on the advice of the Earl of Melfort, his Secretary of State, he decided to call all his regular forces south, leaving only a small garrison with the Duke of Gordon at Edinburgh Castle. No sooner had the army, commanded by Lieutenant-General James Douglas and Major General Graham of Claverhouse, crossed the Border than the Cameronians were on the move. Colin, Earl of Balcarres, later wrote to James in exile, explaining the disastrous consequences of the decision to withdraw the army;

> ...so soon as your Majesty sent orders that the army should be brought together, and be in readiness to march into England, all the discontented in the nation thought they had met with their just time, believing your affairs must be in a miserable condition in England when you was obliged to bring up so inconsiderable a force, and by that to leave a whole nation exposed to your enemies...

Douglas and Claverhouse arrived at London towards the end of October, and prepared to march west with the King to join the main royal army, concentrating at Salisbury. Before he left, James elevated Claverhouse to the peerage as Viscount Dundee, in recognition of his unflinching loyalty. But if Dundee was loyal, others were far less so. Although his army was at least twice the size of William's, successive desertions weakened the King's resolve. Lord Cornberry, son of the Earl of Clarendon, was among the first to go, taking three regiments of horse with him into William's camp. He was followed by John Churchill, victor of the Battle of Sedgemoor and the future Duke of Marlborough, along with the Duke of Grafton; but the cruellest desertion by far was that of Princess Anne, the King's second daughter, a firm Protestant like her sister Mary. With rebellion breaking out across England, James ignored the advice of Dundee and others to make a stand, leaving England in December, never to return, as William advanced steadily from the west.

With the old regime collapsing in the south, the Privy Council, deprived of armed support, began to lose control in Scotland. On 10 December, a mob, many Cameronians among them, ransacked the Chapel Royal at Holyrood. Later in the month, the hated curates were ejected from their manses throughout the south west, a process known as 'rabbling.' Some of these were carried out with considerable cruelty, presumably as a result of years of pent up frustration, or other local causes. At the manse of Kirkpatrick-Juxta in Annandale, the incumbent minister, Archibald Fergusson, was beaten up and stripped naked by a crowd of women. At Kilmarnock, Robert Bell had his gown torn from him, which was burnt at the Cross, along with the Prayer Book.

William was now in control in London, although his exact status had yet to be decided, both in England and Scotland. William Rose, Bishop of Edinburgh, was in London at the time, trying to safeguard the Episcopalian church in Scotland. The situation was not quite as grim as seemed at first; for William was now taking a more objective view of the religious question in Scotland. Rose was told;

> He now knows the state of Scotland much better than he did when he was in Holland, for, while there, he was made believe that Scotland generally all over was Presbyterian, but now sees the great body of the nobility and gentry are for Episcopacy, and 'tis the trading and inferior sort are for Presbytery; wherefore he now bids me tell you that, if you will undertake to serve him to the purpose that he is served here in England, he will take you by the hand, support the Church and Order, and throw off the Presbyterians.

But the Scots' bishops remained loyal to the old dynasty, and to the minority party soon to be known as Jacobites, from *Jacobus*, the Latin for James. By this they ensured that Episcopacy could not be the established form of the Church of Scotland.

With the throne officially empty after the flight of James, William summoned Conventions in both England and Scotland to consider the constitutional question. The English met first, deciding to offer the crown jointly to William and Mary. Sovereignty was thus decided at an assembly of legislators, abandoning for ever the dangerous fiction of the Divine Right of Kings.

With the Scottish Convention due to meet in Edinburgh on 14 March 1689, the Societies held their own assembly at Lesmahagow Church on the 3rd. Once again the Covenants were renewed. But the Cameronians, now virtually the only armed force in southern Scotland, apart from the garrison at Edinburgh Castle, had not yet decided their attitude to the Revolution and the new government. For many, William was – and remained – an Uncovenanted King, no more trustworthy than any of his predecessors. But for others, Cleland among them, a clear choice had to be made between William and the Jacobites. When the Duke of Hamilton, a long standing opponent of Stewart absolutism, arrived in Edinburgh to attend the Convention of Estates, he was accompanied by a large body of Cameronians, many of them armed.

The political situation throughout the British Isles was tense.

At the Revolution, Ireland had remained loyal to the old dynasty. James, with the help of Louis XIV, landed at Kinsale in early March, hoping to launch an offensive to recover all of his lost kingdoms. Soon he had control of all of Ireland, with the exception of Enniskillen and Londonderry in the north, where the Protestant settlers responded to the demand that they open their gates to the King with shouts of 'No Surrender', a cry that was to echo across Irish history. Despite this setback, James hoped to cross to England before the end of the summer, and retained some confidence that the Convention in Scotland would fall into line behind the Jacobites, headed by Dundee and Balcarres.

When the Convention finally opened, the Whigs – now a general term for all those opposed to James – had a majority over their Jacobite opponents, and Hamilton was elected president. But Dundee and his colleagues were still hopeful. Two letters were to be read out, one from James and the other from William, the contents of which were as yet unknown. The Jacobites hoped that James would offer concessions which would swing all moderate opinion behind the old order; after all, the Stewarts had been on the throne of Scotland since 1371, and represented an ancient tradition. But James, trusting in the advice of the criminally incompetent Melfort, made a fatal error. William's letter was conciliatory, offering guarantees for the safety of the Protestant religion. James, in contrast, was arrogant and threatening. Opinion at once swung behind Hamilton.

The Jacobites had lost the political battle, but they still had almost all the force. Gordon's guns loomed ominously over the Convention from the Castle, and Dundee had a party of fifty horsemen from his old regiment, who had remained loyal to their commander. Hamilton had arranged for William to send four of his Scottish regiments under General Mackay to protect the Convention, although they had not yet arrived. In the meantime, he offered the Convention the service of the Cameronians, who, up to now, had been concealed in vaults and cellars around the city. On receiving word, the armed bands from the west emerged from their hiding place, and gathered outside Parliament House. Cleland was there, and was reputed to be the author of a plot to assassinate Dundee. With his enemies concentrating in strength, Edinburgh was too dangerous for Dundee, who left for the north after a brief conference with the Duke of Gordon, immortalised in the ballad by Sir Walter Scott.

With Dundee out of the way, the Jacobite opposition in the Convention collapsed. On 4 April, by a virtually unanimous vote, it was declared that James had vacated the throne. Hamilton followed this by proposing to offer the crown jointly to 'the Prince and Princess of Orange, now king and queen of England.' Seven days later, the Convention also passed the Claim of Right, declaring that any religion but Presbyterianism was 'contrary to the inclination of the generality of the people,' and that Episcopacy ought to be abolished. These documents were carried to London by Archibald Campbell, now tenth Earl of Argyll, and two other commissioners. On 11 May Argyll administered the coronation oath to William and Mary. For his service to the new monarchs, Argyll had hoped to recover the title of Marquis, held by his grandfather; but in time he was to be raised to the even higher honour of Duke. His family, with little reason to love the Stewarts, were to remain the strongest anti-Jacobite force in the Highlands, right through to the Hanoverian succession.

Mackay arrived in Edinburgh in late March and relieved the Cameronian irregulars blockading Edinburgh Castle. But the regular forces were still fairly modest, and Scotland now appeared to be in as much danger as she had been in 1644. Dundee, acting out the role of Montrose, was busy raising forces in the north, and James promised to send him 5,000 men from Ireland. In the Convention, the Laird of Blackwood proposed that a new regiment be raised amongst the western Whigs, 'in this juncture of affairs, when religion, liberty, country and all were in great danger.' Command was to be given to James Douglas, Earl of Angus, and William Cleland was to be Lieutenant-Colonel. A general meeting of the Societies was held on 29 April at the parish church of Douglas in Lanarkshire, to consider this proposal. Most took the strict view that until William took the Covenants, service under him would be sinful. A minority, no doubt recognising the dangers they would face if Dundee triumphed, agreed to form a new regiment of the line, to be known as the Cameronians. After some dispute over the conditions of service, they agreed the following;

> To declare that you engage in this service, of purpose to resist popery and prelacy and arbitrary power, and to recover and establish the work of reformation in Scotland, in opposition to popery, prelacy and arbitrary power in all branches and steps thereof, till the government

in church and state be brought to that lustre and integrity which it had in the best times.

With William and Mary now legally constituted, the Convention was raised to the status of a full Parliament on 5 June, with Hamilton as Commissioner. The bishops, who had been in attendance during the Convention, all stayed away, never to reappear in a legislative assembly. On 22 July Parliament passed an act abolishing prelacy. For the duration of the present emergency nothing was put in its place, although it was declared that the King and Queen 'will settle by law that church government in this kingdom which is most agreeable to the inclination of the people.' One thing, though, was absolutely clear: the question of church government would be settled in true Erastian form by Parliament, not by the Church itself. No one spoke for ecclesiastical independence or the Covenants.

Dundee had managed to gather an army, raised chiefly amongst the western clans, including the MacDonalds. He had also been joined by a small force from Ireland, under Colonel Alexander Cannon, although this was far weaker than James had promised. Mackay with about 4,500 troops, many of them freshly raised Lowland recruits, set off in pursuit into the Highlands. On 27 July 1689 he met the Jacobites, posted on the heights above, as he made his way out of the Pass of Killiecrankie, close to Blair Atholl. Dundee had less than half Mackay's numbers, although he was far better placed. Just after 7 o'clock in the evening, as the summer sun was sinking behind Strath Garry, its rays blinding the Williamites in the valley below, Dundee ordered a charge. Rushing downhill in the fashion of those who had followed Montrose and MacColla, the Jacobites let off a single volley, before falling on the enemy with their broadswords, slicing into Mackay's line, and carrying away virtually the whole of his left wing and much of the centre. But in that wild downhill charge almost a third of the Jacobite army had been killed, a far higher casualty rate than any of Montrose's battles. Their most grievous loss was Dundee himself, killed at the height of his victory. With the Highlanders busy plundering his baggage train, Mackay led the rest of his army off to safety.

News of the Battle of Killiecrankie caused a brief panic in the south. But Cannon, on whom command of the victorious army had now devolved, had not the cavalry to risk a descent on the

Lowlands, and restricted himself to raids and recruiting drives. In an attempt to check enemy raids from Atholl into the Lowlands, the Council on 12 August ordered the Cameronian Regiment, which had arrived too late to take part in Killiecrankie, to advance from Doune in Stirlingshire to Dunkeld. This was a dangerous posting, right on the threshold of the mountains, so much so that many in the regiment believed that they were being deliberately led into destruction.

Dunkeld, an ancient cathedral town, lies on the north bank of the River Tay, and is virtually surrounded by hills. From some low lying hills close to the river on the east side of the town, the main street runs west to the Market Cross. From there it passes by the south wall of the Cathedral, then in a ruinous state. The only other large building, apart from the old chapter houses of the Cathedral, was Dunkeld House, a mansion belonging to the Marquis of Atholl, which formed a square around a courtyard. Apart from these places, the narrow streets and walled enclosures of the town provided good defensive cover.

The Cameronians arrived at Dunkeld on Saturday 17 August, 700 or 800 men in all, with Cleland in command. Wasting no time, Cleland set about making the place secure: the stone walls around Atholl's house, the building itself and the Cathedral were all made defensible. Already worried by the seemingly impossible task of holding this vulnerable outpost, morale was boosted by the arrival of Lord Cardross with five troops of horse and dragoons on Monday morning. By that same evening word came of a great gathering of Highlanders to the north, and, after receiving orders from Perth, Cardross rode off as quickly as he had come. Now close to panic, the Cameronian infantry threatened to abandon their position. To steady their nerve, and to prove that he was not about to leave them, Cleland offered to shoot his horse and those of the other officers. All drew strength from their commander's courage and resolve, returning at once to their duties.

On 21 August the Jacobites appeared in strength in the hills around Dunkeld. Cannon had over 4,000 men, twice as strong as the army Dundee led to victory at Killiecrankie. But Cannon was an uninspiring soldier, who understood little of the Highlanders and their martial traditions. Unlike Montrose and Dundee, he led from behind, failing to provide his men with much needed inspiration. Still worse, he was now committing his troops to a street battle, for which they were ill suited. Morale was still high after Killiecrankie; but Cannon was now about to risk all in a futile encounter.

The Battle of Dunkeld began at 7 o'clock in the morning. Cannon placed his small artillery train on Gallow Hill, to the north of Dunkeld House, where it played a minimal part in the fight to come. On the eastern flank of the town, the Cameronians under Captain Hay held Shioches Hill, an important outpost intersected by dikes, and with woods running down to join the first houses. Once this position was taken, Dunkeld would no longer be defensible from this direction. Under assault from the Maclean regiment, Hay and his men carried out a fighting retreat, dike by dike, back towards a barricade erected at the Cross. Having gained his first objective, Cannon placed two troops of horse to prevent any attempted breakout to the east. At the same time, another two troops rode across Bishop's Hill to the west of the Cathedral, to guard the ford across the Tay. Cleland was now held in a vice. The Highlanders moved for the kill, rushing the barricade in the town centre. As Hay was driven back to Dunkeld House, the Cameronian detachments to the west were attacked in overwhelming numbers, forcing them to retreat back to the Cathedral, where all the civilians who had not managed to escape were taking cover. During this retreat a number of men were trapped in houses and killed.

Cannon's men were now attacking in four places at once. The Appin Stewarts assaulted the Cathedral with such determination, that help had to be brought in to try to hold the position. Bit by Bit, the Cameronians were forced back to Dunkeld House, virtually their final refuge. At about 8 o'clock Cleland was felled by two shots, one in the head and the other in the liver. Mortally wounded, he tried to crawl into a house so that his men would not be discouraged by the sight of his body; but he expired in the attempt. Major Henderson took command, only to fall soon after. Captain Munro took over. This was now the critical point in the battle, for the Jacobites, discouraged by the unexpectedly tough resistance, were beginning to lose impetus. Each fresh troop as it arrived fired off a single musket shot, before crowding in hopeless confusion around the walls of Dunkeld house. For Munro, the greatest danger came from the enemy snipers, posted in the nearby houses. To combat this, he sent out groups of men with burning faggots tied to the ends of their pikes. Doors were locked and houses set on fire. Soon the air filled with the terrible screams of men being burned to death, sixteen in one house alone. By 11 o' clock, with the regiment running out of powder, the men prepared to make a desperate last stand in Dunkeld House, when the Highlanders suddenly drew off. A contemporary report records;

> At length the rebels wearie with so many fruitless and expensive assaults, and finding no abatement of the courage or diligence of their adversories, who treated them with continual shot from all their posts, they gave over and fell back, and run to the hills in great confusion. Whereupon they within beat their drums, and flourished their colours, and hallowed after them, with all expressions of contempt and provocations, to return. Their commanders assay'd to bring them back to a fresh assault, as some prisoners related; but they answered them, they could fight against men, but it was not fit to fight any more against devils.

Expecting a further attack, the Cameronians sung Psalms, repaired their defences, and waited. The Highlanders never came. By the time Cardross reappeared in the afternoon, Cannon had retreated to the north west, leaving 300 dead behind. Although the embers of the revolt were to smoulder into the following year, the back of the first Jacobite rising had been broken by the Cameronians at Dunkeld. Balcarres wrote to James 'Thus all the hopes of your friends were dashed, and your enemies more encouraged than ever.' The following year James was defeated by William at the Battle of the Boyne, and immediately ran back to France, leaving his loyal Irish troops to face the consequences of the adventure. He would never make another serious attempt to recover the crowns he had allowed to slip so casually from his grasp. His daughter Anne, who succeeded William in 1702, was to be the last Stewart monarch to sit on the throne of Britain, finally fulfilling James V's prophecy that the dynasty which came with a lass would pass with a lass.

As well as marking the first serious defeat for the Jacobites, the Battle of Dunkeld is notable in one other regard: it was the last fight of the Covenanter Wars. In June 1690 Parliament passed an act establishing the Presbyterian system of church government, with the Westminster Confession as the basis of its doctrine. All the ministers ejected since 1661 were restored to their former charges, and a General Assembly was called, the first since 1653. Although Hugh Kennedie, a surviving Protestor, was elected Moderator, the members meekly confirmed the Erastian settlement. There was no attempt to raise the doctrine of the two states, or to remind the nation of the forgotten promises of the Covenant. A new national church had been established; and for most people this was enough. Religion had been at the centre of politics for too long.

There were, of course, dissenters. The bishops continued to exist – although stripped of all their political functions and state support – commanding some loyalty, particularly in the Lowlands of the north east. For the hard core of the Cameronian party – which should now be distinguished from the regiment – the settlement of 1690 fell far short of their uncompromising ideals. Some, including Robert Hamilton, who had led the Covenanters so disastrously at Bothwell Bridge, remained outside the mainstream as the 'True Church of Scotland.' Refusing to take the oath of allegiance to William as an 'uncovenanted ruler,' the Society Men played little part in national life in the years to follow. As late as 1712, they renewed the Covenants at Auchensauch Hill in Lanarkshire, finally emerging in 1743, after a series of bewildering splits, as the Reformed Presbyterian Church. In 1876 most of the Reformed Presbyterians joined the Free Church of Scotland, leaving a few congregations to carry the idea of the Covenants down to the present day. As for the Cameronian Regiment, it continued to serve with distinction throughout the world, until disbanded in the defence review of 1968, when, after holding one last conventicle at Douglas in Lanarkshire, it lowered its banners for the last time.

The ideas of the Covenants and the Covenanters have had a deep resonance throughout Scottish history, extending far beyond the confines of religion. In 1706 a group of 300 men, describing themselves as Covenanters, gathered in Dumfries and burned the unpopular Bill of Union, under which the Parliaments of Scotland and England were to be united the following year. Later in the century, Robert Burns, Ayrshireman, patriot and political radical, defined his own feelings in verse;

The Solemn League and Covenant
Cost Scotland blood – cost Scotland tears;
But it seal'd Freedom's sacred cause –
If thou'rt slave, indulge thy sneers.

In reaching out for a new identity, it seemed natural for Scots to return to the idea of a Covenant. In 1949 a group of enthusiasts, headed by John MacCormick, attempted to galvanise opinion by shaping a new Covenant, calling for a Parliament for Scotland. The first to sign was the Duke of Montrose, recalling the actions of his ancestor in 1638. Eventually another two million signatures were collected, although it proved impossible to translate this enthusiasm into real political gains. It is perhaps not too far fetched to suggest that it took Margaret Thatcher, acting as a political reincarnation of Charles I, to remind the Scots, once again, of the dangers of arrogance and absolutism, forcing the nation ever forward on the path of a new destiny.

Select Bibliography

Documentary and Narrative Sources

Acts of the Parliament of Scotland

Account of the Highland Host, Blackwood's Magazine, April, 1817.

Adair, P., *A True Narrative of the Rise and Progress of the Presbyterian Church in Ireland,* 1866.

Baillie, Robert, *Letters and Journals,* 3 vols., 1841.

Balcarres, Colin, Earl of, *Memoirs Touching the Revolution in Scotland, 1688–1690,* 1841.

Balcanquall, Walter, *A Large Declaration Concerning the Late Tumults in Scotland,* 1639.

Balfour, Sir James, *Historical Works,* 4 vols., 1824.

Barnes, Ambrose, *Memoirs,* 1867.

Blackadder, John, *Memoirs,* edited by A Chrichton, 1826.

The Book of Clanranald, in 'Reliquiae Celticae', edited by A. MacBain and J. Kennedy, 2 vols, 1892–94.

Burnet, Gilbert, *Memoirs of the Lifes and Actions Of James and William, dukes of Hamilton,* 1852.

Burnet, Gilbert, *History of my Own Life and Times,* edited by O. Airey and H.C. Foxcroft, 1897–1902.

Calendar of Clarendon State Papers, variously edited, 1869–1970.

Calendar of State Papers, Domestic Series, of the reign of Charles I, 1858–97.

Calendar of State Papers, Domestic Series, 1649–1660, 1875–86.

Calendar of State Papers, Domestic Series, of the Reign of King Charles II, 1860–1939.

Clarendon, Edward, Earl of, *The History of the Rebellion and Cival Wars in England,* 6 vols., edited bt W.D. MaCray, 1888.

Correspondence of the Earl of Ancram and the Earl of Lothian, 2 vols., edited by D. Laing, 1875.

Correspondence of the Scots Commissioners in London, 1644–1646. edited by H.W. Meikle, 1917.

Cromwell, Oliver, *Writings and Speeches,* edited by W.C. Abbot., 1937–47.

Douglas, Robert, *Diary,* in 'Historical Fragments Relative to Scottish Affairs from 1635 to 1664', edited by J. Maidment, 1833.

The Exact Narrative of the Conflict at Dunkeld Betwixt the Earl of Angus's Regiment and the Rebels, in 'Blackwood's Magazine', September 1817.

Extracts from the Council Register of the Burgh of Aberdeen, 1643–1747, edited by J. Stuart, 1847.

Select Bibliography

Extracts from the Records of the Burgh of Edinburgh, 1642–1655, edited by M. Wood, 1938.

Fountainhall, Lord, *Chronological Notes of Scottish Affairs from 1680 to 1701*, 1822.

Fraser, James, *Chronicle of the Frasers. The Wardlaw Manuscript*, 1905.

The Government of Scotland under the Covenanters, edited by D. Stevenson, 1982.

Guthry, Henry, *Memoirs*, 1747.

The Hamilton Papers, edited by S.R. Gardiner, 1880.

His Majesties Declaration Concerning His Proceedings with His Subjects of Scotland, 1640.

The History of the Warr of Ireland from 1641 to 1653, by a British Officer of the Regiment of Sir John Clotworthy, 1873.

Hodgson, John, *Memoirs*, 1806.

Kirkton, James, *A History of the Church of Scotland*, edited by R, Stewart, 1992; first published in 1817 as *The Secret and True History of the Church of Scotland from the Restoration to the Year 1678*.

Lamont, John, *Diary, 1649–1671*, 1839.

The Lauderdale Papers, 3 vols., edited by O. Airy, 1884–85.

Law, Robert, *Memorialls; or the Memorable Things that Fell out Within the Island of Brittain from 1638 to 1684*, edited by C.K. Sharpe, 1818.

Letters and Papers Illustrating the Relations between Charles II and Scotland in 1650, edited by S.R. Gardiner, 1894.

Letters and Papers of the Verney Family, edited by J. Bruce, 1853.

Letters from a Roundhead Officer Written from Scotland, edited by J.Y. Akerman, 1856.

Livingston, John, *A Brief Historical Relation of the Life of John Livingston*, 1754.

McCrie, T., ed., *The Life of Robert Blair...by his son-in-law, Mr William Row*, 1848.

Mackenzie, George, of Rosehaugh, *Memoirs of the Affairs of Scotland*, 1821.

MacDonald, John, *Orian Iain Loim. Songs of John MacDonald, Bard of Keppoch*, edited and translated by A.M. Mackenzie, 1964.

Memoirs of Prince Rupert and the Cavaliers, edited by E. Warburton, 1849.

Memoirs of the Scottish Catholics During the XVIIth and XVIIIth Centuries, edited by W. Forbes Leith, 1909.

Memorialls of the Great Civil War From 1646 to 1652, edited by H. Cary, 1842.

Memorials of Montrose and his Times, edited by M. Napier, 1848–1850.

Montereul, Jean De, *Diplomatic Correspondence*, translated by J.G. Fotheringham, 1898.

A Narrative of the Siege of Carlisle in 1644 and 1645, edited by I. Tullie, 1840.

Newcastle, Margaret, Duchess of, *The Life of William Cavendish, Duke of Newcastle*, n.d.

Nicoll, John, *Diary of Public Transactions*, 1836.

Papers Relating to the Army of the Solemn League and Covenant, 1643–1647, edited by C.S. Terry, 1917.

The Quarrel between the Earl of Manchester and Oliver Cromwell, edited by J. Bruce and D. Masson, 1875.

Records of the Kirk of Scotland, volume 1, edited by A. Peterkin, 1838.

The Register of the Privy Council of Scotland, second and third series, variously edited, 1899–1933.

Rothes, John Leslie, Earl of, *A Relation of the Proceedings of the Affairs of the Kirk of Scotland, from August 1637 to July, 1638*, 1830.

Rothiemay, James Gordon of, *History of Scots Affairs from 1637 to 1641*, 3 vols., 1841.

Rushworth, John, *Historical Collections*, 8 vols., 1721–22.

Rutherford, Samuel, *Letters*, edited by A.A. Bonar, 1894.

Ruthven, Patrick Gordon of, *A Short Abridgement of Britane's Distemper*, 1844.

Scottish Diaries and Memoirs, 1550–1746, arranged and edited by J.G. Fyfie, 1928.

Shargarton, James Ure of, *Narrative of the Rising Suppressed at Bothwell Bridge*, in 'Memoirs of William Veitch and George Brysson', edited by T. McCrie, 1825.

Sommerville, James, Lord, *Memorie of the Sommervilles*, 1815.

Spalding, John, *The History of the Troubles*, 1828.

Spreul, John, *Some Remarkable Passages of the Lord's Providence towards Mr John Spreul, town clerk of Glasgow, 1635–1664*, in 'Historical Fragments', edited by J. Maidment, 1833.

Turner, Sir James, *Memoirs of his own Life and Times, 1632–1670*, 1829.

Wallace, James, *Narrative of the Rising Suppressed at Pentland*, in Memoirs of William Veitch and George Brysson, edited by T. McCrie, 1825.

Warriston, Archibald Johnstone of, *Diaries*, variously edited, 1911–1940.

Whitelock, Bulstrode, *Memorials of English Affairs*, 1853.

Wishart, George, *The Memoirs of James Marquis of Montrose*, translated by A.D. Murdoch and H.F. Morland Simpson, 1893.

Secondary Works

Aiton, W., *A History of the Rencounter at Drumclog and Bothwell Bridge*, 1821.

Anderson, W., *The Scottish Nation* etc, biographical history, 1863.

Ashley, M., *General Monck*, 1977.

Ashton, R., *Counter-Revolution. The Second Civil War and its Origins, 1646–8*, 1994.

Baldock, T.S., *Cromwell as a Soldier*, 1899.

Select Bibliography

Barbour, J., 'The Capture of the Covenanting Town of Dumfries by Montrose etc'., in *Transactions of the Dumfriesshire and Galloway Natural History and Antiquarian Society*, XXI, 1908–09.

Barrett, C.R.B., *Battles and Battlefields of England*, 1896.

Barnes, R.P., 'Scotland and the Glorious Revolution of 1688', in *Albion*, volume 3, pp 116–127, 1971.

Barnes, R.P., 'James VII's Forfieture of the Scottish Throne', in *Albion*, volume 5, pp 299–313, 1973.

Bennett, M., *The Civil Wars in Britain and Ireland*, 1997.

Brotchie, T.C.F., *The Battlefields of Scotland*, 1913.

Broxap, E., *The Great Civil War in Lancashire, 1642–1651*, 1910.

Buchan, J., *Montrose*, 1938.

Buckroyd, J., *Church and State in Scotland, 1660–1681*, 1980.

Buckroyd, J., 'Anti-Clericalism in Scotland During the Restoration', in *Politics and Society: Scotland, 1408–1929*, edited by N. MacDougall, 1983.

Buckroyd, J., *The Life of James Sharp, Archbishop of St Andrews, 1618 – 1679*, 1987.

Burne, A.H., *The Battlefields of England*, 1950.

Burne, A.H. and Young, P., *The Great Civil War*, 1959.

Burrell, S.A., 'The Apocalyptic Vision of the Early Covenanters', in *The Scottish Historical Review*, vol. XLIII, pp 1–24, 1964.

Campbell, A.H., 'Cromwell's Edinburgh Campaign', in the *Scots Magazine*, XVIII, pp 456–463, 1932–33.

Campbell, T., *Standing Witness. An Illustrated Guide to the Scottish Covenanters*, 1996.

Carlton, C., *Charles I. The Personal Monarch*, 1983.

Carlton, C., *Archbishop William Laud*, 1987.

Corish, P.J., 'The Rising of 1641 and the Catholic Confederacy, 1641–5', in *A New History of Ireland*, vol III, edited by T. W. Moody, F. X. Martin and F. J. Bryce, 1991.

Corsar, K.C., 'The Surrender of Edinburgh Castle, December 1650', in *The Scottish Historical Review*, vol. 28, pp 43–54, 1949.

Cowan, E.J., 'Montrose and Argyll', in *The Scottish Nation*, edited by G. Menzies, 1972.

Cowan, E.J., 'The Solemn League and Covenant', in *Scotland and England, 1286–1815*, edited by R. A. Mason, 1987.

Cowan, E.J., *Montrose. For Covenant and King*, 1995.

Cowan, I.B., 'The Covenanters: a Revision Article', in *The Scottish Historical Review*, vol XLVII, pp 35–52, 1968.

Cowan, I.B., *The Scottish Covenanters, 1660–1688*, 1976.

Cowan, I.B., 'The Reluctant Revolutionaries: Scotland in 1688', in *By Force or Default? The Revolution of 1688–1689*, edited by E. Cruickshanks, 1989.

Dalton, C., *The Scottish Army, 1661–1688*, 1989 reprint.

Davies, G. and Hardacre, P.H., 'The Restoration of Scottish Episcopacy, 1660–1661', in *The Journal of British Studies*, pp 32–53, 1961.

Dawson, N.H., *Cromwell's Understudy: the Life and Times of General John Lambert*, 1938.

Donald, P., *An Uncounselled King. Charles I and the Scottish Troubles, 1637–1641*, 1990.

Donaldson, G., *Scotland from James V to James VII*, 1965.

Douglas, W.S., *Cromwell's Scotch Campaigns, 1650–51*, 1898.

Douglas Simpson, W., 'The Topographical Problems of the Battle of Alford', in *The Aberdeen University Review*, vil VI, pp 248–254, 1918–19.

Dow, F.D., *Cromwellian Scotland, 1651–1660*, 1979.

Elder, J.R., *The Highland Host of 1678*, 1914.

Ferguson, W., *Scotland's Relations with England – a Survey to 1707*, 1994.

Ford, D., 'Enterkin and the Covenanters', in *Transactions of the Dumfriesshire and Galloway Natural History and Antiquarian Society*, third series, vol XXXVI pp 132–148, 1957–58.

Foster, W.R., *The Church Before the Covenants, 1596–1638*, 1975.

Firth, C.H., 'Marston Moor', in *Transactions of the Royal Historical Society*, XII, pp 17–79, 1898.

Firth, C.H., 'The Battle of Dunbar', in *Transactions of the Royal Historical Society*, XIV, pp 19–52, 1900.

Firth, C.H., *Cromwell's Army*, 1962, 4th edition.

Fissel, M.C., *The Bishops' War. Charles I's Campaigns against Scotland, 1638–1640*, 1994.

Fraser, A., *Cromwell Our Chief of Men*, 1973.

Fraser, W., *The Book of Carlaverock*, 1873.

Furgol, E.M., *A Regimental History of the Covenanting Armies, 1639–1651*, 1990.

Furgol, E.M., 'Scotland turned Sweden: the Scottish Covenanters and the Military Revolution, 1638–1651', in *The Scottish National Covenant in its British Context, 1638–1651*, edited by J. Morrill, 1990.

Gardiner, S.R., *History of England*, vols VIII to X, 1884.

Gardiner, S.R., *History of the Great Civil War*, 4 vols, 1893.

Gardiner, S.R., *History of the Commonwealth and Protectorate*, 4 vols, 1903.

Gentles, I., *The New Model Army in England, Ireland and Scotland*, 1992.

Gillespie, R., 'An Army Sent from God: Scots at War in Ireland, 1642–9', in *Scotland at War AD 79–1918*, edited by N. Macdougall, 1991.

Grainger, J.D., *Cromwell Against the Scots. The Last Anglo-Scottish War, 1650–1652*, 1997.

Gregg, P., *King Charles I*, 1981.

Guthrie, C.L., 'The Solemn League and Covenant in the Three Kingdoms of England, Scotland and Ireland', in *The Scottish Historical Review*, vol XV, pp 292–309, 1918.

Hamilton, C.L., 'Scotland, Ireland and the English Civil War', in *Albion*, vol 7, pp 120–30, 1975.

Hayes McCoy, G.A., *Irish Battles. A Military History of Ireland*, 1969.

Hazlett, H., 'The Recruitment and Organisation of the Scottish Army in Ulster, 1642–9', in *Essays in British and Irish History in Honour of James Eadie Todd*, edited by H.A. Cronne, T. W. Moody and D.B. Quinn, 1949.

Hewison, J.K., *The Covenanters*, 2 vols, 1913.

Hexter, J.H., *The Reign of King Pym*, 1943.

Hibbard, C.M., *Charles I and the Popish Plot*, 1983.

Hibbard, C.M., 'Episcopal Warrior in the British Wars of Religion', in *War and Government in Britain*, edited by M.C. Fissel, 1991.

Hill, G., *An Historical Account of the MacDonnells of Antrim*, 1873.

Hill, J.M. *Celtic Warfare, 1595–1763*, 1986.

Hill Burton, J., *History of Scotland*, vols 6 and 7, 1897.

Hoenig, F., 'The Battle of Preston', in *Journal of the Royal United Services Institution*, vol XLII, pp 830–843, 1898.

Howie, J., *Biographica Scoticana...Scots Worthies*, 1816.

Hughes, B.P., *Firepower. Weapons Effectiveness in the Battlefield, 1630–1850*, 1974.

Hutton, R., *Charles the Second, King of England, Scotland and Ireland*, 1989.

Hopkins, P., *Glencoe and the End of the Highland War*, 1986.

Irwin, R.A., 'Cromwell in Lancashire: the Campaign of Preston 1648', in *The Army Quarterly*, vol 27, pp 72–87, 1933–34.

Kaplan, L., 'Presbyterians and Independents in 1643', in *The English Historical Review*, vol 84, pp 244–56, 1969.

Kaplan, L., 'Steps to War: the Scots and Parliament, 1642–1643', in the *Journal of British Studies*, vol IX, pp 50–70, 1970.

Kenyon, J., *The Civil Wars of England*, 1988.

Kiernan, V.G., 'The Covenanters: a Problem of Creed and Class', in *History from Below*, edited by K. Frantz, 1988.

Kiernan, V.G., 'A Banner with a Strange Device: the Later Covenanters', in *Covenant, Charter and Party*, edited by T. Brotherstone, 1989.

Kitson, F., *Prince Rupert. Portrait of a Soldier*, 1994.

Lang, A., *A History of Scotland*, vol III, 1904.

Lee, M., 'Scotland and the General Crisis of the Seventeenth Century', in *The Scottish Historical Review*, vol LXIII, pp 136–54, 1984.

Lee, M., *The Road to Revolution. Scotland under Charles I*, 1985.

Linklater, M. and Hesketh, C., *For King and Conscience. John Graham of Claverhouse, Viscount Dundee*, 1989.

Lucas Phillips, C.E., *Cromwell's Captains*, 1938.

Lowe, J., 'Some Aspects of the Wars in Ireland, 1641–1649', in *Irish Sword*, vol 4, pp 81–87, 1959–60.

McCoy, F.N., *Robert Baillie and the Second Scots Reformation*, 1974.

MacInnes, A.I., *Charles I and the Making of the Covenanting Movement,* 1991.

Macleod, R.H., 'The Battle of Auldearn, 9 May 1645', in *The Seventeenth Century in the Highlands,* Inverness Field Club, 1986.

Mackenzie. W.C., *The Life and Times of John Maitland Duke of Lauderdale, 1616–1682,* 1923.

Makey, W., *The Church of the Covenant, 1637–1651,* 1979.

Markham, C.R., *The Great Lord Fairfax,* 1870.

Mason, R., 'The Aristocracy, Episcopacy and the Revolution of 1638', in *Covenant, Charter and Party,* edited by T. Brotherstone, 1989.

Mathieson, W.L., *Politics and Religion. A Study in Scottish History from the Reformation to the Revolution,* 2 vols, 1902.

Mathieson, W.L., 'The Scottish Parliament, 1560–1707', in *The Scottish Historical Review,* vol IV, pp 49–62, 1907.

Matthew, D., *Scotland Under Charles I,* 1955.

Mitchison, R., *Lordship and Patronage, Scotland 1603–1745,* 1983.

Morrah, P., *Prince Rupert of the Rhine,* 1976.

Mulligan, L., 'The Scottish Alliance and the Committee of Both Kingdoms', in *Historical Studies,* vol 14, pp 173–188, 1970.

Murren, P., *Grampian Battlefields,* 1990.

Napier, M., *Memoirs of the Marquis of Montrose,* 2 vols, 1856.

Newman, P., *Marston Moor, 2 July 1644: the Sources and the Site,* 1978.

O'Connel, J.J., *The Irish Wars. A Military History of Ireland from the Norse Invasion to 1798,* 1920.

O'Danachair, C.O., 'Montrose's Irish Regiments', in *Irish Sword,* 4, pp 61–67, 1959–60.

Ohlmeyer, J.H., *Civil War and Restoration in the Three Stuart Kingdoms: the Career of Randal MacDonnell, marquis of Antrim, 1609–1683,* 1993.

Ohlmeyer, J.H., 'The Wars of Religion, 1603–1660', in *A Military History of Ireland,* edited by T. Bartlett and K. Jeffery, 1996.

Ohlmeyer, J.H., 'The Marquis of Antrim: A Stuart Turn-Kilt?', in *History Today,* March 1993.

Orr, R.L., *Alexander Henderson. Churchman and Statesman,* 1919.

Paterson, J., *History of the County of Ayr,* 2 vols, 1847.

Pearl, V., 'Oliver St John, and the middle group in the Long Parliament', in *The English Historical Review,* vol 81, pp 490–519, 1966.

Perceval-Maxwell, M., 'Ireland and Scotland 1638 to 1648', in *The Scottish National Covenant in its British Context, 1638–1651,* edited by J. Morrill, 1990.

Pittock, M.G.H., *The Invention of Scotland. The Stuart Myth and Scottish Identity, 1638 to the Present,* 1991.

Reid, J.S., *History of the Persbyterian Church in Ireland,* 3 vols, 1867.

Reid, S., *Scots Armies of the Civil War, 1639–1651,* 1982.

Reid, S., *The Campaigns of Montrose. A Military History of the Civil War in Scotland 1639 to 1646*, 1990.

Rogers, H.C.B., *Battles and Generals of the Civil Wars, 1642–1651*, 1968.

Ross, A., *The Cameronians (Scottish Rifles)*, 1919.

Rubinstein, H.L., *Captain Luckless. James, First Duke of Hamilton, 1606–1649*, 1975.

Russell, C., *The Fall of the British Monarchies, 1637–1642*, 1991.

Scally, J., 'Counsel in Crisis: James, third Marquis of Hamilton and the Bishops' Wars, 1638–1640', in *Celtic Dimensions of the British Civil Wars*, edited by J.R. Young, 1997.

Sharpe, K., *The Personal Rule of Charles I*, 1992.

Stephen, W., *History of Inverkeithing and Rosyth*, 1921.

Stevenson, D., 'The Battle of Mauchline Moor 1648', in *Ayrshire Collections*, vol 11, pp 3–24, 1973.

Stevenson, D., *The Scottish Revolution, 1637–44*, 1973.

Stevenson, D., 'The Massacre at Dunnaverty 1647', in *Scottish Studies*, vol 19, pp 27–37, 1975.

Stevenson, D., *Revolution and Counter-Revolution in Scotland, 1644–1651*, 1977.

Stevenson, D., *Alisdair MacColla and the Highland Problem in the Seventeenth Century*, 1980.

Stevenson D., *Scottish Covenanters and Irish Confederates*, 1981.

Stevenson, D., 'The Covenanters and the Western Association', in *Ayrshire Archaeological and Natural History Society Collections*, vol 13, 1982.

Stevenson D., 'The Early Covenanters and the Federal Union of Britain', in *Scotland and England, 1286 – 1815*, edited by R.A. Mason. 1987.

Stevenson, D., *King or Covenant? Voices from the Civil War*, 1996.

Stevenson, L., (ed) Dictionary of National Biography, 1885–1900.

Terry, C.S., 'The Siege of Newcastle-Upon-Tyne by the Scots in 1644', in *Archaeologia Aeliana*, 21, pp 180–258, 1899.

Terry, C.S., *The Life and Campaigns of Alexander Leslie*, 1899.

Terry, C.S., *John Graham of Claverhouse, Viscount Dundee, 1648–1689*, 1905.

Terry, C.S., *The Pentland Rising and Rullion Green*, 1905.

Terry, C.S., *A History of Scotland*, 1920.

Treave, G., *Portrait of a Cavalier. William Cavendish, First Duke of Newcastle*, 1979.

Trench, C.C., 'From Arquebus to Rifle: the Pursuit of Perfection', in *History Today*, 23, 1973.

Wardale, H., 'Cromwell in Lancashire', in *Transactions of the Lancashire and Cheshire Antiquarian Society* for 1932, vol XLVIII, pp 76–94, 1934.

Wedgwood, C.V., 'The Covenanters and the First Civil War', in *The Scottish Historical Review*, vol 39, pp 1–15, 1960.

Wedgwood, C.V., *The King's Peace, 1637–1641*, 1955.

Wedgwood, C.V., *The King's War, 1641–1647*, 1958.

Wijn, J.W., 'Military Forces and Warfare, 1610–1648', in *New Cambridge Modern History*, vol 4.

Williams, R., *Montrose, Cavalier in Mourning*, 1975.

Williamson, A.H., 'Scotland and the British Revolutions', in *The Scottish Historical Review*, vol LXXIII, pp 117–127, 1994.

Willis Bund, J.W., *The Civil War in Worcestershire and the Scotch Invasion of 1651*, 1905.

Willcock, J., *The Great Marquess. The Life and Times of Archibald... Marquess of Argyll*, 1903.

Willcock, J., *A Scots Earl in Covenanting Times: Being the Life and Times of Archibald 9th Earl of Argyll*, 1907.

Woolych, A., *Battles of the English Civil War*, 1961.

Woodrow, R., *The History of the Sufferings of the Church of Scotland from the Restoration to the Revolution*, 4 volumes, 1828–1830.

Young, P., *Marston Moor 1644*, 1970.

Young, P., and Holmes, R., *The English Civil War. A Military History of Three Civil Wars*, 1974.

Yule, G., *The Independents in the English Civil War*, 1958.

Index

Aberdeen 11, 24–32, 42, 77, 95, 96, 98, 99, 104, 110, 112, 113, 140
  the battle of (1644) 96–98, 103, 109, 129
Aboyne, James Gordon, Viscount 29, 30, 31, 36, 65, 74, 77, 96, 113, 116, 120, 121, 122, 123, 124, 126, 127, 130, 140, 148, 175
Abjuration Oath (1685) 275, 277
Act of Classes (1646) 135
Act of Classes (1649) 171, 185, 198, 206, 207
Act of Revocation (1625) 4, 5, 9
Airds Moss, clash at (1680) 268, 269
Airlie, James Ogilvie, 1st Earl of 42, 43, 95, 96, 123, 128, 199, 260
Airlie, 2nd Earl, see Ogilvie, James
Alford, the Battle of (1645) 119–121, 130
Anne, Princess, subsequently Queen of Great Britain 284, 291
Antrim, Randal McDonnell, Earl of 18, 24, 25, 27, 62, 65–69, 72, 74, 75, 77, 78, 90, 91, 102. 126, 135, 136, 137, 140, 147, 149, 172
Argyll, Archibald Campbell, Lord Lorne, 8th Earl and 1st Marquis of 7, 10, 18, 19, 23, 24, 27, 37, 39, 42, 43, 44, 55–60, 62, 63, 64, 66, 67, 68, 78, 91, 92, 95, 96, 98, 99, 100, 103, 105, 106, 109, 112, 118, 119, 121, 122, 130, 145, 147, 148–152, 160, 169–174, 177, 179, 184, 189, 190, 199, 200, 205, 207, 222, 223, 225, 228, 229, 236
Argyll, Archibald Campbell, Lord Lorne, 9th Earl of 222, 228, 235, 246, 270, 271, 276, 277, 278, 282
Argyll, Archibald Campbell, Lord Lorne, 10th Earl and 1st Duke of 282, 287
Atholl, John, 1st Earl of in the Murray line 42, 44, 56, 57, 198
Atholl, John, 2nd Earl in the Murray line and 1st Marquis of 276
Auldearn, the Battle of (1645) 114–117, 118, 181
Ayr 221, 227, 245, 250, 259

Baillie, Robert 75, 79, 89, 133, 141, 176, 233
Baillie, General William 73, 82, 86–89, 94, 105, 106, 109, 112–114, 117, 119–121, 122–124, 153, 161, 163, 164, 167, 213
Balcarres, Alexander Lindsay, 1st Earl of 120, 121, 151
Balcarres, Colin Lindsay, 3d Earl of 284
Balmerino, John Elphinstone, Lord 6, 7, 9, 13, 16, 23, 60, 135, 151, 229
Balvenie, the Bourd of (1649) 176, 178, 181, 189, 203
Banff 146, 148
Benburb, the Battle of (1646) 143–144, 145, 170
Berwick-upon-Tweed 21, 30, 32, 33, 37, 40, 44, 58, 154, 169
  the Pacification of (1639) 35, 36, 40, 52
Blackadder, John 234, 237, 249, 256, 265, 266, 269
Blakeston, Sir William 83, 86
Borthwick Castle 201, 202
Bothwell Bridge 202, 259, 260, 261, 267
  the Battle of (1679) 261–263, 264, 266, 268
Braid Hills, Cromwell's camp at 190, 191, 197, 208
Breda 179, 180, 181, 183, 224
Brig o' Dee, the Battle of the (1639) 31, 32
Bristol 68, 130
Brown, Sir John 200, 209, 210, 211
Burleigh, John Balfour of 254, 256, 257, 278
Burleigh, Robert Arnot, Lord 96, 97, 121
Burnet, Alexander, Archbishop of Glasgow, subsequently of St Andrews 236, 237, 246, 248, 249, 266
Burntisland 178, 187, 207, 209, 212
Byron, Lord John 74, 83, 87, 153, 158, 161, 167

Caerlaverock Castle 25, 42, 46, 52
Callendar, James Livingstone, Earl of
    78, 89, 152, 154, 157, 160, 161,
    163–165, 167, 168, 177
Cameron, Richard viii, 265–269, 273
Cameronians viii, 266, 269, 271, 273–
    278, 281, 283–287, 292
Cameronian Regiment 252, 287, 289,
    292
Campbell – see the Earls of Argyll
Campbell, Sir Ducan, of Auchinbreck
    105, 106, 107
Campbell, James, of Lawers 114, 115
Cannon, Alexander 288, 289, 290, 291
Carbisdale, fight at (1650) 181–182,
    189, 203
Cargill, Donald 234, 256, 266, 269,
    273
Carlisle 21, 40, 44, 58, 96, 110, 111,
    113, 118, 154, 158, 159, 169, 201,
    212
Carrickfergus Castle 62, 72, 170
Cassillis, John Kennedy, 6th Earl of
    151, 168, 177, 180, 229, 249
Cassillis, John Kennedy, 7th Earl of
    272
Cessation, the (1643) 70, 71, 102
Charlemont 103, 142, 143
Charles I vii, viii, 1, 4–9, 11–14, 16–
    19, 21, 22, 24, 25, 27–29, 32–41,
    44, 45, 47, 52–61, 63–65, 67, 69,
    70, 72, 74, 75, 80, 89, 98, 101–103,
    107, 108, 110, 113, 118, 122, 125,
    126, 131, 135, 137–141, 145, 146,
    149, 151, 171, 174, 222, 226, 229,
    279, 293
Charles II, formerly Prince of Wales
    156, 168, 173, 174, 177, 179, 180,
    181, 183–186, 189, 198–200, 205,
    207, 212, 213, 214–220, 222–226,
    229, 230, 233, 246, 248, 250, 259,
    260, 264, 265, 267, 269, 274, 275,
    279
Claverhouse, John Graham of,
    Viscount Dundee 233, 254, 256–
    259, 262, 270–273, 275, 277, 280,
    283, 284, 286–288
Cleland, William 252, 254, 257, 258,
    278, 282, 283, 286, 287, 289, 290
Coll Coitach 27, 148, 149
Committee of Both Kingdoms 75, 100,
    110, 111, 118
Confederacy of Kilkenny 61, 65, 91,
    103, 135, 144, 176
Conn, George 16, 24

Conway, Edward Lord 44, 46–51
Craigievar, Sir William Forbes of 96,
    97
Crawford, Lawrence 71, 80, 82, 87,
    140
Crawford, Ludovic, 16th Earl of 59,
    77, 127
Crawford-Lindsay, Earl of, see
    Lindsay, John
Cromwell, Oliver 52, 71, 79, 80, 81,
    83, 87, 89, 90, 100, 101, 102, 133,
    149, 159, 161–168, 169–171, 173,
    174, 176, 179, 185, 187–196, 197–
    202, 205, 207, 208, 210, 211, 212,
    214–220, 222, 223, 224, 229, 261
Cromwell, Richard 223
Cumbernauld, the Bond of (1640) 44,
    56, 78, 92
Cunningham, Lady Ann 19, 28

Dalkeith Castle 25, 27, 201
Dalnaspidel, Highlanders routed at
    (1654) 223
Dalrymple, Sir James 270, 271, 282
Dalyell, Tam, of the Binns 218, 219,
    238, 240–245, 260, 267, 269
Dean, Colonel Richard 164, 218, 222
Digby, Lord George 118, 126, 130,
    131, 133
Dirleton Castle 201, 202
Douglas, William, Marquis of 126,
    127
Drumclog, the Battle of (1679) 256–
    258, 260
Drummond, James, Lord 92, 93, 94
Dumbarton Castle 25, 27, 42, 46, 51
Dumfries 77, 78, 131, 198, 199, 208,
    239, 245, 253, 292
Dunbar 33, 188, 190, 191, 192, 195,
    197
    the Battle of (1650) 187, 193–196,
    197, 198, 200, 206, 218
Dundas, Walter 197, 205
Dundee 95, 112, 113, 220
    the Viscount of, see Claverhouse
Dunkeld 113, 121, 122, 130, 289,
    290
    the Battle of (1689) 289–291
Dunnaverty Castle 136, 148
Dunnotar Castle 31, 78, 220, 277,
    278
Dunstaffnage Castle 92, 105

Eastern Association, the 71, 79, 80,
    81, 82, 83, 87, 100, 102, 154, 198

Edinburgh, town and castle 2, 5, 6, 12, 14, 15, 23, 25, 26, 27, 28, 33, 35, 36, 37, 40, 42, 46, 52, 57, 65, 121, 125, 168, 168, 170, 171, 175, 183, 190, 191, 197, 198, 201, 204, 208, 221, 222, 226, 227, 245, 249, 260, 264, 270, 271, 277, 280, 281, 285, 286, 287
Eglinton, Alexander Montgomery, 6th Earl of 82, 85, 151, 156, 168, 189, 202
Elcho, David Lord 92, 93, 94, 95, 96, 121
Elgin 109, 110
Engagement, the (1647) 150, 151, 152, 155, 172, 177
Essex, the Earl of 32, 70, 100, 102
Eythin, Lord 73, 82

Fairfax, Fernando Lord 68, 76, 79, 81, 82, 83, 86
Fairfax, Sir Thomas 68, 74, 79, 81, 82, 85, 86, 88, 102, 118, 125, 133, 139, 149, 154, 161, 172, 185, 186, 213
Fairfoul, Andrew, Archbishop of Glasgow 213, 236
Fleetwood, Charles 186, 189, 194, 213, 215, 217, 218, 219, 223
Fyfie Castle, clash at (1644) 99, 100, 102

General Assemblies of the Church of Scotland vii, 4, 19, 30. 35, 36, 38, 69, 159, 160, 178, 190, 220, 221, 232, 292, 293
Gillespie, Patrick 199, 206, 229
Glasgow 19, 122, 125, 131, 132, 133, 155, 201, 208, 240, 245, 250, 256, 259, 283
Glencairn, William 9th Earl of 31, 22, 223, 226
Gordon, George, see Huntly, 2nd Marquis of
Gordon, Lord George 26, 77, 78, 95, 96, 99, 109, 110, 113, 116, 120
Gordon, Lord Lewis, subsequently 3d Marquis of Huntly 31, 96, 109, 130, 136, 175, 176, 198
Gordon, 1st Duke of, see Huntly, 4th Marquis of
Gordon, Nathaniel 32, 77, 95, 96, 97, 110, 120, 123, 124, 127, 128, 132
Goring, Lord George 80, 83, 85, 86, 87, 88, 118
Greyfriars Church, Edinburgh 15, 264, 275

Gunn, Colonel William 31, 32
Gustavus Adolphus, King of Sweden ix, 83
Guthrie, James 200, 206, 226, 229, 235, 236

Hackston, David, of Rathilet 254, 256, 257, 261, 268, 269
Haddo, Sir Gordon 77, 78
Halket, Colonel Robert, 176, 197, 203
Hamilton, the Battle of 203–204
Hamilton, James, 3d Marquis and 1st Duke of 13, 17–19, 24, 27–30, 33, 36, 38, 43, 45, 55, 56, 58, 59, 63–67, 74, 95, 136, 141, 146, 147, 150, 151–156, 158, 165, 167, 168, 169, 172, 175
Hamilton, William, Lord Lanark, 2nd Duke of 59, 63, 67, 122, 124, 146, 150, 153, 158, 169, 172, 177, 178, 218, 219
Hamilton, William Douglas, 3d Duke of 230, 265, 272, 285, 286, 287, 288
Hamilton, Sir Robert 254, 255, 256, 257, 260, 261, 262, 292
Hampden, John 17, 21, 52, 63, 68
Harrison, Thomas 89, 212, 213, 215
Heligoland, the Treaty of (1650) 183
Henderson, Alexander 9, 14, 19, 34, 53, 54, 55, 63, 75, 141
Henrietta Maria, Queen 24, 32, 61, 64, 65, 66, 141
Hereford 123, 126, 130, 134
Highland Host, the (1678) 250–252
Hilton, artillery duel at (1644) 76, 77
Hoffman, Augustine 201, 204, 205, 208, 209
Holburne, Lieutenant-General 209, 210, 211
Huntly, George Gordon, 2nd Marquis of 11, 16, 23–27, 29, 30, 42, 77, 78, 91, 96, 110, 130, 133, 136, 140, 146, 147, 148, 152, 155, 156, 175
Huntly, 3d Marquis, see Lord Lewis Gordon
Huntly, George Gordon, 4th Marquis and 1st Duke of 250, 280, 283, 286
Hurry, Sir John 59, 63, 83, 109, 110, 112, 113–117, 140, 155, 157, 165, 181, 182

Incident, the (1641) 60, 64
Indulgences 246, 264, 266, 280, 281
Inverary 42, 104, 160

Inverkeithing, the Battle of (1651) 210–211
Inverlochy Castle 105, 106, 221
the Battle of Inverlochy (1645) 106–107, 108, 109, 110, 113, 125
Inverness 105, 106, 109, 114, 136, 140, 175, 221, 227
Irvine 245, 259

James VI and I, King of Great Britain vii, 1, 2, 3, 5, 8, 12, 14, 19, 39, 230, 270
James VII and II, King of Great Britain 253, 259, 265, 266, 269–272, 275–288, 291
James Stewart, Prince of Wales, the Old Pretender 282

Ker, Colonel Gilbert 176, 197, 201, 202, 203, 204
Killiecrankie, the Battle of (1689) 288, 289, 290
Kilmarnock 157, 259
Kilpont, Lord 92, 93, 94, 95
Kilsyth 122, 123
the Battle of (1645) 122, 124, 125, 126, 135
King, John 256, 257, 258, 264

Lambert, John 82, 85, 154, 155, 157, 158, 159, 160, 161, 168, 171, 186, 189, 193, 194, 195, 195, 202, 203, 208, 209–212, 213, 214–219, 223, 224, 225
Lanark 241, 271
the Declaration of (1682) 271
Lanark, Lord, see Hamilton, William
Laud, William 3, 5, 45, 54, 55, 101
Lauderdale, John Maitland, Earl and subsequently Duke of 75, 101, 150, 151, 153, 158, 172, 174, 177, 212, 224, 225, 226, 227, 230, 231, 235, 236, 237, 245, 246–250, 251, 259, 265, 269
Learmont, Joseph 243, 244
Leighton, Robert 231, 248, 249
Leith 28, 37, 40, 178, 187, 188, 189, 197, 208, 221, 227
Leslie, Alexander, Earl of Leven ix, 22, 25, 28, 33, 34, 36, 37, 41, 42, 45, 48, 49, 50, 51, 59, 60, 70, 72, 73, 75–78, 80–83, 85, 86, 88, 89, 90, 100, 110, 111, 118, 125, 126, 130, 131, 133, 134, 137, 147, 152, 153, 158, 168, 170, 186

Leslie, General David 73, 83, 87, 88, 89, 125, 126, 127, 128, 131, 132, 133, 147, 148, 149, 152, 156, 168, 175, 179, 181, 185, 186, 187–196, 197, 198, 200, 205, 206, 208, 209, 211, 212, 218, 219, 212
Leven, Earl of, see Leslie, Alexander
Lindsay, John, 10th Lord Lindsay, subsequently Earl of Crawford-Lindsay 44, 56, 87, 121
Linlithgow 169, 197, 210
London viii, 51, 52, 53, 63, 79, 100, 138, 213, 224
the Treaty of (1641) 58
Lorne Lord, see Argyll, Earls of
Loudoun, John Campbell, Lord, 1st Earl of 13, 39, 59, 63, 101, 124, 125, 135, 145, 150, 168, 173
Loudoun, James Campbell, 2nd Earl of 250
Louis XIV 134, 280, 282, 286
Lucas, Sir Charles 76, 80, 83, 86

MacColla, Alisdair 27, 66, 90–94, 96, 97, 99, 103, 104, 106, 110, 113, 115–117, 119, 121–123, 126, 127, 130, 133, 135, 136, 140, 147, 148, 149, 181
MacDonald, Coll MacGillespich, see Coll Coitach
McDonnell, James 90, 106, 120
Mackay, Hugh, of Scourie 282, 283, 286, 287, 288
Mackenzie, Sir George, of Rosehaugh
Maclellan, Sir John, of Barscob 239, 243, 249
Maitland, Lord, see Lauderdale
Manchester, Edward Montagu, Earl of 71, 76, 80, 81, 82, 86, 90, 100, 101, 102
Marischal, William Keith, 7th Earl 30, 31, 42
Marston Moor 81, 82
the Battle of (1644) 84–88, 89, 90, 91, 100, 102, 105, 109
Mauchline Muir, the Battle of (1648) 157, 172, 237
Mary II, Queen of Great Britain 282, 284, 285, 287, 288
Melfort, John Drummond, Earl of 280, 283, 286
Melville, Andrew 2, 3, 21, 38, 54
Middleton, John, subsequently Earl of 32, 127, 130, 133, 136, 140, 148, 153, 154, 157, 160, 161, 163, 164,

Index

165, 175, 176, 198, 207, 220, 222–226, 228, 229, 230, 232–235, 236, 246, 247

Monk, George 71, 74, 170, 186, 193, 194, 195, 202, 207, 208, 214, 217, 220, 222, 223, 224, 227

Monmouth, James Duke of 260, 261, 262, 263, 264, 269, 276, 278

Montgomery, Robert 168, 202, 203, 208, 218, 219, 237

Montgomery, Viscount, of Ards 143, 144

Montreuil, Jean de 134, 135, 137, 138, 150

Montrose, James Graham, 5th Earl and 1st Marquis of 11, 14, 23, 25, 26, 27, 30, 31, 37, 38, 39, 42, 43, 44, 56–60, 63, 64–67, 72, 74–78, 80, 89, 90, 91, 92, 93–99, 100, 101, 103, 105, 106–108, 109, 110, 111, 112, 113–117, 118, 119–123, 125–129, 130, 131, 132, 133, 135–138, 140, 142, 150, 153, 155, 156, 165, 168, 171, 172, 174, 175, 177, 178, 179, 180–183, 199, 223, 227, 228, 229, 253

Moss Troopers 211, 202, 207, 208, 222

Munro, George 142, 144, 153, 158, 160, 162, 164, 165, 169, 170, 179

Munro, Robert 62, 72, 91, 103, 106, 111, 135, 142, 143, 144, 218

Musgrave, Sir Philip 153, 154, 158, 160, 165

Musselburgh 188, 189, 190

Nantwich, the Battle of (1644) 74, 186

Napier, Archibald Master of 113, 120

Naseby, the Battle of (1645) 118, 119

National Covenant (1638) vii, 14, 15, 16, 17, 19, 175, 177, 264

Newburn, the Battle of (1640) 49–51

Newcastle 29, 30, 44, 46, 47, 48, 49, 50, 51, 72, 73, 75, 76, 77, 78, 79, 89, 90, 110, 110, 139, 140, 146, 159

Newcastle, William Cavendish, Marquis of 68, 73, 74, 75, 76, 77, 79, 80, 81, 82, 86, 89

Newark 79, 86, 131, 134, 137, 138, 139

Nithsdale, Robert Maxwell, 1st Earl of 11. 16, 24, 25, 42, 46, 65, 66, 77

Nye, Philip 79, 90

Oakey, John 194, 210

O'Cahan, Magnus 90, 99, 106, 120, 132

Ogilvie, Lord James, 2nd Earl of Airlie 74, 77, 132, 175, 176, 199, 242, 250

Ogilvie, Sir Thomas 95, 96, 107

O'Neil, Owen Roe 62, 103, 136, 141, 142, 143, 176

O'Neil, Sir Phelim 60, 61, 62

Orkney Isles 179, 181, 265

Ormonde, James Butler, Earl of 61, 65, 70, 71, 144, 172, 176, 177, 180

Overton, Colonel Robert 209, 210, 221

Oxford 64, 74, 77, 81, 125, 135, 137

Peden, Alexander 234, 237, 249, 265, 279

Pembroke Castle 153, 159

Pentland Rising (1666) 236, 239–244, 246, 247, 250, 260

Perth 4, 78, 92, 94, 95, 96, 105, 112, 122, 199, 207, 212, 221, 227

Perth, James Drummond, 4th Earl of 250, 277, 280

Philiphaugh, the Battle of (1645) 127–129, 130, 132, 133, 134, 135, 136, 228

Pittscottie, Colin 87, 209, 218, 219

Pluscardine, Sir Thomas Mackenzie of 175, 176, 181

Popish Plot (1679) 259, 276, 279

Poyntz, Sydnam 125, 131, 134

Preston, the Battle of (1648) 161–168, 169, 181, 193

Pride, Colonel Thomas 164, 166, 171, 194

Pym, John 41, 52, 53, 58, 60, 63, 68, 70

Queensberry, William Duke of 276, 277, 280

Queensferry Paper (1680) 267, 268

Ralston, Colonel William 203, 204

Reay, Donald Mackay, Lord 77, 176

Renwick, James 271, 273, 274, 275, 278, 279, 281, 282

Rinnuccini, Giovanni Battista 135, 142, 144, 176

Ripon, peace negotiations at (1640) 52, 53, 56

Rollo, Sir William 96, 132

Ross, Lord 254, 256, 258, 259

Rothes, John Leslie, 5th Earl of 13, 14, 18, 23, 25, 34, 37, 41, 57, 58, 59

Rothes, John Leslie, 6th Earl and 1st Duke of 218, 220, 226, 235, 237, 240, 247, 269
Roxburgh, Robert Ker, Earl of
Rullion Green, the Battle of (1666) 242–244, 245, 249, 264
Rupert, Prince 63, 68, 79, 80, 82, 83, 85, 87, 89, 91, 109, 118, 130
Rutherford, Samuel 9, 75, 229
Ruthven, Patrick 37, 40, 42, 46

St Andrews 130, 255
St Giles, Edinburgh vii, 5, 10, 69, 228, 269
Scott, Sir James 93, 94
Seaforth, Colin Mackenzie, Earl of 91, 105, 106, 107, 110, 114, 117, 136, 175, 181, 198
Selby 46, 47, 79
Shaftesbury, the Earl of 259, 260, 264, 276, 279
Sharp, James, minister of Crail, afterwards Archbishop of St Andrews 224, 225, 227, 230, 231, 233, 238, 245, 246, 247, 253, 254, 255, 256, 261, 265, 266, 268, 278
Skippon, Philip 102, 107
Societies, see the Cameronians
Solemn League and Covenant (1643) 69, 70, 75, 91, 100, 111, 139, 146, 147, 150, 151, 169, 175, 177, 183, 222, 229
South Shields, fort at 76, 80, 90
Spottiswood, John, Archbishop of St Andrews 4, 7, 8, 16, 19, 59, 231
Spottiswood, Sir Robert 132, 133
Start, the (1650) 199, 207
Stewart, John, of Ladywell 56, 57
Stirling, town and castle 96, 121, 197, 198, 199, 206, 207, 212, 220
Strachan, Archibald 169, 176, 181, 182, 189, 197, 198, 199, 200, 201, 205, 229
Strafford, Earl of, see Wentworth
Sutherland, John 14th Earl of 114, 117, 181, 182
Sunderland 76, 80
Sydserf, Bishop Thomas 9, 13, 16, 231

Tables, the 13, 14, 37, 42
Tantallon Castle 201, 202, 208
Test Act (1680) 269, 270, 271, 272, 280
Tippermuir, the Battle of (1644) 92–94, 96, 103, 109, 121

Traquair, John Stewart, Earl of 6, 7, 10, 13, 14, 25, 27, 36, 38, 39, 42, 126, 127
Tullibardine, Patrick 3d Earl of 31
Tullibardine, James 4th Earl of 92, 93, 121
Turner, Sir James 70, 154, 156, 157, 160, 164, 204, 235, 236, 237, 238, 239, 245, 246, 247, 253, 280
Turriff 25, 29, 99, 110
   the Trot of (1639) 29
Tweeddale, John Hay, Earl of 235, 246, 265

Uxbridge, the Treaty of (1645) 101, 102, 105, 107, 110, 150

Vane, Sir Henry 45, 55
Vane, Sir Henry, the younger 68, 59, 110, 225

Wallace, Colonel James 240, 241, 242, 243, 244, 245, 258, 260
Waller, Sir William 68, 81
Warriston, Archibald Johnston of 14, 15, 19, 34, 35, 37, 60, 75, 133, 141, 149, 170, 173, 180, 183, 189, 200, 225, 229, 236, 249
Warrington 166, 167, 213, 214
Welsh, John 234, 237, 239, 240, 243, 249, 254, 261, 265, 266
Wentworth, Thomas, 1st Earl of Strafford 15, 16, 24, 25, 27, 29, 34, 39, 40, 42, 45, 48, 49, 53, 55, 61
Western Association 197, 198, 199, 200, 201, 202, 203, 204, 234, 261
Western Remonstrance (1650) 199, 200, 206, 207
Westminster Assembly 68, 69, 75, 79, 90, 133, 147
Whiggamore Raid, the (1648) 168, 169, 198, 202, 237, 241
Wigan 161, 165, 166, 213, 216
William of Orange 270, 282, 283, 284, 285, 286, 287, 288, 291, 292
Winwick, battle at (1648) 166, 167
Wishart, George 155, 183, 232
Worcester 118, 215
   the Battle of (1651) 216–220, 224
Wynrame, George, of Liberton 179, 180

York 22, 27, 48, 51, 64, 78, 79, 80, 81, 89
York, James Duke of, see James VII and II